POETIC GEMS

SELECTED FROM THE WORKS

OF

WILLIAM M^cGONAGALL,

Poet and Tragedian,
Died in Edinburgh 29th September, 1902

WITH

BIOGRAPHICAL SKETCH AND REMINISCENCES

BY THE AUTHOR,

AND PORTRAIT BY D. B. GRAY

DUNDEE:
DAVID WINTER & SON LTD.
15 SHORE TERRACE

LONDON:
GERALD DUCKWORTH & CO. LTD
3 HENRIETTA ST., W.C.2

1969

CONTENTS.

Faithfully Yours
William McGonagall
poet, and Tragedian.

BRIEF AUTOBIOGRAPHY

DEAR READER,—My parents were both born in Ireland, where they spent the great part of their lives after their marriage. They left Ireland for Scotland, and never returned to the Green Isle. I was born in the year of 1830 in the city of Edinburgh, the garden of bonnie Scotland, which is justly famed by all for its magnificent scenery. My parents were poor, but honest, sober, and God-fearing. My father was a hand-loom weaver, and wrought at cotton fabrics during his stay in Edinburgh, which was for about two years. Owing to the great depression in the cotton trade in Edinburgh, he removed to Paisley with his family, where work was abundant for a period of about three years ; but then a crash taking place, he was forced to remove to Glasgow with his family with the hope of securing work there, and enable him to support his young and increasing family, as they were all young at that time, your humble servant included. In Glasgow he was fortunate in getting work as a cotton weaver ; and as trade was in a prosperous state for about two years, I was sent to school, where I remained about eighteen months, but at the expiry of which, trade again becoming dull, my poor parents were compelled to take me from school, being unable to pay for schooling through adverse circumstances ; so that all the education I received was before I was seven years of age.

My father, being forced to leave Glasgow through want of work, came to Dundee, where plenty of work was to be had at the time—such as sacking, cloth, and other fabrics. It was at this time that your humble servant was sent to work in a mill in the Scouringburn, which was owned by Mr Peter Davie, and there I remained for about four years, after which I was taken from the mill, and put to learn the hand-loom in Ex-Provost Reid's factory, which was also situated in the Scouringburn. After I had learned to be an expert hand-loom weaver, I began to take a great delight in reading books, as well as to improve my handwriting, in my leisure hours at night, until I made myself what I am.

The books that I liked best to read were Shakspeare's penny plays, more especially Macbeth, Richard III., Hamlet, and Othello ; and I gave myself no rest until I obtained complete mastery over the above four characters. Many a time in my dear father's absence I enacted entire scenes from Macbeth and Richard III., along with some of my shopmates, until they were quite delighted ; and many a time they regaled me and the other actors that had entertained them to strong ale, biscuits, and cheese.

My first appearance on any stage was in Mr Giles' theatre, which was in Lindsay Street quarry, some years ago : I cannot give the exact date, but it is a very long time ago. The theatre was built of brick, somewhat similar to Mr M'Givern's at the top of Seagate. The character that I appeared in was Macbeth, Mrs Giles sustaining the character of Lady Macbeth on that occasion, which she performed admirably. The way that I was allowed to perform was in terms of the following agreement, which was entered into between Mr Giles and myself—that I had to give Mr Giles one pound in cash before the performance, which I considered rather hard, but as there was no help for it, I made known Mr Giles's terms to my shopmates, who were hand-loom weavers in Seafield Works, Taylor's Lane. No sooner than the terms were made known to them, than they entered heartily into the arrangement, and in a very short time they made up the pound by subscription, and with one accord declared they would go and see me perform the Thane of Fife, *alias* Macbeth. To see that the arrangement with Mr Giles was carried out to the letter, a deputation of two of my shopmates was appointed to wait upon him with the pound. Mr Giles received the deputation, and on receipt of the money cheerfully gave a written agreement certifying that he would allow me to perform Macbeth on the following night in his theatre. When the deputation came back with the news that Mr Giles had consented to allow me to make my *debut* on the following night, my shopmates cheered again and again, and the rapping of the lays I will never forget as long as I live. When the great night arrived my shopmates were in high glee with the hope of getting a Shakspearian treat from your humble servant. And I can assure you, without boasting, they were not disappointed in their anticipations, my shopmates having secured seats before the general public were admitted. It would be impossible for me to describe the scene in Lindsay Street, as it was crowded from head to foot, all being eager to witness my first appearance as an exponent of Shakspeare. When I appeared on the stage I was received with a perfect storm of applause, but when I exclaimed " Command, they make a halt upon the heath," the applause was deafening, and was continued during the entire evening, especially so in the combat scene. The house was crowded during each of the three performances on that ever-memorable night, which can never be forgot by me or my shopmates, and even entire strangers included. At the end of each performance I was called before the curtain, and received plaudit after plaudit of applause in recognition of my able impersonation of Macbeth.

What a sight it was to see such a mass of people struggling to gain admission! hundreds failing to do so, and in the struggle numbers were trampled under foot, one man having lost one of his shoes in the scrimmage ; others were carried bodily into the theatre along with the press. So much then for the true account of my first appearance on any stage.

The most startling incident in my life was the time I discovered myself to be a poet, which was in the year 1877. During the Dundee holiday week, in the bright and balmy month of June, when trees and flowers were in full bloom, while lonely and sad in my room, I sat thinking about the thousands of people who were away by rail and steamboat, perhaps to the land of Burns, or poor ill-treated Tannahill, or to gaze upon the Trossachs in Rob Roy's country, or elsewhere wherever their minds led them. Well, while pondering so, I seemed to feel as it were a strange kind of feeling stealing over me, and remained so for about five minutes. A flame, as Lord Byron has said, seemed to kindle up my entire frame, along with a strong desire to write poetry ; and I felt so happy, so happy, that I was inclined to dance, then I began to pace backwards and forwards in the room, trying to shake off all thought of writing poetry ; but the more I tried, the more strong the sensation became. It was so strong, I imagined that a pen was in my right hand, and a voice crying, " Write Write! " So I said to myself, ruminating, let me see ; what shall I write ? then all at once a bright idea struck me to write about my best friend, the late Reverend George Gilfillan ; in my opinion I could not have chosen a better subject, therefore I immediately found paper, pen, and ink, and set myself down to immortalize the great preacher, poet, and orator. These are the lines I penned, which I dropped into the box of the *Weekly News* office surreptitiously, which appeared in that paper as follows :—

" W. M'G., Dundee, who modestly seeks to hide his light under a bushel, has surreptitiously dropped into our letter-box an address to the Rev. George Gilfillan. Here is a sample of this worthy's powers of versification : —

' Rev. George Gilfillan of Dundee,
　　There is none can you excel ;
You have boldly rejected the Confession of Faith,
　　And defended your cause right well.

' The first time I heard him speak,
　　'Twas in the Kinnaird Hall,
Lecturing on the Garibaldi movement,
　　As loud as he could bawl.

' He is a liberal gentleman
　　To the poor while in distress,
And for his kindness unto them
　　The Lord will surely bless.

' My blessing on his noble form,
　　And on his lofty head,
May all good angels guard him while living,
　　And hereafter when he's dead.' "

P.S.—This is the first poem that I composed while under the divine inspiration, and is true, as I have to give an account to God at the day of judgment for all the sins I have committed.

With regard to my far-famed Balmoral journey, I will relate it truly as it happened. 'Twas on a bright summer morning in the month of July 1878, I left Dundee *en route* for Balmoral, the Highland home of Her Most Gracious Majesty, Queen of Great Britain and Empress of India. Well, my first stage for the day was the village of Alyth. When I arrived there I felt weary, foot-sore, and longed for rest and lodgings for the night. I made enquiry for a good lodging-house, and found one very easily, and for the lodging I paid fourpence to the landlady before I sat down, and when I had rested my weary limbs for about five minutes I rose and went out to purchase some provisions for my supper and breakfast—some bread, tea, sugar, and butter—

7

nd when I had purchased the provisions I returned to my lodgings and prepared for myself a hearty tea, which I relished very much, I can assure you, for I felt very hungry, not having tasted food of any kind by the way during the travel, which caused me to have a raven ous appetite, and to devour it greedily ; and after supper I asked the landlady to oblige me with some water to wash my feet, which she immediately and most cheerfully supplied me with ; then I washed my sore blistered feet and went to bed, and was soon in the arms of Morpheus, the god of sleep. Soundly I slept all the night, until the landlady awoke me in the morning, telling me it was a fine sunshiny morning. Well, of course I arose, and donned my clothes, and I felt quite refreshed after the refreshing sleep I had got during the night ; then I gave myself a good washing, and afterwards prepared my breakfast, which I devoured quickly, and left the lodging-house, bidding the landlady good morning, and thanking her for her kindness ; then I wended my way the next day as far as the Spittal o' Glenshee—

Which is the most dismal to see—
With its bleak, rocky mountains,
And clear, crystal fountains,
With their misty foam ;
And thousands of sheep there together do roam,
Browsing on the barren pasture, blasted-like to see,
Stunted in heather, and scarcely a tree ;
And black-looking cairns of stones, as monuments to show,
Where people have been found that were lost in the snow—
Which is cheerless to behold—
And as the traveller gazes thereon it makes his blood run cold,
And almost makes him weep,
For a human voice is seldom heard there,
Save the shepherd crying to his sheep.

The chain of mountains there is most frightful to see,
Along each side of the Spittal o' Glenshee ;
But the Castleton o' Braemar is most beautiful to see,
With its handsome whitewashed houses, and romantic scenery,
And bleak-looking mountains, capped with snow,
Where the deer and the roe do ramble to and fro,
Near by the dark river Dee,
Which is most beautiful to see.

And Balmoral Castle is magnificent to be seen,
Highland home of the Empress of India, Great Britain's Queen,
With its beautiful pine forests, near by the river Dee,
Where the rabbits and hares do sport in mirthful glee,
And the deer and the roe together do play
All the live long summer day,
In sweet harmony together,
While munching the blooming heather,
With their hearts full of glee,
In the green woods of Balmoral, near by the river Dee.

8

And, my dear friends, when I arrived at the Spittal o' Glenshee, a dreadful thunder-storm came on, and the vivid flashes of the forked lightning were fearful to behold, and the rain poured down in torrents, until I was drenched to the skin, and longed to be under cover from the pitiless rain. Still God gave me courage to proceed on my weary journey, until I arrived at a shepherd's house near by the wayside, and I called at the house, as God had directed me to do, and knocked at the door fearlessly. I was answered by the servant maid, who asked me kindly what I wanted, and I told her I wanted lodgings for the night, and that I was wet to the skin with the rain, and that I felt cold and hungry, and that I would feel thankful for any kind of shelter for the night, as it was still raining and likely to be for the night. Then she told me there was no accommodation ; then the shepherd himself came to the door, and he asked me what I wanted, and I told him I wanted a lodging for the night, and at first he seemed unwilling, eyeing me with a suspicious look, perhaps taking me for a burglar, or a sheep-stealer, who had come to steal his sheep—at least that was my impression. But when I showed him Her Most Gracious Majesty's royal letter, with the royal black seal, that I had received from her for my poetic abilities, he immediately took me by the hand and bade me come in, and told me to " gang in ower to the fire and to warm mysel'," at the same time bidding the servant maid make some supper ready for the poet ; and while the servant girl was making some porridge for me, I showed him a copy of my poems, which I gave to him as a present for his kindness towards me, which he read during the time I was taking my supper, and seemed to appreciate very much. Then when I had taken my supper, he asked me if I would be afraid to sleep in the barn, and I told him so long as I put my trust in God I had nought to fear, and that these were the principles my dear parents had taught me. When I told him so he felt quite delighted, and bade me warm my feet before I would " gang oot to my bed i' the barn," and when I had warmed my feet, he accompanied me to the barn, where there was a bed that might have pleased Her Most Gracious Majesty, and rolling down the bed-clothes with his own hands, he wished me a sound sleep, and bade me good night. Then I instantly undressed and tumbled into bed, and was soon sound asleep, dreaming that I saw Her Most Gracious Majesty riding in her carriage-and-pair, which was after-wards truly verified. Well, when I awoke the next morning I felt rather chilled, owing to the wetting I had got, and the fatigue of the distance I had travelled ; but, nothing daunted, I still resolved to see Her Majesty. So I dressed myself quickly, and went over to the house to bid the shepherd good morning, and thank him for the kindness I had received at his hands, but I was told by the girl he was away tending the sheep, but that he had told her to give me my breakfast, and she bade me come in and sit down and get it. So of course I went in, and got a good breakfast of porridge and good Highland milk, enough to make a hungry soul to sing with joy, especially in a strange country, and far from home. Well, having breakfasted, I arose and bade the servant girl good-bye, at the same time thanking her and the shepherd—her master—for their kindness towards me. Then, taking to the road again, I soon came in sight of the Castleton o' Braemar.

9

with its beautiful whitewashed houses and romantic scenery, which I have referred to in my poem. When I arrived at the Castleton o' Braemar it was near twelve o'clock noon, and from the Castleton it is twelve miles to Balmoral; and I arrived at the lodge gates of the palace of Balmoral just as the tower clock chimed three; and when I crossed the little bridge that spans the river Dee, which has been erected by Her Majesty, I walked boldly forward and knocked loudly at the porter lodge door, and it was immediately answered by the two constables that are there night and day, and one of them asked me in a very authoritative tone what I wanted, and of course I told him I wanted to see Her Majesty, and he repeated, " Who do you want to see ? " and I said I was surprised to think that he should ask me again after telling him distinctly that I wanted to see Her Majesty. Then I showed him Her Majesty's royal letter of patronage for my poetic abilities, and he read it, and said it was not Her Majesty's letter; and I said " Who's is it then ? do you take me for a forger ? " Then he said Sir Thomas Biddulph's signature was not on the letter, but I told him it was on the envelope, and he looked and found it to be so. Then he said, " Why didn't you tell me that before ? " I said I forgot. Then he asked me what I wished him to do with the letter, and I requested him to show it to Her Majesty or Sir Thomas Biddulph. He left me, pretending to go up to the palace with the letter, standing out in the cold in front of the lodge, wondering if he would go up to the palace as he pretended. However, be that as it may, I know not, but he returned with an answer as follows :—" Well, I've been up at the Castle with your letter, and the answer I got for you is they cannot be bothered with you," said with great vehemence. " Well," I replied, " it cannot be helped "; and he said it could not, and began to question me when I left Dundee, and the way I had come from Dundee, and where I had lodged by the way; and I told him, and he noted it all down in his memorandum book, and when he had done so he told me I would have to go back home again the same way I came; and then he asked me if I had brought any of my poetry with me, and I said I had, and showed him the second edition, of which I had several copies, and he looked at the front of it, which seemed to arrest his attention, and said, " You are not poet to Her Majesty; Tennyson's the real poet to Her Majesty." Then I said, " Granted; but, sir, you cannot deny that I have received Her Majesty's patronage." Then he said, " I should like very well to hear you give some specimens of your abilities," and I said, " Where ? " and he said, " Just where you stand "; and I said, " No, sir, nothing so degrading in the open air. When I give specimens of my abilities it is either in a theatre or some hall, and if you want to hear me take me inside of the lodge, and pay me before I begin; then you shall hear me. These are my conditions, sir; do you accept my terms ? " Then he said, " Oh, you might to oblige the young lady there." So I looked around to see the young lady he referred to, and there she was, looking out at the lodge entrance; and when I saw her I said, " No, sir, I will not; if it were Her Majesty's request I wouldn't do it in the open air, far less do it to please the young lady." Then the lady shut the lodge door, and he said, " Well, what do you charge for this book of poems ? " and I said " 2d.," and he gave it me, telling me to go straight home and not to think of coming back again to Balmoral. So I bade him good-bye and retraced my steps in search of a lodging for the night, which I obtained at the first farmhouse I called at ; and when I knocked at the door I was told to come in and warm my feet at the fire, which I accordingly did, and when I told the good wife and man who I was, and about me being at the palace, they felt very much for me, and lodged me for the night, and fed me likewise, telling me to stay with them for a day or two, and go to the roadside and watch Her Majesty, and speak to her, and that I might be sure she would do something for me, but I paid no heed to their advice. And when I had got my supper, I was shown out to the barn by the gudeman, and there was prepared for me a bed which might have done a prince, and the gudeman bade me good night. So I closed the barn door and went to bed, resolving to be up very early the next morning and on the road, and with the thought thereof I couldn't sleep. So as soon as daylight appeared, I got up and donned my clothes, and went to the farmer's door and knocked, for they had not arisen, it being so early, and I bade them good-bye, thanking them at the same time for their kindness ; and in a few minutes I was on the road again for Dundee—it being Thursday morning I refer to—and lodging in the same houses on my homeward journey, which I accomplished in three days, by arriving in Dundee on Saturday early in the day, foot-sore and weary, but not the least discouraged. So ends my ever-memorable journey to Balmoral.

My next adventure was going to New York, America, in the year 1887, March the 10th. I left Glasgow on board the beautiful steamer "Circassia," and had a very pleasant voyage for a fortnight at sea ; and while at sea I was quite a favourite amongst the passengers, and displayed my histrionic abilities, to the delight of the passengers, but received no remuneration for so doing ; but I was well pleased with the diet I received ; also with the kind treatment I met with from the captain and chief steward—Mr Hendry. When I arrived at Castle Garden, New York, I wasn't permitted to pass on to my place of destination until the officials there questioned me regarding the place in New York I was going to, and how old I was, and what trade I was ; and, of course, I told them I was a weaver, whereas if I had said I was a poet, they wouldn't allowed me to pass, but I satisfied them in their interrogations, and was allowed to pass on to my place of destination. During my stay in New York with a Dundee man, I tried occasionally to get an engagement from theatrical proprietors and music-hall proprietors, but alas ! 'twas all in vain, for they all told me they didn't encourage rivalry, but if I had the money to secure a hall to display my abilities, or a company of my own, I would make lots of money ; but I am sorry to say I had neither, therefore I considered wisely it was time to leave, so I wrote home to a Dundee gentleman requesting him to take me home, and he granted my request cheerfully, and secured for me a passage on board the " Circassia " again, and I had a very pleasant return voyage home again to bonnie Dundee. Since I came home to Dundee I have been very well treated by the more civilised community, and have made several appearances before the public in Baron Zeigler's circus and Transfield's circus, to delighted and crowded audiences; and the more that I was treated unkindly by a few ignorant boys and the Magistrates of the city, nevertheless my heart still clings to Dundee; and, while in Glasgow, my thoughts, night and day, were always towards Dundee; yet I must confess, during a month's stay in Glasgow, I gave three private entertainments to crowded audiences, and was treated like a prince by them, but owing to declining health, I had to leave the city of Glasgow. Since this Book of Poems perhaps will be my last effort,—

I earnestly hope the inhabitants of the beautiful city of Dundee
Will appreciate this little volume got up by me,
And when they read its pages, I hope it will fill their hearts with
   delight,
While seated around the fireside on a cold winter's night;
And some of them, no doubt, will let a silent tear fall
In dear remembrance of

WILLIAM M'GONAGALL.

REMINISCENCES.

MY DEARLY BELOVED READERS,—I will begin with giving an account of my experiences amongst the publicans. Well, I must say that the first man who threw peas at me was a publican, while I was giving an entertainment to a few of my admirers in a public-house in a certain little village not far from Dundee; but, my dear friends, I wish it to be understood that the publican who threw the peas at me was not the landlord of the public-house, he was one of the party who came to hear me give my entertainment. Well, my dear readers, it was while I was singing my own song, " The Rattling Boy from Dublin Town," that he threw the peas at me. You must understand that the Rattling Boy was courting a lass called Biddy Brown, and the Rattling Boy chanced to meet his Biddy one night in company with another lad called Barney Magee, which, of course, he did not like to see, and he told Biddy he considered it too bad for her to be going about with another lad, and he would bid her good-bye for being untrue to him. Then Barney Magee told the Rattling Boy that Biddy Brown was his ass, and that he could easily find another—and come and have a glass, and be friends. But the Rattling Boy told Barney Magee to give his glass of strong drink to the devil! meaning, I suppose, it was only fit for devils to make use of, not for God's creatures. Because, my friends, too often has strong drink been the cause of seducing many a beautiful young woman away from her true lover, and from her parents also, by a false seducer, which, no doubt, the Rattling Boy considered Barney Magee to be. Therefore, my dear friends, the reason, I think, for the publican throwing the peas at me is because I say, to the devil with your glass, in my song, " The Rattling Boy from Dublin," and he, no doubt, considered it had a teetotal tendency about it, and, for that reason, he had felt angry, and had thrown the peas at me.

My dear readers, my next adventure was as follows :—During the Blue Ribbon Army movement in Dundee, and on the holiday week of the New-year, I was taken into a public-house by a party of my friends and admirers, and requested to give them an entertainment, for which I was to be remunerated by them. Well, my friends, after the party had got a little refreshment, and myself along with the rest, they proposed that I should give them a little entertainment, which I most willingly consented to do, knowing I would be remunerated by the company for so doing, which was the case ; the money I received from them I remember amounted to four shillings and sixpence. All had gone on as smoothly as a marriage bell, and every one of the party seemed to be highly delighted with the entertainment I had given them. Of course, you all ought to know that while singing a good song, or giving a good recitation, it helps to arrest the company's attention from the drink ; yes! in many cases it does, my friends. Such, at least, was the case with me—at least the publican thought so —for—what do you think ?—he devised a plan to bring my entertainment to an end abruptly, and the plan was, he told the waiter to throw a wet towel at me, which, of course, the waiter did, as he was told, and I received the wet towel, full force, in the face, which staggered me no doubt, and had the desired effect of putting an end to me giving any more entertainments in his house. But, of course, the company I had been entertaining felt angry with the publican for being guilty of such a base action towards me, and I felt indignant myself, my friends, and accordingly I left the company I had been entertaining and bade them good-bye. My dear friends, a publican is a creature that would wish to decoy all the money out of the people's pockets that enter his house ; he does not want them to give any of their money away for an intellectual entertainment. No, no! by no means ; give it all to him, and crush out entertainments altogether, thereby he would make more money if he could only do so. My dear friends, if there were more theatres in society than public-houses, it would be a much better world to live in, at least more moral ; and oh! my dear friends, be advised by me. Give your money to the baker, and the butcher, also the shoemaker and the clothier, and shun the publicans ; give them no money at all, for this sufficient reason, they would most willingly deprive us of all moral entertainment if we would be as silly as to allow them. They would wish us to think only about what sort of strong drink we should make use of, and to place our affections on that only, and give the most of our earnings to them ; no matter whether your families starve or not, or go naked or shoeless ; they care not, so as their own families are well clothed from the cold, and well fed. My dear friends, I most sincerely entreat of you to shun the publicans as you would shun the devil, because nothing good can emanate from indulging in strong drink, but only that which is evil. Turn ye, turn ye! why be a slave to the bottle ? Turn to God, and He will save you.

> I hope the day is near at hand,
> When strong drink will be banished from our land.

I remember a certain publican in the city that always pretended to have a great regard for me. Well, as I chanced to be passing by his door one day he was standing in the doorway, and he called on me to come inside, and, as he had been in the habit of buying my poetry, he asked me if I was getting on well, and, of course, I told him the truth, that I was not getting on very well, that I had nothing to do, nor I had not been doing anything for three weeks past, and, worse than all, I had no poetry to sell. Then he said that was a very bad job, and that he was very sorry to hear it, and he asked me how much I would take to give an entertainment in his large back-room, and I told him the least I would take would be five shillings. Oh! very well, he replied I will invite some of my friends and acquaintances for Friday night first, and mind, you will have to be here at seven o'clock punctual to time, so as not to keep the company waiting. So I told him I would remember the time, and thanked him for his kindness, and bade him good-bye. Well, when Friday came, I was there punctually at seven o'clock, and, when I arrived, he told me I was just in time, and that there was a goodly company gathered to hear me. So he bade me go ben to the big room, and that he would be ben himself—as I supposed more to look after the money than to hear me give my entertainment. Well, my readers, when I made my appearance before the company I was greeted with applause, and they told me they had met together for the evening to hear me give my entertainment. Then a round of drink was called for, and the publican answered the call. Some of the company had whisky to drink, and others had porter or ale, whichever they liked best ; as for myself, I remember I had gingerbeer. Well, when we had all partaken of a little drink, it was proposed by some one in the company that a chairman should be elected for the evening, which seemed to meet with the publican's approbation. Then the chairman was elected, and I was introduced to the company by the chairman as the great poet M'Gonagall, who was going to give them an entertainment from his own productions ; hoping they would keep good order and give me a fair hearing, and, if they would, he was sure I would please them. And when he had delivered himself so, he told me to begin, and accordingly I did so, and entertained the company for about an hour and a half. The company was highly satisfied with the entertainment I gave them, and everyone in the company gave three-pence each, or sixpence each—whatever they liked, I suppose—until it amounted to five shillings. Then the chairman told the publican that five shillings had been subscribed anent the entertainment I had given, and handed it to him. Then the publican gave it to me, and I thanked him and the company for the money I received from them anent the entertainment I had given them. Then the chairman proposed that I should sing " The Rattling Boy from Dublin " over again, and that would conclude the evening's entertainment, and that I would get another subscription, which was unanimously carried by the company, but opposed by the publican ; and he told me and the company I had no right to get any more than I had bargained for. But, my friends, his motive for objecting to me getting any more money was to get it himself anent another round of drink he guessed the party would have after I left. And such was the case, as I was told by one of the party the next day, who stayed well up to eleven o'clock, and it was after ten o'clock when I left. Now, my friends, here was a man, a publican, I may say, that pretended to be my friend, that was not satisfied with the money that he got from the company for so many rounds of drink, all through me, of course, that had brought them there to hear me give an entertainment. My opinion is, if I had been as simple to have spent my five shillings that I got for giving my entertainment, he would not have felt satisfied either. In my opinion, he would have laughed at my simplicity for doing so. May heaven protect me from all such friends for ever, and protect everyone that reads my experiences amongst the publicans in this little Book of Poetic Gems!

I remember another night while giving an entertainment in a certain public-house to my admirers, and as soon as the publican found out I was getting money for giving the entertainment, he immediately wrote a letter and addressed it to me, or caused some one else to do it for him, and one of the waiters gave it to me. As soon as I received it in my hand I gave it to one of the company to read, and before he broke open the letter I told him it was a hoax, in my opinion, got up to make me leave his house ; and, my dear friends, it was just as I thought—a hoax. I was told in that letter, by particular request, to go to Gray's Hall. where a ball was held that evening, and, at the request of the master of the ceremonies, I was requested to come along to the hall, and recite my famous poem, " Bruce of Bannockburn " and I would be remunerated for it, and to hire a cab immediately, for the company at the ball were all very anxious to hear me. So I left the public-house directly, but I was not so foolish as to hire a cab to take me to Gray's Hall. No, my friends, I walked all the way, and called at the hall and shewed the letter to a man that was watching the hall door, and requested him to read it, and to show it to the master of the ball ceremonies, to see if I was wanted to recite my poem, " Bruce of Bannockburn." So the man took the letter from me and shewed it to the master of the ceremonies, and he soon returned with the letter, telling me it was a hoax, which I expected. My dear friends, this lets you see so far, as well as me, that these publicans that won't permit singing or reciting in their houses are the ones that are selfish or cunning. They know right well that while anyone is singing a song in the company, or reciting, it arrests the attention of the audience from off the drink. That is the reason, my dear friends for the publican not allowing moral entertainments to be carried on in their houses, which I wish to impress on your minds. It is not for the sake of making a noise in their houses, as many of them say by way of an excuse. No! believe me, they know that pleasing entertainment arrests the attention of their customers from off the drink for the time being, and that is the chief reason for them not permitting it, and, from my own experience, I know it to be the case.

I remember another night while in a public-house. This was on a Saturday night, and the room I was in was quite full, both of men and women, and, of course, I was well known to the most of them. However, I was requested to sing them a song, or give them a recitation, which, of course, I consented to do on one condition, that I was paid for it, which the company agreed to do. So accordingly I sang " The Rattling Boy from Dublin," which was well received by the company. Then they proposed I should recite my Bannockburn poem, which I did, and after I had finished, and partaken of a little refreshment, the company made up for me a handsome collection. Then I began to think it was time for me to leave, as they seemed rather inclined to sing and enjoy themselves. However, when I got up to leave the company, I missed my stick. Lo and behold! it was gone from the place I had left it, and was nowhere to be seen by me or anyone else in the company. And while I was searching for it, and making a great fuss about it, one of the waiters chanced to come in with drink to the company, and he told me it had been taken away ; for what purpose, my friends, if you know not, I will tell you : to make me leave the house, because I was getting too much money from the company, and the landlady guessed I would leave the house when I missed my stick, which was really the case.

I remember another Saturday night I was in the same public-house. and I was entertaining a number of gentlemen, and had received a second collection of money from them, and as soon as the landlady found out I was getting so much money, she rushed into the room and ordered me out at once, telling me to " hook it " out of here, and laid hold of me by the arm and showed me to the door.

Another case, I remember, happened to me in Perth ; worse, in my opinion, than that. Well, my friends, I chanced to be travelling at the time, and, being in very poor circumstances, I thought I would call at a public-house where I was a little acquainted with the landlord, and ask him if he would allow me to give an entertainment in one of his rooms, and I would feel obliged to him if he would be so kind. Well, however, he consented with a little flattery. Sometimes flattery does well ; and in reference to flattery I will quote the beautiful lines of John Dryden the poet :—

> " Flattery, like ice, our footing does betray,
> Who can tread sure on the smooth slippery way ?
> Pleased with the fancy, we glide swiftly on,
> And see the dangers which we cannot shun."

The entertainment was to come off that night, and to commence at eight o'clock. So, my friends, I travelled around the city—God knows, tired, hungry, and footsore—inviting the people to come and hear me give my entertainment ; and, of course, a great number of

16

rich men and poor men came to hear me, and the room was filled by seven o'clock. But, remember, my dear friends, when I wanted to begin, the publican would not allow me until he had almost extracted every penny from the pockets of the company. And when he told me to begin, I remember I felt very reluctant to do so, for I knew I would get but a small recompense for my entertainment. And it just turned out to be as I expected. My dear friends, I only received eighteenpence for my entertainment from, I daresay, about sixty of a company. I ask of you, my dear readers, how much did the publican realise from the company that night by selling drink ? In my opinion, the least he would have realised would be eighteen shillings or a pound. But, depend upon it, they will never take the advantage of me again.

My dear friends, I entreat of you all, for God's sake and for the furtherance of Christ's kingdom, to abstain from all kinds of intoxicating liquor, because seldom any good emanates from it. In the first place, if it was abolished, there would not be so much housebreaking, for this reason : When the burglar wants to break into a house, if he thinks he hasn't got enough courage to do so, he knows that if he takes a few glasses of either rum, whisky, or brandy, it will give him the courage to rob and kill honest disposed people. Yet the Government tolerates such a demon, I may call it, to be sold in society ; to help burglars and thieves to rob and kill ; also to help the seducer to seduce our daughters ; and to help to fill our prisons, and our lunatic asylums, and our poorhouses. Therefore, for these few sufficient reasons, I call upon you, fathers and mothers, and the friends of Christianity, and the friends of humanity,

> To join each one, with heart and hand,
> And help to banish the bane of society from our land,
> And trust in God, and worship Him,
> And denounce the publicans, because they cause sin ;
> Therefore cease from strong drink,
> And you will likely do well,
> Then there's not so much danger of going to hell!

My dear friends, along with my experiences amongst the publicans, I will relate to you a rather dangerous adventure that happened to me some years ago, as follows. Being on travel in the parish of Liff, that is, I think, about six miles from Dundee, and as I was very hard up for money at the time, and being rather at a loss how to get a little of that filthy lucre, as some people term it. But, my dear readers, I never considered it to be either filthy or bad. Money is most certainly the most useful commodity in society that I know of. It is certainly good when not abused ; but, if abused, the fault rests with the abuser —the money is good nevertheless. For my own part, I have always found it to be one of my best friends. Well, being near to a smithy at the time I refer to, I resolved to call on the smith at the smithy and ask his permission to be allowed to give an entertainment from my own works in the smithy that same night. And when I called on the smith and asked his permission to give my entertainment, and told him who I was, he granted me permission of the smithy cheerfully to give my entertainment. So I went from house to house in the district,

17

inviting the people to come to my entertainment, which was to commence at eight o'clock. Admission—adults, twopence each; children, one penny each. When it drew near to eight o'clock there was a very respectable audience gathered to hear me, and gave me a very hearty welcome and a patient hearing; and they all felt highly delighted with the entertainment I had given them, and many of them inviting me to hurry back again, and give them another entertainment. The proceeds, I remember, for the entertainment I gave amounted to four shillings and ninepence, which I was very thankful for. Well, my dear friends, after I had thanked the smith for the liberty of his smithy, and had left and had drawn near to Liff school-room, I heard the pattering of men's feet behind me, and an undefinable fear seized me. Having my umbrella with me I grasped it firmly, and waited patiently until three men came up to me near Liff school-room, and there they stood glaring at me as the serpent does before it leaps upon its prey. Then the man in the centre of the three whispered to his companions, and, as he did so, he threw out both his hands, with the intention, no doubt, of knocking me down, and, with the assistance of the other two, robbing me of the money I had realised from my entertainment. But when he threw out his arms to catch hold of me, as quick as lightning I struck him a blow across the legs with my umbrella, which made him leap backwards, and immediately they then went away round to the front of the school-master's house, close by the road side, and planted themselves there. And when I saw they were waiting for me to come that way as they expected, I resolved to make my escape from them the best way I could. But how? ah, that was the rub. However, I went round to the front of the school-master's house, and reviewed them in the distance, and, the night being dark, the idea struck me if I could manage to get away from their sight they would give up the chase, and go home to Lochee without satisfying their evil intentions. Well, my friends, the plan I adopted was by lowering my body slowly downwards until my knees were touching the ground, and, in that position, I remained for a few seconds; then I threw myself flat on my face on the road, and I remained in that way watching them in the greatest fear imaginable. But, thank God the plan I adopted had the desired effect of saving me from being robbed, or perhaps murdered. Then I thought it advisable to go home by Birkhill, for fear of meeting the night poachers or prowlers again. And when I arrived at Birkhill I resolved to go home by passing through Lord Duncan's woods. I considered it would be safer doing so than by going home the way the poachers had gone, and, just as I made my entry into Lord Duncan's woods, I began to sing—

> Yea, though I walk in death's dark vale,
> Yet will I fear none ill,
> For Thou art with me, and Thy rod
> And staff me comfort still.

So, my dear readers, I arrived safe home, and thanked God for delivering me from the hands of evil-doers, as He has done on all occasions

TRIBUTE FROM THREE STUDENTS AT GLASGOW UNIVERSITY.

The University,
Glasgow, February 1891.

To WILLIAM M'GONAGALL,
    Poet and Tragedian,
      City of Dundee.

Dear Sir,—We, the undersigned, beg to send you herewith an Ode we have composed in your honour. We have had the extreme pleasure of reading your " Poetic Gems," and have embodied our sentiments in the poem referred to. We do not hope to receive a very favourable criticism upon our small effort, but as young men desirous to imitate the master of poetic art we have discovered in you, we trust you will be as lenient as possible with your enthusiastic disciples. We do not wish to rival your splendid achievements, as that would be as presumptuous as it would be futile, but if we can, afar off, emulate the performances of the poet of Dundee, or in a remote way catch any of his inspiration, our reward will be truly great. We beg, therefore, that you will write us, and inform us what you think of our poem. You might also reply, as far as you are able, to the following questions :—

    I. What grammar would you recommend as a preliminary study to the writing of poetry ?

    II. Is a College education an aid to write poetry, and what University would you recommend ?

    III. Is the most intellectual benefit to be derived from a study of the M'Gonagallian or Shakespearian school of poetry ?

    IV. Does your own success in the realms of poetry enable you to estimate what special capacity any of us may have for lyric poetry or the drama ?

    V. Would you recommend any of us to try our chance at the histrionic art ; and if not, why not ? Is Macbeth or Richard III. the best character to take up ?

    VI. Would you recommend us to write direct to the Queen as a patron of poetry ; or should we go to Balmoral to see her there ?

    VII. What chances do you consider we have in knocking out Tennyson as Poet Laureate ?

    VIII. If we should resolve upon going to Balmoral, which route would you recommend ? Also name any " models " that may be known to you in that direction ; stating landlady's name, and if married or single.

We are, your admiring followers,

HENRY JOHN MACDONALD.
A. F. CAMPBELL.
S. DONALD STEWART.

ODE TO WILLIAM M'GONAGALL,

POET AND TRAGEDIAN, DUNDEE.

AMONG the poets of the present day
There is no one on earth who can possibly be able for to gainsay
But that William M'Gonagall, poet and tragedian,
Is truly the greatest poet that was ever found above or below the
    meridian.

'Twas in year '91, in the first month of spring,
On a very cold night, and the frost in full swing,
I met my friend Mactavish walking along the street,
And he gave me your " Poetic Gems " for to read them as a treat.

I took them home, and read them, and exclaimed,
Eureka! Eureka! M'Gonagall I proclaim
To have the deepest insight into human nature of any man I know,
As the reading of his " Gems " doth most emphatically show.

He reaches with poetic power the higher flights of song,
And like the eagle near the clouds, he soars serene and strong ;
No common fowl is he, to roost on fence or crow about a barn,
He warbles sweet his wood-notes wild, and tell no common " yarn."

A better poet was never seen in the city of Dundee at any time,
And never again shall be, as far as I can see in the meantime :
His poem on the Tay Bridge is most beautiful to be read,
As I found by reading it one cold night before I went to bed.

Also his poem about the Emperor of Germany's funeral is the work of
    a master-mind,
And rivals in merit the greatest plays that the " Bard of Avon " left
    behind,
And it will be read when Milton's " Paradise Lost " is totally forgotten,
And all other poetic gems save those of William M'Gonagall are rotten.

But not till then will the world ever come to see
The wealth and beauty of the " Poetic Gems " of M'Gonagall, poet
    and tragedian, of Dundee ;
And though his book can now be bought at the modest price of a
    shilling,
You can never get anywhere, at any price, a product quite so thrilling.

At the beginning of the volume is to be seen the classic head
Of the greatest tragedian that ever the boards did tread,
For to act the Thane of Fife, or discourse with spirits from beneath,
And cry in tones of thunder : " Command! they stand upon the
    heath."

20

Also his ode on the death of George Gilfillan
Shows that he was a true gentleman and no villain;
His poem on the funeral of the illustrious Prince Leopold
Would almost make any one weep for to behold.

Any one who would read his lines on Queen Victoria
Would never again be troubled with melancholia,
Because she has been a good Queen, and by no means bad,
Which, if she were, would indeed be sad.

And though she did not receive M'Gonagall at her castle of Balmoral
The wreath that binds the poet's brow should be something more
    than floral,—
A wreath that will flourish evergreen in all the coming time,
When the name of the great M'Gonagall shall be known from clime to
    clime.

They will one day yet rear him monuments of brass, and weep upon
    his grave,
Though when he was living they would hardly have given him the
    price of a shave;
But his peerless, priceless " Poetic Gems " will settle once for all
The claim to immortality of William M'Gonagall.

TRIBUTE FROM ZULULAND.

The Royal Scots, Fort Curtis, Eokowe,
Zululand, 26th January 1891.

Poet M'Gonagall,—I received a copy of your poems recently from
home, and take the first opportunity of congratulating you on the
production of such a splendid work. Your poems show a taste not to
be met with in many of the writings of the present age, and one can
only wonder how you could have produced such a selection of poems,
commencing as you did at such a late stage in life. I lent your book
to a large number of my friends in the regiment who hail both from
England and Scotland, and they one and all assert that it surpasses,
in tone and clearness of expression, any of the writings of the so-called
" poets " of the present day. I am confident your book would
command an extraordinary sale if you arranged for its being sent out
to the Cape or Natal Colonies, wherein so many well-known men
reside who hail from the " land o' cakes." In Kimberley your work
is extensively read and highly appreciated, but it is mainly obtained
from friends at home, and not from local publishers. Trusting you
may enjoy many years of excellent health, so as you can give us yet
another proof of your poetical abilities, I remain, your sincere
well-wisher.

FRED. ROLLO, 1st Royal Scots.

TESTIMONIALS.

We willingly certify that the bearer, Mr William M'Gonagall, has considerable ability in recitation. We have heard him recite some passages from Shakspeare with great force ; and are of opinion that he is quite competent to read or recite passages from the poets and orators in villages and country towns with pleasure and profit to his audience. We also believe him to be a respectable man.

> ISLAY BURNS, Minister of St. Peter's F. Church.
> JOHN ALEX. BANKS, M.A. Edin., Headmaster,
> Propy. School, Dundee.
> WILLIAM KNIGHT, Assistant, Free St. John's Ch.,
> Dundee (now Professor, St. Andrews Univ.).

29th March 1864.

Dundee, 30th May 1865.

I certify that William M'Gonagall has for some time been known to me. I have heard him speak, he has a strong proclivity for the elocutionary department, a strong voice, and great enthusiasm. He has had a good deal of experience too, having addressed audiences. nd enacted parts here and elsewhere

> GEORGE GILFILLAN.

POETIC GEMS.

AN ODE TO THE QUEEN

ON HER JUBILEE YEAR.

Sound drums and trumpets, far and near!
And let all Queen Victoria's subjects loudly cheer!
And show by their actions that her they revere,
Because she's served them faithfully fifty long year!

All hail to the Empress of India and Great Britain's Queen!
Long may she live happy and serene!
And as this is now her Jubilee year,
I hope her subjects will show their loyalty without fear.

Therefore let all her subjects rejoice and sing,
Until they make the welkin ring :
And let young and old on this her Jubilee be glad,
And cry, " Long Live our Queen! " and don't be sad.

She has been a good Queen, which no one dare gainsay,
And I hope God will protect her for many a day ;
May He enable her a few more years to reign,
And let all her lieges say—Amen!

Let all hatred towards her be thrown aside
All o'er her dominions broad and wide ;
And let all her subjects bear in mind,
By God kings and queens are put in trust o'er mankind.

Therefore rejoice and be glad on her Jubilee day,
And try and make the heart of our Queen feel gay ;
Oh! try and make her happy in country and town,
And not with Shakspeare say, " uneasy lies the head that
wears a crown."

And as this is her first Jubilee year,
And will be her last, I rather fear ;
Therefore, sound drums and trumpets cheerfully,
Until the echoes are heard o'er land and sea.

And let the innocent voices of the children at home or abroad
Ascend with cheerful shouts to the throne of God ;
And sing aloud, " God Save our Gracious Queen ! "
Because a good and charitable Sovereign she has been.

Therefore, ye sons of Great Britain, come join with me,
And welcome in our noble Queen's Jubilee ;
Because she has been a faithful Queen, ye must confess,
There hasn't been her equal since the days of Queen Bess

Therefore let all her lieges shout and cheer,
" God Save our Gracious Queen ! " for many a year ;
Let such be the cry in the peasant's cot, and hall,
With stentorian voices, as loud as they can bawl.

And let bonfires be kindled on every hill,
And her subjects dance around them at their freewill ;
And try to drive dull care away
By singing and rejoicing on the Queen's Jubilee day.

May God protect her for many a day,
At home or abroad when she's far away ;
Long may she be spared o'er her subjects to reign,
And let each and all with one voice say—Amen !

Victoria is a good Queen, which all her subjects know,
And for that may God protect her from every foe ;
May He be as a hedge around her, as He's been all along,
And let her live and die in peace—is the end of my song.

THE DEATH OF PRINCE LEOPOLD.

Alas! noble Prince Leopold, he is dead!
Who often has his lustre shed :
Especially by singing for the benefit of Esher School,—
Which proves he was a wise prince, and no conceited fool.

Methinks I see him on the platform singing the *Sands o' Dee*,
The generous-hearted Leopold, the good and the free,
Who was manly in his actions, and beloved by his mother ;
And in all the family she hasn't got such another.

He was of a delicate constitution all his life,
And he was his mother's favourite, and very kind to his wife,
And he had also a particular liking for his child,
And in his behaviour he was very mild.

Oh! noble-hearted Leopold, most beautiful to see,
Who was wont to fill your audience's hearts with glee,
With your charming songs, and lectures against strong drink:
Britain had nothing else to fear, as far as you could think.

A wise prince you were, and well worthy of the name,
And to write in praise of thee I cannot refrain ;
Because you were ever ready to defend that which is right,
Both pleasing and righteous in God's eye-sight.

And for the loss of such a prince the people will mourn,
But, alas! unto them he can never more return,
Because sorrow never could revive the dead again,
Therefore to weep for him is all in vain.

'Twas on Saturday the 12th of April, in the year 1884,
He was buried in the royal vault, never to rise more
Until the great and fearful judgment-day,
When the last trump shall sound to summon him away.

When the Duchess of Albany arrived she drove through the
    Royal Arch,—
A little before the Seaforth Highlanders set out on the funeral
    march ;
And she was received with every sympathetic respect,
Which none of the people present seem'd to neglect.

Then she entered the memorial chapel and stayed a short time,
And as she viewed her husband's remains it was really sublime,
While her tears fell fast on the coffin lid without delay,
Then she took one last fond look, and hurried away.

At half-past ten o'clock the Seaforth Highlanders did appear,
And every man in the detachment his medals did wear ;
And they carried their side-arms by their side,
With mournful looks, but full of love and pride.

Then came the Coldstream Guards headed by their band,
Which made the scene appear imposing and grand ;
Then the musicians drew up in front of the guard-room,
And waited patiently to see the prince laid in the royal tomb.

First in the procession were the servants of His late Royal
    Highness,
And next came the servants of the Queen in deep mourning
    dress,
And the gentlemen of his household in deep distress,
Also General Du Pla, who accompanied the remains from
    Cannes.

The coffin was borne by eight Highlanders of his own regiment,
And the fellows seemed to be rather discontent
For the loss of the prince they loved most dear,
While adown their cheeks stole many a silent tear.

Then behind the corpse came the Prince of Wales in field
    marshal uniform,
Looking very pale, dejected, careworn, and forlorn ;
Then followed great magnates, all dressed in uniform,
And last, but not least, the noble Marquis of Lorne.

The scene in George's Chapel was most magnificent to behold,
The banners of the knights of the garter embroidered with gold;
Then again it was most touching and lovely to see
The Seaforth Highlanders' inscription to the Prince's memory:

It was wrought in violets, upon a background of white flowers,
And as they gazed upon it their tears fell in showers ;
But the whole assembly were hushed when Her Majesty did
    appear,
Attired in her deepest mourning, and from her eye there fell
    a tear.

Her Majesty was unable to stand long, she was overcome
    with grief,
And when the Highlanders lowered the coffin into the tomb
    she felt relief ;
Then the ceremony closed with singing " Lead, kindly light,"
Then the Queen withdrew in haste from the mournful sight.

Then the Seaforth Highlanders' band played " Lochaber no
    more,"
While the brave soldiers' hearts felt depressed and sore ;
And as homeward they marched they let fall many a tear
For the loss of the virtuous Prince Leopold they loved so dear

THE DEATH OF LORD AND LADY DALHOUSIE.

Alas! Lord and Lady Dalhousie are dead, and buried at last,
Which causes many people to feel a little downcast;
And both lie side by side in one grave,
But I hope God in His goodness their souls will save.

And may He protect their children that are left behind,
And may they always food and raiment find;
And from the paths of virtue may they ne'er be led,
And may they always find a house wherein to lay their head.

Lord Dalhousie was a man worthy of all praise,
And to his memory I hope a monument the people will raise,
That will stand for many ages to come
To commemorate the good deeds he has done.

He was beloved by men of high and low degree,
Especially in Forfarshire by his tenantry:
And by many of the inhabitants in and around Dundee.
Because he was affable in temper, and void of all vanity.

He had great affection for his children, also his wife,
'Tis said he loved her as dear as his life;
And I trust they are now in heaven above,
Where all is joy, peace, and love.

At the age of fourteen he resolved to go to sea,
So he entered the training-ship Britannia belonging the
    navy,
And entered as a midshipman as he considered most fit,
Then passed through the course of training with the greatest
    credit.

In a short time he obtained the rank of lieutenant,
Then to her Majesty's ship Galatea he was sent ;
Which was under the command of the Duke of Edinburgh,
And during his service there he felt but little sorrow.

And from that he was promoted to be commander of the
    Britannia,
And was well liked by the men, for what he said was law ;
And by him Prince Albert Victor and Prince George received
    a naval education,
Which met with the Prince of Wales' most hearty approbation

'Twas in the year 1877 he married the Lady Ada Louisa
    Bennett,
And by marrying that noble lady he ne'er did regret ;
And he was ever ready to give his service in any way,
Most willingly and cheerfully by night or by day.

'Twas in the year of 1887, and on Thursday the 1st of
    December,
Which his relatives and friends will long remember
That were present at the funeral in Cockpen churchyard,
Because they had for the noble Lord a great regard.

About eleven o'clock the remains reached Dalhousie,
And were met by a body of the tenantry ;
They conveyed them inside the building, all seemingly woe
    begone,
And among those that sent wreaths was Lord Claude
    Hamilton.

Those that sent wreaths were but very few,
But one in particular was the Duke of Buccleuch ;
Besides Dr. Herbert Spencer, and Countess Rosebery, and
    Lady Bennett,
Which no doubt were sent by them with heartfelt regret.

Besides those that sent wreaths in addition were the Earl
    and Countess of Aberdeen,
Especially the Prince of Wales' was most lovely to be seen,
And the Earl of Dalkeith's wreath was very pretty too,
With a mixture of green and white flowers, beautiful to
    view.

Amongst those present at the interment were Mr Marjori-
    banks, M.P.,
Also ex-Provost Ballingall from Bonnie Dundee ;
Besides the Honourable W. G. Colville, representing the
    Duke and Duchess of Edinburgh,
While in every one's face standing at the grave was depicted
    sorrow.

The funeral service was conducted in the Church of Cockpen
By the Rev. J. Crabb, of St. Andrew's Episcopal Church,
    town of Brechin ;
And as the two coffins were lowered into their last resting-
    place,
Then the people retired with sad hearts at a quick pace.

THE FUNERAL OF THE GERMAN EMPEROR.

YE sons of Germany, your noble Emperor William now is
    dead,
Who oft great armies to battle hath led ;
He was a man beloved by his subjects all,
Because he never tried them to enthral.

The people of Germany have cause now to mourn
The loss of their hero, who to them will ne'er return ;
But his soul I hope to Heaven has fled away,
To the realms of endless bliss for ever and aye.

He was much respected throughout Europe by the high and
    the low,
And all over Germany people's hearts are full of woe ;
For in the battlefield he was a hero bold,
Nevertheless, a lover of peace, to his credit be it told.

'Twas in the year of 1888, and on March the 16th day,
That the peaceful William's remains were conveyed away
To the royal mausoleum of Charlottenburg, their last resting-
    place,
The God-fearing man that never did his country disgrace.

The funeral service was conducted in the cathedral by the
    court chaplain, Dr. Kogel,
Which touched the hearts of his hearers, as from his lips it
    fell,
And in conclusion he recited the Lord's Prayer
In the presence of kings, princes, dukes, and counts assembled
    there.

And at the end of the service the infantry outside fired
    volley after volley,
While the people inside the cathedral felt melancholy,
As the sound of the musketry smote upon the ear,
In honour of the illustrious William, whom they loved most dear.

Then there was a solemn pause as the kings and princes
    took their places,
Whilst the hot tears are trickling down their faces,
And the mourners from shedding tears couldn't refrain ;
And in respect of the good man, above the gateway glared a
    bituminous flame.

Then the coffin was placed on the funeral car,
By the kings and princes that came from afar ;
And the Crown Prince William heads the procession alone,
While behind him are the four heirs-apparent to the throne.

Then followed the three Kings of Saxony, and the King of
    the Belgians also,
Together with the Prince of Wales, with their hearts full of woe,
Besides the Prince of Naples and Prince Rudolph of Austria
    were there,
Also the Czarevitch, and other princes in their order I do
    declare.

And as the procession passes the palace the blinds are drawn
    completely,
And every house is half hidden with the sable drapery ;
And along the line of march expansive arches were erected,
While the spectators standing by seemed very dejected.

And through the Central Avenue, to make the decorations
    complete,
There were pedestals erected, rising fourteen to fifteen feet,

And at the foot and top of each pedestal were hung decora
tions of green bay,
Also beautiful wreaths and evergreen festoons all in grand
array.

And there were torches fastened on pieces of wood stuck in
the ground ;
And as the people gazed on the wierd-like scene, their silence
was profound ;
And the shopkeepers closed their shops, and hotel-keepers
closed in the doorways,
And with torchlight and gaslight, Berlin for once was all ablaze.

The authorities of Berlin in honour of the Emperor considered
it no sin,
To decorate with crape the beautiful city of Berlin ;
Therefore Berlin I declare was a city of crape,
Because few buildings crape decoration did escape.

First in the procession was the Emperor's bodyguard,
And his great love for them nothing could it retard ;
Then followed a squadron of the hussars with their band,
Playing " Jesus, Thou my Comfort," most solemn and grand.

And to see the procession passing the sightseers tried their best,
Especially when the cavalry hove in sight, riding four abreast ;
Men and officers with their swords drawn, a magnificent sight
to see
In the dim sun's rays, their burnished swords glinting dimly.

Then followed the footguards with slow and solemn tread,
Playing the " Dead March in Saul," most appropriate for the
dead ;
And behind them followed the artillery, with four guns
abreast,
Also the ministers and court officials dressed in their best.

The whole distance to the grave was covered over with laurel
and bay,
So that the body should be borne along smoothly all the way ;
And the thousands of banners in the procession were beautiful
to view,
Because they were composed of cream-coloured silk and light
blue.

There were thousands of thousands of men and women
gathered there,
And standing ankle deep in snow, and seemingly didn't care
So as they got a glimpse of the funeral car,
Especially the poor souls that came from afar.

And when the funeral car appeared there was a general hush,
And the spectators in their anxiety to see began to crush ;
And when they saw the funeral car by the Emperor's charger
led,
Every hat and cap was lifted reverently from off each head.

And as the procession moved on to the royal mausoleum,
The spectators remained bareheaded and seemingly quite
dumb ;
And as the coffin was borne into its last resting-place,
Sorrow seemed depicted in each one's face.

And after the burial service the mourners took a last farewell
Of the noble-hearted William they loved so well ;
Then rich and poor dispersed quietly that were assembled
there,
While two batteries of field-guns fired a salute which did
rend the air
In honour of the immortal hero they loved so dear,
The founder of the Fatherland Germany, that he did revere.

THE BATTLE OF TEL-EL-KEBIR.

YE sons of Great Britain, come join with me,
And sing in praise of Sir Garnet Wolseley ;
Sound drums and trumpets cheerfully,
For he has acted most heroically.

Therefore loudly his praises sing
Until the hills their echoes back doth ring ;
For he is a noble hero bold,
And an honour to his Queen and country, be it told.

He has gained for himself fame and renown,
Which to posterity will be handed down ;
Because he has defeated Arabi by land and by sea,
And from the battle of Tel-el-Kebir he made him to flee.

With an army about fourteen thousand strong,
Through Egypt he did fearlessly march along,
With the gallant and brave Highland brigade,
To whom honour is due, be it said.

Arabi's army was about seventy thousand in all,
And, virtually speaking, it wasn't very small ;
But if they had been as numerous again,
The Irish and Highland brigades would have beaten them, it
    is plain.

'Twas on the 13th day of September, in the year of 1882,
Which Arabi and his rebel horde long will rue ;
Because Sir Garnet Wolseley and his brave little band
Fought and conquered them on Kebir land.

He marched upon the enemy with his gallant band
O'er the wild and lonely desert sand,
And attacked them before daylight,
And in twenty minutes he put them to flight.

The first shock of the attack was borne by the Second Brigade,
Who behaved most manfully, it is said,
Under the command of brave General Grahame,
And have gained a lasting honour to their name.

But Major Hart and the 18th Royal Irish, conjoint,
Carried the trenches at the bayonet's point ;
Then the Marines chased them about four miles away,
At the charge of the bayonet, without dismay!

General Sir Archibald Alison led on the Highland Brigade,
Who never were the least afraid.
And such has been the case in this Egyptian war,
For at the charge of the bayonet they ran from them afar!

With their bagpipes playing, and one ringing cheer,
And the 42nd soon did the trenches clear ;
Then hand to hand they did engage,
And fought like tigers in a cage.

Oh! it must have been a glorious sight
To see Sir Garnet Wolseley in the thickest of the fight!
In the midst of shot and shell, and the cannon's roar,
Whilst the dead and the dying lay weltering in their gore.

Then the Egyptians were forced to yield,
And the British were left masters of the field ;
Then Arabi he did fret and frown
To see his army thus cut down.

Then Arabi the rebel took to flight,
And spurred his Arab steed with all his might :
With his heart full of despair and woe,
And never halted till he reached Cairo.

Now since the Egyptian war is at an end,
Let us thank God! Who did send
Sir Garnet Wolseley to crush and kill
Arabi and his rebel army at Kebir hill.

THE FAMOUS TAY WHALE.

'Twas in the month of December, and in the year 1883,
That a monster whale came to Dundee,
Resolved for a few days to sport and play,
And devour the small fishes in the silvery Tay.

So the monster whale did sport and play
Among the innocent little fishes in the beautiful Tay,
Until he was seen by some men one day,
And they resolved to catch him without delay.

When it came to be known a whale was seen in the Tay,
Some men began to talk and to say,
We must try and catch this monster of a whale,
So come on, brave boys, and never say fail.

Then the people together in crowds did run,
Resolved to capture the whale and to have some fun!
So small boats were launched on the silvery Tay,
While the monster of the deep did sport and play.

Oh! it was a most fearful and beautiful sight,
To see it lashing the water with its tail all its might,
And making the water ascend like a shower of hail,
With one lash of its ugly and mighty tail.

Then the water did descend on the men in the boats,
Which wet their trousers and also their coats ;
But it only made them the more determined to catch the **whale**,
But the whale shook at them his tail.

Then the whale began to puff and to blow,
While the men and the boats after him did go,
Armed well with harpoons for the fray,
Which they fired at him without dismay.

And they laughed and grinned just like wild baboons,
While they fired at him their sharp harpoons :
But when struck with the harpoons he dived below,
Which filled his pursuers' hearts with woe :

Because they guessed they had lost a prize,
Which caused the tears to well up in their eyes ;
And in that their anticipations were only right,
Because he sped on to Stonehaven with all his might :

And was first seen by the crew of a Gourdon fishing boat,
Which they thought was a big coble upturned afloat ;
But when they drew near they saw it was a whale,
So they resolved to tow it ashore without fail.

So they got a rope from each boat tied round his tail,
And landed their burden at Stonehaven without fail ;
And when the people saw it their voices they did raise,
Declaring that the brave fishermen deserved great praise.

And my opinion is that God sent the whale in time of need,
No matter what other people may think or what is their creed ;
I know fishermen in general are often very poor,
And God in His goodness sent it to drive poverty from their
    door.

So Mr John Wood has bought it for two hundred and twenty-
    six pound,
And has brought it to Dundee all safe and all sound ;
Which measures 40 feet in length from the snout to the tail,
So I advise the people far and near to see it without fail.

Then hurrah! for the mighty monster whale,
Which has got 17 feet 4 inches from tip to tip of a tail!
Which can be seen for a sixpence or a shilling,
That is to say, if the people all are willing.

THE RAILWAY BRIDGE OF THE SILVERY TAY.

BEAUTIFUL Railway Bridge of the Silvery Tay!
With your numerous arches and pillars in so grand array,
And your central girders, which seem to the eye
To be almost towering to the sky.
The greatest wonder of the day,
And a great beautification to the River Tay,
Most beautiful to be seen,
Near by Dundee and the Magdalen Green.

Beautiful Railway Bridge of the Silvery Tay!
That has caused the Emperor of Brazil to leave
His home far away, *incognito* in his dress,
And view thee ere he passed along *en route* to Inverness.

Beautiful Railway Bridge of the Silvery Tay!
The longest of the present day
That has ever crossed o'er a tidal river stream,
Most gigantic to be seen,
Near by Dundee and the Magdalen Green.

Beautiful Railway Bridge of the Silvery Tay!
Which will cause great rejoicing on the opening day,
And hundreds of people will come from far away,
Also the Queen, most gorgeous to be seen,
Near by Dundee and the Magdalen Green.

Beautiful Railway Bridge of the Silvery Tay!
And prosperity to Provost Cox, who has given
Thirty thousand pounds and upwards away
In helping to erect the Bridge of the Tay,
Most handsome to be seen,
Near by Dundee and the Magdalen Green.

Beautiful Railway Bridge of the Silvery Tay!
I hope that God will protect all passengers
By night and by day,
And that no accident will befall them while crossing
The Bridge of the Silvery Tay,
For that would be most awful to be seen
Near by Dundee and the Magdalen Green.

Beautiful Railway Bridge of the Silvery Tay!
And prosperity to Messrs Bouche and Grothe,
The famous engineers of the present day,
Who have succeeded in erecting the Railway
Bridge of the Silvery Tay,
Which stands unequalled to be seen
Near by Dundee and the Magdalen Green.

THE NEWPORT RAILWAY.

Success to the Newport Railway,
Along the braes of the Silvery Tay,
And to Dundee straightway,
Across the Railway Bridge o' the Silvery Tay,
Which was opened on the 12th of May,
In the year of our Lord 1879,
Which will clear all expenses in a very short time
Because the thrifty housewives of Newport
To Dundee will often resort,
Which will be to them profit and sport,
By bringing cheap tea, bread, and jam,
And also some of Lipton's ham,
Which will make their hearts feel light and gay,
And cause them to bless the opening day
Of the Newport Railway.

The train is most beautiful to be seen,
With its long, white curling cloud of steam,
As the train passes on her way
Along the bonnie braes o' the Silvery Tay.

And if the people of Dundee
Should feel inclined to have a spree,
I am sure 'twill fill their hearts with glee
By crossing o'er to Newport,
And there they can have excellent sport,
By viewing the scenery beautiful and gay,
During the livelong summer day,

And then they can return at night
With spirits light and gay,
By the Newport Railway,
By night or by day,
Across the Railway Bridge o' the Silvery Tay.

Success to the undertakers of the Newport Railway
Hoping the Lord will their labours repay,
And prove a blessing to the people
For many a long day
Who live near by Newport,
On the bonnie braes o' the Silvery Tay.

THE TAY BRIDGE DISASTER.

BEAUTIFUL Railway Bridge of the Silv'ry Tay!
Alas! I am very sorry to say
That ninety lives have been taken away
On the last Sabbath day of 1879,
Which will be remember'd for a very long time.

'Twas about seven o'clock at night,
And the wind it blew with all its might,
And the rain came pouring down,
And the dark clouds seem'd to frown,
And the Demon of the air seem'd to say—
" I'll blow down the Bridge of Tay."

When the train left Edinburgh
The passengers' hearts were light and felt no sorrow,
But Boreas blew a terrific gale,
Which made their hearts for to quail,
And many of the passengers with fear did say—
" I hope God will send us safe across the Bridge of Tay."

But when the train came near to Wormit Bay,
Boreas he did loud and angry bray,
And shook the central girders of the Bridge of Tay
On the last Sabbath day of 1879,
Which will be remember'd for a very long time.

So the train sped on with all its might,
And Bonnie Dundee soon hove in sight,
And the passengers' hearts felt light,
Thinking they would enjoy themselves on the New Year,
With their friends at home they lov'd most dear,
And wish them all a happy New Year.

So the train mov'd slowly along the Bridge of Tay,
Until it was about midway,
Then the central girders with a crash gave way,
And down went the train and passengers into the Tay!
The Storm Fiend did loudly bray,
Because ninety lives had been taken away,
On the last Sabbath day of 1879,
Which will be remember'd for a very long time.

As soon as the catastrophe came to be known
The alarm from mouth to mouth was blown,
And the cry rang out all o'er the town,
Good Heavens! the Tay Bridge is blown down,
And a passenger train from Edinburgh,
Which fill'd all the people's hearts with sorrow,
And made them for to turn pale,
Because none of the passengers were sav'd to tell the tale
How the disaster happen'd on the last Sabbath day of 1879
Which will be remember'd for a very long time.

It must have been an awful sight,
To witness in the dusky moonlight,
While the Storm Fiend did laugh, and angry did bray,
Along the Railway Bridge of the Silv'ry Tay.
Oh! ill-fated Bridge of the Silv'ry Tay,
I must now conclude my lay
By telling the world fearlessly without the least dismay,
That your central girders would not have given way,
At least many sensible men do say,
Had they been supported on each side with buttresses,
At least many sensible men confesses,
For the stronger we our houses do build,
The less chance we have of being killed.

43

AN ADDRESS TO THE NEW TAY BRIDGE.

BEAUTIFUL new railway bridge of the Silvery Tay,
With your strong brick piers and buttresses in so grand array,
And your thirteen central girders, which seem to my eye
Strong enough all windy storms to defy.
And as I gaze upon thee my heart feels gay,
Because thou are the greatest railway bridge of the present day,
And can be seen for miles away
From north, south, east, or west of the Tay
On a beautiful and clear sunshiny day,
And ought to make the hearts of the " Mars " boys feel gay,
Because thine equal nowhere can be seen,
Only near by Dundee and the bonnie Magdalen Green.

Beautiful new railway bridge of the Silvery Tay,
With thy beautiful side-screens along your railway,
Which will be a great protection on a windy day,
So as the railway carriages won't be blown away,
And ought to cheer the hearts of the passengers night and day
As they are conveyed along thy beautiful railway,
And towering above the silvery Tay,
Spanning the beautiful river shore to shore
Upwards of two miles and more,
Which is most wonderful to be seen
Near by Dundee and the bonnie Magdalen Green.

Thy structure to my eye seems strong and grand,
And the workmanship most skilfully planned ;
And I hope the designers, Messrs Barlow & Arrol, will prosper
    for many a day
For erecting thee across the beautiful Tay.
And I think nobody need have the least dismay
To cross o'er thee by night or by day,
Because thy strength is visible to be seen
Near by Dundee and the bonnie Magdalen Green.

44

Beautiful new railway bridge of the Silvery Tay
I wish you success for many a year and a day,
And I hope thousands of people will come from far away,
Both high and low without delay,
From the north, south, east, and the west,
Because as a railway bridge thou are the best ;
Thou standest unequalled to be seen
Near by Dundee and the bonnie Magdalen Green.

And for beauty thou art most lovely to be seen
As the train crosses o'er thee with her cloud of steam ;
And you look well, painted the colour of marone,
And to find thy equal there is none,
Which, without fear of contradiction, I venture to say,
Because you are the longest railway bridge of the present day
That now crosses o'er a tidal river stream,
And the most handsome to be seen
Near by Dundee and the bonnie Magdalen Green.

The New Yorkers boast about their Brooklyn Bridge,
But in comparison to thee it seems like a midge,
Because thou spannest the silvery Tay
A mile and more longer I venture to say ;
Besides the railway carriages are pulled across by a rope,
Therefore Brooklyn Bridge cannot with thee cope ;
And as you have been opened on the 20th day of June,
I hope Her Majesty Queen Victoria will visit thee very soon,
Because thou are worthy of a visit from Duke, Lord, or Queen,
And strong and securely built, which is most worthy to be seen
Near by Dundee and the bonnie Magdalen Green.

THE LATE SIR JOHN OGILVY.

ALAS! Sir John Ogilvy is dead, aged eighty-seven,
But I hope his soul is now in heaven ;
For he was a generous-hearted gentleman I am sure,
And, in particular, very kind unto the poor.

He was a Christian gentleman in every degree,
And, for many years, was an M.P. for Bonnie Dundee,
And, while he was an M.P., he didn't neglect
To advocate the rights of Dundee in every respect.

He was a public benefactor in many ways,
Especially in erecting an asylum for imbecile children to
    spend their days ;
Then he handed the institution over as free,—
As a free gift and a boon to the people of Dundee.

He was chairman of several of the public boards in Dundee,
And among these were the Asylum Board and the Royal
    Infirmary ;
In every respect he was a God-fearing true gentleman,
And to gainsay it there's nobody can.

He lived as a Christian gentleman in his time,
And he now lies buried in the family vault in Strathmartine ;
But I hope his soul has gone aloft where all troubles cease,
Amongst the blessed saints where all is joy and peace.

To the people around Baldovan he will be a great loss,
Because he was a kind-hearted man and a Soldier of the Cross.
He had always a kind word for every one he met,
And the loss of such a good man will be felt with deep regret.

Because such men as Sir John Ogilvy are hard to be found,
Especially in Christian charity his large heart did abound,
Therefore a monument should be erected for him most hand-
    some to behold,
And his good deeds engraven thereon in letters of gold.

THE RATTLING BOY FROM DUBLIN.

I'M a rattling boy from Dublin town,
I courted a girl called Biddy Brown,
Her eyes they were as black as sloes,
She had black hair and an aquiline nose.

Chorus—

Whack fal de da, fal de darelido,
Whack fal de da, fal de darelay,
Whack fal de da, fal de darelido,
Whack fal de da, fal de darelay.

One night I met her with another lad,
Says I, Biddy, I've caught you, by dad ;
I never thought you were half so bad
As to be going about with another lad.

Chorus.

Says I, Biddy, this will never do,
For to-night you've prov'd to me untrue,
So do not make a hullaballoo,
For I will bid farewell to you.

Chorus.

Says Barney Magee, She is my lass,
And the man that says no, he is an ass,
So come away, and I'll give you a glass,
Och, sure you can get another lass.

Chorus.

47

Says I, To the devil with your glass,
You have taken from me my darling lass,
And if you look angry, or offer to frown,
With my darling shillelah I'll knock you down.
Chorus.

Says Barney Magee unto me,
By the hokey I love Biddy Brown,
And before I'll give her up to thee,
One or both of us will go down.
Chorus.

So, with my darling shillelah, I gave him a whack,
Which left him lying on his back,
Saying, botheration to you and Biddy Brown,—
For I'm the rattling boy from Dublin town.
Chorus.

So a policeman chanced to come up at the time,
And he asked of me the cause of the shine,
Says I, he threatened to knock me down
When I challenged him for walking with my Biddy Brown
Chorus.

So the policeman took Barney Magee to jail,
Which made him shout and bewail
That ever he met with Biddy Brown,
The greatest deceiver in Dublin town.
Chorus.

So I bade farewell to Biddy Brown,
The greatest jilter in Dublin town,
Because she proved untrue to me,
And was going about with Barney Magee.
Chorus.

48

THE BURIAL OF THE REV. GEORGE GILFILLAN

On the Gilfillan burial day,
In the Hill o' Balgay,
It was a most solemn sight to see,
Not fewer than thirty thousand people assembled in Dundee,
All watching the funeral procession of Gilfillan that day,
That death had suddenly taken away,
And was going to be buried in the Hill o' Balgay.

There were about three thousand people in the procession alone,
And many were shedding tears, and several did moan,
And their bosoms heaved with pain,
Because they knew they would never look upon his like again.

There could not be fewer than fifty carriages in thep rocession
    that day,
And gentlemen in some of them that had come from far away,
And in whispers some of them did say,
As the hearse bore the precious corpse away,
Along the Nethergate that day.
I'm sure he will be greatly missed by the poor,
For he never turned them empty-handed away from his door ;
And to assist them in distress it didn't give him pain,
And I'm sure the poor will never look upon his like again.

On the Gilfillan burial day, in the Hill o' Balgay,
There was a body of policemen marshalled in grand array,
And marched in front of the procession all the way ;
Also the relatives and friends of the deceas'd,
Whom I hope from all sorrows has been releas'd,
And whose soul I hope to heaven has fled away,
To sing with saints above for ever and aye.

The Provost, Magistrates, and Town Council were in the
    procession that day ;
Also Mrs Gilfillan, who cried and sobbed all the way
For her kind husband, that was always affable and gay,
Which she will remember until her dying day.

When the procession arrived in the Hill o' Balgay,
The people were almost as hush as death, and many of them
    did say—
As long as we live we'll remember the day
That the great Gilfillan was buried in the Hill o' Balgay.

When the body of the great Gilfillan was lowered into the grave,
'Twas then the people's hearts with sorrow did heave ;
And with tearful eyes and bated breath,
Mrs Gilfillan lamented her loving husband's death.

Then she dropped a ringlet of immortelles into his grave,
Then took one last fond look, and in sorrow did leave ;
And all the people left with sad hearts that day,
And that ended the Gilfillan burial in the Hill o' Balgay.

THE BATTLE OF EL-TEB.

YE sons of Great Britain, I think no shame
To write in praise of brave General Graham !
Whose name will be handed down to posterity without any
    stigma,
Because, at the battle of El-Teb, he defeated Osman Digna.

With an army about five thousand strong,
To El-Teb, in the year 1884, he marched along,
And bivouacked there for the night ;
While around their fires they only thought of the coming fight.

They kept up their fires all the long night,
Which made the encampment appear weird-like to the sight ;
While the men were completely soaked with the rain,
But the brave heroes disdained to complain.

The brave heroes were glad when daylight did appear,
And when the reveille was sounded, they gave a hearty cheer
And their fires were piled up higher again,
Then they tried to dry their clothes that were soaked with
    the rain.

Then breakfast was taken about eight o'clock,
And when over, each man stood in the ranks as firm as a rock,
And every man seemed to be on his guard—
All silent and ready to move forward.

The first movement was a short one from where they lay—
Then they began to advance towards El-Teb without dismay,
And showed that all was in order for the fray,
While every man's heart seemed to feel light and gay.

The enemy's position could be seen in the distance far away
But the brave heroes marched on without delay—
Whilst the enemy's banners floated in the air,
And dark swarms of men were scattered near by there.

Their force was a large one—its front extended over a mile,
And all along the line their guns were all in file ;
But, as the British advanced, they disappeared,
While our brave kilty lads loudly cheered.

Thus slowly and cautiously brave General Graham proceeded,
And to save his men from slaughter, great caution was needed,
Because Osman Digna's force was about ten thousand strong ;
But he said, Come on, my brave lads, we'll conquer them
    ere long!

It was about ten o'clock when they came near the enemy's lines,
And on the morning air could be heard the cheerful chimes
Coming from the pipes of the gallant Black Watch,
Which every ear in the British force was eager to catch.

Then they passed by the enemy about mid-day,
While every Arab seemed to have his gun ready for the fray;
When a bullet strikes down General Baker by the way,
But he is soon in the saddle again without delay,

And ready for any service that he could perform ;
Whilst the bullets fell around them in a perfect storm
That they had to lie down, but not through fear,
Because the enemy was about 800 yards on their left rear

Then General Graham addressed his men,
And said, If they won't attack us, we must attack them,
So start to your feet my lads, and never fear,
And strike up your bagpipes, and give a loud cheer.

So they leapt to their feet, and gave a loud cheer,
While the Arabs swept down upon them without the least fear,
And put aside their rifles, and grasped their spears ;
Whilst the British bullets in front of them the earth uptears.

Then the British charged them with their cold steel,
Which made the Arabs backward for to reel ;
But they dashed forward again on their ranks without dismay,
But before the terrible fire of their musketry they were
    swept away.

Oh, God of Heaven! it was a terrible sight
To see, and hear the Arabs shouting with all their might
A fearful oath when they got an inch of cold steel,
Which forced them backwards again, and made them reel.

By two o'clock they were fairly beat,
And Osman Digna, the false prophet, was forced to retreat
After three hours of an incessant fight ;
But Heaven, 'tis said, defends the right.

And I think he ought to be ashamed of himself ;
For I consider he has acted the part of a silly elf,
By thinking to conquer the armies of the Lord
With his foolish and benighted rebel horde.

THE BATTLE OF ABU KLEA.

YE sons of Mars, come join with me,
And sing in praise of Sir Herbert Stewart's little army,
That made ten thousand Arabs flee
At the charge of the bayonet at Abu Klea.

General Stewart's force was about fifteen hundred all told,
A brave little band, but, like lions bold,
They fought under their brave and heroic commander,
As gallant and as skilful as the great Alexander.

And the nation has every reason to be proud,
And in praise of his little band we cannot speak too loud,
Because that gallant fifteen hundred soon put to flight
Ten thousand Arabs, which was a most beautiful sight.

The enemy kept up a harmless fire all night,
And threw up works on General Stewart's right ;
Therefore he tried to draw the enemy on to attack,
But they hesitated, and through fear drew back.

But General Stewart ordered his men forward in square,
All of them on foot, ready to die and to dare ;
And he forced the enemy to engage in the fray,
But in a short time they were glad to run away.

But not before they penetrated through the British square,
Which was a critical moment to the British, I declare,
Owing to the great number of the Arabs,
Who rushed against their bayonets and received fearful stabs.

Then all was quiet again until after breakfast,
And when the brave little band had finished their repast,
Then the firing began from the heights on the right,
From the breastworks they had constructed during the night.

By eight o'clock the enemy was of considerable strength,
With their banners waving beautifully and of great length,
And creeping steadily up the grassy road direct to the wells,
But the British soon checked their advance by shot and shells.

At ten o'clock brave General Stewart made a counter-attack,
Resolved to turn the enemy on a different track ;
And he ordered his men to form a hollow square,
Placing the Guards in the front, and telling them to prepare.

And on the left was the Mounted Infantry,
Which truly was a magnificent sight to see ;
Then the Sussex Regiment was on the right,
And the Heavy Cavalry and Naval Brigade all ready to fight.

Then General Stewart took up a good position on a slope,
Where he guessed the enemy could not with him cope,
Where he knew the rebels must advance,
All up hill and upon open ground, which was his only chance.

Then Captain Norton's battery planted shells amongst the
    densest mass,
Determined with shot and shell the enemy to harass ;
Then came the shock of the rebels against the British square,
While the fiendish shouts of the Arabs did rend the air.

But the steadiness of the Guards, Marines, and Infantry
    prevailed,
And for the loss of their brother officers they sadly bewailed,
Who fell mortally wounded in the bloody fray,
Which they will remember for many a long day.

For ten minutes a desperate struggle raged from left to rear,
While Gunner Smith saved Lieutenant Guthrie's life without
    dread or fear ;
When all the other gunners had been borne back,
He took up a handspike, and the Arabs he did whack.

The noble hero hard blows did strike,
As he swung round his head the handspike ;
He seemed like a destroying angel in the midst of the fight,
The way he scattered the Arabs left and right.

Oh ! it was an exciting and terrible sight,
To see Colonel Burnaby engaged in the fight :
With sword in hand, fighting with might and main,
Until killed by a spear-thrust in the jugular vein.

A braver soldier ne'er fought on a battle-field,
Death or glory was his motto, rather than yield ;
A man of noble stature and manly to behold,
And an honour to his country be it told.

It was not long before every Arab in the square was killed,
And with a dense smoke and dust the air was filled ;
General Stewart's horse was shot, and he fell to the ground,
In the midst of shot and shell on every side around.

And when the victory was won they gave three British cheers,
While adown their cheeks flowed many tears
For their fallen comrades that lay weltering in their gore ;
Then the quare was re-formed and the battle was o'er.

A CHRISTMAS CAROL

WELCOME, sweet Christmas, blest be the morn
That Christ our Saviour was born!
Earth's Redeemer, to save us from all danger,
And, as the Holy Record tells, born in a manger.

> *Chorus*—Then ring, ring, Christmas bells,
> Till your sweet music o'er the kingdom swells
> To warn the people to respect the morn
> That Christ their Saviour was born.

The snow was on the ground when Christ was born,
And the Virgin Mary His mother felt very forlorn
As she lay in a horse's stall at a roadside inn,
Till Christ our Saviour was born to free us from sin.

Oh! think of the Virgin Mary as she lay
In a lowly stable on a bed of hay,
And angels watching o'er her till Christ was born,
Therefore all the people should respect Christmas morn

The way to respect Christmas time
Is not by drinking whisky or wine,
But to sing praises to God on Christmas morn,
The time that Jesus Christ His Son was born ;

Whom He sent into the world to save sinners from hell,
And by believing in Him in heaven we'll dwell ;
Then blest be the morn that Christ was born,
Who can save us from hell, death, and scorn.

Then be warned, and respect the Saviour dear,
And treat with less respect the New Year,
And respect always the blessed morn
That Christ our Saviour was born.

For each new morn to the Christian is dear,
As well as the morn of the New Year,
And he thanks God for the light of each new morn,
Especially the morn that Christ was born.

Therefore, good people, be warned in time,
And on Christmas morn don't get drunk with wine,
But praise God above on Christmas morn,
Who sent His Son to save us from hell and scorn.

There the heavenly babe He lay
In a stall among a lot of hay,
While the Angel Host by Bethlehem
Sang a beautiful and heavenly anthem.

Christmas time ought to be held most dear,
Much more so than the New Year,
Because that's the time that Christ was born,
Therefore respect Christmas morn.

And let the rich be kind to the poor,
And think of the hardships they do endure,
Who are neither clothed nor fed,
And many without a blanket to their bed

THE CHRISTMAS GOOSE.

Mr Smiggs was a gentleman,
  And lived in London town ;
His wife she was a good kind soul,
  And seldom known to frown.

'Twas on Christmas eve,
  And Smiggs and his wife lay cosy in bed,
When the thought of buying a goose
  Came into his head.

So the next morning,
  Just as the sun rose,
He jump'd out of bed,
  And he donn'd his clothes,

Saying, " Peggy, my dear,
  You need not frown,
For I'll buy you the best goose
  In all London town."

So away to the poultry shop he goes,
  And bought the goose, as he did propose,
And for it he paid one crown,
  The finest, he thought, in London town.

When Smiggs bought the goose
  He suspected no harm,
But a naughty boy stole it
  From under his arm.

Then Smiggs he cried, " Stop, thief !
  Come back with my goose ! "
But the naughty boy laugh'd at him,
  And gave him much abuse.

But a policeman captur'd the naughty boy,
    And gave the goose to Smiggs,
And said he was greatly bother'd
    By a set of juvenile prigs.

So the naughty boy was put in prison
    For stealing the goose,
And got ten days' confinement
    Before he got loose.

So Smiggs ran home to his dear Peggy,
    Saying, " Hurry, and get this fat goose ready,
That I have bought for one crown ;
    So, my darling, you need not frown."

" Dear Mr Smiggs, I will not frown :
    I'm sure 'tis cheap for one crown,
Especially at Christmas time—
    Oh! Mr Smiggs, it's really fine."

" Peggy, it is Christmas time,
    So let us drive dull care away,
For we have got a Christmas goose,
    So cook it well, I pray.

" No matter how the poor are clothed,
    Or if they starve at home,
We'll drink our wine, and eat our goose,
    Aye, and pick it to the bone."

AN AUTUMN REVERIE.

Alas! beautiful Summer now hath fled,
And the face of Nature doth seem dead,
And the leaves are withered, and falling off the trees,
By the nipping and chilling autumnal breeze.

The pleasures of the little birds are all fled,
And with the cold many of them will be found dead,
Because the leaves of the trees are scattered in the blast,
And makes the feathered creatures feel downcast.

Because there are no leaves on the trees to shield them from
    the storm
On a windy, and rainy, cloudy morn ;
Which makes their little hearts throb with pain,
By the chilling blast and the pitiless rain.

But still they are more contented than the children of God,
As long as they can pick up a worm from the sod,
Or anything they can get to eat,
Just, for instance, a stale crust of bread or a grain of wheat.

Oh! think of the little birds in the time of snow,
Also of the little street waifs, that are driven to and fro,
And trembling in the cold blast, and chilled to the bone,
For the want of food and clothing, and a warm home.

Besides think of the sorrows of the wandering poor,
That are wandering in the cold blast from door to door ;
And begging, for Heaven's sake, a crust of bread,
And alas! not knowing where to lay their head.

While the rich are well fed and covered from the cold,
While the poor are starving, both young and old ;
Alas! it is the case in this boasted Christian land,
Whereas the rich are told to be kind to the poor, is God's
command.

Oh! think of the working man when he's no work to do,
Who's got a wife and family, perhaps four or two,
And the father searching for work, and no work can be had,
The thought, I'm sure, 'tis enough to drive the poor man mad.

Because for his wife and family he must feel,
And perhaps the thought thereof will cause him to steal
Bread for his family, that are starving at home,
While the thought thereof makes him sigh heavily and groan.

Alas! the pangs of hunger are very hard to thole,
And few people can their temper control,
Or become reconciled to their fate,
Especially when they cannot find anything to eat.

Oh! think of the struggles of the poor to make a living,
Because the rich unto them seldom are giving ;
Whereas they are told he that giveth to the poor lendeth
unto the Lord,
But alas! they rather incline their money to hoard.

Then there's the little news-vendors in the street,
Running about perhaps with bare feet ;
And if the rich chance to see such creatures in the street,
In general they make a sudden retreat.

THE WRECK OF THE STEAMER "LONDON'

WHILE ON HER WAY TO AUSTRALIA.

'TWAS in the year of 1866, and on a very beautiful day,
That eighty-two passengers, with spirits light and gay,
Left Gravesend harbour, and sailed gaily away
On board the steamship " London,"
Bound for the city of Melbourne,
Which unfortunately was her last run,
Because she was wrecked on the stormy main,
Which has caused many a heart to throb with pain,
Because they will ne'er look upon their lost ones again.

'Twas on the 11th of January they anchored at the Nore ;
The weather was charming—the like was seldom seen before
Especially the next morning as they came in sight
Of the charming and beautiful Isle of Wight,
But the wind it blew a terrific gale towards night,
Which caused the passengers' hearts to shake with fright,
And caused many of them to sigh and mourn,
And whisper to themselves, We will ne'er see Melbourne

Amongst the passengers was Gustavus V. Brooke,
Who was to be seen walking on the poop,
Also clergymen, and bankers, and magistrates also,
All chatting merrily together in the cabin below ;
And also wealthy families returning to their dear native land,
And accomplished young ladies, most lovely and grand,
All in the beauty and bloom of their pride,
And some with their husbands sitting close by their side.

'Twas all on a sudden the storm did arise,
Which took the captain and passengers all by surprise,
Because they had just sat down to their tea,
When the ship began to roll with the heaving of the sea,
And shipped a deal of water, which came down on their heads,
Which wet their clothes and also their beds ;
And caused a fearful scene of consternation,
And amongst the ladies great tribulation,
And made them cry out, Lord, save us from being drowned,
And for a few minutes the silence was profound.

Then the passengers began to run to and fro,
With buckets to bale out the water between decks below,
And Gustavus Brooke quickly leapt from his bed
In his Garibaldi jacket and drawers, without fear or dread,
And rushed to the pump, and wrought with might and main ;
But alas! all their struggling was in vain,
For the water fast did on them gain ;
But he enacted a tragic part until the last,
And sank exhausted when all succour was past ;
While the big billows did lash her o'er,
And the Storm-fiend did laugh and roar.

Oh, Heaven! it must have really been
A most harrowing and pitiful scene
To hear mothers and their children loudly screaming,
And to see the tears adown their pale faces streaming,
And to see a clergyman engaged in prayer,
Imploring God their lives to spare, ...
Whilst the cries of the women and children did rend the air.

Then the captain cried, Lower down the small boats,
And see if either of them sinks or floats ;
Then the small boats were launched on the stormy wave,
And each one tried hard his life to save
From a merciless watery grave.   .   .   .   .   .   .

A beautiful young lady did madly cry and rave,
" Five hundred sovereigns, my life to save! "
But she was by the sailors plainly told
For to keep her filthy gold, ...
Because they were afraid to overload the boat,
Therefore she might either sink or float,
Then she cast her eyes to Heaven, and cried, Lord, save me,
Then went down with the ship to the bottom of the sea,
Along with Gustavus Brooke, who was wont to fill our hearts
    with glee
While performing Shakespearian tragedy.

And out of eighty-two passengers only twenty were saved,
And that twenty survivors most heroically behaved.
For three stormy days and stormy nights they were tossed to
    and fro
On the raging billows, with their hearts full of woe,
Alas! poor souls, not knowing where to go,
Until at last they all agreed to steer for the south,
And they chanced to meet an Italian barque bound for
    Falmouth,
And they were all rescued from a watery grave,
And they thanked God and Captain Cavassa, who did their
    lives save.

THE WRECK OF THE " THOMAS DRYDEN "

IN PENTLAND FIRTH.

As I stood upon the sandy beach
  One morn near Pentland Ferry,
I saw a beautiful brigantine,
  And all her crew seem'd merry.

When lo! the wind began to howl,
  And the clouds began to frown,
And in the twinkling of an eye
  The rain came pouring down.

Then the sea began to swell,
  And seem'd like mountains high,
And the sailors on board that brigantine
  To God for help did loudly cry.

Oh! it was an awful sight
  To see them struggling with all their might
And imploring God their lives to save
  From a merciless watery grave.

Their cargo consisted of window-glass,
  Also coal and linseed-oil,
Which helped to calm the raging sea
  That loud and angry did boil.

Because when the bottoms of the barrels
  Were with the raging billows stove in,
The oil spread o'er the water,
  And smoothed the stormy billows' din!

Then she began to duck in the trough of the sea
  Which was fearful to behold ;
And her crossyards dipped in the big billows
  As from side to side she rolled.

She was tossed about on the merciless sea,
  And received some terrible shocks,
Until at last she ran against
  A jagged reef of rocks.

'Twas then she was rent asunder,
  And the water did rush in—
It was most dreadful to hear it,
  It made such a terrific din.

Then the crew jumped into the small boats
  While the Storm-fiend did roar,
And were very near being drowned
  Before they got ashore.

Then the coal-dust blackened the water
  Around her where she lay,
And the barrels of linseed-oil
  They floated far away.

And when the crew did get ashore,
  They were shaking with cold and fright,
And they went away to Huna inn,
  And got lodgings for the night!

ATTEMPTED ASSASSINATION OF THE QUEEN.

God prosper long our noble Queen,
  And long may she reign!
Maclean he tried to shoot her,
  But it was all in vain.

For God He turned the ball aside
  Maclean aimed at her head ;
And he felt very angry
  Because he didn't shoot her dead.

66

There's a divinity that hedgeth a king,
   And so it does seem,
And my opinion is, it has hedged
   Our most gracious Queen.

Maclean must be a madman,
   Which is obvious to be seen,
Or else he wouldn't have tried to shoot
   Our most beloved Queen.

Victoria is a good Queen,
   Which all her subjects know,
And for that God has protected her
   From all her deadly foes.

She is noble and generous,
   Her subjects must confess ;
There hasn't been her equal
   Since the days of good Queen Bess.

Long may she be spared to roam
   Among the bonnie Highland floral,
And spend many a happy day
   In the palace of Balmoral.

Because she is very kind
   To the old women there,
And allows them bread, tea, and sugar,
   And each one to get a share.

And when they know of her coming,
   Their hearts feel overjoy'd,
Because, in general, she finds work
   For men that's unemploy'd.

And she also gives the gipsies money
    While at Balmoral, I've been told,
And, mind ye, seldom silver,
    But very often gold.

I hope God will protect her
    By night and by day,
At home and abroad
    When she's far away.

May He be as a hedge around her,
    As He's been all along,
And let her live and die in peace
    Is the end of my song.

SAVING A TRAIN.

'Twas in the year of 1869, and on the 19th of November,
Which the people in Southern Germany will long remember,
The great rain-storm which for twenty hours did pour down,
That the rivers were overflowed and petty streams all around.

The rain fell in such torrents as had never been seen before,
That it seemed like a second deluge, the mighty torrents' roar,
At nine o'clock at night the storm did rage and moan,
When Carl Springel set out on his crutches all alone—

From the handsome little hut in which he dwelt,
With some food to his father, for whom he greatly felt,
Who was watching at the railway bridge,
Which was built upon a perpendicular rocky ridge.

The bridge was composed of iron and wooden blocks,
And crossed o'er the Devil's Gulch, an immense cleft of rocks ,
Two hundred feet wide and one hundred and fifty feet deep'
And enough to make one's flesh to creep.

Far beneath the bridge a mountain-stream did boil and rumble,
And on that night did madly toss and tumble ;
Oh! it must have been an awful sight
To see the great cataract falling from such a height.

It was the duty of Carl's father to watch the bridge on
    stormy nights,
And warn the on-coming trains of danger with the red lights ;
So, on this stormy night, the boy Carl hobbled along
Slowly and fearlessly upon his crutches, because he wasn't
    strong.

He struggled on manfully with all his might
Through the fearful darkness of the night,
And half-blinded by the heavy rain,
But still resolved the bridge to gain.

But, when within one hundred yards of the bridge, it gave
    way with an awful crash,
And fell into the roaring flood below, and made a fearful
    splash,
Which rose high above the din of the storm,
The like brave Carl never heard since he was born.

Then father! father! cried Carl in his loudest tone,
Father! father! he shouted again in very pitiful moans ;
But no answering voice did reply,
Which caused him to heave a deep-fetched sigh.

And now to brave Carl the truth was clear
That he had lost his father dear,
And he cried, My poor father's lost, and cannot be found
He's gone down with the bridge, and has been drowned.

But he resolves to save the on-coming train,
So every nerve and muscle he does strain,
And he trudges along dauntlessly on his crutches,
And tenaciously to them he clutches.

And just in time he reaches his father's car
To save the on-coming train from afar,
So he seizes the red light, and swings it round,
And cries with all his might, The bridge is down! The
    bridge is down!

So forward his father's car he drives,
Determined to save the passengers' lives,
Struggling hard with might and main,
Hoping his struggle won't prove in vain.

So on comes the iron-horse snorting and rumbling,
And the mountain-torrent at the bridge kept roaring **and**
    tumbling ;
While brave Carl keeps shouting, The bridge is down! **The**
    bridge is down!
He cried with a pitiful wail and sound.

But, thank heaven, the engine-driver sees the red light
That Carl keeps swinging round his head with all his **might** ;
But bang! bang! goes the engine with a terrible crash,
And the car is dashed all to smash.

But the breaking of the car stops the train,
And poor Carl's struggle is not in vain ;
But, poor soul, he was found stark dead,
Crushed and mangled from foot to head!

And the passengers were all loud in Carl's praise,
And from the cold wet ground they did him raise,
And tears for brave Carl fell silently around,
Because he had saved two hundred passengers from being
    drowned.

In a quiet village cemetery he now sleeps among the silent
    dead,
In the south of Germany, with a tombstone at his head,
Erected by the passengers he saved in the train,
And which to his memory wil¹ long remain.

THE MOON.

Beautiful Moon, with thy silvery light,
Thou seemest most charming to my sight ;
As I gaze upon thee in the sky so high,
A tear of joy does moisten mine eye.

Beautiful Moon, with thy silvery light,
Thou cheerest the Esquimau in the night ;
For thou lettest him see to harpoon the fish,
And with them he makes a dainty dish.

Beautiful Moon, with thy silvery light,
Thou cheerest the fox in the night,
And lettest him see to steal the grey goose away
Out of the farm-yard from a stack of hay.

Beautiful Moon, with thy silvery light,
Thou cheerest the farmer in the night,
And makest his heart beat high with delight
As he views his crops by the light in the night.

Beautiful Moon, with thy silvery light,
Thou cheerest the eagle in the night,
And lettest him see to devour his prey
And carry it to his nest away.

Beautiful Moon, with thy silvery light,
Thou cheerest the mariner in the night
As he paces the deck alone,
Thinking of his dear friends at home.

Beautiful Moon, with thy silvery light,
Thou cheerest the weary traveller in the night ;
For thou lightest up the wayside around
To him when he is homeward bound.

O Beautiful Moon, with thy silvery light,
Thou cheerest the lovers in the night
As they walk through the shady groves alone,
Making love to each other before they go home.

Beautiful Moon, with thy silvery light,
Thou cheerest the poacher in the night ;
For thou lettest him see to set his snares
To catch the rabbits and the hares.

THE BEAUTIFUL SUN.

BEAUTIFUL SUN! with thy golden rays,
To God, the wise Creator, be all praise ;
For thou nourisheth all the creation,
Wherever there is found to be animation.

Without thy heat we could not live,
Then praise to God we ought to give ;
For thou makest the fruits and provisions to grow,
To nourish all creatures on earth below.

Thou makest the hearts of the old feel glad,
Likewise the young child and the lad,
And the face of Nature to look green and gay,
And the little children to sport and play.

Thou also giveth light unto the Moon,
Which certainly is a very great boon
To all God's creatures here below,
Throughout the world where'er they go.

How beautiful thou look'st on a summer morn,
When thou sheddest thy effulgence among the yellow corn,
Also upon lake, and river, and the mountain tops,
Whilst thou leavest behind the most lovely dewdrops!

How beautiful thou seem'st in the firmament above,
As I gaze upon thee, my heart fills with love
To God, the great Creator, Who has placed thee there,
Who watches all His creatures with an eye of care!

Thou makest the birds to sing on the tree,
Also by meadow, mountain, and lea :
And the lark high poised up in air,
Carolling its little song with its heart free from care.

Thou makest the heart of the shepherd feel gay
As he watches the little lambkins at their innocent play :
While he tends them on the hillside all day,
Taking care that none of them shall go astray.

Thou cheerest the weary traveller while on his way
During the livelong summer day,
As he admires the beautiful scenery while passing along,
And singing to himself a stave of a song.

Thou cheerest the tourist while amongst the Highland hills,
As he views their beautiful sparkling rills
Glittering like diamonds by thy golden rays,
While the hills seem to offer up to God their praise.

While the bee from flower to flower does roam
To gather honey, and carry it home ;
While it hums its little song in the beautiful sunshine,
And seemingly to thank the Creator divine—

For the honey it hath gathered during the day,
In the merry month of May,
When the flowers are in full bloom,
Also the sweet honeysuckle and the broom.

How beautiful thy appearance while setting in the west,
Whilst encircled with red and azure, 'tis then thou look'st best!
Then let us all thank God for thy golden light
In our prayers every morning and night !

GRACE DARLING;

THE WRECK OF THE "FORFARSHIRE."

As the night was beginning to close in one rough September
    day
In the year of 1838, a steamer passed through the Fairway
Between the Farne Islands and the coast, on her passage
    northwards ;
But the wind was against her, and the steamer laboured hard.

There she laboured in the heavy sea against both wind and
    tide,
While a dense fog enveloped her on every side ;
And the mighty billows made her timbers creak,
Until at last, unfortunately, she sprung a leak.

Then all hands rushed to the pumps, and wrought with
    might and main.
But the water, alas! alarmingly on them did gain ;
And the thick sleet was driving across the raging sea,
While the wind it burst upon them in all its fury.

And the fearful gale and the murky aspect of the sky
Caused the passengers on board to lament and sigh
As the sleet drove thick, furious, and fast,
And as the waves surged mountains high, they stood aghast.

And the screaming of the sea-birds foretold a gathering storm,
And the passengers, poor souls, looked pale and forlorn,
And on every countenance was depicted woe
As the " Forfarshire " steamer was pitched to and fro.

And the engine-fires with the water were washed out ;
Then, as the tide set strongly in, it wheeled the vessel about,
And the ill-fated vessel drifted helplessly along ;
But the fog cleared up a little as the night wore on.

Then the terror-stricken crew saw the breakers ahead,
And all thought of being saved from them fled ;
And the Farne lights were shining hazily through the gloom,
While in the fore-cabin a woman lay with two children in a
swoon.

Before the morning broke, the " Forfarshire " struck upon a
rock,
And was dashed to pieces by a tempestuous shock,
Which raised her for a moment, and dashed her down again,
Then the ill-starred vessel was swallowed up in the briny main.

Before the vessel broke up, some nine or ten of the crew intent
To save their lives, or perish in the attempt,
Lowered one of the boats while exhausted and forlorn,
And, poor souls, were soon lost sight of in the storm.

Around the windlass on the forecastle some dozen poor
wretches clung,
And with despair and grief their weakly hearts were rung
As the merciless sea broke o'er them every moment ;
But God in His mercy to them Grace Darling sent.

By the first streak of dawn she early up had been,
And happened to look out upon the stormy scene,
And she descried the wreck through the morning gloom ;
But she resolved to rescue them from such a perilous doom.

Then she cried, Oh! father dear, come here and see the wreck,
See, here take the telescope, and you can inspect ;
Oh! father, try and save them, and heaven will you bless ;
But, my darling, no help can reach them in such a storm as this.

Oh! my kind father, you will surely try and save
These poor souls from a cold and watery grave ;
Oh! I cannot sit to see them perish before mine eyes,
And, for the love of heaven, do not my pleading despise!

Then old Darling yielded, and launched the little boat,
And high on the big waves the boat did float ;
Then Grace and her father took each an oar in hand,
And to see Grace Darling rowing the picture was grand.

And as the little boat to the sufferers drew near,
Poor souls, they tried to raise a cheer ;
But as they gazed upon the heroic Grace,
The big tears trickled down each sufferer's face.

And nine persons were rescued almost dead with the cold
By modest and lovely Grace Darling, that heroine bold ;
The survivors were taken to the light-house, and remained
    there two days,
And every one of them was loud in Grace Darling's praise.

Grace Darling was a comely lass, with long, fair floating hair,
With soft blue eyes, and shy, and modesty rare ;
And her countenance was full of sense and genuine kindliness,
With a noble heart, and ready to help suffering creatures in
    distress.

But, alas! three years after her famous exploit,
Which, to the end of time, will never be forgot,
Consumption, that fell destroyer, carried her away
To heaven, I hope, to be an angel for ever and aye.

Before she died, scores of suitors in marriage sought her hand ;
But no, she'd rather live in Longstone light-house on Farne
    island,
And there she lived and died with her father and mother,
And for her equal in true heroism we cannot find another.

TO MR JAMES SCRYMGEOUR, DUNDEE.

Success to James Scrymgeour,
  He's a very good man,
And to gainsay it,
  There's few people can ;

Because he makes the hearts
  Of the poor o'erjoyed
By trying to find work for them
  When they're unemployed.

And to their complaints
  He has always an attentive ear,
And ever ready to help them
  When unto him they draw near.

And no matter what your occupation is,
  Or what is your creed,
He will try to help you
  In the time of need ;

Because he has the fear
  Of God within his heart,
And the man that fears God
  Always takes the poor's part.

And blessed is the man
  That is kind to the poor ;
For his reward in heaven,
  'Tis said in the Scripture, is sure.

And I hope heaven will be
  Mr James Scrymgeour's reward ;
For his struggles on behalf of the poor
  Are really vexatious and hard.

For he is to be seen daily
  Walking along our streets,
With a Christian-looking countenance,
  And a kind word to all he meets.

Besides, he is void of all pride,
  And wouldn't feel ashamed
To be seen with a beggar
  Or a tinker walking by his side.

Fellow-citizens of Dundee,
  Isn't it really very nice
To think of James Scrymgeour trying
  To rescue fallen creatures from the paths of vice ?

And in the winter he tries to provide
  Hot dinners for the poor children of Dundee,
Who are starving with hunger no doubt,
  And in the most abject poverty.

He is a little deaf, no doubt,
  But not deaf to the cries of hungry men ;
No! he always tries to do his best
  To procure bread for them.

And at the Sabbath-morning free-breakfasts
  He is often seen there,
Administering to the wants of the hungry,
  And joining in prayer.

He is a man of noble principles,
  As far as I can think,
And the noblest principle he has got
  Is, he abhors the demon drink.

And, in my opinion, he is right
  As far as I can see,
And I hereby proclaim that such a man
  Is an honour to Dundee :

Because he is always working
    For the poor people's good,
Kind soul, trying hard
    To procure for them clothing and food.

Success to him and his family,
    And may God them defend :
Why ? fellow-citizens of Dundee,
    Because he is the poor man's friend.

THE BATTLE OF BANNOCKBURN.

SIR ROBERT the Bruce at Bannockburn
Beat the English in every wheel and turn,
And made them fly in great dismay
From off the field without delay.

The English were a hundred thousand strong,
And King Edward passed through the Lowlands all along,
Determined to conquer Scotland, it was his desire,
And then to restore it to his own empire.

King Edward brought numerous waggons in his train,
Expecting that most of the Scottish army would be slain,
Hoping to make the rest prisoners, and carry them away
In waggon-loads to London without delay.

The Scottish army did not amount to more than thirty
    thousand strong ;
But Bruce had confidence he'd conquer his foes ere long ;
So, to protect his little army, he thought it was right
To have deep-dug pits made in the night ;

And caused them to be overlaid with turf and brushwood
Expecting the plan would prove effectual where his little
    army stood,
Waiting patiently for the break of day,
All willing to join in the deadly fray.

Bruce stationed himself at the head of the reserve,
Determined to conquer, but never to swerve,
And by his side were brave Kirkpatrick and true De
    Longueville,
Both trusty warriors, firm and bold, who would never him
    beguile.

By daybreak the whole of the English army came in view,
Consisting of archers and horsemen, bold and true ;
The main body was led on by King Edward himself,
An avaricious man, and fond of pelf.

The Abbot of Inchaffray celebrated mass,
And all along the Scottish lines barefoot he did pass,
With the crucifix in his hand, a most beautiful sight to see,
Exhorting them to trust in God, and He would set them free.

Then the Scottish army knelt down on the field,
And King Edward he thought they were going to yield,
And he felt o'erjoyed, and cried to Earl Percy,
" See! See! the Scots are crying for mercy."

But Percy said, " Your Majesty need not make such a fuss,
They are crying for mercy from God, not from us ;
For, depend upon it, they will fight to a man, and find their
    graves
Rather than yield to become your slaves."

Then King Edward ordered his horsemen to charge,
Thirty thousand in number, it was very large ;
They thought to o'erwhelm them ere they could rise from
    their knees,
But they met a different destiny, which did them displease.
For the horsemen fell into the spik'd pits in the way,
And, with broken ranks and confusion, they all fled away

But few of them escap'd death from the spik'd pits,
For the Scots with their swords hack'd them to bits ;
De Valence was overthrown and carried off the field
Then King Edward he thought it was time to yield.

And he uttered a fearful cry
To his gay archers near by,
Ho! archers! draw your arrows to the head,
And make sure to kill them dead ;
Forward, without dread, and make them fly,
Saint George for England, be our cry!

Then the arrows from their bows swiftly did go,
And fell amongst them as thick as the flakes of snow ;
Then Bruce he drew his trusty blade,
And in heroic language said,
Forward! my heroes, bold and true!
And break the archers' ranks through and through!
And charge them boldly with your swords in hand,
And chase these vultures from off our land,
And make King Edward mourn
The day he came to Bannockburn.

See proud Edward on his milk-white steed,
One of England's finest breed,
Coming here in grand array,
With horsemen bold and archers gay,
Thinking he will us dismay,
And sweep everything before him in his way ;
But I swear by yon blessed sun
I'll make him and his army run
From off the field of Bannockburn.

By St. Andrew and our God most high,
We'll conquer these epicures or die!

And make them fly like chaff before the wind
Until they can no refuge find ;
And beat them off the field without delay,
Like lions bold and heroes gay.
Upon them!—charge!—follow me,
For Scotland's rights and liberty!

Then the Scots charged them with sword in hand,
And made them fly from off their land ;
And King Edward was amazed at the sight,
And he got wounded in the fight ;
And he cried, Oh, heaven! England's lost, and I'm undone,
Alas! alas! where shall I run ?
Then he turned his horse, and rode on afar,
And never halted till he reached Dunbar.

Then Bruce he shouted, Victory!
We have gained our rights and liberty ;
And thanks be to God above
That we have conquered King Edward this day,
A usurper that does not us love.

Then the Scots did shout and sing,
Long live Sir Robert Bruce our King!
That made King Edward mourn
The day he came to Bannockburn!

EDINBURGH.

BEAUTIFUL city of Edinburgh!
Where the tourist can drown his sorrow
By viewing your monuments and statues fine
During the lovely summer-time.
I'm sure it will his spirits cheer
As Sir Walter Scott's monument he draws near,
That stands in East Princes Street
Amongst flowery gardens, fine and neat.
And Edinburgh castle is magnificent to be seen
With its beautiful walks and trees so green,
Which seems like a fairy dell ;
And near by its rocky basement is St. Margaret's well,
Where the tourist can drink at when he feels dry,
And view the castle from beneath so very high,
Which seems almost towering to the sky.
Then as for Nelson's monument that stands on the Calton hill,
As the tourist gazes thereon, with wonder his heart does fill
As he thinks on Admiral Nelson who did the Frenchmen kill.
Then, as for Salisbury crags, they are most beautiful to be seen,
Especially in the month of June, when the grass is green ;
There numerous mole-hills can be seen,
And the busy little creatures howking away,
Searching for worms amongst the clay ;
And as the tourist's eye does wander to and fro
From the south side of Salisbury crags below,
His bosom with admiration feels all aglow
As he views the beautiful scenery in the valley below ;
And if, with an observant eye, the little loch beneath he scans,
He can see the wild ducks swimming about and beautiful
    white swans.

Then, as for Arthur's seat, I'm sure it is a treat
Most worthy to be seen, with its rugged rocks and pastures
    green,
And the sheep browsing on its sides
To and fro, with slow-paced strides,
And the little lambkins at play
During the livelong summer-day.
Beautiful city of Edinburgh! the truth to express,
Your beauties are matchless I must confess,
And which no one dare gainsay,
But that you are the grandest city in Scotland at the present
    day!

GLASGOW.

BEAUTIFUL city of Glasgow, with your streets so neat and clean,
Your stately mansions, and beautiful Green!
Likewise your beautiful bridges across the river Clyde,
And on your bonnie banks I would like to reside.

    Chorus—
    Then away to the West—to the beautiful West!
    To the fair city of Glasgow that I like the best,
    Where the river Clyde rolls on to the sea,
    And the lark and the blackbird whistle with glee.

'Tis beautiful to see the ships passing to and fro,
Laden with goods for the high and the low ;
So let the beautiful city of Glasgow flourish,
And may the inhabitants always find food their bodies to
    nourish.

    Chorus

The statue of the Prince of Orange is very grand,
Looking terror to the foe, with a truncheon in his hand,
And well mounted on a noble steed, which stands in the
Trongate,
And holding up its foreleg, I'm sure it looks first-rate.

Chorus.

Then there's the Duke of Wellington's statue in Royal
Exchange Square—
It is a beautiful statue I without fear declare,
Besides inspiring and most magnificent to view,
Because he made the French fly at the battle of Waterloo.

Chorus.

And as for the statue of Sir Walter Scott that stands in
George Square,
It is a handsome statue—few can with it compare,
And most elegant to be seen,
And close beside it stands the statue of Her Majesty the
Queen.

Chorus.

Then there's the statue of Robert Burns in George Square,
And the treatment he received when living was very unfair ;
Now, when he's dead, Scotland's sons for him do mourn,
But, alas! unto them he can never return.

Chorus.

Then as for Kelvin Grove, it is most lovely to be seen
With its beautiful flowers and trees so green,
And a magnificent water-fountain spouting up very high,
Where the people can quench their thirst when they feel dry

Chorus.

86

Beautiful city of Glasgow, I now conclude my muse,
And to write in praise of thee my pen does not refuse ;
And, without fear of contradiction, I will venture to say
You are the second grandest city in Scotland at the present day !

    Chorus.

OBAN.

OH ! beautiful Oban with your lovely bay,
Your surroundings are magnificent on a fine summer-day ;
There the lover of the picturesque can behold,
As the sun goes down, the scenery glittering like gold.

And on a calm evening, behind the village let him climb the hill,
And as he watches the sun go down, with delight his heart
    will fill
As he beholds the sun casting a golden track across the sea,
Clothing the dark mountains of Mull with crimson brilliancy.

And on a sunny morning 'tis delightful to saunter up the
    Dunstaffnage road,
Where the green trees spread out their branches so broad ;
And as you pass the Lovers' Loan your spirits feel gay
As you see the leaflet float lightly on the sunny pathway.

And when you reach the little gate on the right hand,
Then turn and feast your eyes on the scene most grand,
And there you will see the top of Balloch-an-Righ to your right,
Until at last you will exclaim, Oh ! what a beautiful sight !

And your mind with wonder it must fill
As you follow the road a couple of miles further, till
You can see Bennefure Loch on the left hand,
And the Castle of Dunstaffnage most ancient and grand.

Then go and see the waters of Loch Etive leaping and
    thundering
And flashing o'er the reef, splashing and dundering,
Just as they did when Ossian and Fingal watched them from
    the shore,
And, no doubt, they have felt delighted by the rapids'
    thundering roar.

Then there's Ganevan with its sparkling bay,
And its crescent of silver sand glittering in the sun's bright
    array,
And Dunolly's quiet shores where sea crabs abide,
And its beautiful little pools left behind by the tide.

Then take a sail across to Kerrera some day,
And see Gylen Castle with its wild-strewn shore and bay,
With its gigantic walls and towers of rocks
Shivered into ghastly shapes by the big waves' thundering
    shocks.

Then wander up Glen Crootyen, past the old village churchyard,
And as you pass, for the dead have some regard ;
For it is the road we've all to go,
Sooner or later, both the high and the low!

And as you return by the side of the merry little stream,
That comes trotting down the glen most charming to be seen,
Sometimes wimpling along between heather banks,
And slipping coyly away to hide itself in its merry pranks.

Then on some pleasant evening walk up the Glen Shellach road,
Where numberless sheep the green hillside often have trod,
And there's a little farmhouse nestling amongst the trees,
And its hazel woods climbing up the brae, shaking in the
    breeze.

And Loch Avoulyen lies like a silver sea with its forests
    green,
With its fields of rushes and headlands most enchanting to
    be seen,
And on the water, like a barge anchored by some dreamland
    shore,
There wild fowls sit, mirrored, by the score.

And this is beautiful Oban, where the tourist seldom stays
    above a night,
A place that fills the lover of the picturesque with delight ;
And let all the people that to Oban go
View it in its native loveliness, and it will drive away all
    woe.

Oh! beautiful Oban, with your silvery bay,
'Tis amongst your Highland scenery I'd like to stray
During the livelong summer-day,
And feast my eyes on your beautiful scenery, enchanting and
    gay.

THE BATTLE OF FLODDEN FIELD.

'Twas on the 9th of September, a very beautiful day,
That a numerous English army came in grand array,
And pitched their tents on Flodden field so green
In the year of our Lord fifteen hundred and thirteen.

And on the ridge of Braxton hill the Scottish army lay,
All beautifully arrayed, and eager for the fray,
And near by stood their noble king on that eventful day,
With a sad and heavy heart, but in it no dismay.

And around him were his nobles, both in church and state,
And they felt a little dispirited regarding the king's fate ;
For the independence of bonnie Scotland was at stake,
And if they lost the battle, many a heart would break.

And as King James viewed the enemy he really wondered,
Because he saw by them he was greatly outnumbered,
And he knew that the struggle would be desperate to the last,
And for Scotland's weal or woe the die was cast.

The silence of the gathered armies was very still
Until some horsemen began to gallop about the brow of the
    hill,
Then from rank to rank the signal for attack quickly flew,
And each man in haste to his comrade closely drew.

Then the Scottish artillery opened with a fearful cannonade ;
But the English army seemed to be not the least afraid,
And they quickly answered them by their cannon on the plain ;
While innocent blood did flow, just like a flood of rain.

But the artillery practice very soon did cease,
Then foe met foe foot to foot, and the havoc did increase,
And, with a wild slogan cry, the Highlanders bounded down
    the hill,
And many of the English vanguard, with their claymores,
    they did kill.

Then, taken by surprise and the suddenness of the attack,
The vanguard of the English army instantly fell back,
But rallied again immediately—to be beaten back once more,
Whilst beneath the Highlanders' claymores they fell by the
    score.

But a large body of horsemen came to the rescue,
And the wing of the Scottish army they soon did subdue ;
Then swords and spears clashed on every side around,
While the still air was filled with a death-wailing sound.

Then King James thought he'd strike an effective blow—
So he ordered his bodyguard to the plain below,
And all the nobles that were in his train,
To engage the foe hand to hand on that bloody plain.

And to them the din of battle was only a shout of glory ;
But for their noble king they felt a little sorry,
Because they knew he was sacrificing a strong position,
Which was to his army a very great acquisition.

But King James was resolved to have his own will,
And he wouldn't allow the English to come up the hill,
Because he thought he wasn't matching himself equally
    against the foe ;
So the nobles agreed to follow their leader for weal or woe.

'Twas then they plunged down into the thick of the fight,
And the king fought like a lion with all his might ;
And in his cause he saw his nobles falling on every side around,
While he himself had received a very severe wound.

And the English archers were pouring in their shafts like hail
And swords and spears were shivered against coats of mail,
And the king was manfully engaged contesting every inch of
    ground,
While the cries of the dying ascended up to heaven with a
    pitiful sound.

And still around the king the battle fiercely raged,
While his devoted followers were hotly engaged,
And the dead and the dying were piled high all around,
And alas! the brave king had received the second wound.

The Scottish army was composed of men from various
    northern isles,
Who had travelled, no doubt, hundreds of miles ;
And with hunger and fatigue many were like to faint,
But the brave heroes uttered no complaint.

And heroically they fought that day on behalf of their king,
Whilst around him they formed a solid ring ;
And the king was the hero of the fight,
Cutting, hacking, and slashing left and right.

But alas! they were not proof against the weapons of the foe,
Which filled their hearts with despair and woe ;
And, not able to maintain their close form, they were beaten
    back,
And Lennox and Argyle, their leaders, were slain, alack!

And the field became so slippery with blood they could
    scarcely stand,
But in their stocking-feet they fought hand to hand,
And on both sides men fell like wheat before the mower,
While the cheers from both armies made a hideous roar.

Then King James he waved his sword on high,
And cried, " Scotchmen, forward! and make the Saxons fly ;
And remember Scotland's independence is at stake,
So charge them boldly for Scotland's sake."

So grooms, lords, and knights fought all alike,
And hard blows for bonnie Scotland they did strike,
And swords and spears loudly did clatter,
And innocent blood did flow like water.

But alas! the king and his nobles fought in vain,
And by an English billman the king was slain;
Then a mighty cheer from the English told Scotland's power
    had fled,
And King James the Fourth of Scotland, alas! was dead!

GREENLAND'S ICY MOUNTAINS.

GREENLAND'S icy mountains are fascinating and grand,
And wondrously created by the Almighty's command;
And the works of the Almighty there's few can understand:
Who knows but it might be a part of Fairyland?

Because there are churches of ice, and houses glittering like
    glass,
And for scenic grandeur there's nothing can it surpass,
Besides there's monuments and spires, also ruins,
Which serve for a safe retreat from the wild bruins.

And there's icy crags and precipices, also beautiful waterfalls,
And as the stranger gazes thereon, his heart it appals
With a mixture of wonder, fear, and delight,
Till at last he exclaims, Oh! what a wonderful sight!

The icy mountains they're higher than a brig's topmast,
And the stranger in amazement stands aghast
As he beholds the water flowing off the melted ice
Adown the mountain sides, that he cries out, Oh! how nice!

Such sights as these are truly magnificent to be seen,
Only that the mountain tops are white instead of green,
And rents and caverns in them, the same as on a rugged
    mountain side,
And suitable places, in my opinion, for mermaids to reside.

Sometimes these icy mountains suddenly topple o'er
With a wild and rumbling hollow-startling roar ;
And new peaks and cliffs rise up out of the sea,
While great cataracts of uplifted brine pour down furiously.

And those that can witness such an awful sight
Can only gaze thereon in solemn silence and delight,
And the most Godfearless man that hath this region trod
Would be forced to recognise the power and majesty of God.

Oh ! how awful and grand it must be on a sunshiny day
To see one of these icy mountains in pieces give way !
While, crack after crack, it falls with a mighty crash
Flat upon the sea with a fearful splash.

And in the breaking up of these mountains they roar like
    thunder,
Which causes the stranger no doubt to wonder ;
Also the Esquimaux of Greenland betimes will stand
And gaze on the wondrous work of the Almighty so grand.

When these icy mountains are falling, the report is like big
    guns,
And the glittering brilliancy of them causes mock-suns,
And around them there's connected a beautiful ring of light,
And as the stranger looks thereon, it fills his heart with delight.

Oh! think on the danger of seafaring men
If any of these mighty mountains were falling on them ;
Alas! they would be killed ere the hand of man could them save
And, poor creatures, very likely find a watery grave!

'Tis most beautiful to see and hear the whales whistling and
blowing,
And the sailors in their small boats quickly after them
rowing,
While the whales keep lashing the water all their might
With their mighty tails, left and right.

In winter there's no sunlight there night or day,
Which, no doubt, will cause the time to pass tediously away,
And cause the Esquimaux to long for the light of day,
So as they will get basking themselves in the sun's bright array.

In summer there is perpetual sunlight,
Which fill the Esquimaux' hearts with delight ;
And is seen every day and night in the blue sky,
Which makes the scenery appear most beautiful to the eye.

During summer and winter there the land is covered with snow,
Which sometimes must fill the Esquimaux' hearts with woe
As they traverse fields of ice, ten or fifteen feet thick,
And with cold, no doubt, their hearts will be touched to the
quick.

And let those that read or hear this feel thankful to God
That the icy fields of Greenland they have never trod ;
Especially while seated around the fireside on a cold winter
night,
Let them think of the cold and hardships Greenland sailors
have to fight.

A TRIBUTE TO HENRY M. STANLEY,

THE GREAT AFRICAN EXPLORER.

WELCOME, thrice welcome, to the City of Dundee
The great African explorer, Henry M. Stanley,
Who went out to Africa its wild regions to explore,
And travelled o'er wild and lonely deserts, fatigued and
    footsore.

And what he and his little band suffered will never be forgot
Especially one in particular, Major Edmund Barttelot,
Alas! the brave heroic officer by a savage was shot,
The commandant of the rear column—O hard has been his lot!

O think of the noble Stanley and his gallant little band,
While travelling through gloomy forests and devastated land
And suffering from all kinds of hardships under a burning sun!
But the brave hero has been successful, and the victory's won!

While in Africa he saw many wonderful sights,
And was engaged, no doubt, in many savage fights,
But the wise Creator was with him all along,
And now he's home again to us, I hope quite strong.

And during his travels in Africa he made strange discoveries,
He discovered a dwarfish race of people called pigmies,
Who are said to be the original natives of Africa,
And when Stanley discovered them he was struck with awe.

One event in particular is most worthy to relate,
How God preserved him from a very cruel fate :
He and his officers were attacked, while sailing in their boat,
By the savages of Bumbireh, all eager to cut his throat.

They seized him by the hair, and tugged it without fear,
While one of his men received a poke in the ribs with a spear ;
But Stanley, having presence of mind, instantly contrives
To cry to his men, Shove off the boat, and save your lives!

Then savages swarmed into three canoes very close by,
And every bow was drawn, while they savagely did cry ;
But the heroic Stanley quickly shot two of them dead,
Then the savages were baffled, and immediately fled.

This incident is startling, but nevertheless true,
And in the midst of all dangers, the Lord brought him through,
Then, welcome him, thrice welcome him, right cheerfully,
Shouting, Long live the great African explorer, Henry M.
    Stanley!

Therefore throw open the gates of the City of Dundee,
And receive him with loud cheers, three times three,
And sound your trumpets and beat your drums,
And play up, See the Conquering Hero Comes!

JOTTINGS OF NEW YORK :

A DESCRIPTIVE POEM.

OH mighty City of New York! you are wonderful to behold,
Your buildings are magnificent, the truth be it told,
They were the only thing that seemed to arrest my eye,
Because many of them are thirteen storeys high.

And as for Central Park, it is lovely to be seen,
Especially in the summer season when its shrubberies and
    trees are green ;
And the Burns' statue is there to be seen,
Surrounded by trees, on the beautiful sward so green ;
Also, Shakespeare and Sir Walter Scott,
Which by Englishmen and Scotchmen will ne'er be forgot.

There the people on the Sabbath-day in thousands resort,
All loud in conversation and searching for sport,
Some of them viewing the menagerie of wild beasts there,
And also beautiful black swans, I do declare.

And there's beautiful boats to be seen there,
And the joyous shouts of the children do rend the air,
While the boats sail along with them o'er Lohengrin Lake,
And the fare is five cents for children and adults ten is all
    they take.

And there's also summer-house shades and merry-go-rounds,
And with the merry laughter of the children the Park resounds
During the livelong Sabbath-day,
Enjoying the merry-go-round play.

Then there's the elevated railroads, about five storeys high,
Which the inhabitants can see and hear night and day
    passing by,
Oh! such a mass of people daily do throng,
No less than five hundred thousand daily pass along,
And all along the City you can get for five cents,
And, believe me, among the passengers there are few
    discontent.

And the tops of the houses are all flat,
And in the warm weather the people gather to chat,
Besides on the house-tops they dry their clothes,
And also many people all night on the house-tops repose.

And numerous ships and steamboats are there to be seen
Sailing along the East River Water so green ;
'Tis certainly a most beautiful sight
To see them sailing o'er the smooth water day and night.

And Brooklyn Bridge is a very great height,
And fills the stranger's heart with wonder at first sight,
But with all its loftiness, I venture to say,
For beauty it cannot surpass the new Railway Bridge of the
    Silvery Tay.

And there's also ten thousand rumsellers there,
Oh! wonderful to think, I do declare!
To accommodate the people of that city therein,
And to encourage them to commit all sorts of sin.

And on the Sabbath-day, ye will see many a man
Going for beer with a tin can,
And seems proud to be seen carrying home the beer
To treat his neighbours and family dear.

Then at night numbers of the people dance and sing,
Making the walls of their houses to ring
With their songs and dancing on Sabbath night,
Which I witnessed with disgust, and fled from the sight.

And with regard to New York and the sights I did see,
One street in Dundee is more worth to me,
And, believe me, the morning I sailed from New York
For Bonnie Dundee, my heart it felt as light as a cork.

BEAUTIFUL MONIKIE.

BEAUTIFUL Monikie! with your trees and shrubberies green,
And your beautiful walks, most charming to be seen :
'Tis a beautiful place for pleasure-seekers to resort,
Because there they can have innocent sport,
By taking a leisure walk all round about,
And see the anglers fishing in the pond for trout.

Besides, there's lovely white swans swimming on the pond,
And Panmure Monument can be seen a little distance beyond;
And the scenery all round is enchanting I declare,
While sweet-scented fragrance fills the air.

Then away, pleasure-seekers of bonnie Dundee,
And have a day's outing around Monikie,
And inhale the pure air, on a fine summer day,
Which will help to drive dull care away ;
As ye gaze on the beautiful scenery there,
Your spirits will feel o'erjoyed and free from care.

Then near to the pond there's a beautiful green sward,
Where excursionists can dance until fatigue does them retard:
And if they feel thirsty, the Monikie water's near by,
Where they can quench their thirst if very dry.

Then, after that, they can have a walk at their ease,
Amongst the green shrubbery and tall pine trees ;
And in the centre of the pond they can see
Three beautiful little islets dressed in green livery.

Monikie is as bonnie a place as ye could wish to see,
And about eleven or twelve miles from bonnie Dundee ;
It's the only place I know of to enjoy a holiday,
Because there's a hall of shelter there to keep the rain away.

Then there's a large park, a very suitable place,
For the old and the young, if they wish to try a race ;
It's there they can enjoy themselves during the live-long
    summer day,
Near to the little purling burn, meandering on its way,
And emptying itself into the pond of Monikie,
Which supplies the people with water belonging Dundee.

A TRIBUTE TO MR MURPHY AND THE

BLUE RIBBON ARMY.

ALL hail to Mr Murphy, he is a hero brave,
That has crossed the mighty Atlantic wave,
For what purpose let me pause and think—
I answer, to warn the people not to taste strong drink.

And, I'm sure, if they take his advice, they never will rue
The day they joined the Blue Ribbon Army in the year 1882 ;
And I hope to their colours they will always prove true,
And shout, Hurrah! for Mr Murphy and the Ribbon of Blue.

What is strong drink ? Let me think—I answer 'tis a thing
From whence the majority of evils spring,
And causes many a fireside with boisterous talk to ring,
And leaves behind it a deadly sting.

Some people do say it is good when taken in moderation,
But, when taken to excess, it leads to tribulation,
Also to starvation and loss of reputation,
Likewise your eternal soul's damnation.

The drunkard, he says he can't give it up,
For I must confess temptation's in the cup ;
But he wishes to God it was banished from the land,
While he holds the cup in his trembling hand.

And he exclaims in the agony of his soul—
Oh, God, I cannot myself control
From this most accurs'd cup!
Oh, help me, God, to give it up!

Strong drink to the body can do no good ;
It defiles the blood, likewise the food,
And causes the drunkard with pain to groan,
Because it extracts the marrow from the bone :

And hastens him on to a premature grave,
Because to the cup he is bound a slave ;
For the temptation is hard to thole,
And by it he will lose his immortal soul.

The more's the pity, I must say,
That so many men and women are by it led astray,
And decoyed from the paths of virtue and led on to vice
By drinking too much alcohol and acting unwise.

Good people all, of every degree,
I pray, ye all be warned by me :
I advise ye all to pause and think,
And never more to taste strong drink.

Because the drunkard shall never inherit the kingdom of God
And whosoever God loves he chastens with his rod :
Therefore, be warned, and think in time,
And don't drink any more whisky, rum, or wine.

But go at once—make no delay,
And join the Blue Ribbon Army without dismay,
And rally round Mr Murphy, and make a bold stand,
And help to drive the Bane of Society from our land.

I wish Mr Murphy every success,
Hoping he will make rapid progress ;
And to the Blue Ribbon Army may he always prove true,
And adhere to his colours—the beautiful blue.

LOCH KATRINE.

BEAUTIFUL Loch Katrine in all thy majesty so grand,
Oh! how charming and fascinating is thy silver strand!
Thou certainly art most lovely, and worthy to be seen,
Especially thy beautiful bay and shrubberies green.

Then away to Loch Katrine in the summer time,
And feast on its scenery most lovely and sublime ;
There's no other scene can surpass in fair Scotland,
It's surrounded by mountains and trees most grand.

And as I gaze upon it, let me pause and think,
How many people in Glasgow of its water drink,
That's conveyed to them in pipes from its placid lake,
And are glad to get its water their thirst to slake.

Then away to Loch Katrine in the summer time,
And feast on its scenery most lovely and sublime ;
There's no other scene can surpass in fair Scotland,
It's surrounded by mountains and trees most grand.

The mountains on either side of it are beautiful to be seen,
Likewise the steamers sailing on it with their clouds of steam:
And their shadows on its crystal waters as they pass along,
Is enough to make the tourist burst into song.

Then away to Loch Katrine in the summer time,
And feast on its scenery most lovely and sublime ;
There's no other scene can surpass in fair Scotland,
It's surrounded by mountains and trees most grand.

'Tis beautiful to see its tiny wimpling rills,
And the placid Loch in the hollow of a circle of hills,
Glittering like silver in the sun's bright array,
Also many a promontory, little creek, and bay.

Then away to Loch Katrine in the summer time,
And feast on its scenery most lovely and sublime ;
There's no other scene can surpass in fair Scotland,
It's surrounded by mountains and trees most grand.

Then to the east there's the finely wooded Ellen's Isle,
There the tourist can the tedious hours beguile,
As he gazes on its white gravelled beautiful bay,
It will help to drive dull care away.

Then away to Loch Katrine in the summer time,
And feast on its scenery most lovely and sublime ;
There's no other scene can surpass in fair Scotland,
It's surrounded by mountains and trees most grand.

The mountains Ben-An and Ben-Venue are really very grand,
Likewise the famous and clear silver strand ;
Where the bold Rob Roy spent many a happy day,
With his faithful wife, near by its silvery bay.

Then away to Loch Katrine in the summer time,
And feast on its scenery most lovely and sublime ;
There's no other scene can surpass in fair Scotland,
It's surrounded by mountains and trees most grand.

FORGET-ME-NOT.

A GALLANT knight and his betroth'd bride,
Were walking one day by a river side,
They talk'd of love, and they talk'd of war,
And how very foolish lovers are.

At length the bride to the knight did say,
There have been many young ladies led astray
By believing in all their lovers said,
And you are false to me I am afraid.

No, Ellen, I was never false to thee ,
I never gave thee cause to doubt me ;
I have always lov'd thee and do still,
And no other woman your place shall fill.

Dear Edwin, it may be true, but I am in doubt,
But there's some beautiful flowers here about,
Growing on the other side of the river,
But how to get one, I cannot discover.

Dear Ellen, they seem beautiful indeed,
But of them, dear, take no heed ;
Because they are on the other side,
Besides, the river is deep and wide.

Dear Edwin, as I doubt your love to be untrue,
I ask one favour now from you :
Go! fetch me a flower from across the river,
Which will prove you love me more than ever.

Dear Ellen! I will try and fetch you a flower
If it lies within my power   *   *   *
To prove that I am true to you,
And what more can your Edwin do ?

So he leap'd into the river wide,
And swam across to the other side,
To fetch a flower for his young bride,
Who watched him eagerly on the other side.

So he pluck'd a flower right merrily,
Which seemed to fill his heart with glee,
That it would please his lovely bride ;
But, alas! he never got to the other side.

For when he tried to swim across,
All power of his body he did loss,
But before he sank in the river wide,
He flung the flowers to his lovely bride.

And he cried, Oh, Heaven! hard is my lot,
My dearest Ellen! Forget me not :
For I was ever true to you,
My dearest Ellen! I bid thee adieu!

Then she wrung her hands in wild despair,
Until her cries did rend the air ;
And she cried, Edwin, dear, hard is our lot,
But I'll name this flower Forget-me-not.

And I'll remember thee while I live,
And to no other man my hand I'll give,
And I will place my affection on this little flower,
And it will solace me in a lonely hour.

THE ROYAL REVIEW :

AUGUST 25, 1881.

ALL hail to the Empress of India, Great Britain's Queen—
Long may she live in health, happy and serene—
That came from London, far away,
To review the Scottish Volunteers in grand array :
Most magnificent to be seen,
Near by Salisbury Crags and its pastures green,
Which will long be remembered by our gracious Queen—

And by the Volunteers, that came from far away,
Because it rain'd most of the day.
And with the rain their clothes were wet all through,
On the 25th day of August, at the Royal Review.
And to the Volunteers it was no lark,
Because they were ankle deep in mud in the Queen's Park,
Which proved to the Queen they were loyal and true,
To endure such hardships at the Royal Review.

106

Oh! it was a most beautiful scene
To see the Forfarshire Artillery marching past the Queen ;
Her Majesty with their steady marching felt content,
Especially when their arms to her they did present.

And the Inverness Highland Volunteers seemed verygran',
And marched by steady to a man
Amongst the mud without dismay,
And the rain pouring down on them all the way.
And the bands they did play, God Save the Queen,
Near by Holyrood Palace and the Queen's Park so green.

Success to our noble Scottish Volunteers!
I hope they will be spared for many long years,
And to Her Majesty always prove loyal and true.
As they have done for the second time at the Royal Review.

To take them in general, they behaved very well,
The more that the rain fell on them pell-mell.
They marched by Her Majesty in very grand array,
Which will be remembered for many a long day,
Bidding defiance to wind and rain,
Which adds the more fame to their name.

And I hope none of them will have cause to rue
The day that they went to the Royal Review.
And I'm sure Her Majesty ought to feel proud,
And in their praise she cannot speak too loud,
Because the more that it did rain they did not mourn,
Which caused Her Majesty's heart with joy to burn,
Because she knew they were loyal and true
For enduring such hardships at the Royal Review.

107

THE NITHSDALE WIDOW AND HER SON.

'Twas in the year of 1746, on a fine summer afternoon,
When trees and flowers were in full bloom,
That widow Riddel sat knitting stockings on a little rustic seat,
Which her only son had made for her, which was very neat.

The cottage she lived in was in the wilds of Nithsdale,
Where many a poor soul had cause to bewail
The loss of their shealings, that were burned to the ground,
By a party of fierce British dragoons that chanced to come round.

While widow Riddel sat in her garden she heard an unusual
    sound,
And near by was her son putting some seeds into the ground,
And as she happened to look down into the little strath below,
She espied a party of dragoons coming towards her very slow.

And hearing of the cruelties committed by them, she shook
    with fear.
And she cried to her son, "Jamie, thae sodgers are coming here!"
While the poor old widow's heart with fear was panting,
And she cried, " Mercy on us, Jamie, what can they be
    wanting ? "

Next minute the dragoons were in front of the cottage door,
When one of them dismounted, and loudly did roar,
" Is there any rebels, old woman, skulking hereabouts ? "
" Oh, no, Sir, no! believe my word without any doubts."

" Well, so much the better, my good woman, for you and them;
But, old girl, let's have something to eat, me, and my men " :
" Blithely, sir, blithely! ye're welcome to what I hae,"
When she bustled into the cottage without delay.

And she brought out oaten cakes, sweet milk, and cheese,
Which the soldiers devoured greedily at their ease,
And of which they made a hearty meal,
But, for such kind treatment, ungrateful they did feel.

Then one of the soldiers asked her how she got her living :
She replied, " God unto her was always giving ;
And wi' the bit garden, alang wi' the bit coo,
And wi' what the laddie can earn we are sincerely thankfu'."

To this pitiful detail of her circumstances the villain made
no reply,
But drew a pistol from his holster, and cried, " Your cow
must die! "
Then riding up to the poor cow, discharged it through her
head,
When the innocent animal instantly fell down dead.

Not satisfied with this the merciless ruffian leaped the little
garden wall,
And with his horse trod down everything, the poor widow's all,
Then having finished this barbarous act of direst cruelty,
The monster rejoined his comrades shouting right merrily :

" There, you old devil, that's what you really deserve,
For you and your rascally rebels ought to starve " ;
Then the party rode off, laughing at the mischief that was
done,
Leaving the poor widow to mourn and her only son.

When the widow found herself deprived of her all,
She wrung her hands in despair, and on God did call,
Then rushed into the cottage and flung herself on her bed,
And, with sorrow, in a few days she was dead.

And, during her illness, her poor boy never left her bedside,
There he remained, night and day, his mother's wants to
provide,
And make her forget the misfortunes that had befallen them,
All through that villainous and hard-hearted party of men.

On the fourth day her son followed her remains to the grave.
And during the burial service he most manfully did behave,
And when the body was laid in the grave, from tears he
could not refrain,
But instantly fled from that desolated place, and never
returned again.

Thirteen years after this the famous battle of Minden was fought
By Prince Ferdinand against the French, who brought them
to nought ;
And there was a large body of British horse, under Lord
George Sackville,
And strange! the widow's son was at the battle all the while.

And on the evening after the battle there were assembled in
a tavern
A party of British dragoons, loudly boasting and swearing,
When one of them swore he had done more than any of them—
A much more meritorious action—which he defied them to
condemn.

" What was that, Tam, what was that, Tam ? " shouted his
companions at once.
" Tell us, Tam ; tell us, Tam, was that while in France ? "
" No! " he cried, " it was starving an old witch, while in
Nithsdale,
By shooting her cow and riding down her greens, that is the
tale."

"And don't you repent it?" exclaimed a young soldier,
    present.
"Repent what?" cried the braggart; "No! I feel quite
    content."
"Then, villain!" cried the youth, unsheathing his sword,
"That woman was my mother, so not another word!

"So draw, and defend yourself, without more delay,
For I swear you shall not live another day!"
Then the villain sprang to his feet, and a combat ensued,
But in three passes he was entirely subdued.

Young Riddel afterwards rose to be a captain
In the British service, and gained a very good name
For being a daring soldier, wherever he went,
And as for killing the ruffian dragoon he never did repent.

JACK O' THE CUDGEL.

PART I.

'Twas in the famous town of Windsor, on a fine summer morn,
Where the sign of Windsor Castle did a tavern adorn;
And there sat several soldiers drinking together,
Resolved to make merry in spite of wind or weather.

And old Simon the landlord was at the head of the table,
Cutting slices of beef as quick as he was able;
And one of the soldiers was of rather superior rank,
And on his dress trinkets of gold and silver together did clank.

He was a free companion, but surly and hard,
And a soldier of fortune, and was named Croquard;
And he had all the appearance of his martial calling,
But on this particular morning he was rudely bawling.

So the other soldiers laughed, for their spirits felt gay,
And they applauded his jokes, and let him have his own way,
Because he could command as desperate a gang of men as
    any in the world,
So many a joke and slur at the soldiers he hurled.

And the mirth increased as the day wore on,
And Croquard didn't seem the least woe-begone ;
But, as he was trolling out a very merry song,
A wandering minstrel sat down beside him, and thought it
    no wrong.

By my troth, shouted Croquard, Come here, minstrel,
And give us a stave of love, or war, which is my will :
But the minstrel didn't appear to comply with this request,
And he tried to withdraw, as he thought it was best.

Ho! didst thou hear me, varlet ? then Croquard did cry ;
Oh! gentle sir, replied the minstrel, I cannot with your wish
    comply ;
Believe me, I sing best to the ladies at the court,
And, in doing so, find it more profitable sport.

What, varlet! cried Croquard, Dost thou refuse me ?
By heaven, proud cur, you shall see
And feel the weight of my hand before thou are much older :
Then he instantly sprang up, and seized the minstrel by the
    shoulder.

Then the youth began to tremble, and seemed terrified to
    death,
And appeared ready to faint for the want of breath ;
While Croquard shook him roughly, just like an ugly whelp
And he looked from one to another, imploring help.

At this moment a youth observed what was going on,
And he cried out to Croquard, Inhuman monster, begone!
Leave the minstrel, thou pig-headed giant, or I'll make you
    repent,
For thou must know my name is Jack, and I hail from Kent.

Then Croquard relaxed his hold of the minstrel boy,
Which caused the minstrel's heart to leap with joy ;
As Jack placed himself before Croquard the giant,
And stood on his guard with a stout oak cudgel defiant.

Then the fist of the giant descended in a crack,
But Jack dealt Croquard a heavy blow upon the back
With his cudgel, so that the giant's hand fell powerless down
    by his side,
And he cursed and roared with pain, and did Jack deride.

Then the giant tried to draw his sword for to fight,
But Jack danced around him like a young sprite,
And struck him a blow with his cudgel upon the back of the
    head,
And from the effects of the blow he was nearly killed dead.

Then down sank the carcase of the giant to the ground,
While the soldiers about Jack did quickly gather round ;
And Jack cried, Ha! lie thou there overgrown brute,
And defiantly he spurned Croquard's body with his foot.

There, lad, cried Vintner Simon, thou hast shown English
    spirit to-day,
By chastising yon overbearing giant in a very proper way ;
So come, my lad, and drink a flagon of my very best sack,
For you handled your cudgel well, and no courage did lack

Then no sooner had our hero finished his goblet of sack,
He cried, Go and fetch the minstrel back ;
For the giant by this time had fled far away,
Therefore the minstrel's tender heart need not throb with
dismay.

Then the minstrel was brought back without delay,
Which made Jack's heart feel light and gay ;
And the minstrel thanked Jack for saving him on that
eventful day,
So the soldiers drank to Jack's health, and then went away.

And when King Edward III. heard what Jack had done,
He sent for Jack o' the Cudgel, the noble Saxon,
And he made him his page, and Jack uttered not a word,
But he unwillingly gave up the cudgel for the honour of the
sword.

PART II.

AFTER the battle of Calais, King Edward returns to fair
England,
And he invited his nobles to a banquet most grand,
That the like hadn't been in England for many a day ;
And many of the guests invited had come from far away.

The large hall of Windsor Castle was ablaze with light,
And there sat King Edward and his Queen, a most beautiful
sight—
To see them seated upon two thrones of burnished gold ;
And near the King sat Jack o' the Cudgel, like a warrior bold.

And when the banquet was prepared, King Edward arose,
And said, My honoured guests, I have called you together
for a special purpose!
To celebrate our victories so gloriously achieved in France
By my noble and heroic troops at the charge of the lance.

And now, since the war in France with us is o'er,
And Edward, our son, about to marry the lady he does adore,
The most amiable and lovely Countess of Kent ;
Therefore, I hope they will live happy together and never
 repent.

Then King Edward took the Countess by the hand, and said,
Come, Edward, take your bride by the hand, and don't be
 afraid ;
And do not think, my beloved son, that with you I feel wroth,
Therefore, take the Countess by the hand, and plight your troth

Then the Prince arose and took the fair Countess by the hand,
As King Edward, his father, had given the royal command ;
Then he led the Countess Joan to the foot of the throne,
Then King Edward and his Queen welcomed the Countess
 to their palatial home.

Then the Prince unto his father said, I must not forget
 whatever betide,
That to Sir Jack o' the Cudgel I do owe my bride ;
Because he rescued her from the hands of a fierce brigand,
Therefore 'twould be hard to find a braver knight in fair
 England.

Then a cheer arose, which made the lofty hall to ring,
As Jack advanced towards the throne, on the motion of the
 King ;
Then Jack fell on one knee before King Edward,
Then said the Monarch, Arise, brave youth, and I will thee
 reward.

Sir Jack, I give thee land to the value of six hundred marks
In thine own native county of Kent, with beautiful parks,
Also beautiful meadows and lovely flowers and trees,
Where you can reside and enjoy yourself as you please.

115

And remember, when I need your service you will be at my
    command,
Then Jack o' the Cudgel bowed assent, and kissed King
    Edward's hand ;
Then the Countess Joan took a string of rarest pearls from
    her hair,
And placed the pearls around Jack's neck, most costly and
    rare.

Then the tumult became uproarious when Jack received the
    presentation,
And he thanked the Lady Joan for the handsome donation ;
Then all the ladies did loudly cheer, and on Jack smilingly
    did fan,
And Sir Walter Manny cried aloud, Sir Jack, you are a
    lucky man.

Then the mirth increased, and louder the applause,
And the Countess Joan asked, after a pause,
Tell me who has gained the love of the Knight o' the Cudgel ;
Then Jack replied, My lady, you know her right well.

She is the lovely daughter of noble John of Aire,
Then, replied the Countess, she is a lovely creature, I must
    declare ;
And I hope the choice that you have made won't make you
    grieve,
Then Jack kissed the Countess's hand, and took his leave.

And he wended his way to his beautiful estate in Kent,
And many a happy day there he spent ;
And he married the lovely daughter of John of Aire,
And they lived happy together, and free from all care.

116

THE BATTLE OF CULLODEN:

A HISTORICAL POEM.

'Twas in the year of 1746, and in April the 14th day,
That Prince Charles Stuart and his army marched on without
    delay,
And on the 14th of April they encamped on Culloden Moor,
But the army felt hungry, and no food could they procure.

And the calls of hunger could not brook delay,
So they resolved to have food, come what may;
They, poor men, were hungry and in sore distress,
And many of them, as well as officers, slipped off to Inverness

The Prince gave orders to bring provisions to the field,
Because he knew without food his men would soon yield
To the pangs of hunger, besides make them feel discontent,
So some of them began to search the neighbourhood for
    refreshment.

And others, from exhaustion, lay down on the ground,
And soon in the arms of Morpheus they were sleeping sound;
While the Prince and some of his officers began to search for
    food,
And got some bread and whisky, which they thought very
    good.

The Highland army was drawn up in three lines in grand
    array,
All eager for the fray in April the 16th day,
Consisting of the Athole Brigade, who made a grand display
On the field of Culloden on that ever-memorable day.

Likewise the Camerons, Stewarts, and Macintoshes, Mac-
lachlans and Macleans,
And John Roy Stewart's regiment, united into one, these
are their names ;
Besides the Macleods, Chisholms, Macdonalds of Clanranald
and Glengarry,
Also the noble chieftain Keppoch, all eager the English to
harry.

The second line of the Highland army formed in column on
the right,
Consisting of the Gordons, under Lord Lewis Gordon, ready
for the fight ;
Besides the French Royal Scots, the Irish Piquets or Brigade,
Also Lord Kilmarnock's Foot Guards, and a grand show they
made.

Lord John Drummond's regiment and Glenbucket's were
flanked on the right
By Fitz-James's Dragoons and Lord Elcho's Horse Guards,
a magnificent sight ;
And on the left by the Perth squadron under Lord Strath-
allan,
A fine body of men, and resolved to fight to a man.

And there was Pitsligo, and the Prince's body guards under
Lord Balmerino,
And the third line was commanded by General Stapleton, a
noble hero ;
Besides, Lord Ogilvy was in command of the third line or
reserve,
Consisting of the Duke of Perth's regiment and Lord
Ogilvy's—men of firm nerve.

The Prince took his station on a very small eminence,
Surrounded by a troop of Fitz-James's horse for his defence,
Where he had a complete view of the whole field of battle,
Where he could see the front line and hear the cannons rattle.

Both armies were about the distance of a mile from each
    other,
All ready to commence the fight, brother against brother,
Each expecting that the other would advance
To break a sword in combat, or shiver a lance.

To encourage his men the Duke of Cumberland rode along
    the line,
Addressing himself hurriedly to every regiment, which was
    really sublime ;
Telling his men to use their bayonets, and allow the High-
    landers to mingle with them,
And look terror to the rebel foe, and have courage, my men.

Then Colonel Belford of the Duke's army opened fire from
    the front line,
After the Highlanders had been firing for a short time ;
The Duke ordered Colonel Belford to continue the cannonade,
To induce the Highlanders to advance, because they seemed
    afraid.

And with a cannon-ball the Prince's horse was shot above
    the knee,
So that Charles had to change him for another immediately ;
And one of his servants who led the horse was killed on the
    spot,
Which by Prince Charles Stuart was never forgot.

119

'Tis said in history, before the battle began

The Macdonalds claimed the right as their due of leading the van,

And because they wouldn't be allowed, with anger their hearts did burn,

Because Bruce conferred that honour upon the Macdonalds at the battle of Bannockburn.

And galled beyond endurance by the fire of the English that day,

Which caused the Highlanders to cry aloud to be led forward without delay,

Until at last the brave Clan Macintosh rushed forward without dismay,

While with grape-shot from a side battery hundreds were swept away.

Then the Athole Highlanders and the Camerons rushed in sword in hand,

And broke through Barrel's and Monro's regiments, a sight most grand ;

After breaking through these two regiments they gave up the contest,

Until at last they had to retreat after doing their best.

Then, stung to the quick, the brave Keppoch, who was abandoned by his clan,

Boldly advanced with his drawn sword in hand, the brave man.

But, alas! he was wounded by a musket-shot, which he manfully bore,

And in the fight he received another shot, and fell to rise no more

Nothing could be more disastrous to the Prince that day,
Owing to the Macdonalds refusing to join in the deadly fray ;
Because if they had all shown their wonted courage that day,
The proud Duke of Cumberland's army would have been
    forced to run away.

And, owing to the misconduct of the Macdonalds, the
    Highlanders had to yield,
And General O'Sullivan laid hold of Charles's horse, and led
    him off the field,
As the whole army was now in full retreat,
And with the deepest concern the Prince lamented his sore
    defeat.

Prince Charles Stuart, of fame and renown,
You might have worn Scotland's crown,
If the Macdonalds and Glengarry at Culloden had proved
    true ;
But, being too ambitious for honour, that they didn't do,
Which, I am sorry to say, proved most disastrous to you,
Looking to the trials and struggles you passed through.

THE BATTLE OF SHERIFFMUIR:

A HISTORICAL POEM.

'Twas in the year 1715, and on the 10th of November,
Which the people of Scotland have cause to remember ;
On that day the Earl of Mar left Perth bound for Sheriffmuir,
At the same time leaving behind a garrison under Colonel
    Balfour.

Besides leaving a force of about three thousand men
    quartered in different parts of Fife,
To protect the people's property, and quell party strife,
The army along with him amounted to three thousand foot
    and twelve hundred cavalry,
All in the best of order, a most pleasant sight to see.

The two armies bivouacked near Sheriffmuir during the night,
And around their camp-fires they talked concerning the
    coming fight.
The Duke of Argyle's English army numbered eight thousand
    strong,
Besides four hundred horse, posted in the rear all along.

And the centre of the first line was composed of ten battalions
    of foot,
Consisting of about four thousand, under the command of
    Clanranald and Glengarry to boot ;
And at the head of these battalions Sir John Maclean and
    Brigadier Ogilvie,
And the two brothers of Sir Donald Macdonald of Sleat, all
    in high glee.

The Marquis of Huntly's squadron of horse was also there ;
Likewise the Stirling squadron, carrying the Chevalier's
    standard, I do declare ;
And the Perthshire squadron formed the left wing,
And with their boisterous shouts they made the welkin ring.

The centre of the second line consisted of eight battalions of
    infantry,
And three of the Earl of Seaforth's foot, famous for their
    bravery ;
There were also two battalions of the Marquis of Huntly,
Besides the Earl of Panmure's battalion, all men of high degree.

And those of the Marquis of Tullibardine, commanded by the
      Viscount of Strathallan,
And of Logie Almond, and likewise Robertson of Strowan ;
Besides two squadrons of horse under the Earl Marischal,
And the Angus squadron was on the left : these include
      them all.

During this formation, the Duke of Argyle was watching all
      the time,
But owing to the ground occupied by them he couldn't see
      their line,
Which was unfortunately obstructed by the brow of a hill,
At the thought thereof the Duke's heart with fear did fill.

The hill was occupied by a party of Earl Mar's troops looking
      towards Dunblane,
Which the Earl of Mar no doubt resolved to maintain ;
Then the Duke returned to the army, and ordered the drums
      to beat,
But an hour elapsed before his army were ready Mar's to meet.

As soon as the Earl of Mar perceived Argyle's line was
      partially formed,
He gave orders that Argyle's army should be instantly stormed.
Then Mar placed himself at the head of the clans, and led
      forward his men,
As a noble hero would do, which no one can condemn.

Then he pulled off his hat, which he waved in his right hand,
And when he arrived within pistol-shot the Highlanders
      made a bold stand,
And they poured in a volley upon the English infantry,
And to the dismay of the Highlanders the English returned
      fire instantly.

And to the horror of the Highlanders Alan Muidartach was
  wounded mortally,
Then he was carried off the field, a most pitiful sight to see ;
And as his men clustered around him they stood aghast,
And before he died he told them to hold their posts fast.

While lamenting the death of the Captain of Clanranald
  most pitifully,
Glengarry at this juncture sprang forward right manfully,
And throwing his bonnet into the air, he cried, heroically,
Revenge! revenge! revenge to-day! and mourning to-morrow
  ye shall see!

No sooner had he pronounced these words than the High
  landers rushed forward, sword in hand,
Upon the royal battalions with the utmost fury, which they
  could not withstand,
And with their broadswords among the enemy they spread
  death and dismay,
Until the three battalions on Argyle's left wing instantly
  gave way.

Then a complete rout ensued, and the Earl of Mar pursued
  them half-a-mile ;
Then he ordered his men to halt and rest a while,
Until he should put them into order right speedily,
Then follow the enemy at the double-march and complete
  the victory.

Then the Highlanders chased them and poured in a volley,
Besides they hewed them down with their broadswords
  mercilessly ;
But somehow both armies got mixed together, and a general
  rout ensued,
While the Highlanders eagerly the English army hotly pursued.

The success on either side is doubtful to this day,
And all that can be said is, both armies ran away ;
And on whichsoever side success lay it was toward the
    Government,
And to allay all doubts about which party won, we mu
    feel content.

THE EXECUTION OF JAMES GRAHAM,
MARQUIS OF MONTROSE :

A HISTORICAL POEM.

'Twas in the year of 1650, and on the twenty-first of May,
The city of Edinburgh was put into a state of dismay
By the noise of drums and trumpets, which on the air arose,
That the great sound attracted the notice of Montrose.

Who enquired at the Captain of the guard the cause of it,
Then the officer told him, as he thought most fit,
That the Parliament dreading an attempt might be made to
    rescue him,
The soldiers were called out to arms, and that had made the din.

Do I, said Montrose, continue such a terror still ?
Now when these good men are about my blood to spill,
But let them look to themselves, for after I am dead,
Their wicked consciences will be in continual dread.

After partaking of a hearty breakfast, he commenced his
    toilet,
Which, in his greatest trouble, he seldom did forget.
And while in the act of combing his hair,
He was visited by the Clerk Register, who made him stare,

When he told him he shouldn't be so particular with his
    head,
For in a few hours he would be dead ;
But Montrose replied, While my head is my own I'll dress
    it at my ease,
And to-morrow, when it becomes yours, treat it as you please.

He was waited upon by the Magistrates of the city,
But, alas! for him they had no pity.
He was habited in a superb cloak, ornamented with gold and
    silver lace ;
And before the hour of execution an immense assemblage of
    people were round the place.

From the prison, bareheaded, in a cart, they conveyed him
    along the Watergate
To the place of execution on the High Street, where about
    thirty thousand people did wait,
Some crying and sighing, a most pitiful sight to see,
All waiting patiently to see the executioner hang Montrose,
    a man of high degree.

Around the place of execution, all of them were deeply
    affected,
But Montrose, the noble hero, seemed not the least dejected;
And when on the scaffold he had, says his biographer
    Wishart,
Such a grand air and majesty, which made the people start.

As the fatal hour was approaching when he had to bid the
    world adieu,
He told the executioner to make haste and get quickly
    through,
But the executioner smiled grimly, but spoke not a word,
Then he tied the Book of Montrose's Wars round his neck
    with a cord.

Then he told the executioner his foes would remember him
hereafter,
And he was as well pleased as if his Majesty had made him
Knight of the Garter ;
Then he asked to be allowed to cover his head,
But he was denied permission, yet he felt no dread.

He then asked leave to keep on his cloak,
But was also denied, which was a most grievous stroke ;
Then he told the Magistrates, if they could invent any more
tortures for him,
He would endure them all for the cause he suffered, and
think it no sin.

On arriving at the top of the ladder with great firmness,
His heroic appearance greatly did the bystanders impress,
Then Montrose asked the executioner how long his body
would be suspended,
Three hours was the answer, but Montrose was not the
least offended.

Then he presented the executioner with three or four pieces
of gold,
Whom he freely forgave, to his honour be it told,
And told him to throw him off as soon as he uplifted his hands,
While the executioner watched the fatal signal, and in
amazement stands.

And on the noble patriot raising his hands, the executioner
began to cry,
Then quickly he pulled the rope down from the gibbet on high,
And around Montrose's neck he fixed the rope very gently,
And in an instant the great Montrose was launched into
eternity.

127

Then the spectators expressed their disapprobation by a
    general groan,
And they all dispersed quietly, and wended their way home,
And his bitterest enemies that saw his death that day,
Their hearts were filled with sorrow and dismay.

Thus died, at the age of thirty-eight, James Graham,
    Marquis of Montrose,
Who was brought to a premature grave by his bitter foes ;
A commander who had acquired great military glory
In a short space of time, which cannot be equalled in story.

BALDOVAN.

THE scenery of Baldovan
    Is most lovely to see,
Near by Dighty Water,
    Not far from Dundee.

'Tis health for any one
    To be walking there,
O'er the green swards of Baldovan,
    And in the forests fair.

There the blackbird and the mavis
    Together merrily do sing
In the forest of Baldovan,
    Making the woodlands to ring.

'Tis delightful to hear them
    On a fine summer day,
Carolling their cheerful notes
    So blythe and so gay.

Then there's the little loch near by,
    Whereon can be seen every day
Numerous wild ducks swimming
    And quacking in their innocent play.

LOCH LEVEN.

BEAUTIFUL Loch Leven, near by Kinross,
For a good day's fishing the angler is seldom at a loss,
For the loch it abounds with pike and trout,
Which can be had for the catching without any doubt ;
And the scenery around it is most beautiful to b · seen,
Especially the Castle, wherein was imprisoned Scotland's
  ill-starred Queen.

Then there's the lofty Lomond Hills on the eastern side,
And the loch is long, very deep, and wide ;
Then on the southern side there's Benarty's rugged hills,
And from the tops can be seen the village of Kinross with
  its spinning mills.

The big house of Kinross is very handsome to be seen,
With its beautiful grounds around it, and lime trees so green
And 'tis a magnificent sight to see, on a fine summer
  afternoon,
The bees extracting honey from the leaves when in full
  bloom.

There the tourist can enjoy himself and while away the hours,
Underneath the lime trees shady bowers,
And listen to the humming of the busy bees,
While they are busy gathering honey from the lime trees.

Then there's the old burying ground near by Kinross,
And the dead that lie there turned into dusty dross,
And the gravestones are all in a state of decay,
And the old wall around it is mouldering away.

MONTROSE.

BEAUTIFUL town of Montrose, I will now commence my
    lay,
And I will write in praise of thee without dismay,
And in spite of all your foes, ...
I will venture to call thee Bonnie Montrose.
Your beautiful Chain Bridge is magnificent to be seen,
Spanning the river Esk, a beautiful tidal stream,
Which abounds with trout and salmon,
Which can be had for the catching without any gammon.

Then as for the Mid Links, it is most beautiful to be
    seen,
And I'm sure is a very nice bowling green,
Where young men can enjoy themselves and inhale the pure
    air,
Emanating from the sea and the beautiful flowers there,
And as for the High Street, it's most beautiful to see,
There's no street can surpass it in the town of Dundee,
Because it is so long and wide,   .   .   .
That the people can pass on either side
Without jostling one another or going to any bother.

Beautiful town of Montrose, near by the seaside,
With your fine shops and streets so wide,
'Tis health for the people that in you reside,
Because they do inhale the pure fragrant air,
Emanating from the pure salt wave and shrubberies growing
    there ;
And the inhabitants of Montrose ought to feel gay,
Because it is one of the bonniest towns in Scotland at the
    present day.

THE CASTLE OF MAINS.

ANCIENT Castle of the Mains,
With your romantic scenery
And surrounding plains,
Which seem most beautiful to the eye ;
And the little rivulet running by,
Which the weary traveller can drink of when he feels dry,
And the heaven's breath smells sweetly there,
And scented perfumes fill the air,
Emanating from the green trees and beautiful wild flowers
  growing there.

There the people can enjoy themselves
And wile away the time,
By admiring the romantic scenery
In the beautiful sunshine ;
And pull the little daisy,
As they carelessly recline
Upon the grassy green banks,
Which is most charming to see,
Near by the Castle of the Mains,
Not far from Dundee.

Then there's the old burying-ground,
Most solemn to see,   . . .
And the silent dead reposing silently
Amid the shady trees,
In that beautiful fairy dell
Most lovely to see,
Which in the summer season
Fills the people's hearts with glee,
To hear the birds singing and the humming of the bee.

BROUGHTY FERRY.

ANCIENT Castle of Broughty Ferry
With walls as strong as Londonderry ;
Near by the sea-shore,
Where oft is heard and has been heard the cannon's roar
In the present day and days of yore,
Loudly echoing from shore to shore.

From your impregnable ramparts high
Like the loud thunder in the sky,
Enough to frighten a foreign foe away
That would dare to come up the river Tay,
To lay siege to Bonnie Dundee,
I'm sure your cannon-balls would make them flee—

Home again to their own land
Because your cannon shot they could not withstand,
They would soon be glad to get away
From the beautiful shores of the silvery Tay.

Ancient Castle, near by Tayside,
The soldiers ought to feel happy that in you reside,
Because from the top they can have a view of Fife,
Which ought to drown their sorrow and give them fresh life,
And make their spirits feel light and gay
As they view the beautiful scenery of the silvery Tay.

The village of Broughty Ferry is most beautiful to see,
With its stately mansions and productive fishery,
Which is a great boon to the villagers and the people of
    Dundee,
And ought to make them thankful, and unto God to pray
For creating plenty of fish for them in the beautiful Tay.

And the city of Dundee seems beautiful to the eye
With her mill stalks and Old Steeple so high,
Which can be seen on a clear summer day
From the top of Broughty Castle near the mouth of Tay.

Then there's beautiful Reres Hill,
Where the people can ramble at their will
Amongst its beautiful shrubberies and trees so green
Which in the summer season is most charming to be seen,
And ought to drive dull care away,
Because the people can see every clear day
From the top the ships sailing on the silvery Tay.

ROBERT BURNS.

IMMORTAL Robert Burns of Ayr,
There's but few poets can with you compare ;
Some of your poems and songs are very fine :
To " Mary in Heaven " is most sublime ;
And then again in your " Cottar's Saturday Night,"
Your genius there does shine most bright,
As pure as the dewdrops of night.

Your " Tam o' Shanter " is very fine,
Both funny, racy, and divine,
From John o' Groats to Dumfries
All critics consider it to be a masterpiece,
And, also, you have said the same,
Therefore they are not to blame.

And in my own opinion both you and they are right,
For your genius there does sparkle bright,
Which I most solemnly declare
To thee, Immortal Bard of Ayr!

Your " Banks and Braes of Bonnie Doon "
Is sweet and melodious in its tune,
And the poetry is moral and sublime,
And in my opinion nothing can be more fine.

Your " Scots wha hae wi' Wallace bled "
Is most beautiful to hear sung or read ;
For your genius there does shine as bright,
Like unto the stars of night   .   .   .   .   .

Immortal Bard of Ayr! I must conclude, my muse
To speak in praise of thee does not refuse,
For you were a mighty poet, few could with you compare,
And also an honour to Scotland, for your genius it is rare.

ADVENTURES OF KING ROBERT THE BRUCE.

KING ROBERT THE BRUCE's deadly enemy, John of Lorn,
Joined the English with eight hundred Highlanders one fine
    morn,
All strong, hardy, and active fearless mountaineers,
But Bruce's men attacked them with swords and spears.

And while they were engaged, a new enemy burst upon them,
Like a torrent of raging water rushing down a rocky glen :
It was John of Lorn and his Highlanders that came upon
    them,
So the tide of battle was too much for them to stem.

And with savage yells they made the valley ring,
Then made a long circuit, and stole in behind the King,
Whirling their broadswords and Lochaber axes left and right;
And the enemy being thrice their number, they relinquished
    the fight.

134

Then to a certain house Bruce quickly hied,
And sitting by the door the housewife he spied ;
And she asked him who he was, and he said, A wanderer,
Then she said, All wanderers are welcome here, kind sir.

Then the King said, Good dame, tell me the reason why,
How you respect all wanderers that chance to pass by,
And for whose sake you bear such favour to homeless men ?
Then she said, King Robert the Bruce, if you want to ken,

The lawful King of this country, whom I hope to see;
Then Bruce said, My good woman, your King stands before
    thee ;
And she said, Ah! sire, where are your men gone ?
Then the King told her that he's come alone.

Then she said, Ah, my lawful King, this must not be,
For I have two stout sons, and they shall follow thee,
And fight to the death for your Majesty,
Aye, in faith, my good King, by land or sea.

Then she brought her sons before the King, and thus did say,
Now swear, my sons, to be true to your King without dismay;
Then they knelt and cried, Mother, we'll do as you desire,
We willingly will fight on behalf of our noble sire.

Who has been hunted like a felon by night and by day,
By foul plotters devising to take his life away ;
But God will protect him in the midst of the strife,
And, mother dear, we'll fight for him during life.

Then the King said, Noble lads, it's you shall follow me,
And ye shall be near me by land or sea,
And for your loyalty towards me your mother I'll reward;
When all on a sudden the tramping of horses was heard.

135

Then the King heard voices he knew full well,
But what had fetched his friends there he couldn't tell;
'Twas Edward his brother and Lord Douglas, with one
    hundred and fifty men,
That had travelled far, to find their King, o'er mountain
    and glen.

And when they met they conversed on the events of the day,
Then the King unto them quickly did say,
If we knew where the enemy were, we would work them skaith;
Then Lord James said, I'll lead you where they are, by my faith.

Then they marched upon the enemy just as the morning broke,
To a farm house where they were lodged, and, with one bold
    stroke,
They, the Scots, rushed in and killed two-thirds of them dead;
And such was the life, alas! King Robert the Bruce led!

A TALE OF THE SEA.

A PATHETIC tale of the sea I will unfold,
Enough to make one's blood run cold;
Concerning four fishermen cast adrift in a dory.
As I've been told, I'll relate the story.

'Twas on the 8th April, on the afternoon of that day,
That the little village of Louisburg was thrown into a wild
    state of dismay,
And the villagers flew to the beach in a state of wild uproar
And in a dory they found four men were cast ashore.

Then the villagers, in surprise, assembled about the dory,
And they found that the bottom of the boat was gory;
Then their hearts were seized with sudden dread,
When they discovered that two of the men were dead.

And the two survivors were exhausted from exposure,
    hunger, and cold,
Which caused the spectators to shudder when them they did
    behold ;
And with hunger the poor men couldn't stand on their feet,
They felt so weakly on their legs for want of meat.

They were carried to a boarding-house without delay,
But those that were looking on were stricken with dismay,
When the remains of James and Angus M'Donald were found
    in the boat,
Likewise three pieces of flesh in a pool of blood afloat.

Angus M'Donald's right arm was missing from the elbow,
And the throat was cut in a sickening manner, which filled
    the villagers hearts with woe,
Especially when they saw two pieces of flesh had been cut
    from each thigh,
'Twas then the kind-hearted villagers did murmur and sigh.

Angus M'Donald must have felt the pangs of hunger before
    he did try
To cut two pieces of flesh from James M'Donald's thigh ;
But, Oh, heaven! the pangs of hunger are very hard to thole,
And anything that's eatable is precious unto an hungry soul.

Alas! it is most pitiful and horrible to think,
That with hunger Christians will each other's blood drink,
And eat each other's flesh to save themselves from starvation;
But the pangs of hunger makes them mad , and drives them
    to desperation.

An old American soldier, that had passed through the Civil War,
Declared the scene surpassed anything he's seen by far,
And at the sight, the crowd in horror turned away,
Which no doubt they will remember for many a day.

Colin Chisholm, one of the survivors, was looking very pale,
Stretched on a sofa, at the boarding-house, making his wail ;
Poor fellow! his feet were greatly swollen, and with a melan-
　　choly air,
He gave the following account of the distressing affair :

We belonged to the American fishing schooner, named
　　" Cicely,"
And our captain was a brave man, called M'Kenzie ;
And the vessel had fourteen hands altogether,
And during the passage we had favourable weather.

'Twas on March the 17th we sailed from Gloucester, on the
　　Wednesday,
And all our hearts felt buoyant and gay ;
And we arrived on the Western banks on the succeeding
　　Tuesday,
While the time unto us seemed to pass merrily away.

About eight o'clock in the morning, we left the vessel in a
　　dory,
And I hope all kind Christians will take heed to my story :
Well, while we were at our work, the sky began to frown,
And with a dense fog we were suddenly shut down.

Then we hunted and shouted, and every nerve did strain,
Thinking to find our schooner, but, alas! it was all in vain :
Because the thick fog hid the vessel from our view,
And to keep ourselves warm we closely to each other drew.

We had not one drop of water, nor provisions of any kind,
Which, alas! soon began to tell on our mind ;
Especially upon James M'Donald, who was very thinly clad,
And with the cold and hunger he felt almost mad.

And looking from the stern where he was lying,
He said, Good-bye, mates, Oh! I am dying!
Poor fellow, we kept his body, thinking the rest of us would
be saved,
Then, with hunger, Angus M'Donald began to cry and
madly raved.

And he cried, Oh, God! send us some kind of meat,
Because I'm resolved to have something to eat ;
Oh! do not let us starve on the briny flood,
Or else I will drink of poor Jim's blood.

Then he suddenly seized his knife and cut off poor Jim's arm,
Not thinking in his madness he'd done any harm ;
Then poor Jim's blood he did drink, and his flesh did eat,
Declaring that the blood tasted like cream, and was a treat.

Then he asked me to taste it, saying, It was good without
doubt,
Then I tasted it, but in disgust I instantly spat it out ;
Saying, If I was to die within an hour on the briny flood,
I would neither eat the flesh nor drink the blood.

Then in the afternoon again he turned to me,
Saying, I'm going to cut Jim's throat for more blood d'ye see ;
Then I begged of him, for God's sake, not to cut the throat of
poor Jim,
But he cried, Ha! ha! to save my own life I consider it no sin.

I tried to prevent him, but he struck me without dismay,
And cut poor Jim's throat in defiance of me, or all I could say,
Also a piece of flesh from each thigh, and began to eat away,
But poor fellow he sickened about noon, and died on the
Sunday.

Now it is all over, and I will thank God all my life,
Who has preserved me and my mate, M'Eachern, in the
    midst of danger and strife ;
And I hope that all landsmen of low and high degree,
Will think of the hardships of poor mariners while at sea.

DESCRIPTIVE JOTTINGS OF LONDON.

As I stood upon London Bridge and viewed the mighty throng
Of thousands of people in cabs and 'busses rapidly whirling
    along,
All furiously driving to and fro,
Up one street and down another as quick as they could go :

Then I was struck with the discordant sounds of human
    voices there,
Which seemed to me like wild geese cackling in the air :
And the river Thames is a most beautiful sight,
To see the steamers sailing upon it by day and by night.

And the Tower of London is most gloomy to behold,
And the crown of England lies there, begemmed with
    precious stones and gold ;
King Henry the Sixth was murdered there by the Duke of
    Glo'ster,
And when he killed him with his sword he called him an
    imposter.

St. Paul's Cathedral is the finest building that ever I did see,
There's no building can surpass it in the city of Dundee,
Because it's magnificent to behold,
With its beautiful dome and spire glittering like gold.

And as for Nelson's Monument that stands in Trafalgar
Square,
It is a most stately monument I most solemnly declare,
And towering defiantly very high,
Which arrests strangers' attention while passing by.

Then there's two beautiful water-fountains spouting up very
high,
Where the weary traveller can drink when he feels dry;
And at the foot of the monument there's three bronze lions
in grand array,
Enough to make the stranger's heart throb with dismay.

Then there's Mr Spurgeon, a great preacher, which no one
dare gainsay,
I went to hear him preach on the Sabbath-day,
And he made my heart feel light and gay,
When I heard him preach and pray.

And the Tabernacle was crowded from ceiling to floor,
And many were standing outside the door ;
He is an eloquent preacher I honestly declare,
And I was struck with admiration as on him I did stare.

Then there's Petticoat Lane I venture to say,
It's a wonderful place on the Sabbath-day ;
There wearing-apparel can be bought to suit the young or old,
For the ready cash, silver, coppers, or gold.

Oh! mighty city of London! you are wonderful to see,
And thy beauties no doubt fill the tourist's heart with glee ;
But during my short stay, and while wandering there,
Mr Spurgeon was the only man I heard speaking proper
English I do declare.

ANNIE MARSHALL THE FOUNDLING.

ANNIE MARSHALL was a foundling, and lived in Downderry,
And was trained up by a coast-guardsman, kind-hearted and
    merry,
And he loved Annie Marshall as dear as his life,
And he resolved to make her his own loving wife.

The night was tempestuous, most terrific, and pitch dark,
When Matthew Pengelly rescued Annie Marshall from an
    ill-fated barque,
But her parents were engulfed in the briny deep,
Which caused poor Annie at times to sigh and weep.

One day Matthew asked Annie if she would be his wife,
And Annie replied, I never thought of it in all my life ;
Yes, my wife, Annie, replied Matthew, hold hard a bit,
Remember, Annie, I've watched you grow up, and consider
    you most fit.

Poor Annie did not speak, she remained quite mute,
And with agitation she trembled from head to foot,
The poor girl was in a dilemma, she knew not what to say,
And owing to Matthew training her, she couldn't say him nay.

Oh! Matthew, I'm afraid I would not make you a good wife,
And in that respect there would be too much strife,
And the thought thereof, believe me, makes me feel ill,
Because I'm unfit to be thy wife, Matthew, faltered the poor girl.

Time will prove that, dear Annie, but why are you so calm ?
Then Annie put her hand shyly into Matthew's brown palm.
Just then the flashing lightning played upon Annie's face,
And the loud thunder drowned Matthew's words as Annie
    left the place.

But Matthew looked after her as she went home straightway,
And his old heart felt light and gay,
As he looked forward for his coming marriage day,
Because he knew that Annie Marshall couldn't say him nay.

Then the sky grew dark, and the sea lashed itself into foam,
But he heeded it not as he sat there alone,
Till the sound of a gun came booming o'er the sea,
Then Matthew had to attend to his duty immediately.

A ship, he muttered, Lord, help them! and coming right in
      by the sound,
And in a few minutes she will run aground.
And the vessel was dashed against the rocks with her helpless
      crew,
Then in hot haste for assistance Matthew instantly flew.

Then Matthew returned with a few men all willing to lend
      their aid,
But amongst them all Matthew seemed the least afraid ;
Then an old man cried, Save my boy, for his mother's sake,
Oh! Matthew, try and save him, or my heart will break!

I will, Heaven helping me, Matthew said solemnly,
Come, bear a hand, mates, and lower me over the cliff quietly ;
Then Matthew was lowered with ropes into what seemed a
      watery grave,
At the risk of his own life, old Jonathan Bately's on to ave.

So Matthew Pengelly saved Jonathan Bately's son,
And the old man thanked God and Matthew for what he had
      d ne,
And the mother's heart was full of gratitude and joy,
For the restoration of her darling boy.

So Matthew resolved to marry Annie Marshall,
But first he'd go to sea whatever did befall,
To earn a few pounds to make the marriage more grand,
So he joined a whaling vessel and went to Greenland.

And while Matthew was away at Greenland,
David Bately wanted to marry Annie Marshall right offhand,
But Annie refused to marry David Bately,
So in anger David Bately went another voyage to sea.

A few nights after David Bately had gone to sea,
Annie's thoughts reverted to Matthew Pengelly,
And as she sat in the Downderry station watching the
     boiling waves below,
The wind blew a terrific gale, which filled her heart with woe.

And as she sat there the big waves did loudly roar,
When a man cried, Help! help! there's a corpse washed ashore;
Then Annie rushed madly to the little beach,
And when she saw the corpse she gave a loud screech.

So there is but little more to tell of this sad history,
Only that Annie Marshall mourned long for Matthew
     Pengelly,
Who had floated home to be buried amongst his own kin,
But, alas! the rest of the crew were buried in the sea, save
     him.

BILL BOWLS THE SAILOR.

'TWAS about the beginning of the present century,
Bill Bowls was pressed, and sent to sea ;
And conveyed on board the Waterwitch without delay,
Scarce getting time to bid farewell to the villagers of Fairway.

And once on board the " Waterwitch," he resolved to do his
   duty,
And God willing, he'd marry Nelly Blyth, the village beauty ;
And he'd fight for Old England, like a jolly British tar,
And he'd think of Nelly Blyth during the war.

The poor fellow little imagined what he had to go through,
But in all his trials at sea, he never did rue ;
No ; the brave tar became reconciled to his fate,
And he felt proud of his commander, Captain Ward the great.

And on board the " Waterwitch " was Tom Riggles, his old
   comrade,
And with such a one as Tom Riggles he seldom felt afraid,
Because the stories they told on board made the time fly away,
And made the hearts of their messmates feel light and gay.

'Twas on a sunny morning, and clear to the view,
Captain Ward the close attention of his men he drew :
Look! he cried, there's two Frenchmen of war on our right,
Therefore, prepare my men immediately to commence the
   fight.

Then the " Waterwitch " was steered to the ship most near,
While every man resolved to sell his life most dear ;
But the French commander, disinclined to commence the fight,
Ordered his men to put on a press of canvas and take to flight.

But Captain Ward quickly gave the order to fire,
Then Bill Bowls cried, Now we'll get fighting to our heart's
   desire!
And for an hour and more a running fight was maintained,
Until the two ships of the enemy near upon the " Waterwitch "
   gained.

Captain Ward walked the deck with a firm tread,
When a shot from the enemy pierced the ship's side above
  his head ;
And with a splinter Bill Bowls was wounded on the left arm,
And he cried, Death to the frog-eaters! they have done me
  little harm.

Then Captain Ward cried, Fear not, we will win the day,
Now, courage my men, pour in broadsides without delay ;
Then they sailed round the " St. Denis " and the " Gloire,"
And in at their cabin windows they poured a deadly fire.

The effect on the two ships was fearful to behold,
But still the Frenchmen stuck to their guns with courage, be
  it told ;
And the crash and din of artillery was deafening to the ear,
And the cries of the wounded men on deck were pitiful to hear.

Then Captain Ward to his men did say,
We must board these French ships without dismay ;
Then he seized his cutlass, as he fearlessly spoke,
And jumped on board the " St. Denis " in the midst of the
  smoke.

Then Bill Bowls and Tom Riggles quickly followed him,
Then hand to hand the battle in earnest did begin ;
And the men sprang upon their foes and beat them back,
And they hauled down their colours, and hoisted the Union Jack.

But the men on board the " St. Denis " fought desperately hard,
But, alas! as the " St. Denis " was captured, a ball struck
  Captain Ward
Right on the forehead, and he fell dead with a groan
And for the death of Captain Ward the sailors did cry and moan.

Then the first lieutenant, who was standing near by,
Loudly to the men did cry :
Come men, and carry your noble commander to his cabin
    below,
But there is one consolation, we have beaten the foe.

And thus fell Captain Ward in the prime of his life,
And I hope he is now in the better land, free from strife :
But, alas! 'tis sad to think he was buried in the mighty deep,
Where too many of our brave seamen do silently sleep.

The " St. Denis " and the " Gloire " were towed to Gibraltar,
    the nearest port,
But by the capturing of them, they felt but little sport,
Because, for the loss of Captain Ward, the men felt woe-
    begone,
Because in bravery, they said, he was next to Admiral Nelson.

YOUNG MUNRO THE SAILOR.

'Twas on a sunny morning in the month of May,
I met a pretty damsel on the banks o' the Tay ;
I said, My charming fair one, come tell to me I pray,
Why you do walk alone on the banks o' the Tay.

She said, Kind sir, pity me, for I am in great woe
About my young sailor lad, whose name is James Munro ;
It's he has been long at sea, seven years from this day,
And I come here sometimes to weep for him that's far, far
    away.

Lovely creature, cease your weeping and consent to marry
me,
And my houses and all my land I will give to thee,
And we shall get married without any delay,
And live happy and contented on the banks o' the Tay.

Believe me, my sweet lady, I pity the sailor's wife,
For I think she must lead a very unhappy life ;
Especially on a stormy night, I'm sure she cannot sleep,
Thinking about her husband whilst on the briny deep.

Oh, sir! it is true, what you to me have said,
But I must be content with the choice I've made ;
For Munro he's young and handsome, I will ne'er deny,
And if I don't get him for a husband, believe me, I will
die.

Because, when last we parted, we swore to be true,
And I will keep my troth, which lovers ought to do ;
And I will pray for his safe return by night and by day,
That God may send him safe home to the banks o' the
Tay.

Forgive me, noble heart, for asking to marry you,
I was only trying your love, if it was really true ;
But I've found your love is pure towards your sailor lad,
And the thought thereof, believe me, makes my heart feel
glad.

As homeward we retraced our steps her heart seemed
glad,
In hopes of seeing again her brave sailor lad,
Who had promised to marry her when he would return,
So I bade her keep up her spirits and no longer mourn.

148

Dear creature, the lass that's true to her sweetheart deserves
   great praise,
And I hope young Munro and you will spend many happy
   days,
For unto him I know you will ever prove true,
And perchance when he comes home he will marry you.

What you have said, kind sir, I hope will come true,
And if it does, I'll make it known to you ;
And you must come to the marriage, which you musn't
   gainsay,
And dance and rejoice with us on the marriage-day.

When we arrived in Dundee she bade me good-bye,
Then I told her where I lived, while she said with a sigh,
Kind sir, I will long remember that morning in May,
When I met you by chance on the banks o' the Tay.

When three months were past her sailor lad came home,
And she called to see me herself alone,
And she invited me to her marriage without delay,
Which was celebrated with great pomp the next day.

So I went to the marriage with my heart full of joy,
And I wished her prosperity with her sailor boy ;
And I danced and sang till daylight, and then came away,
Leaving them happy and contented on the banks o' the Tay.

So all ye pretty fair maids, of high or low degree,
Be faithful to your sweethearts when they have gone to sea,
And never be in doubts of them when they are far away,
Because they might return and marry you some unexpected
   day.

THE DEATH OF THE OLD MENDICANT.

THERE was a rich old gentleman
Lived on a lonely moor in Switzerland,
And he was very hard to the wandering poor,
'Tis said he never lodged nor served them at his door.

'Twas on a stormy night, and Boreas blew a bitter blast,
And the snowflakes they fell thick and fast,
When a poor old mendicant, tired and footsore,
Who had travelled that day fifteen miles and more,
Knocked loudly at the rich man's door.

The rich man was in his parlour counting his gold,
And he ran to the door to see who was so bold,
And there he saw the mendicant shivering with the cold

Then the mendicant unto him said,
My dear sir, be not afraid,
Pray give me lodgings for the night,
And heaven will your love requite ;
Have pity on me, for I am tired and footsore,
I have travelled fifteen miles to-day and more.

Begone! you vagabond, from my door!
I never give lodgings to the poor ;
So be off, take to your heels and run,
Or else I'll shoot you with my gun!
Now do not think I'm making fun ;
Do you hear, old beggar, what I say ?
Now be quick! and go away.

Have mercy, sir, I cannot go,
For I shall perish in the snow ;
Oh! for heaven's sake, be not so hard,
And God will your love reward.

My limbs are tired, I cannot go away,
Oh! be so kind as let me stay.
'Twas vain! the rich man said, I shan't,
And shut his door on the mendicant,
And said, That is the way I'll serve the poor
While I live on this lonely moor.

Then the old mendicant did go away,
And, murmuring to himself, did say,
Oh, woe's me that ever I was born!
Oh, God, protect me from the storm
My feeble limbs refuse to go,
And my poor heart does break with woe.

Then he lay down and died among the snow.
He was found by the rich man's shepherd next day,
While he was searching for sheep that had gone astray
And he was struck with fear and woe
To see the body lying dead among the snow.

So the shepherd ran home and told his master
About the very sad disaster ;
That he had found a dead body in the snow,
But whose it was he did not know.

Then the rich man ordered the body to be brought to his house
And to be instantly dressed by his loving spouse,
For his conscience smote him with fear and woe,
When he heard of the old mendicant being found dead in
    the snow.

So the poor old mendicant was buried without delay
In a very respectable way ;
And from that very day the rich man was kind to the poor
And never turned any one away from his door.

AN ADVENTURE IN THE LIFE OF
KING JAMES V. OF SCOTLAND.

ON one occasion King James the Fifth of Scotland, when
    alone, in disguise,
Near by the Bridge of Cramond met with rather a dis-
    agreeable surprise.
He was attacked by five gipsy men without uttering a word,
But he manfully defended himself with his sword.

There chanced to be a poor man threshing corn in a barn
    near by,
Who came out on hearing the noise so high ;
And seeing one man defending himself so gallantly,
That he attacked the gipsies with his flail, and made them flee

Then he took the King into the barn,
Saying, " I hope, sir, you've met with no great harm ;
And for five men to attack you, it's a disgrace ;
But stay, I'll fetch a towel and water to wash your face."

And when the King washed the blood off his face and hands,
" Now, sir, I wish to know who you are," the King demands.
" My name, sir, is John Howieson, a bondsman on the farm
    of Braehead."
" Oh, well," replied the King, " your company I need not
    dread."

" And perhaps you'll accompany me a little way towards
    Edinburgh,
Because at present I'm not free from sorrow.
And if you have any particular wish to have gratified,
Let me know it, and it shall not be denied."

Then honest John said, thinking it no harm,
" Sir, I would like to be the owner of Braehead farm ;
But by letting me know who you are it would give my mind
    relief."
Then King James he answered that he was the Gudeman of
    Ballingeich.

" And if you'll meet me at the palace on next Sunday,
Believe me, for your manful assistance, I'll you repay.
Nay, honest John, don't think of you I'm making sport,
I pledge my word at least you shall see the royal court."

So on the next Sunday John put on his best clothes,
And appeared at the palace gate as you may suppose.
And he inquired for the Gudeman of Ballingeich ;
And when he gained admittance his heart was freed from
    grief.

For John soon found his friend the Gudeman,
And the King took John by the han',
Then conducted John from one apartment to another,
Just as kindly as if he'd been his own brother.

Then the King asked John if he'd like to see His Majesty.
" Oh, yes," replied John, " His Majesty I would really like
    to see."
And John looked earnestly into the King's face,
And said, " How am I to know His Grace ? "

" Oh, John, you needn't be the least annoyed about that,
For all heads will be uncovered : the King will wear his hat."
Then he conducted John into a large hall,
Which was filled by the nobility, crown officers, and all.

Then said John to the King, when he looked round the room,
" Sir, I hope I will see the King very soon,"
Because to see the King, John rather dreaded,
At last he said to the King, " 'Tis you! the rest are bare-
      headed."

Then the King said, " John, I give you Braehead farm as it
      stands,
On condition you provide a towel and basin of water to wash
      my hands,
If ever I chance to come your way."
Then John said, " Thanks to your Majesty, I'll willingly obey."

THE CLEPINGTON CATASTROPHE.

'TWAS on a Monday morning, and in the year of 1884,
That a fire broke out in Bailie Bradford's store,
Which contained bales of jute and large quantities of waste,
Which the brave firemen ran to extinguish in great haste.

They left their wives that morning without any dread,
Never thinking, at the burning pile, they would be killed dead
By the falling of the rickety and insecure walls ;
When I think of it, kind Christians, my heart it appals !

Because it has caused widows and their families to shed briny
      tears,
For there hasn't been such a destructive fire for many years ;
Whereby four brave firemen have perished in the fire,
And for better fathers or husbands no family could desire.

'Twas about five o'clock in the morning the fire did break out,
While one of the workmen was inspecting the premises round
      about—
Luckily before any one had begun their work for the day—
So he instantly gave the alarm without delay.

At that time only a few persons were gathered on the spot,
But in a few minutes some hundreds were got,
Who came flying in all directions, and in great dismay ;
So they help'd to put out the fire without delay.

But the spreading flames, within the second flats, soon began
    to appear,
Which filled the spectators' hearts with sympathy and
    fear,
Lest any one should lose their life in the merciless fire,
When they saw it bursting out and ascending higher and
    higher.

Captain Ramsay, of the Dundee Fire Brigade, was the first
    to arrive,
And under his directions the men seemed all alive,
For they did their work heroically, with all their might and
    main,
In the midst of blinding smoke and the burning flame.

As soon as the catastrophe came to be known,
The words, Fire! Fire! from every mouth were blown ;
And a cry of despair rang out on the morning air,
When they saw the burning pile with its red fiery glare.

While a dense cloud of smoke seemed to darken the sky,
And the red glaring flame ascended up on high,
Which made the scene appear weird-like around ;
While from the spectators was heard a murmuring sound.

But the brave firemen did their duty manfully to the last,
And plied the water on the burning pile, copiously and fast ;
But in a moment, without warning, the front wall gave way,
Which filled the people's hearts with horror and dismay :

155

Because four brave firemen were killed instantaneously on
    the spot,
Which by the spectators will never be forgot ;
While the Fire Fiend laughingly did hiss and roar,
As he viewed their mangled bodies, with the *debris* covered
    o'er.

But in the midst of dust and fire they did their duty well,
Aye! in the midst of a shower of bricks falling on them
    pell-mell,
Until they were compelled to let the water-hose go ;
While the blood from their bruised heads and arms did flow.

But brave James Fyffe held on to the hose until the last,
And when found in the *debris*, the people stood aghast.
When they saw him lying dead, with the hose in his hand,
Their tears for him they couldn't check nor yet command.

Oh, heaven! I must confess it was no joke
To see them struggling in the midst of suffocating smoke,
Each man struggling hard, no doubt, to save his life,
When he thought of his dear children and his wife.

But still the merciless flame shot up higher and higher ;
Oh, God! it is terrible and cruel to perish by fire ;
Alas! it was saddening and fearful to behold,
When I think of it, kind Christians, it makes my blood run
    cold.

What makes the death of Fyffe the more distressing,
He was going to be the groomsman at his sister's bridal
    dressing,
Who was going to be married the next day ;
But, alas! the brave hero's life was taken away.

156

But accidents will happen by land and by sea,
Therefore, to save ourselves from accidents, we needn't **try**
    to flee,
For whatsoever God has ordained will come to pass ;
For instance, ye may be killed by a stone or a piece of glass.

I hope the Lord will provide for the widows in their distress,
For they are to be pitied, I really must confess ;
And I hope the public of Dundee will lend them a helping
    hand ;
To help the widows and the fatherless is God's command.

THE REBEL SURPRISE NEAR TAMAI.

'Twas on the 22nd of March, in the year 1885,
That the Arabs rushed like a mountain torrent in full drive,
And quickly attacked General M'Neill's transport-zereba,
But in a short time they were forced to withdraw.

And in the suddenness of surprise the men were carried away,
Also camels, mules, and horses were thrown into wild
    disarray,
By thousands of the Arabs that in ambush lay,
But our brave British heroes held the enemy at bay.

There was a multitude of camels heaped upon one another,
Kicking and screaming, while many of them did smother,
Owing to the heavy pressure of the entangled mass,
That were tramping o'er one another as they lay on the grass.

The scene was indescribable, and sickening to behold,
To see the mass of innocent brutes lying stiff and cold,
And the moaning cries of them were pitiful to hear,
Likewise the cries of the dying men that lay wounded in the
    rear.

Then General M'Neill ordered his men to form in solid square,
Whilst deafening shouts and shrieks of animals did rend the
    air,
And the rush of stampeded camels made a fearful din,
While the Arabs they did yell, and fiendishly did grin.

Then the gallant Marines formed the east side of the square,
While clouds of dust and smoke did darken the air,
And on the west side the Berkshire were engaged in the fight,
Firing steadily and coolly with all their might.

Still camp followers were carried along by the huge animal
    mass,
And along the face of the zereba 'twas difficult to pass,
Because the mass of brutes swept on in wild dismay,
Which caused the troops to be thrown into disorderly array.

Then Indians and Bluejackets were all mixed together back
    to back,
And for half-an-hour the fire and din didn't slack ;
And none but steady troops could have stood that fearful shock,
Because against overwhelming numbers they stood as firm
    as a rock.

The Arabs crept among the legs of the animals without any
    dread,
But by the British bullets many were killed dead,
And left dead on the field and weltering in their gore,
Whilst the dying moans of the camels made a hideous roar.

Then General M'Neill to his men did say,
Forward ! my lads, and keep them at bay !
Come, make ready, my men, and stand to your arms,
And don't be afraid of war's alarms!

So forward! and charge them in front and rear,
And remember you are fighting for your Queen and country
    dear,
Therefore, charge them with your bayonets, left and right,
And we'll soon put this rebel horde to flight.

Then forward at the bayonet-charge they did rush,
And the rebel horde they soon did crush ;
And by the charge of the bayonet they kept them at bay,
And in confusion and terror they all fled away.

The Marines held their own while engaged hand-to-hand,
And the courage they displayed was really very grand ;
But it would be unfair to praise one corps more than
    another,
Because each man fought as if he'd been avenging the death
    of a brother.

The Berkshire men and the Naval Brigade fought with
    might and main,
And, thank God! the British have defeated the Arabs once
    again,
And have added fresh laurels to their name,
Which will be enrolled in the book of fame.

'Tis lamentable to think of the horrors of war,
That men must leave their homes and go abroad afar,
To fight for their Queen and country in a foreign land,
Beneath the whirlwind's drifting scorching sand.

But whatsoever God wills must come to pass,
The fall of a sparrow, or a tiny blade of grass ;
Also, man must fall at home by His command,
Just equally the same as in a foreign land.

BURNING OF THE EXETER THEATRE.

'Twas in the year of 1887, which many people will long
    remember,
The burning of the Theatre at Exeter on the 5th of September,
Alas! that ever-to-be-remembered and unlucky night,
When one hundred and fifty lost their lives, a most agonising
    sight.

The play on this night was called " Romany Rye,"
And at act four, scene third, Fire! Fire! was the cry ;
And all in a moment flames were seen issuing from the stage,
Then the women screamed frantically, like wild beasts in a
    cage.

Then a panic ensued, and each one felt dismayed,
And from the burning building a rush was made ;
And soon the theatre was filled with a blinding smoke,
So that the people their way out had to grope.

The shrieks of those trying to escape were fearful to hear,
Especially the cries of those who had lost their friends most
    dear ;
Oh, the scene was most painful in the London Inn Square,
To see them ringing their hands and tearing their hair!

And as the flames spread, great havoc they did make,
And the poor souls fought heroically in trying to make their
    escape ;
Oh, it was horrible to see men and women trying to reach the
    door!
But in many cases death claimed the victory, and their
    struggles were o'er.

160

Alas! 'twas pitiful the shrieks of the audience to hear,
Especially as the flames to them drew near ;
Because on every face were depicted despair and woe,
And many of them jumped from the windows into the street
    below.

The crushed and charred bodies were carried into London
    Hotel yard,
And to alleviate their sufferings the doctors tried hard ;
But, alas! their attendance on many was thrown away,
But those that survived were conveyed to Exeter Hospital
    without delay.

And all those that had their wounds dressed proceeded home,
Accompanied by their friends, and making a loud moan ;
While the faces and necks of others were sickening to behold,
Enough to chill one's blood, and make the heart turn cold,

Alas! words fail to describe the desolation,
And in many homes it will cause great lamentation ;
Because human remains are beyond all identification,
Which will cause the relatives of the sufferers to be in great
    tribulation.

Oh, Heaven! it must have been an awful sight,
To see the poor souls struggling hard with all their might,
Fighting hard their lives to save,
While many in the smoke and burning flame did madly rave!

It was the most sickening sight that ever anybody saw,
Human remains, beyond recognition, covered with a heap of
    straw ;
And here and there a body might be seen, and a maimed
    hand,
Oh, such a sight, that the most hard-hearted person could
    hardly withstand!

K   **161**

The number of the people in the theatre was between seven
and eight thousand,
But, alas! one hundred and fifty by the fire have been found
dead ;
And the most lives were lost on the stairs leading from the
gallery,
And these were roasted to death, which was sickening to see.

The funerals were conducted at the expense of the local
authority,
And two hours and more elapsed at the mournful ceremony ;
And at one grave there were two thousand people, a very
great crowd,
And most of the men were bareheaded and weeping aloud.

Alas! many poor children have been bereft of their fathers
and mothers,
Who will be sorely missed by little sisters and brothers ;
But, alas! unto them they can ne'er return again,
Therefore the poor little innocents must weep for them in vain.

I hope all kind Christian souls will help the friends of the dead,
Especially those that have lost the winners of their bread ;
And if they do, God surely will them bless,
Because pure Christianity is to help the widows and orphans
in distress.

I am very glad to see Henry Irving has sent a hundred
pound,
And I hope his brother actors will subscribe their mite all
round ;
And if they do it will add honour to their name,
Because whatever is given towards a good cause they will it
regain.

JOHN ROUAT THE FISHERMAN.

MARGARET SIMPSON was the daughter of humble parents in
  the county of Ayr,
With a comely figure, and face of beauty rare,
And just in the full bloom of her womanhood
Was united to John Rouat, a fisherman good.

John's fortune consisted of his coble, three oars, and his
  fishing-gear,
Besides his two stout boys, John and James, he loved most
  dear.
And no matter how the wind might blow, or the rain pelt,
Or scarcity of fish, John little sorrow felt.

While sitting by the clear blazing hearth of his home,
With beaming faces around it, all his own.
But John, the oldest son, refused his father obedience,
Which John Rouat considered a most grievous offence.

So his father tried to check him, but all wouldn't do,
And John joined a revenue cutter as one of its crew ;
And when his father heard it he bitterly did moan,
And angrily forbade him never to return home.

Then shortly after James ran away to sea without his
  parents' leave,
So John Rouat became morose, and sadly did grieve.
But one day he received a letter, stating his son John was
  dead,
And when he read the sad news all comfort from him fled.

Then shortly after that his son James was shot,
For allowing a deserter to escape, such was his lot ;
And through the death of his two sons he felt dejected,
And the condolence of kind neighbours by him was rejected.

'Twas near the close of autumn, when one day the sky
    became o'ercast,
And John Rouat, contrary to his wife's will, went to sea at
    last,
When suddenly the sea began to roar, and angry billows
    swept along,
And, alas! the stormy tempest for John Rouat proved too
    strong.

But still he clutched the oars, thinking to keep his coble
    afloat,
When one 'whelming billow struck heavily against the boat,
And man and boat were engulfed in the briny wave,
While the Storm Fiend did roar and madly did rave.

When Margaret Rouat heard of her husband's loss, her
    sorrow was very great,
And the villagers of Bute were moved with pity for her sad
    fate,
And for many days and nights she wandered among the
    hills,
Lamenting the loss of her husband and other ills.

Until worn out by fatigue, towards a ruinous hut she did
    creep,
And there she lay down on the earthen floor, and fell
    asleep,
And as a herd boy by chance was passing by,
He looked into the hut and the body of Margaret he did espy.

Then the herd boy fled to communicate his fears,
And the hut was soon filled with villagers, and some shed
tears.
When they discovered in the unhappy being they had found
Margaret Rouat, their old neighbour, then their sorrow was
profound.

Then the men from the village of Bute willingly lent their aid,
To patch up the miserable hut, and great attention to her
was paid.
And Margaret Rouat lived there in solitude for many years,
Although at times the simple creature shed many tears.

Margaret was always willing to work for her bread,
Sometimes she herded cows without any dread,
Besides sometimes she was allowed to ring the parish bell,
And for doing so she was always paid right well.

In an old box she kept her money hid away,
But being at the kirk one beautiful Sabbath day,
When to her utter dismay when she returned home,
She found the bottom forced from the box, and the money gone.

Then she wept like a child, in a hysteric fit,
Regarding the loss of her money, and didn't very long
survive it.
And as she was wont to descend to the village twice a week,
The villagers missed her, and resolved they would for her
seek.

Then two men from the village, on the next day
Sauntered up to her dwelling, and to their dismay,
They found the door half open, and one stale crust of bread,
And on a rude pallet lay poor Margaret Rouat cold and dead.

THE SORROWS OF THE BLIND.

PITY the sorrows of the poor blind,
For they can but little comfort find ;
As they walk along the street,
They know not where to put their feet.
They are deprived of that earthly joy
Of seeing either man, woman, or boy ;
Sad and lonely through the world they go,
Not knowing a friend from a foe :
Nor the difference betwixt day and night,
For the want of their eyesight ;
The blind mother cannot see her darling boy,
That was once her soul's joy.
By day and night,
Since she lost her precious sight ;
To her the world seems dark and drear,
And she can find no comfort here.
She once found pleasure in reading books,
But now pale and careworn are her looks.
Since she has lost her eyesight,
Everything seems wrong and nothing right.

The face of nature, with all its beauties and livery green.
Appears to the blind just like a dream.
All things beautiful have vanished from their sight,
Which were once their heart's delight.
The blind father cannot see his beautiful child, nor wife,
That was once the joy of his life ;
That he was wont to see at morn and night,
When he had his eyesight.
All comfort has vanished from him now,
And a dejected look hangs on his brow.

Kind Christians all, both great and small,
Pity the sorrows of the blind,
They can but little comfort find ;
Therefore we ought to be content with our lot,
And for the eyesight we have got,
And pray to God both day and night
To preserve our eyesight ;
And be always willing to help the blind in their distress,
And the Lord will surely bless
And guard us by night and day,
And remember us at the judgment day.

GENERAL GORDON,

THE HERO OF KHARTOUM.

ALAS! now o'er the civilised world there hangs a gloom
For brave General Gordon, that was killed in Khartoum ;
He was a Christian hero, and a soldier of the Cross,
And to England his death will be a very great loss.

He was very cool in temper, generous and brave,
The friend of the poor, the sick, and the slave ;
And many a poor boy he did educate,
And laboured hard to do so both early and late.

He was a man that did not care for worldly gear,
Because the living and true God he did fear ;
And the hearts of the poor he liked to cheer,
And by his companions in arms he was loved most dear.

He always took the Bible for his guide,
And he liked little boys to walk by his side ;
He preferred their company more so than men,
Because he knew there was less guile in them.

And in his conversation he was modest and plain,
Denouncing all pleasures he considered sinful and vain,
And in battle he carried no weapon but a small cane,
Whilst the bullets fell around him like a shower of rain.

He burnt the debtors' books that were imprisoned in
Khartoum,
And freed them from a dismal prison gloom,
Those that were imprisoned for debt they couldn't pay,
And sent them rejoicing on their way.

While engaged in the Russian war, in the midst of the fight,
He stood upon a rising ground and viewed them left and right,
But for their shot and shell he didn't care a jot,
While the officers cried, Gordon, come down, or else you'll be
shot.

His cane was christened by the soldiers Gordon's wand of
victory,
And when he waved it the soldiers' hearts were filled with
glee,
While with voice and gesture he encouraged them in the strife,
And he himself appeared to possess a charmed life.

Once when leading a storming party the soldiers drew back,
But he quickly observed that courage they did lack,
Then he calmly lighted a cigar, and turned cheerfully round,
And the soldiers rushed boldly on with a bound.

And they carried the position without delay,
And the Chinese rebels soon gave way,
Because God was with him during the day,
And with those that trust Him for ever and aye.

He was always willing to conduct meetings for the poor,
Also meat and clothing for them he tried to procure,
And he always had little humorous speeches at command,
And to hear him deliver them it must have been grand.

In military life his equal couldn't be found,
No! if you were to search the wide world around,
And 'tis pitiful to think he has met with such a doom
By a base *traitor knave* while in Khartoum.

Yes, the black-hearted traitor opened the gates of Khartoum,
And through that the Christian hero has met his doom,
For when the gates were opened the Arabs rushed madly in,
And foully murdered him while they laughingly did grin.

But he defended himself nobly with axe and sword in hand,
But, alas! he was soon overpowered by that savage band,
And his body received a hundred spear wounds and more,
While his murderers exultingly did loudly shriek and roar.

But heaven's will, 'tis said, must be done,
And according to his own opinion his time was come ;
But I hope he is now in heaven reaping his reward,
Although his fate on earth was really very hard.

I hope the people will his memory revere,
And take an example from him, and worship God in fear,
And never be too fond of worldly gear,
And walk in General Gordon's footsteps while they are here.

THE BATTLE OF CRESSY.

'Twas on the 26th of August, the sun was burning hot,
In the year of 1346, which will never be forgot,
Because the famous field of Cressy was slippery and gory,
By the loss of innocent blood which I'll relate in story.

To the field of Cressy boldly King Philip did advance,
Aided by the Bohemian Army and chosen men of France,
And treble the strength of the English Army that day,
But the lance thrusts of the English soon made them give
way.

The English Army was under the command of the Prince of
Wales,
And with ringing cheers the soldiers his presence gladly hails,
As King Edward spoke to the Prince, his son, and said,
My son put thou thy trust in God and be not afraid,
And he will protect thee in the midst of the fight,
And remember God always defends the right.

Then the Prince knelt on one knee before the King,
Whilst the soldiers gathered round them in a ring ;
Then the King commanded that the Prince should be
carefully guarded,
And if they were victorious each man would be rewarded.

These arrangements being made, the Prince rode away,
And as he rode past the ranks, his spirits felt gay ;
Then he ordered the men to refresh themselves without
delay,
And prepare to meet the enemy in the coming deadly fray.

Then contentedly the men seated themselves upon the grass,
And ate and drank to their hearts content, until an hour did
    pass ;
Meanwhile the French troops did advance in disorganised
    masses,
But as soon as the English saw them they threw aside their
    glasses.

And they rose and stood in the ranks as solid as the rock,
All ready and eager to receive the enemy's shock ;
And as the morning was advancing a little beyond noon,
They all felt anxious for the fight, likewise to know their doom.

Then the French considered they were unable to begin the
    attack,
And seemed rather inclined for to draw back ;
But Count D'Alencon ordered them on to the attack,
Then the rain poured down in torrents and the thunder did
    crack.

Then forward marched the French with mock shrill cries,
But the English their cries most bravely defies ;
And as the sun shone out in all its brilliant array,
The English let fly their arrows at them without the least
    dismay.

And each man fought hard with sword and lance pell mell,
And the ranks were instantly filled up as soon as a man fell ;
And the Count D'Alencon, boldly charged the Black Prince,
And he cried, yield you, Sir Knight, or I'll make you wince.

Ha, by St. George! thou knowest not what thou sayest,
Therefore yield thyself, Sir Frenchman, for like an ass thou
    brayest ;
Then planting his lance he ran at the Count without fear,
And the Count fell beneath the Black Prince's spear.

And the Black Prince and his men fought right manfully,
By this time against some forty thousand of the enemy,
Until the Prince recognised the banner of Bohemia floating in
    the air ;
Then he cried that banner shall be mine, by St. George
    I do swear.

On! on! for old England, he cried, on! gentlemen on!
And spur your chargers quickly, and after them begone ;
Then the foremost, a slight youth, to the Prince did reply,
My Prince, I'll capture that banner for you else I will die

Ha! cried the Prince, is it thou my gallant Jack of Kent,
Now charge with me my brave lad for thou has been sent
By God, to aid me in the midst of the fight,
So forward, and wield your cudgel with all your might.

Then right into the midst of the Bohemian Knights they
    fought their way,
Brave Jack o' the Cudgel and the Prince without dismay ;
And Jack rushed at the Standard Bearer without any dread,
And struck him a blow with his cudgel which killed him dead.

Then Jack bore off the Standard, to the Prince's delight,
Then the French and the Bohemians instantly took to flight ;
And as the last rays of the sun had faded in the west,
The wounded and dying on both sides longed for rest.

And Philip, King of France, was wounded twice in the fray,
And was forced to fly from the field in great dismay ;
And John of Hainault cried, come sire, come away,
I hope you will live to win some other day.

Then King Edward and his army, and the Prince his son,
Knelt down and thanked God for the victory won ;
And the King's heart was filled with great delight,
And he thanked Jack for capturing the Bohemian Standard
    during the fight.

THE WRECK OF THE BARQUE " WM. PATERSON,"
OF LIVERPOOL.

Ye landsmen all attend my verse, and I'll tell to ye a tale
Concerning the barque " Wm. Paterson " that was lost in a
    tempestuous gale ;
She was on a voyage from Bangkok to the Clyde with a cargo
    of Teakwood,
And the crew numbered fifteen in all of seamen firm and good.

'Twas on the 8th of March, when a violent gale from the
    southward broke out,
And for nine days during tempestuous weather their ship was
    tossed about
By the angry sea, and the barque she sprang a leak,
Still the crew wrought at the pumps till their hearts were like
    to break.

And the pumps were kept constantly going for fourteen long
    hours,
And the poor men were drenched to the skin with sea spray
    showers ;
Still they wrought at the pumps till they became rather clogged
Until at last the barque became thoroughly water-logged.

Oh! hard was the fate of these brave men,
While the water did rush in from stern to stem,
Poor souls 'twas enough to have driven them frantic,
To be drifting about water-logged in the Atlantic.

At last she became unmanageable and her masts had to be
    cut away,
Which the brave crew performed quickly without delay ;
Still gales of more or less violence prevailed every day,
Whilst the big waves kept dashing o'er them, likewise the
    spray.

And with the fearful hurricane the deckhouse and galley
were carried away,
Yet the thought of a speedy deliverance kept up their courage
day by day,
And the captain prepared for the breaking up of the ship
without dismay,
And to save his rations he reduced each man to two biscuits a
day.

The brave heroes managed to save a pinnace about fifteen
feet long,
And into it thirteen of the crew quickly and cautiously did
throng,
With two bags of biscuits and a cask of water out of the tank,
And for these precious mercies, God they did thank ;

Who is the giver of all good things,
And to those that put their trust in him often succour brings,
And such has been the case with these brave men at sea,
That sent Captain M'Mullan to save them and bring them to
Dundee.

When once into the pinnace they improvised a sail into a tent,
Which to the crew some little shelter lent ;
Still every day they were drifting towards the coast of
Greenland,
Yet they hoped in God that speedy deliverance might be
near at hand.

And as every day passed by they felt woe begone,
Because no sail could they see on the horizon ;
And they constructed a sea anchor to keep the boat's head to
sea,
Andnotwithstanding their hardships they stood out bravely

174

And on the 19th of March a ship hove in sight,

Which proved to be the " Slieve Roe " to their delight ;

Then they hoisted a signal of distress when they espied the
" Slieve Roe,"

But it was not seen on account of the wreck being in the
water so low.

But as soon as Captain M'Mullan knew it was a signal of
distress,

Then heroically and quickly his men he did address,

He cried! come my men keep the ship close to the wind,

And let's try if we can these unfortunate souls find.

And as the " Slieve Roe " to them drew near,

Poor souls they gave a hearty cheer ;

Then they were immediately taken on board,

And they thanked Captain M'Mullan for saving them,
likewise the Lord.

Then a crew from the " Slieve Roe " were sent away,

For the two remaining members of the crew without delay ;

The Captain and a Sailor, together with a cat and a pet dog,

Which had been the companions of the sailors, and seemed as
frisky as a frog.

And when they had all got safe on board,

With one accord they thanked the Lord ;

And Captain M'Mullan kindly did them treat,

By giving them dry clothing and plenty of meat.

And for his kind treatment unto them he deserves great
praise,

For his many manly and kindly ways,

By saving so many lives during the time he has been at sea,

And in particular for fetching the crew of the "Wm. Paterson"
safe to Dundee

HANCHEN, THE MAID OF THE MILL

Near the village of Udorf, on the banks of the Rhine,
There lived a miller and his family, once on a time ;
And there yet stands the mill in a state of decay,
And concerning the miller and his family, attend to my lay

The miller and his family went to Church one Sunday morn,
Leaving behind their darling child, the youngest born,
In charge of brave Hanchen, the servant maid,
A kind-hearted girl and not the least afraid.

As Hanchen was engaged preparing dinner for the family
She chanced to turn round, and there she did see
Heinrich Bottler, her lover, and she sincerely loved him,
Then she instantly got him something to eat and bade him
    begin.

And in the midst of her business she sat down beside him,
While he did justice to the meat and thought it no sin,
But while he was eating he let fall his knife,
Then he commanded Hanchen to pick it up or else he'd take
    her life.

Then as she stooped down to pick up the knife,
The villain caught her by the throat, and swore he'd take her
    life,
Then he drew a dagger from under his coat,
Crying tell me where your master's money is, or I'll cut your
    throat

And still he threatened to kill her with the dagger in his hand,
If the poor girl didn't comply with his demand,
While in his choking grasp her breath was fleeting faster and
faster,
Therefore she had no other choice but to die or betray her
master.

Then she cried, mercy, for Heaven's sake let go thy hold,
And I'll tell thee where my master keeps his gold ;
Then he let go his hold without delay,
And she unto him thus boldly did say.

Here, take this axe and use it, while I run upstairs,
To gather all my money, besides all my wares,
Because I'm resolved to fly along with you,
When you've robbed my master of his gold and bid France
adieu.

Then deceived by her plan he allowed her to leave the room,
Telling her to make haste and come back very soon,
Then to her master's bedroom she led the way,
And showed him the coffer where her master's money lay.

Then Heinrich with the axe broke the coffer very soon,
While Hanchen instead of going upstairs to her room,
Bolted all the doors upon him without dismay,
While Heinrich was busy preparing to carry her master's
money away.

Then she rushed to the mill to give the alarm,
Resolved to protect her master's money, while she could
wield an arm ;
And the only being in sight, was her master's boy of five
years old,
Then she cried, run! run! and tell father there's a robber
taking his gold.

L   177

Then the boy did as she bid him without any doubt,
And set off, running on the road she pointed out ;
But at this moment, a shrill whistle made her stand aghast,
When she heard Heinrich, crying, catch that child that's
running so fast.

But still the boy ran on with might and main,
Until a ruffian sprang up from the bed of a natural drain ;
And snatching the boy in his arms, and hastening towards
the mill,
While brave Hanchen was afraid the boy he would kill.

Then the villain came rushing with the boy towards the mill,
Crying, open the door, or the child I'll kill ;
But she cried, never will I open the door to thee,
No ! I will put my trust in God, and He'll save the child and me.

Then the ruffian set down the child, for a moment to look
about,
Crying, open the door, or I'll fire the mill without doubt ;
And while searching for combustibles, he discovered an inlet
to the mill,
Saying, my pretty maid, once I get in, it's you I will kill.

Then he tied the hands and feet of the poor child,
Which caused it to scream with fear, very wild ;
Then he stole back to the aperture to effect an entrance,
And when Hanchen saw him, she said now is my chance.

So the ruffian got safely in the great drum wheel,
Then Hanchen set on the engine, which made the ruffian reel ;
And as he was whirled about, he screamed aloud,
And when Hanchen saw him like a rat in a trap, she felt very
proud.

At length the master arrived and his family,
And when she heard his kindly voice her heart was full of glee,
Then she opened the mill door and let him in,
While her eyes with tears of joy were full to the brim.

Then the master set off the engine without delay,
And the ruffian was dragged forth while he shook with
  dismay,
And Heinrich and he were bound together under a strong
  escort,
And conveyed to Bonn Prison where villains resort.

So thus ends the story of Hanchen, a heroine brave,
That tried hard her master's gold to save,
And for her bravery she got married to the miller's eldest son,
And Hanchen on her marriage night cried Heaven's will be
  done.

WRECK OF THE SCHOONER
"SAMUEL CRAWFORD."

'Twas in the year of 1886, and on the 29th of November,
Which the surviving crew of the " Samuel Crawford " will
  long remember,
She was bound to Baltimore with a cargo of pine lumber ;
But, alas! the crew suffered greatly from cold and hunger.

'Twas on December 3rd when about ten miles south-west
Of Currituck light, and scudding at her best ;
That a heavy gale struck her a merciless blow,
Which filled the hearts of the crew with fear and woe.

179

Then the merciless snow came down, hiding everything from
    view,
And as the night closed in the wind tempestuous blew ;
Still the brave crew reefed the spanker and all the sails,
While not one amongst them with fear bewails.

Still the gallant little schooner ploughed on the seas,
Through the blinding snow and the stormy breeze ;
Until it increased to a fearful hurricane,
Yet the crew wrought manfully and didn't complain.

But during the night the wind it harder blew,
And the brave little schooner was hove to ;
And on the morning of December the 4th the wind died
    out,
But it rent the schooner from stem to stern without any
    doubt.

And the seas were running mountains high,
While the poor sailors, no doubt, heaved many a sigh ;
Because they must have felt cold, and the schooner sprung a
    leak,
Still they wrought while their hearts were like to break.

Then the wind it sprang up in terrific fury again,
But the crew baled out the water with might and main ;
But still the water fast on them did gain,
Yet the brave heroes disdained to complain.

On the morning of December the 4th she was scudding before
    a hurricane,
And the crew were exhausted, but managed the poop to gain ;
And the vessel was tossed like a cork on the wave,
While the brave crew expected to meet with a watery grave.

And huge beams and pine planks were washed overboard,
While Captain Tilton looked on and said never a word ;
And the crew likewise felt quite content,
Until the fore-and-aft rigging overboard went.

Then loudly for help to God they did cry,
And to their earnest prayer He did draw nigh ;
And saved them from a watery grave,
When help from Him they did crave.

Poor souls they expected to be engulfed every hour,
And to appease their hunger they made dough with salt
    water and flour ;
And made a sort of hard cake placed over a griddle hole,
To satisfy their hunger, which, alas! is hard to thole.

And two of these cakes each man got per day,
Which the poor creatures devoured in a ravenous way ;
Along with a little fresh water to wash it down,
Which they most thankfully praised God for and didn't
    frown.

And on the 10th of December when they had burned their
    last light,
The ship " Orinoco " bound for New York hove in sight ;
And they were rescued safely and taken on board,
And they thanked the Captain, and likewise the Lord.

Then the Captain of the " Orinoco " ordered her to be set
    on fire,
Which was quickly done as he did desire ;
Which caused the rescued crew to stare in amaze,
And to take the last look of their schooner in a blaze

THE FIRST GRENADIER OF FRANCE.

'Twas in a certain regiment of French Grenadiers,
A touching and beautiful custom was observed many years ;
Which was meant to commemorate the heroism of a departed
    comrade,
And when the companies assembled for parade,
There was one name at roll call to which no answer was made.

It was that of the noble La Tour d'Auvergne,
The first Grenadier of France, heroic and stern ;
And always at roll call the oldest sergeant stepped forward a
    pace,
And loudly cried, " died on the field of battle," then fell back
    into his place.

He always refused offers of high promotion,
Because to be promoted from the ranks he had no notion ;
But at last he was in command of eight thousand men,
Hence he was called the first Grenadier of France, La Tour
    d'Auvergne.

When forty years of age he went on a visit to a friend,
Never thinking he would have a French garrison to defend
And while there he made himself acquainted with the country,
But the war had shifted to that quarter unfortunately.

But although the war was there he felt undaunted,
Because to fight on behalf of France was all he wanted ;
And the thought thereof did his mind harass,
When he knew a regiment of Austrians was pushing on to
    occupy a narrow pass.

They were pushing on in hot haste and no delaying,
And only two hours distant from where the Grenadier was
    staying,
But when he knew he set off at once for the pass,
Determined if 'twere possible the enemy to harass.

He knew that the pass was defended by a stout tower,
And to destroy the garrison the enemy would exert all their
power ;
But he hoped to be able to warn the French of their danger,
But to the thirty men garrisoned there he was quite a
stranger.

Still the brave hero hastened on, and when he came there,
He found the thirty men had fled in wild despair ;
Leaving their thirty muskets behind,
But to defend the garrison to the last he made up his mind.

And in searching he found several boxes of ammunition not
destroyed,
And for a moment he felt a little annoyed ;
Then he fastened the main door, with the articles he did find,
And when he had done so he felt satisfied in mind.

Then he ate heartily of the provisions he had brought,
And waited patiently for the enemy, absorbed in thought ;
And formed the heroic resolution to defend the tower,
Alone, against the enemy, while he had the power.

There the brave hero sat alone quite content,
Resolved to hold the garrison, or die in the attempt ;
And about midnight his practised ear caught the tramp of
feet,
But he had everything ready for the attack and complete.

There he sat and his mind absorbed in deep distress,
But he discharged a couple of muskets into the darkness ;
To warn the enemy that he knew they were there,
Then he heard the Austrian officers telling their men to
beware.

So until morning he was left unmolested,
And quietly till daylight the brave Grenadier rested ;
But at sunrise the Austrian commander called on the garrison
 to surrender,
But the Grenadier replied, " never, I am its sole defender."

Then a piece of artillery was brought to bear upon the tower,
But the Grenadier from his big gun rapid fire on it did
 shower ;
He kept up a rapid fire, and most accurate,
And when the Austrian commander noticed it he felt irate.

And at sunset the last assault was made,
Still the noble Grenadier felt not the least afraid ;
But the Austrian commander sent a second summons of
 surrender,
Hoping that the garrison would his injunctions remember.

Then the next day at sunrise the tower door was opened wide,
And a bronzed and scarred Grenadier forth did glide ;
Literally laden with muskets, and passed along the line of
 troops,
While in utter astonishment the Austrian Colonel upon him
 looks.

Behold! Colonel, I am the garrison, said the soldier proudly,
What! exclaimed the Colonel, do you mean to tell me—
That you alone have held that tower against so many men,
Yes! Colonel, I have indeed, replied La Tour d'Auvergne.

Then the Colonel raised his cap and said, you are the bravest
 of the brave,
Grenadier, I salute you, and I hope you will find an honourable
 grave ;
And you're at liberty to carry the muskets along with you,
So my brave Grenadier I must bid thee adieu.

At last in action the brave solider fell in June 1800,
And the Emperor Napoleon felt sorry when he heard he was
    dead ;
And he commanded his regiment to remember one thing
    above all,
To cry out always the brave Grenadier's name at the roll call.

THE TRAGIC DEATH OF
THE REV. A. H. MACKONOCHIE.

FRIENDS of humanity, of high and low degree,
I pray ye all come listen to me ;
And truly I will relate to ye,
The tragic fate of the Rev. Alexander Heriot Mackonochie

Who was on a visit to the Bishop of Argyle
For the good of his health, for a short while ;
Because for the last three years his memory had been affected
Which prevented him from getting his thoughts collected

'Twas on Thursday, the 15th of December, in the year of 1887,
He left the Bishop's house to go and see Loch Leven ;
And he was accompanied by a little skye terrier and a
    deerhound,
Besides the Bishop's two dogs, that knew well the ground.

And as he had taken the same walk the day before,
The Bishop's mind was undisturbed and easy on that score :
Besides the Bishop had been told by some men,
That they saw him making his way up a glen.

From which a river flows down with a mighty roar,
From the great mountains of the Mamore ;
And this route led him towards trackless wastes eastward,
And no doubt to save his life he had struggled very hard.

And as Mr Mackonochie had not returned at dinner time,
The Bishop ordered two men to search for him, which they
    didn't decline ;
Then they searched for him along the road he should have
    returned,
But when they found him not, they sadly mourned.

And when the Bishop heard it, he procured a carriage and pair,
While his heart was full of woe, and in a state of despair ;
He organised three search parties without delay,
And headed one of the parties in person without dismay.

And each party searched in a different way,
But to their regret at the end of the day ;
Most unfortunately no discovery had been made,
Then they lost hope of finding him, and began to be afraid.

And as a last hope, two night searches were planned,
And each party with well lighted lamps in hand
Started on their perilous mission, Mr Mackonochie to try and
    find,
In the midst of driving hail, and the howling wind.

One party searched a distant sporting lodge with right good
    will,
Besides through brier, and bush, and snow, on the hill ;
And the Bishop's party explored the Devil's Staircase with
    hearts full of woe,
A steep pass between the Kinloch hills, and the hills of
    Glencoe.

Oh! it was a pitch dark and tempestuous night,
And the searchers would have lost their way without lamp
    light ;
But the brave searchers stumbled along for hours, but slow,
Over rocks, and ice, and sometimes through deep snow.

And as the Bishop's party were searching they met a third
    party from Glencoe side,
Who had searched bracken and burn, and the country wide ;
And sorrow was depicted in each one's face,
Because of the Rev. Mr Mackonochie they could get no trace

But on Saturday morning the Bishop set off again,
Hoping that the last search wouldn't prove in vain ;
Accompanied with a crowd of men and dogs,
All resolved to search the forest and the bogs.

And the party searched with might and main,
Until they began to think their search would prove in vain ;
When the Bishop's faithful dogs raised a pitiful cry,
Which was heard by the searchers near by.

Then the party pressed on right manfully,
And sure enough there were the dogs guarding the body of
    Mackonochie ;
And the corpse was cold and stiff, having been long dead,
Alas! almost frozen, and a wreath of snow around the head.

And as the searchers gathered round the body in pity they
    did stare,
Because his right foot was stained with blood, and bare ;
But when the Bishop o'er the corpse had offered up a prayer,
He ordered his party to carry the corpse to his house on a bier.

So a bier of sticks was most willingly and quickly made,
Then the body was most tenderly upon it laid ;
And they bore the corpse and laid inside the Bishop's private
    chapel,
Then the party took one sorrowful look and bade the corpse,
    farewell.

THE BURNING OF THE STEAMER

" CITY OF MONTREAL."

A SAD tale of the sea I will relate, which will your hearts appal,
Concerning the burning of the steamship " City of Montreal,"
Which had on board two hundred and forty-nine souls in all,
But, alas! a fearful catastrophe did them befall.

The steamer left New York on the 6th August with a general
cargo,
Bound for Queenstown and Liverpool also ;
And all went well until Wednesday evening the 10th,
When in an instant an alarming fire was discovered at length.

And most of the passengers had gone to their berths for the
night,
But when the big bell rang out, oh! what a pitiful sight ;
To see mothers and their children crying, was most heart-
rending to behold,
As the blinding smoke began to ascend from the main hold.

And the smoke before long drifted down below,
Which almost choked the passengers, and filled their hearts
with woe ;
Then fathers and mothers rushed madly upon the deck,
While the crew were struggling manfully the fire to check.

Oh, it was a soul-harrowing and horrible sight,
To see the brave sailors trying hard with all their might ;
Battling furiously with the merciless flames—
With a dozen of hose, but still the fire on them gains.

At length it became apparent the steamer couldn't be saved,
And the passengers were huddled together, and some of them
madly raved ;
And the family groups were most touching to see,
Especially husbands and wives embracing each other tenderly.

The mothers drew their little ones close to them,
Just like little lambs huddled together in a pen ;
While the white foaming billows was towering mountains high,
And one and all on God for protection did cry.

And when the Captain saw the steamer he couldn't save,
He cried, come men, prepare the boats to be launched on the
    briny wave ;
Be quick, and obey my orders, let each one bear a hand—
And steer the vessel direct for Newfoundland.

Then the men made ready the boats, which were eight on board,
Hurriedly and fearlessly with one accord ;
And by eight o'clock on Thursday morning, everything was
    ready
For the passengers to leave the burning steamer that was
    rolling unsteady.

Then Captain Land on his officers loudly did call,
And the cheery manliness of him inspired confidence in all ;
Then he ordered the men to lower the boats without delay,
So the boats were launched on the stormy sea without dismay.

Then women and children were first put into them,
Also a quantity of provisions, then followed the men ;
And as soon as the boats were loaded they left the steamer's
    side,
To be tossed to and fro on the ocean wide.

And just as they left the burning ship, a barque hove in sight,
Which filled the poor creatures hearts with delight ;
And the barque was called the " Trebant," of Germany,
So they were all rescued and conveyed to their homes in
    safety.

But before they left the barque, they thanked God that did
    them save
From a cold and merciless watery grave ;
Also the Captain received their thanks o'er and o'er,
Whilst the big waves around the barque did sullenly roar.

So good people I warn ye all to be advised by me,
To remember and be prepared to meet God where'er ye may
    be ;
For death claims his victims, both on sea and shore,
Therefore be prepared for that happy land where all troubles
    are o'er.

THE WRECK OF THE WHALER " OSCAR."

'Twas on the 1st of April, and in the year of Eighteen thirteen,
That the whaler "Oscar" was wrecked not far from Aberdeen ;
'Twas all on a sudden the wind arose, and a terrific blast it
    blew,
And the " Oscar " was lost, and forty-two of a gallant crew.

The storm burst forth with great violence, but of short
    duration,
And spread o'er a wide district, and filled the people's hearts
    with consternation,
And its effects were such that the people will long mind,
Because at Peterhead the roof was torn off a church by the
    heavy wind.

The " Oscar " joined other four ships that were lying in
    Aberdeen Bay,
All ready to start for Greenland without delay,
While the hearts of each ship' crew felt light and gay,
But, when the storm burst upon them, it filled their hearts
    with dismay.

The wind had been blowing westerly during the night,
But suddenly it shifted to the North-east, and blew with all
    its might,
And thick and fast fell the blinding snow,
Which filled the poor sailors' hearts with woe.

And the " Oscar " was exposed to the full force of the
    gale,
But the crew resolved to do their best, allowing they should
    fail,
So they weighed anchor, and stood boldly out for sea,
While the great crowds that had gathered cheered them
    encouragingly.

The ill-fated " Oscar," however, sent a boat ashore
For some of her crew that were absent, while the angry sea
    did roar,
And 'twas with great difficulty the men got aboard,
And to make the ship alright they wrought with one
    accord.

Then suddenly the wind shifted, and a treacherous calm
    ensued,
And the vessel's deck with snow was thickly strewed ;
And a heavy sea was running with a strong flood tide,
And it soon became apparent the men wouldn't be able the
    ship to guide.

And as the " Oscar " drifted further and further to leeward,
The brave crew tried hard her backward drifting to retard,
But all their efforts proved in vain, for the storm broke out
    anew,
While the drifting snow hid her from the spectators'
    view.

And the position of the " Oscar " was critical in the extreme
And as the spray washed o'er the vessel, O what a soul-
harrowing scene!
And notwithstanding the fury of the gale and the blinding
snow,
Great crowds watched the " Oscar " as she was tossed to and
fro.

O heaven! it was a most heart-rending sight
To see the crew struggling against wind and blinding snow
with all their might,
While the mighty waves lashed her sides and angry did
roar,
Which to their relatives were painful to see that were
standing on shore,

All eagerly watching her attempt to ride out the storm,
Especially their friends and relatives, who seemed very forlorn,
Because the scene was awe-inspiring and made them stand
aghast,
For every moment seemed to be the " Oscar's " last.

Oh! it was horrible to see the good ship in distress,
Battling hard against wind and tide to clear the Girdleness.
A conspicuous promontory on the south side of Aberdeen Bay,
Where many a stout ship and crew have gone down passing
that way.

At last the vessel was driven ashore in the bay of Greyhope,
And the " Oscar " with the elements no longer could cope.
While the big waves lashed her furiously, and she received
fearful shocks,
Until a mighty wave hurled her among large boulders of
rocks.

192

And when the vessel struck, the crew stood aghast,
But they resolved to hew down the mainmast,
Which the spectators watched with eager interest,
And to make it fall on the rocks the brave sailors tried their
best.

But, instead of falling on the rocks, it dropped into the angry
tide,
Then a groan arose from those that were standing on the
shore side ;
And the mainmast in its fall brought down the foremast,
Then all hope of saving the crew seemed gone at last.

And a number of the crew were thrown into the boiling surge
below,
While loud and angry the stormy wind did blow,
And the good ship was dashed to pieces from stern to stem,
Within a yard or two of their friends, who were powerless to
save them.

Oh! it was an appalling sight to see the " Oscar " in distress,
While to the forecastle was seen clinging brave Captain Innes
And five of a crew, crying for help, which none could afford,
Alas! poor fellows, crying aloud to God with one accord!

But their cry to God for help proved all in vain,
For the ship and men sank beneath the briny main,
And out of a crew of forty-four men, only two were saved,
But, landsmen, think how manfully that unfortunate crew
behaved.

And also think of the mariners while you lie down to sleep,
And pray to God to protect them while on the briny deep,
For their hardships are many, and hard to endure,
There's only a plank between them and a watery grave,
which makes their lives unsure.

JENNY CARRISTER,

THE HEROINE OF LUCKNOW-MINE.

A HEROIC story I will unfold,
Concerning Jenny Carrister, a heroine bold,
Who lived in Australia, at a gold mine called Lucknow,
And Jenny was beloved by all the miners, somehow.

Jenny was the only daughter of the old lady who owned the
    mine—
And Jenny would come of an evening, like a gleam of
    sunshine,
And by the presence of her bright face and cheery voice,
She made the hearts of the unlucky diggers rejoice.

There was no pride about her, and day after day,
She walked with her young brother, who was always gay,
A beautiful boy he was, about thirteen years old,
And Jenny and her brother by the miners were greatly extolled.

Old Mrs Carrister was every inch a lady in her way,
Because she never pressed any of the miners that weren't
    able to pay
For the liberty of working the gold-field,
Which was thirty pounds per week for whatever it might yield.

It was in the early part of the year 1871,
That Jack Allingford, a miner, hit on a plan,
That in the mine, with powder, he'd loosen the granite-
    bound face,
So he selected, as he thought, a most suitable place.

And when all his arrangements had been made,
He was lowered down by a miner that felt a little afraid,
But most fortunately Jenny Carrister came up at the time,
Just as Jack Allingford was lowered into the mine.

Then she asked the man at the windlass if he'd had any luck,
But he picked up a piece of candle and then a match he struck ;
Then Jenny asked the miner, What is that for ?
And he replied to blast the mine, which I fear and abhor.

Then with a piece of rope he lowered the candle and matches
    into the mine,
While brave Jenny watched the action all the time ;
And as the man continued to turn round the windlass handle,
Jenny asked him, Isn't it dangerous to lower the matches and
    candle ?

Then the man replied, I hope there's no danger, Jenny my lass,
But whatsoever God has ordained will come to pass ;
And just as he said so the windlass handle swung round,
And struck him on the forehead, and he fell to the ground.

And when Jenny saw the blood streaming from the fallen
    man's head,
She rushed to the mouth of the shaft without any dread,
And Jenny called loudly, but received no reply,
So to her brother standing near by she heaved a deep sigh.

Telling him to run for assistance, while she swung herself on
    to the hand-rope,
Resolved to save Jack Allingford's life as she earnestly did
    hope ;
And as she proceeded down the shaft at a quick pace,
The brave heroine knew that death was staring her in the face

And the rope was burning her hands as she descended,
But she thought if she saved Jack her task would be ended;
And when she reached the bottom of the mine she did not
hesitate,
But bounded towards Jack Allingford, who was lying
seemingly inanimate.

And as she approached his body the hissing fuse burst upon
her ears,
But still the noble girl no danger fears ;
While the hissing of the fuse was like an engine grinding upon
her brain,
Still she resolved to save Jack while life in her body did remain.

She noticed a small jet of smoke issuing from a hole near his
head,
And if he'd lain a few seconds longer there he'd been killed dead,
But God had sent an angel to his rescue,
For seizing him by the arms his body to the air shaft she drew.

It was a supernatural effort, but she succeeded at last,
And Jenny thanked God when the danger was past,
But at the same instant the silence was broke
By a loud explosion, which soon filled the mine with smoke.

But, oh, God be thanked! the greatest danger was past,
But when Jenny saw Jack Allingford, she stood aghast,
Because the blood was issuing from his nose and ears,
And as Jenny viewed his wounds she shed many tears.

But heroic Jenny was not one of the fainting sort,
For immediately to the mouth of the mine she did resort,
And she called loudly for help, the noble lass,
And her cry was answered by voices above at the windlass.

So there were plenty to volunteer their services below,
And the rope was attached to the windlass, and down they did
    go,
And Jack Allingford and Jenny were raised to the top,
While Jenny, noble soul, with exhaustion was like to drop.

And when the miners saw her safe above there was a burst of
    applause,
Because she had rescued Jack Allingford from death's jaws ;
So all ye that read or hear this story, I have but to say,
That Jenny Carrister was the noblest heroine I've ever heard
    of in my day.

THE HORRORS OF MAJUBA.

'Twas after the great Majuba fight :
And the next morning, at daylight,
Captain Macbean's men were ordered to headquarters camp,
So immediately Captain Macbean and his men set out on
    tramp.

And there they were joined by the Blue Jackets and 58th men,
Who, for unflinching courage, no man can them condemn ;
And that brave little band was commissioned to bury their
    dead,
And the little band numbered in all about one hundred

And they were supplied with a white flag, fit emblem of death,
Then they started off to O'Neill's farm, with bated breath,
Where their comrades had been left the previous night,
And were lying weltering in their gore, oh! what a horrible
    sight.

And when they arrived at the foot of Majuba Hill,
They were stopped by a Boer party, but they meant no ill,
Who asked them what they wanted without dismay,
And when they said, their dead, there was no further delay.

Then the brave heroes marched on, without any dread,
To the Hill of Majuba to collect and bury their dead ;
And to see them climbing Majuba it was a fearful sight,
And much more so on a dark pitch night.

And on Majuba there was a row of dead men,
Numbering about forty or fifty of them ;
There were also numbers of wounded men lying on the ground,
And when Captain Macbean's party gazed on them their sorrow was profound.

Oh, heaven! what a sight of blood and brains!
While the grass was red all o'er with blood-stains ;
Especially at the edge of the Hill, where the 92nd men were killed,
'Twas there that the eyes of Macbean's party with tears filled,

When they saw their dead and dying comrades in arms,
Who were always foremost in the fight during war's alarms ;
But who were now lying dead on Majuba Hill,
And, alas! beyond the aid of all human skill.

They then went about two hundred yards down the Hill,
And collected fourteen more bodies, which made their blood run chill ;
And, into one grave, seventy-five bodies they buried there,
All mostly 92nd men, who, I hope, are free from all care.

Oh! think of that little gallant British band,
Who, at Majuba, made such a heroic stand,
And, take them altogether, they behaved like brave men,
But, alas! they were slaughtered like sheep in a pen.

Poor fellows! there were few of them left to retire,
Because undauntedly they faced that murderous fire,
That the mighty host poured in upon them, left and right,
From their numerous rifles, day and night.

The conduct of the 92nd was most brave throughout,
Which has always been the case, without any doubt ;
At least, it has been the case in general with the Highland
    Brigade,
Because in the field they are the foremost, and seldom
    afraid.

And to do the British justice at Majuba they behaved right
    well,
But by overwhelming numbers the most of them fell,
Which I'm very sorry to relate,
That such a brave little band met with such a fate.

The commanders and officers deserve great praise,
Because they told their men to hold Majuba for three days ;
And so they did, until the most of them fell,
Fighting nobly for their Queen and country they loved right
    well.

But who's to blame for their fate I'm at a loss to know,
But I think 'twas by fighting too numerous a foe ;
But there's one thing I know, and, in conclusion, will say,
That their fame will be handed down to posterity for many
    a day!

THE MIRACULOUS ESCAPE OF ROBERT ALLAN,

THE FIREMAN.

'Twas in the year of 1888, and on October the fourteenth
day,
That a fire broke out in a warehouse, and for hours blazed
away ;
And the warehouse, now destroyed, was occupied by the
Messrs R. Wylie, Hill & Co.,
Situated in Buchanan Street, in the City of Glasgow.

The flames burst forth about three o'clock in the
afternoon,
And intimation of the outbreak spread very soon ;
And in the spectators' faces were depicted fear and consterna
tion ;
While the news flew like lightning to the Fire Brigade
Station.

And when the Brigade reached the scene of the fire,
The merciless flames were ascending higher and higher,
Raging furiously in all the floors above the street,
And within twenty minutes the structure was destroyed by
the burning heat.

Then the roof fell in, pushing out the front wall,
And the loud crash thereof frightened the spectators one and
all,
Because it shook the neighbouring buildings to their
foundation,
And caused throughout the City a great sensation

And several men were injured by the falling of the wall,
And as the bystanders gazed thereon, it did their hearts
    appal ;
But the poor fellows bore up bravely, without uttering a
    moan,
And with all possible speed they were conveyed home.

The firemen tried to play upon the building where the fire
    originated,
But, alas! their efforts were unfortunately frustrated,
Because they were working the hose pipes in a building
    occupied by Messrs Smith & Brown,
But the roof was fired, and amongst them it came crashing
    down.

And miraculously they escaped except one fireman,
The hero of the fire, named Robert Allan,
Who was carried with the debris down to the street
    floor,
And what he suffered must have been hard to endure.

He travelled to the fire in Buchanan Street
On the first machine that was ordered, very fleet,
Along with Charles Smith and Dan. Ritchie,
And proceeded to Brown & Smith's buildings that were
    burning furiously.

And in the third floor of the building he took his
    stand
Most manfully, without fear, with the hose in his
    hand,
And played on the fire through a window in the gable
With all his might, the hero, as long as he was able.

And he remained there for about a quarter of an hour,
While from his hose upon the building the water did pour,
When, without the least warning, the floor gave way,
And down he went with it : oh, horror! and dismay!

And with the debris and flooring he got jammed,
But Charlie Smith and Dan. Ritchie quickly planned
To lower down a rope to him, without any doubt,
So, with a long pull and a strong pull, he was dragged
    out.

He thought he was jammed in for a very long time,
For, instead of being only two hours jammed, he thought
    'twas months nine,
But the brave hero kept up his spirits without any dread,
Then he was taken home in a cab, and put in bed.

Oh, kind Christians! think of Robert Allan, the heroic
    man,
For he certainly is a hero, deny it who can ?
Because, although he was jammed, and in the midst of the
    flame,
He tells the world fearlessly he felt no pain.

The reason why, good people, he felt no pain
Is because he put his trust in God, to me it seems plain.
And in conclusion, I most earnestly pray,
That we will all put our trust in God, night and day.

And I hope that Robert Allan will do the same,
Because He saved him from being burnt while in the
    flame ;
And all those that trust in God will do well,
And be sure to escape the pains of hell.

THE BATTLE OF SHINA, IN AFRICA,

FOUGHT IN 1800.

KING SHUAC, the Giant of Mizra, war did declare
Against Ulva, King of Shina, telling him to prepare
And be ready for to meet him in the fight,
Which would commence the next morning before daylight.

When King Ulva heard the news, he told his warriors to
  prepare,
Then suddenly the clatter of arms sounded in the night
  air ;
And the pale beams of the moon shone on coats of mail,
But not one bosom beneath them with fear did quail.

And bugles rang out their hoarse call,
And armed men gathered quickly, not in dread of their
  downfall ;
For King Ulva resolved to go and meet Shuac,
So, by doing so, King Ulva's men courage didn't lack.

Therefore, the temple was lighted up anew,
And filled with armed warriors, bold and true ;
And the King stood clad in his armour, and full of pride,
As he gazed upon his warriors, close by his side.

And he bowed himself to the ground,
While there was a deep silence around ;
And he swore, by his false god of the all-seeing eye,
That he would meet Shuac, King of Mizra, and make
  him fly.

And I swear that in Shina peace shall remain,
And whatever thou desireth, supreme one, will not be in vain;
For thou shalt get what thou considereth to be most fit,
Though it be of my own flesh and blood, I swear it.

Then, when all was in readiness, they marched before the dawn,
Sixty thousand in number, and each a picked man ;
And they marched on silently to take Shuac's army by
    surprise,
And attack him, if possible, before sunrise.

King Shuac's army were about one hundred thousand strong,
And, when King Ulva heard so, he cried, We'll conquer them
    ere long,
Therefore, march on, brave men, we'll meet them before
    daybreak,
So, be resolute and conquer, and fight for Shina's sake.

Within a mile of the enemy's camp they lay all night,
Scarcely taking well-earned repose, they were so eager for
    the fight ;
And when the morning broke clear and cloudless, with a
    burning sun,
Each warrior was wishing that the fight was begun.

And as the armies neared one another, across the fertile land,
It was a most imposing sight, and truly grand,
To see the warriors clad in armour bright,
Especially the form of Shuac, in the midst of the fight.

The royal guard, forming the vanguard, made the first attack,
Under the command of King Ulva, who courage didn't lack ;
And cries of " King Ulva!" and " King Shuac!" rent the air,
While Shuac cried, I'll burn Shina to the ground, I now do
    swear!

King Shuac was mounted on a powerful steed,
Which pressed its way through the ranks with lightning
    speed ;
And with its hoofs the earth it uptears,
Until, with a bound, it dashes through the ranks of opposing
    spears.

Then the two Kings met each other at last,
And fire flashed from their weapons, and blows fell fast ;
But Shuac was the strongest of the two,
But King Ulva was his match with the club, Ulva knew.

Then, with his club, he gave Shuac a blow, which wounded
    him deep,
Crying out, Shuac, thy blood is deserting thee! thou art a
    sheep!
Cried Ulva, dealing him another fearful blow,
Then Shuac raised his club and rushed on his foe.

Then his blow fell, and knocked Ulva's club from his hand,
While both armies in amazement stand
To watch the hand-to-hand fight,
While Shuac's warriors felt great delight.

But there chanced to be a Scotchman in Ulva's army
That had a loaded pistol, and he fired it immediately,
And shot King Shuac through the head,
And he toppled over to the ground killed stone dead!

Then the men of Mizra laid down their arms and fled
When they saw that their King was killed dead ;
Then King Ulva said to the Scotchman, I am thy servant for
    ever,
For to thee I owe my life, and nought but death will us sever.

205

THE COLLISION IN THE ENGLISH CHANNEL.

'Twas on a Sunday morning, and in the year of 1888,
The steamer " Saxmundham," laden with coal and coke for
    freight,
Was run into amidships by the Norwegian barque
    " Nor,"
And sunk in the English Channel, while the storm fiend did
    roar.

She left Newcastle on Friday, in November, about two
    o'clock,
And proceeded well on her way until she received a
    shock ;
And the effects of the collision were so serious within,
That, within twenty minutes afterwards, with water she was
    full to the brim.

The effects of the collision were so serious the water couldn't
    be staunched,
So immediately the " Saxmundham's " jolly-boat was
    launched ;
While the brave crew were busy, and loudly did clatter,
Because, at this time, the stem of the steamer was under
    water.

Then the bold crew launched the lifeboat, without dismay,
While their hearts did throb, but not a word did they
    say ;
Then they tried to launch the port lifeboat, but in that they
    failed,
Owing to the heavy sea, so their sad fate they bewailed.

Then into the jolly-boat and lifeboat jumped fifteen men in all,
And immediately the steamer foundered, which did their
    hearts appal,
As the good ship sank beneath the briny wave,
But they thanked God fervently that did them save.

Oh! it was a miracle how any of them were saved,
But it was by the aid of God, and how the crew behaved ;
Because God helps those that help themselves,
And those that don't try to do so are silly elves.

So the two boats cruised about for some time,
Before it was decided to pull for St. Catherine ;
And while cruising about they must have been ill,
But they succeeded in picking up an engineer and fireman,
    also Captain Milne.

And at daybreak on Sunday morning the men in the lifeboat
Were picked up by the schooner " Waterbird " as towards
    her they did float,
And landed at Weymouth, and made all right
By the authorities, who felt for them in their sad plight.

    .   .   .   .

But regarding the barque " Nor," to her I must return,
And, no doubt, for the drowned men, many will mourn ;
Because the crew's sufferings must have been great,
Which, certainly, is soul-harrowing to relate.

The ill-fated barque was abandoned in a sinking state,
But all her crew were saved, which I'm happy to relate ;
They were rescued by the steamer " Hagbrook " in the
    afternoon,
When after taking to their boats, and brought to Portland
    very soon.

The barque " Nor " was bound from New York to Stettin,
And when she struck the " Saxmundham," oh! what a
    terrible din!
Because the merciless water did rush in,
Then the ship carpenters to patch the breach did begin.

But, alas! all their efforts proved in vain,
For still the water did on them gain ;
Still they resolved to save her whatever did betide,
But, alas! the ill-fated " Nor " sank beneath the tide.

But thanks be to God, the major part of the men have been
    saved,
And all honour to both crews that so manfully behaved ;
And may God protect the mariner by night and by day
When on the briny deep, far, far away!

THE PENNSYLVANIA DISASTER.

'Twas in the year of 1889, and in the month of June,
Ten thousand people met with a fearful doom,
By the bursting of a dam in Pennsylvania State,
And were burned, and drowned by the flood—oh! pity their
    fate!

The embankment of the dam was considered rather weak,
And by the swelled body of water the embankment did break,
And burst o'er the valley like a leaping river,
Which caused the spectators with fear to shiver.

And on rushed the mighty flood, like a roaring big wave,
Whilst the drowning people tried hard their lives to save ;
But eight thousand were drowned, and their houses swept
away,
While the spectators looked on, stricken with dismay.

And when the torrent dashed against the houses they
instantly toppled o'er,
Then many of the houses caught fire, which made a terrific
roar ;
And two thousand people, by the fire, lost their lives,
Consisting of darling girls and boys, also men and their wives.

And when the merciless flood reached Johnstown it was
fifty feet high,
While, in pitiful accents, the drowning people for help did
cry ;
But hundreds of corpses, by the flood, were swept away,
And Johnstown was blotted out like a child's toy house of clay

Alas! there were many pitiful scenes enacted,
And many parents, for the loss of their children, have gone
distracted,
Especially those that were burned in the merciless flame,
Their dear little ones they will never see again.

And among the sad scenes to be witnessed there,
Was a man and his wife in great despair,
Who had drawn from the burning mass a cradle of their child,
But, oh, heaven! their little one was gone, which almost
drove them wild.

Oh, heaven! it was a pitiful and a most agonising sight,
To see parents struggling hard with all their might,
To save their little ones from being drowned,
But 'twas vain, the mighty flood engulfed them, with a
roaring sound.

There was also a beautiful girl, the belle of Johnstown,
Standing in bare feet, on the river bank, sad and forlorn,
And clad in a loose petticoat, with a shawl over her head,
Which was all that was left her, because her parents were dead.

Her parents were drowned, and their property swept away
with the flood,
And she was watching for them on the bank where she stood,
To see if they would rise to the surface of the water again,
But the dear girl's watching was all in vain.

And as for Conemaugh river, there's nothing could it surpass,
It was dammed up by a wall of corpses in a confused mass ;
And the charred bodies could be seen dotting the burning
debris,
While the flames and sparks ascended with a terrific hiss.

The pillaging of the houses in Johnstown is fearful to describe,
By the Hungarians and ghouls, and woe betide
Any person or party that interfered with them,
Because they were mad with drink, and yelling like tigers
in a den.

And many were to be seen engaged in a hand-to-hand fight,
And drinking whisky, and singing wild songs, oh! what a
shameful sight!
But a number of the thieves were lynched and shot
For robbing the dead of their valuables, which will not be
forgot.

Mrs Ogle, like a heroine, in the telegraph office stood at her post,
And wired words of warning, else more lives would have been lost ;
Besides she was warned to flee, but from her work she wouldn't stir,
Until at last the merciless flood engulfed her.

And as for the robbery and outrage at the hands of the ghouls,
I must mention Clara Barton and her band of merciful souls,
Who made their way fearlessly to the wounded in every street,
And the wounded and half-crazed survivors they kindly did treat.

Oh, heaven! it was a horrible sight, which will not be forgot,
So many people drowned and burned—oh! hard has been their lot!
But heaven's will must be done, I'll venture to say,
And accidents will happen until doomsday!

THE SPRIG OF MOSS.

THERE lived in Munich a poor, weakly youth,
But for the exact date, I cannot vouch for the truth,
And of seven of a family he was the elder,
Who was named, by his parents, Alois Senefelder.

But, poor fellow, at home his father was lying dead,
And his little brothers and sisters were depending upon him for bread,
And one evening he was dismissed from his employment,
Which put an end to all his peace and enjoyment.

211

The poor lad was almost mad, and the next day
His parent's remains to the cemetery were taken away ;
And when his father was buried, distracted like he grew,
And he strolled through the streets crying, What shall
    I do!

And all night he wandered on sad and alone,
Until he began to think of returning home,
But, to his surprise, on raising his head to look around,
He was in a part of the country which to him was unknown
    ground.

And when night came on the poor lad stood aghast,
For all was hushed save the murmuring of a river which
    flowed past ;
And the loneliness around seemed to fill his heart with awe,
And, with fatigue, he sat down on the first stone he saw.

And there resting his elbows and head on his knees,
He sat gazing at the running water, which did him please ;
And by the light of the stars which shone on the water blue,
He cried, I will drown myself, and bid this harsh world adieu.

Besides, I'm good for nothing, to himself he said,
And will only become a burden to my mother, I'm afraid ;
And there, at the bottom of that water, said he
From all my misfortunes death will set me free.

But, happily for Alois, more pious thoughts rushed into his
    mind,
And courage enough to drown himself he couldn't find,
So he resolved to go home again whatever did betide,
And he asked forgiveness of his Creator by the river side.

And as he knelt, a few incoherent words escaped him,
And the thought of drowning himself he considered a great
    sin,
And the more he thought of it, he felt his flesh creep,
But in a few minutes he fell fast asleep.

And he slept soundly, for the stillness wasn't broke,
And the day was beginning to dawn before he awoke ;
Then suddenly he started up as if in a fright,
And he saw very near him a little stone smooth and white,

Upon which was traced the delicate design of a Sprig of Moss,
But to understand such a design he was at a loss,
Then he recollected the Sprig of Moss lying on the stone,
And with his tears he'd moistened it, but it was gone.

But its imprint was delicately imprinted on the stone ;
Then, taking the stone under his arm, he resolved to go home,
Saying, God has reserved me for some other thing,
And with joy he couldn't tell how he began to sing.

And on drawing near the city he met his little brother,
Who told him his uncle had visited his mother,
And on beholding their misery had left them money to buy
    food,
Then Alois cried, Thank God, the news is good!

Then 'twas on the first day after Alois came home,
He began the printing of the Sprig of Moss on the stone ;
And by taking the impressions of watch-cases he discovered,
    one day,
What is now called the art of Lithography.

So Alois plodded on making known his great discovery,
Until he obtained the notice of the Royal Academy,
Besides, he obtained a gold Medal, and what was more dear
    to his heart,
He lived to see the wide extension of his art.

And when life's prospects may at times appear dreary to ye,
Remember Alois Senefelder, the discoverer of Lithography,
How God saved him from drowning himself in adversity,
And I hope ye all will learn what the Sprig of Moss teaches ye.

And God that made a way through the Red Sea,
If ye only put your trust in Him, He will protect ye,
And light up your path, and strew it with flowers,
And be your only Comforter in all your lonely hours.

THE END.

DAVID WINTER AND SON LTD. PRINTERS, DUNDEE

MORE

POETIC GEMS

SELECTED FROM THE WORKS

OF

WILLIAM McGONAGALL

Poet and Tragedian
Died in Edinburgh 29th September, 1902

WITH

BIOGRAPHICAL SKETCH AND REMINISCENCES

BY THE AUTHOR

EDITED BY Dr. D. W. SMITH

DUNDEE:
DAVID WINTER & SON LTD.
15 SHORE TERRACE

LONDON:
GERALD DUCKWORTH & CO. LTD
3 HENRIETTA ST.. W.C.2

1969

CONTENTS

THE AUTOBIOGRAPHY

OF

SIR WILLIAM TOPAZ M'GONAGALL

POET AND TRAGEDIAN

Knight of the White Elephant, Burmah

My Dear Readers of this autobiography, which I am the author of,
I beg leave to inform you that I was born in Edinburgh. My parents
were born in Ireland, and my father was a handloom weaver, and he
learned me the handloom weaving while in Dundee, and I followed it for
many years, until it began to fail owing to machinery doing the weaving
instead of the handloom. So much so as I couldn't make a living from it.
But I may say Dame Fortune has been very kind to me by endowing
me with the genius of poetry. I remember how I felt when I received the
spirit of poetry. It was in the year of 1877, and in the month of June,
when trees and flowers were in full bloom. Well, it being the holiday week
in Dundee, I was sitting in my back room in Paton's Lane, Dundee,
lamenting to myself because I couldn't get to the Highlands on holiday
to see the beautiful scenery, when all of a sudden my body got inflamed,
and instantly I was seized with a strong desire to write poetry, so strong,
in fact, that in imagination I thought I heard a voice crying in my ears—

"WRITE! WRITE!"

I wondered what could be the matter with me, and I began to walk
backwards and forwards in a great fit of excitement, saying to myself—
"I know nothing about poetry." But still the voice kept ringing in my
ears—"Write, write," until at last, being overcome with a desire to write
poetry, I found paper, pen, and ink, and in a state of frenzy, sat me down
to think what would be my first subject for a poem. All at once I thought
of the late Rev. George Gilfillan, and composed a poem of four stanzas
in his praise as a preacher, and orator, and poet. Then I sent it to the
"Weekly News" for publication, not sending my name with it, only my
initials—W. M'G., Dundee. It was published, along with a short com-
ment by the editor in its praise, as follows :—"W. M'G., Dundee, has
sent us a poem in praise of the Rev. George Gilfillan, and he sung his
praises truly and well, but he modestly seeks to hide his light under a
bushel," so when I read the poem in the "Weekly News" I was highly
pleased no doubt to see such a favourable comment regarding it. Then
my next poem, or second, was the "Railway Bridge of the Silvery Tay,"
which caused a great sensation in Dundee and far away. In fact, gentle
readers, it was the only poem that made me famous universally. The
reading of the poem abroad caused the Emperor of Brazil to leave his
home far away incognito and view the bridge as he passed along *en route*

to Inverness. But, my dear readers, the Tay Bridge poem is out of print, and I do not intend to publish it again, owing to the fall of the bridge in the year of 1879, which will be remembered for a very long time.

I may also state in this short autobiography of mine that my parents are dead some years ago—I don't remember how many, but they are buried in the Eastern Necropolis, Dundee, and I may say they were always good to me.

And now concerning something more attractive, my dear readers, I must inform ye that as early as ten years of age I was very fond of reading Shakespeare's Penny Plays (Vicker's edition), and from them I received great knowledge regarding the histrionic art. The plays or tragedies I studied most were Macbeth, Hamlet, Richard III, and Othello, the Moor of Venice, and these four characters I have impersonated in my time. During my stay in Dundee my

FIRST APPEARANCE ON THE STAGE

was in the character of Macbeth in Mr Giles' Penny Theatre, Lindsay Street, Dundee, to an overflowing and crowded audience, and I received unbounded applause. I was called before the curtain several times during the performance, and I remember the actors of the company felt very jealous owing to me getting the general applause, and several were as bold as tell me so; and when it came to the combat scene betwixt me and Macduff the actor who was playing Macduff against my Macbeth tried to spoil me in the combat by telling me to cut it short, so as the audience, in his opinion, would say it was a poor combat, but I was too cute for him, guessing his motive for it. I continued the combat until he was fairly exhausted, and until there was one old gentleman in the audience cried out, " Well done, M'Gonagall! Walk into him! " And so I did until he was in a great rage, and stamped his foot, and cried out, " Fool! Why don't you fall ? " And when I did fall the cry was " M'Gonagall! M'Gonagall! Bring him out! Bring him out! " until I had to come before the curtain and receive an ovation from the audience. Such was the case in my second appearance, under the management of Forrest Knowles in the Grocers' Hall, Castle Street, Dundee. The characters I appeared in under his management were Macbeth, Richard III, and Hamlet. These three characters I performed to crowded and delighted audiences. I remember Mr Knowles told me in the dressing-room that I looked the character so well in the dress that I should wear it, and not throw it off, but I told him it was too great a joke to say so. I also remember on that night there were several gentlemen in the audience who were from Edinburgh, and they came to my dressing-room to congratulate me on my great success, and shook hands with me, telling me that few professionals could do it so well; but perhaps they were only flattering me. If so, I will say with the poet, John Dryden—

> Flattery, like ice, our footing does betray,
> Who can tread sure on the smooth slippery way ?
> Pleased with the fancy, we glide swiftly on,
> And see the dangers which we cannot shun.

6

My dear readers the next strange adventure in my life was my

JOURNEY TO BALMORAL

to see the bonnie Highland flora and Her Gracious Majesty the Queen, who was living in Balmoral Castle, near by the River Dee. Well, I left Dundee in the month of June, 1878. I remember it was a beautiful sunshiny day, which made my heart feel light and gay, and I tramped to Alyth that day, and of course I felt very tired and footsore owing to the intense heat. The first thing I thought about was to secure lodgings for the night, which I secured very easily without any trouble, and then I went and bought some groceries for my supper and breakfast, such as tea, sugar, butter, and bread. Then I prepared my supper, and ate heartily, for I had not tasted food of any kind since I had left Dundee, and the distance I had travelled was fifteen miles, and with the fresh air I had inhaled by the way it gave me a keen appetite, and caused me to relish my supper, and feel content. Then the landlady of the house, being a kind-hearted woman, gave me some hot water to wash my feet, as she thought it would make my feet feel more comfortable, and cause me to sleep more sound. And after I had gone to bed I slept as sound as if I'd been dead, and arose in the morning quite refreshed and vigorous after the sound sleep I got. Then I washed my hands and face, and prepared my breakfast, and made myself ready for the road again, with some biscuits in my pocket and a pennyworth of cheese. I left Alyth about ten o'clock in the morning, and crossed over a dreary moor, stunted and barren in its aspect, which was a few miles in length—I know not how many—but I remember there were only two houses to be met with all the way, which caused me to feel rather discontented indeed. The melancholy screams of the peesweeps overhead were rather discordant sounds ringing in my ears, and, worst of all, the rain began to fall heavily, and in a short time I felt wet to the skin ; and the lightning began to flash and the thunder to roar. Yet I trudged on manfully, not the least daunted, for I remembered of saying to my friends in Dundee I would pass through fire and water rather than turn tail, and make my purpose good, as I had resolved to see Her Majesty at Balmoral. I remember by the roadside there was a big rock, and behind it I took shelter from the rain a few moments, and partook of my bread and cheese, while the rain kept pouring down in torrents. After I had taken my luncheon I rose to my feet, determined to push on in spite of rain and thunder, which made me wonder, because by this time I was about to enter

> On the Spittal of Glenshee,
> Which is most dismal for to see,
> With its bleak and rugged mountains,
> And clear, crystal, spouting fountains
> With their misty foam ;
> And thousands of sheep there together doth roam,
> Browsing on the barren pasture most gloomy to see.
> Stunted in heather, and scarcely a tree,
> Which is enough to make the traveller weep,
> The loneliness thereof and the bleating of the sheep.

7

However, I travelled on while the rain came pouring down copiously, and I began to feel very tired, and longed for rest, for by this time I had tr..velled about thirteen miles, and the road on

THE SPITTAL OF GLENSHEE

I remember was very stony in some parts. I resolved to call at the first house I saw by the way and ask lodgings for the night. Well, the first house chanced to be a shepherd's, and I called at the door and gently knocked, and my knock was answered by the mistress of the house. When she saw me she asked me what I wanted, and I told her I wanted a night's lodging and how I was wet to the skin. Then she bade me come inside and sit down by the fireside and dry my claes, and tak' aff my shoon and warm my feet at the fire, and I did so. Then I told her I came from Dundee, and that I was going to Balmoral to see Her Majesty the Queen, and that I was a poet. When I said I was a poet her manner changed altogether, and she asked me if I would take some porridge if she made some, and I said I would and feel very thankful for them. So in a short time the porridge were made, and as quickly partaken, and in a short time the shepherd came in with his two collie dogs, and the mistress told him I was a traveller from Dundee and a poet. When he heard I was a poet he asked me my name, and I told him I was M'Gonagall, the poet. He seemed o'erjoyed when he heard me say so, and told me I was welcome as a lodger for the night, and to make myself at home, and that he had heard often about me. I chanced to have a few copies of a twopence edition of poems with me from Dundee and I gave him a copy, and he seemed to be highly pleased with reading the poems during the evening, especially the one about the late George Gilfillan, and for the benefit of my readers I will insert it as follows. I may also state this is the first poem I composed, when I received the gift of poetry, which appeared in the " Weekly News " :—

LINES IN PRAISE OF THE REV. GEORGE GILFILLAN

All hail to the Rev. George Gilfillan, of Dundee,
He is the greatest preacher I did ever hear or see.
He preaches in a plain, straightforward way,
The people flock to hear him night and day,
And hundreds from his church doors are often
   turned away,
Because he is the greatest preacher of the present
   day.
The first time I heard him speak 'twas in the
   Kinnaird Hall,
Lecturing on the Garabaldi movement as loud as
   he could bawl.
He is a charitable gentlemen to the poor while in
   distress,
And for his kindness unto them the Lord will
   surely bless.
My blessing on his noble form and on his lofty head.
May all good angels guard him while living and
   hereafter when dead.

Well, my dear readers, after the shepherd and me had a social confab together concerning Gilfillan and poetry for some time his wife came in, and she said, " Guidman, I've been out making a bed for you in the barn. But maybe ye'll be feared tae sleep in the barn." But I said, " Oh, no, my good woman, not in the least." So she told her husband to show me the way to the barn, and he said, " Oh, yes, I'll do that, and feel highly honoured in doing so." Accordingly he got a lantern and lighted it, and then said—" Come along with me, sir, and I'll show you where to sleep for the night." Then he led the way to the barn, and when he entered he showed me the bed, and I can assure you it was a bed suitable for either King or Queen.

> And the blankets and sheets
> Were white and clean,
> And most beautiful to be seen,
> And I'm sure would have pleased Lord Aberdeen.

Then the shepherd told me I could bar the barn door if I liked if I was afraid to sleep without it being barred, and I said I would bar the door, considering it much safer to do so. Then he bade me good-night, hoping I would sleep well and come in to breakfast in the morning.

A STRANGE DREAM

After the shepherd had bidden me good-night I barred the door, and went to bed, as I expected to sleep ; but for a long time I couldn't—until at last I was in the arms of Morpheus, dreaming I was travelling betwixt a range of mountains, and seemingly to be very misty, especially the mountain tops. Then I thought I saw a carriage and four horses, and seemingly two drivers, and also a lady in the carriage, who I thought would be the Queen. Then the carriage vanished all of a sudden, and I thought I had arrived at Balmoral Castle, and in front of the Castle I saw a big Newfoundland dog, and he kept barking loudly and angry at me But I wasn't the least afraid of him, and as I advanced towards the front door of the Castle he sprang at me, and seized my right hand, and bit it severely, until it bled profusely. I seemed to feel it painful, and when I awoke, my dear readers, I was shaking with fear, and considered it to be a warning or a bad omen to me on my journey to Balmoral. But, said I to myself—

> " Hence babbling dreams!
> You threaten me in vain."

Then I tried hard to sleep, but couldn't. So the night stole tediously away, and morning came at last, peeping through the chinks of the barn door. So I arose, and donned my clothes, then went into the shepherd's house, but the shepherd wasn't in. He'd been away two hours ago, the mistress said, to look after the sheep on the rugged mountains. " But sit ye down, guidman," said she, " and I'll mak' some porridge for ye before ye tak' the road, for it's a dreary road to Balmoral." So I thanked her and husband for their kindness towards me, and telling her to give my best wishes to her husband bade her good-bye and left the shepherd's house for the Queen's Castle.

It was about ten o'clock in the morning when I left the shepherd's house at the Spittal of Glenshee on my journey to Balmoral. I expected to be there about three o'clock in the afternoon. Well, I travelled on courageously, and, when Balmoral Castle hove in sight, I saw the Union Jack unfurled to the breeze. Well, I arrived at the Castle just as the tower clock was chiming the hour of three. But my heart wasn't full of glee, because I had a presentiment that I wouldn't succeed. When I arrived at the lodge gate, I knocked loudly at the door of the lodge, and it was answered by a big, burly-looking man, dressed in a suit of pilot cloth. He boldly asked me what I wanted and where I had come from. I told him I had travelled all the way from Dundee expecting to see Her Majesty, and to be permitted to give an entertainment before her in the Castle from my own works and from the works of Shakespeare. Further, I informed him that I was the Poet M'Gonagall, and how I had been patronised by Her Majesty. I showed him Her Majesty's letter of patronage, which he read, and said it was a forgery. I said, if he thought so, he could have me arrested. He said this thinking to frighten me, but, when he saw he couldn't, he asked me if I would give him a recital in front of the Lodge as a specimen of my abilities. "No, sir," I said; "nothing so low in my line of business. I am

NOT A STROLLING MOUNTEBANK

that would do the like in the open air for a few coppers. Take me into one of the rooms in the Lodge, and pay me for it, and I will give you a recital, and upon no consideration will I consent to do it in the open air."

Just at that time there was a young lady concealed behind the Lodge door hearkening all the time unknown to me. The man said, "Will you not oblige the young lady here?" And when I saw the lady I said, "No, sir. Nor if Her Majesty would request me to do it in the open air, I wouldn't yield to her request." Then he said, "So I see, but I must tell you that nobody can see Her Majesty without an introductory letter from some nobleman to certify that they are safe to be ushered into Her Majesty's presence, and remember, if ever you come here again, you are liable to be arrested." So I bade him good-bye, and came away without dismay, and crossed o'er a little iron bridge there which spans the River Dee, which is magnificent to see. I went in quest of lodgings for the night, and, as I looked towards the west, I saw a farmhouse to the right of me, about half a mile from the highway. To it I went straightaway, and knocked at the door gently, and a voice from within cried softly, "Come in." When I entered an old man and woman were sitting by the fireside, and the man bade me sit down. I said I was very thankful for the seat, because I was tired and footsore, and required lodging for the night, and that I had been at Balmoral Castle expecting to see Her Majesty, and had been denied the liberty of seeing her by the constable at the Lodge gate. When I told him I had travelled all the way on foot from Dundee, he told me very feelingly he would allow me to stay with him for two or three days, and I could go to the roadside, where Her Majesty passed almost every day, and he was sure she would speak to me, as she always spoke to the gipsies and gave them money. The old woman, who was sitting in the corner at her tea, said, " Ay, and mind ye, guidman, it's no silver she gives them, it's gold. I'm sure Her Majesty's a richt guid lady. Mind ye, this is the Queen's bread I'm eating. Guidman, the mair, I canna see you. I'm blind, born blind, and I maun tell ye, as you're a poet, as I heard ye say, the Queen alloos a' the auld wimmen in the district here a loaf of bread, tea, and sugar, and a' the cold meat that's no used at the Castle, and, mind ye, ilka ane o' them gets an equal share." I said it was very kind of Her Majesty to do so, and she said, " That's no' a', guidman. She aye finds wark for idle men when she comes here—wark that's no needed, no' for hersel, athegether, but just to help needy folk, and I'm sure if you see her she will help you." So I thanked her for the information I had got, and then was conducted to my bed in the barn—a very good one—after I had got a good supper of porridge and milk. Then I went to bed,

NOT TO SLEEP, BUT TO THINK

of the treatment I had met with from the constable at the lodge of Balmoral Castle. I may state also that I showed the constable at the lodge a copy of my poems—twopence edition—I had with me, and he asked me the price tof it, and I said, " Twopence, please." Then he chanced to notice on he front of it, " Poet to Her Majesty," and he got into a rage and said, " You're not poet to Her Majesty." Then I said, " You cannot deny that I am patronised by Her Majesty." Then he said, " Ah, but you must know Lord Tennyson is the real poet to Her Majesty. However, I'll buy this copy of your poems." But, as I said before, when I went to bed it was to think, not to sleep, and I thought in particular what the constable told me—if ever I chanced to come the way again I would be arrested, and the thought thereof caused an undefinable fear to creep all over my body. I actually shook with fear, which I considered to be a warning not to attempt the like again. So I resolved that in the morning I would go home again the way I came. All night through I tossed and turned from one side to another, thinking to sleep, but to court it was all in vain, and as soon as daylight dawned I arose and made ready to take the road. Then I went to the door of the farmhouse and knocked, and it was answered by the farmer, and he said, " 'Odsake, guidman, hoo have ye risen sae early ? It's no' five o'clock yet. Gae awa' back to your bed and sleep twa or three hours yet, and ye will hae plenty o' time after that tae gang tae the roadside to see Her Majesty." But I told him I had given up all thought of it, that I was afraid the constable at the lodge would be on the lookout for me, and if he saw me loitering about the roadside he would arrest me and swear falsely against me. Then he said, " Guidman, perhaps it's the safest way no' to gang, but, however, you'll need some breakfast afore ye tak' the road, sae come in by and sit doon there." Then he asked me if I could sup brose, and I said I could, and be thankful for the like. Then he cried, " Hi! lassie, come here and bile the kettle quick and mak' some brose for this guidman before he gangs awa'." Then the lassie came ben. She might have been about sixteen or seventeen years old, and in a short time she had the kettle boiling, and prepared for me a cog of brose and milk, which

11

I supped greedily and cheerfully, owing no doubt to the pure Highland air I had inhaled, which gave me a keen appetite. Then the farmer came ben and bade me good-bye, and told me to be sure and call again if ever I came the way, and how I would be sure to get a night's lodging or two or three if I liked to stay. So I bade him good-bye and the lassie and the old blind woman, thanking them for their kindness towards me. But the farmer said to the lassie, " Mak' up a piece bread and cheese for him for fear he'll no' get muckle meat on the Spittal o' Glenshee." So when I got the piece of bread and cheese again I bade them good-bye, and took the road for Glenshee, bound for Dundee, while the sun shone out bright and clear, which did my spirits cheer. After I had travelled about six miles, my feet got very hot, and in a very short time both were severely blistered. So I sat me down to rest me for a while, and while I rested I ate of my piece bread and cheese, which, I'm sure, did me please, a nd gave me fresh strength and enabled me to resume my travel again. I travelled on another six miles until I arrived at a lodging-house by the roadside, called

THE MILLER'S LODGING-HOUSE

because he had been a meal miller at one time. There I got a bed for the night, and paid threepence for it, and I can assure ye it was a very comfortable one ; and the mistress of the house made some porridge for me by my own request, and gave me some milk, for which she charged me twopence. When I had taken my porridge, she gave me some hot water in a little tub to wash my feet, because they were blistered, and felt very sore. And when my feet were washed I went to my bed, and in a short time I was sound asleep. About eight o'clock the next morning I awoke quite refreshed, because I had slept well during the night, owing to the goodness of the bed and me being so much fatigued with travelling. Then I chanced to have a little tea and sugar in my pocket that I had bought in Alyth, so I asked the landlady if she could give me a teapot, as I had some tea with me in my pocket, and I would infuse it for my breakfast, as I hadn't got much tea since I had left Dundee. So she gave me a teapot, and I infused the tea, and drank it cheerfully, and ate the remainder of my cheese and bread. I remember it was a lovely sunshiny morning when I bade my host and hostess good-bye, and left, resolved to travel to Blairgowrie, and lodge there for the night. So I travelled on the best way I could. My feet felt very sore, but

> As I chanced to see trouts louping in the River o'
> Glenshee,
> It helped to fill my heart with glee,
> And to anglers I would say without any doubt
> There's plenty of trouts there for pulling out.

When I saw them louping and heard the birds singing o'erhead it really seemed to give me pleasure, and to feel more contented than I would have been otherwise. At Blairgowrie I arrived about seven o'clock at night, and went in quest of a lodging-house, and found one easy enough, and for my bed I paid fourpence in advance. And when I had secured my bed I went out to try to sell a few copies of my poems. I had with me from Dundee the twopence edition, and I managed to sell half a dozen of copies with a great struggle. However, I was very thankful, because it would tide me over until I would arrive in Dundee. So with the shilling I had earned from my poems I bought some grocery goods, and prepared my supper—tea, of course, and bread and butter. Then I had my feet washed, and went to bed, and slept as sound as if I'd been dead. In the morning I arose about seven o'clock, and prepared my breakfast—tea again, and bread and butter. Then after my breakfast I washed my hands and face, and started for Dundee at a rapid pace, and thought it no disgrace. Still the weather kept good, and the sun shone bright and clear, which did my spirits cheer, and weary and footsore I trudged along, singing a verse of a hymn, not a song, as follows :—

> Our poverty and trials here
> Will only make us richer there,
> When we arrive at home, &c., &c.

When at the ten milestone from Dundee I sat down and rested for a while, and partook of a piece bread and butter. I toiled on manfully, and arrived in Dundee about eight o'clock, unexpectedly to my friends and acquaintances. So this, my dear friends, ends my famous journey to Balmoral. Next morning I had a newspaper reporter wanting the particulars regarding my journey to Balmoral, and in my simplicity of heart I gave him all the information regarding it, and when it was published in the papers it

CAUSED A GREAT SENSATION.

In fact, it was the only thing that made me famous—it and the Tay Bridge poem. I was only one week in Dundee after coming from Balmoral when I sent a twopence edition of my poems to the late Rev. George Gilfillan, who was on a holiday tour at Stonehaven at the time for the good of his health. He immediately sent me a reply, as follows :—

" Stonehaven, June, 1878.

" Dear Sir,—I thank you for your poems, especially the kind lines addressed to myself. I have read of your famous journey to Balmoral, for which I hope you are none the worse. I am here on holiday, but return in a few days.—Believe me, yours truly,

" GEORGE GILFILLAN."

Well, the next stirring event in my life which I consider worth narrating happened this way. Being out one day at the little village of Fowlis, about six miles from Dundee, and being in rather poor circumstances, I thought of trying to get a schoolroom to give an entertainment. But when I applied for the schoolroom I met with a refusal. Therefore, not to be beat, I resolved to try to get the smithy, and was fortunate in getting it. Then I went all over the village, or amongst the people, inviting them to my entertainment, chiefly from my own works and from Shakespeare. The prices were to be—Adults 2d., boys and girls 1d.,

13

and the performance was to commence at eight o'clock precisely. Well, when I had made it known amongst the villagers, some of them promised to come—chiefly ploughmen and some of the scholars. To while away the time, I called at the smith's house. The family had just sat down to supper, and the smith bade me draw in a chair to the table and take some supper, which consisted of tea and plenty of oaten cakes and loaf bread; also ham, cheese, and butter. So of course I drew in by my chair to the table, and fared very sumptuously, because I had got no refreshment since the morning before leaving Dundee. After supper, the smith said he would gang doon to the smithy wi' me, and gie it a bit redd up and get the lamp lighted.

THE SMITHY ENTERTAINMENT.

In a short time a few ploughmen came, and of course I was at the door to take the money, and they asked me the charge of admission, and I said—" Twopence, please." Then a few more people came—old and young—and they all seemed to be quite happy in expectation of the coming entertainment. When it was near eight o'clock the smith told me I would need to make ready to begin, so I told him to take the money at the door, and I would begin. He said he would do that cheerfully, and he took his stand at the door, and I addressed the audience as follows :—" Ladies and gentlemen, with your permission, I will now make a begnning by reciting my famous poem, ' Bruce at Bannockburn.' " Before it wias half finished I received great app'ause ; and when finished they were all delighted. Then followed " The Battle of Tel-El-Kebir " and a scene from " Macbeth " ; also " The Rattling Boy from Dublin," which concluded the evening's entertainment. The proceeds taken at the door amounted to 4s. 9d., and of course I was well pleased with what I had realised, because it is a very poor locality in that part of the country. Well, I thanked the audience for their patronage ; also the smith for allowing me the use of his smithy, and, bidding him good-night, I came away resolving to travel home again straightway. Well, as I drew near to Fowlis Schoolroom I heard the pattering of feet behind me and the sound of men's voices. So I was instantly seized with an indefinable fear, and I grasped my stick firmly in my right hand, and stood stock still, resolved to wait until the party behind would come up, and stood right in front of me, and neither of us spoke, when the centre man of the three whispered something to the two men that was with him, and then he threw out both arms, with the intention, no doubt, as I thought, of pulling my hat down over my eyes ; but no sooner were his arms thrown out than my good oaken cudgel came across his body with full force.

My Dear Friends,—I cannot describe to you my feelings at that moment. The cold sweat started to my forehead, but I was resolved to strike out in self-defence. Well, when I brought my good oaken cudgel over the ringleader's body he sprang back, and whispered to his companions, and they were forced to retire. As they were going the same road home as I was going, I thought it advisable not to go, so I took a back road, which leads up to the village of Birkhill, five miles from Dundee, and when I arrived at the village it was past eleven o'clock at night. I went direct to the constable's house and rapped at the door, and it was answered by himself demanding who was there. I said, " A friend," so he opened the door, and he said—" Oh, it's you, Mr M'Gonagall. Come in. Well, sir, what do you want at this late hour ? " " Well, sir," I said, " I've been down to-night giving an entertainment in the Smithy of Fowlis, and I've been attacked near to the Schoolroom of Fowlis by three men that followed me. One of the three, the centre one, threw out both of his arms, with the intention, no doubt, of pulling my hat down over my eyes ; but this stick, sir, of mine, went whack against his body, which made him and his companions retire from the field. And now, as I am rather afraid to pass through Lord Duncan's woods, which are rather dreary and lonely, and the night being so dark, I want you, sir, to escort me through the woods." Then he said he couldn't do that, looking to the lateness of the night, but, said he, " Just you go on, and if anyone offers to molest you, just shout as loud as you can, and I'll come to you." " But, my dear sir," I said, " three men could have me murdered before you could save me." " Well," he said, " I'll stand at the door for a little to see if anyone molests you, and I'll bid you good-night, Mr M'Gonagall, and safe home." I remember while passing through Lord Duncan's woods I recited to myself—

> Yet though I walk through death's dark vale,
> Yet will I fear none ill,
> For Thou art with me, and Thy rod
> And staff me comfort still.

Well, thank God, my dear friends, I arrived safe home to Dundee shortly after twelve o'clock, and my family were very glad to see me safe home again, asking me why I had been so late in coming home. When I told them what I had been doing, giving an entertainment in the Smithy of Fowlis, and had been set upon by three men, they were astonished to hear it, and said that I should thank God that had saved me from being murdered. However, the four shillings and ninepence I fetched home with me—that I had gained from my entertainment—I gave all to my wife, and she was very thankful to get it, because the wolf was at the door, and it had come very opportune. Well, after I had warmed myself at the fire, and taken a cup of tea, and bread and butter, I went to bed, but didn't sleep very sound. I suppose that was owing to the three men that attacked me in the home-coming. Well, my dear readers, the next stirring event that I will relate is

MY TRIP TO AMERICA.

In my remembrance, that is about fourteen years ago, and on the 9th of March I left Dundee. But before I left it I went amongst all my best friends and bade them good-bye, but one particular good friend I must mention, the late Mr Alexander C. Lamb, proprietor of the Temperance Hotel, Dundee. Well, when I called to bid him good-bye, and after we had shaken hands warmly, he asked me if any of my pretended friends had promised to take me home again from America if I failed in my enterprise. So I told him not one amongst them had promised. " Well," says he, " write to me and I will fetch you home."

Then on the next day, after bidding good-bye to my frends and relations in Dundee, I left Dundee with the train bound for Glasgow, and arrived safe about four o'clock in the afternoon. When I arrived I went to a good temperance hotel, near to the Broomielaw Bridge, and secured lodgings for the night, and before going to bed I prepared my supper— tea, of course, and bread and butter—and made a good meal of it. Then I went to bed, but I didn't sleep very sound, because my mind was too much absorbed regarding the perilous adventure I was about to undertake. Well, at an early hour the next morning I got up and washed myself, and prepared my breakfast, and made ready to embark on board the good steamship " Circassia," bound for the city of New York. When I went on board all was confusion, and there was a continuous babel of voices amongst the passengers, each one running hither and thither in search of a berth. And I can assure ye, my friends, it was with a great deal of trouble I secured a berth, because there were so many passengers on board. Well, when all the passengers had got their berths secured for the voyage, and the anchor had been weighed, and the sails hoisted, the big steamer left the Clyde with upwards of 500 souls, bound for New York. Some of them were crying, and some were singing, and some were dancing to the stirring strains of the pibroch. Such is life I say, throughout the world every day, and it was on the 10th of March we sailed away bound for America. As the stout steamer entered the waters of the Atlantic Ocean some snow began to fall, and a piercing gale of wind sprang up, but the snow soon ceased, and the wind ceased also, and the vessel sped on rapidly through the beautiful blue sea, while the cooks on board were preparing the passengers' tea. Yes, my dear readers, that's the supper the passengers get every night—plenty of bread, butter, and tea ; and coffee, bread, and butter for breakfast ; and for dinner, broth or soup and bread and beef. This is the fare in general going and coming. Well, when a week at sea all of a sudden the vessel began to roll, and the sea got into a billowy swell. The vessel began to heave fearfully, and the big waves began to lash her sides and sweep across her deck, so that all the boxes and chests on deck and below had to be firmly secured to prevent them from getting tossed about, and to prevent them from making a roaring sound like thunder. Many of the passengers felt seasick, and were vomiting, but I didn't feel sick at all. Well, the next day was a beautiful sunny day, and all the passengers felt gay, and after tea was over it was proposed amongst a few of them to get up

A CONCERT ON BOARD

that night. I was invited by a few gentlemen, and selected as one of the performers for the evening, and was told to dress in Highland costume, and that I would receive a collection for the recitations I gave them. The concert was to begin at eight o'clock. Well, I consented to take part in the concert, and got a gentleman to dress me, and when dressed I went to the second cabin, where the concert was to be held, and when I entered the cabin saloon I received a hearty round of applause from the passengers gathered there. Among them were the chief steward of the vessel. He

was elected as chairman for the evening, and addressed us as follows :—
" Ladies and gentlemen,—I wish it to be understood that all collections
of money taken on board this vessel at concerts go for the benefit of the
Lifeboat Fund, and I also hope you will also enjoy yourselves in a decent
way, and get through with the concert about ten o'clock, say. As Mr
M'Gonagall, the great poet, is first on the programme, I will call on him
to recite his own poem ' Bruce at Bannockburn.' "

So I leapt to my feet and commenced, and before I was right begun
I received a storm of applause, but that was all I received for it. Well,
when I came to the thrusts and cuts with my sword my voice was drowned
with applaus e, and when I had finished I bade them all good-night, and
retired immediately to my berth in the steerage, and undressed myself
quickly, and went to bed, resolving in my mind not to dress again if I
was requested on the home-coming voyage. Well, my friends, the vessel
made the voyage to New York in twelve days—of course night included
as well—and when she arrived at the jetty or harbour of New York some
of the passengers, when they saw it, felt glad, and others felt sad,
especially those that had but little money with them. As for myself, I
had but eight shillings, which made me feel very downcast, because all
the passengers are examined at Castle Gardens by the officials there
regarding the money they have with them, and other properties. Well,
when I came to the little gate where all the passengers are questioned
regarding their trades and names before they are allowed to pass, and if
they want their British money changed for American money, I saw at
once how I could manage. So after the man had entered my name and
trade in his book as a weaver, I took from my purse the eight shillings,
and laid it down fearlessly, and said—" Change that! It is all I require
in the meantime." So the man looked at me dubiously, but I got passed
without any more trouble after receiving the American money.   Then I
passed on quickly until I saw a car passing along the way I was going.
So I got into the car, and I asked the carman where was Forty-Nine
Street. He said he was just going along that way, and he would let me
off the car when he came to it. So he did, honestly. Then I went to an
old acquaintance of mine while in Dundee, and rang the door bell, and
it was answered by my friend. When he saw me he stood aghast in
amazement, but he bade me come in, and when I entered the house
his wife bade me sit down, and sit near to the fire, for nae doubt I would
feel cold after being on the sea sae lang. So the mistress said I'll mak' ye
a cup o' tea, for ye'll be hungry, nae doubt, and I said I was so. Tea was
prepared immediately, and my friend and his wife sat down at the table
together, and made a hearty meal, and seemingly they were very sociable
until we had finished eating, and the table removed. Then my friend
asked me why I had ventured to come to New York. So I told him it was
in expectation of getting engagements in music halls in the city, and he
said he was afraid I wouldn't succeed in getting an engagement. As he said
it came to pass, for when I went three days after being in New York to
look for engagements at the music halls I was told by all the managers
I saw that they couldn't give me an engagement, because there was a
combination on foot

and how I had come at a very bad time. When I couldn't get an engage-
ment I thought I would try and sell some of my poems I had fetched with
me from Dundee. Well, the first day I tried to sell them it was a complete
failure for this reason—When they saw the Royal coat of arms on the
top of the poems they got angry, and said, "To the deuce with that. We
won't buy that here. You'll better go home again to Scotland." Well,
of course, I felt a little angry, no doubt, and regretted very much that I
had been so unlucky as to come to New York, and resolved in my mind
to get home again as soon as possible. When I came back to my friend's
house, or my lodging-house in New York, I told him how I had been
treated when I offered my poems for sale, and he said to me, "I'll tell
you what to do. You'll just cut off the Royal coat-of-arms, and then the
people will buy them from you." And when he told me to do so I was
astonished to hear him say so, and told him "No!" I said, "I decline
to do so. I am not ashamed of the Royal coat-of-arms yet, and I think
you ought to be ashamed for telling me so, but you may think as you like,
I will still adhere to my colours wherever I go."

WEARYING FOR HOME.

Well, after I had been three weeks in New York without earning a
cent I thought I would write home to Dundee to Mr Alexander C. Lamb,
proprietor of the Temperance Hotel, Dundee. Well, I remember when
writing to my dear friend, the late Mr Lamb, I told him for God's sake to
take me home from out of this second Babylon, for I could get no one to
help me, and when writing it the big tears were rolling down my cheeks,
and at the end of the letter I told him to address it to the Anchor Line
Steam Shipping Company's office, to lie till called for. So, when the
letter was finished I went out to the Post Office and posted it. Well, to
be brief, I remember the next day was Sunday, and in the evening of the
same day my friend invited the most of his neighbours to his house, as
there was going to be a concert held amongst them, and, of course, I was
invited to the concert and expected to recite, of course. And after the
neighbours had been all seated and ready to begin my friend was elected
by the neighbours to occupy the chair for the evening, and he said,
"Ladies and gentlemen,—As we are all assembled here to-night to enjoy
ourselves in a sociable manner, it is expected that all those that can sing
a song will do so, and those that can recite will do the same, and as my
friend here, the great Poet, M'Gonagall, can recite, I request him to open
the concert by reciting his own poem, ' Bruce at Bannockburn.' "

I leapt to my feet and said, "Mr Chairman, ladies and gentlemen,—I
refuse to submit to such a request, because I believe in God, and He has
told us to remember the Sabbath day to keep it holy, and I consider it
is an act of desecration to hold a concert on the Sabbath. Therefore, I
refuse to recite or sing."

"Oh, but," the Chairman said, "it is all right here in New York.
quite common here."

18

Then there chanced to be a Jew in the company, and he said to me, "What you know about God? Did ever He pay your rint?" And I said, "Perhaps He did. If He didn't come down from Heaven and pay it Himself, He put it in the minds of some other persons to do it for Him." Then the Jew said, "You'll petter go home again to Scotland. That won't do here." Then the lady of the house said—" If ye dinna recite to obleege the company ye'll juist need tae gang oot. Ye ought to be ashamed o' yersel, for look how ye have affronted me before my neighbours."

Then I said—" But I haven't affronted God." Then the Jew said—"What you know about God? Did you ever see Him?" "Not in this company at least," I replied. And then I arose and left the company, considering it to be very bad, and retired to my bed for the night, thinking before I fell asleep that I was in dangerous company, because, from my own experience, the people in New York in general have little or no respect for the Sabbath. The theatres are open, also the music halls, and all of them are well patronised. My dear readers, I will now insert in this autobiography of mine a poem, "Jottings of New York," which will give you a little information regarding the ongoings of the people, which runs as follows :—

DESCRIPTIVE POEM—JOTTINGS OF NEW YORK

Oh, mighty city of New York, you are wonderful to behold—
Your buildings are magnificent—the truth be it told—
They were the only thing that seemed to arrest my eye,
Because many of them are thirteen storeys high ;
And as for Central Park, it is lovely to be seen—
Especially in the summer season when its shrubberies are green ;
And the Burns Statue is there to be seen,
Surrounded by trees on the beautiful sward so green ;
Also Shakespeare and the immortal Sir Walter Scott,
Which by Scotchmen and Englishmen will never be forgot.

There are people on the Sabbath day in thousands resort—
All lov'd, in conversation, and eager for sport ;
And some of them viewing the wild beasts there,
While the joyous shouts of children does rend the air—
And also beautiful black swans, I do declare.

And there's beautiful boats to be seen there,
And joyous shouts of children does rend the air,
While the boats sail along with them o'er Lohengrin Lake,
And fare is 5 cents for children, and adults ten is all they take.

And there's also summer-house shades, and merry-go-rounds,
And with the merry laughter of the children the park resounds,
During the live-long Sabbath day,
Enjoying themselves at the merry-go-round play.

Then there's the elevated railroads about five storeys high,
Which the inhabitants can hear night and day passing by ;
Of, such a mass of people there daily do throng—
No less than five 100,000 daily pass along ;
And all along the city you can get for five cents—
And, believe me, among the passengers there's few discontent.

And the tops of the houses are mostly all flat,
And in the warm weather the people gather to chat ;
Besides, on the housetops they dry their clothes ;
And, also, many people all night on the housetops repose.

And numerous ships and steamboats are there to be seen,
Sailing along the East River water, which is very green—
Which is certainly a most beautiful sight
To see them sailing o'er the smooth water day and night.

And as for Brooklyn Bridge, it's a very great height,
And fills the stranger's heart with wonder at first sight ;
And with all its loftiness I venture to say
It cannot surpass the new railway bridge of the Silvery Tay.

And there's also ten thousand rumsellers there—
Oh, wonderful to think of, I do declare!
To accommodate the people of New York therein,
And to encourage them to commit all sorts of sin.

And on the Sabbath day ye will see many a man
Going for beer with a big tin can,
And seems proud to be seen carrying home the beer
To treat his neighbours and his family dear.

Then at night numbers of the people dance and sing,
Making the walls of their houses to ring
With their songs and dancing on Sabbath night,
Which I witnessed with disgust, and fled from the sight.

And with regard to New York and the sights I did see—
Believe me, I never saw such sights in Dundee ;
And the morning I sailed from the city of New York
My heart it felt as light as a cork.

Well, my dear readers, to resume my autobiography, I've told ye I
sent a letter to Mr Alexander C. Lamb in Dundee requesting him to fetch
me to Dundee as he had promised, and when about three weeks had
expired I called at the Anchor Line Steam Shipping Company's office on
a Monday morning, I remember, to see if a letter had come from Dundee.
Well, when I asked Mr Stewart if there was any news from Dundee, he
said, " Yes," smiling at me, and, continuing—" Yes, I received a cable-
gram from Dundee on Saturday night telling me to give you a passage

20

home again—a second class cabin, not the steerage this time." And he asked me how much money I would require, and I told him about three pounds. " But," he said, " I've been told to give you **six**," and when he told me so I felt overjoyed, and thanked him and my dear friend, Mr Alexander C. Lamb. Then he asked me if I would take British money or American, and I said I would take American one half and British the other, and along with it he gave me a certificate for my passage on board the " Circassia," which would sail from New York harbour in about a fortnight or so, telling me to be sure and not forget the time the steamer would leave New York for Glasgow, and bidding me to be watchful regarding my money, for there were many bad characters in New York.

Well, my dear friends, I bade him good-bye, telling him I would take his good advice, and, if alive and well, I would be on the lookout for the steamer that was to take me to Bonnie Scotland, and left him with my heart full of glee.

Well, my dear friends, at last the longed-for day arrived that I was to leave New York, and everything I required being ready, I bade farewell to my old Dundee friend and his mistress, and made my way down to the jetty or harbour of New York, where the beautiful steamer "Circassia" lay that I was to embark in, which would carry me safe to Glasgow and the rest of the passengers, God willing. And when I arrived at the jetty there were a great number of intending passengers gathered ready to go on board, and there was a great deal of hand-shaking amongst them, bidding each other good-bye. Some of them were crying bitterly, I noticed, and others were seemingly quite happy. Such is life.

> Some do weep, and some feel gay,
> Thus runs the world away.

Well, when the hand-shakings were over, the intending passengers went on board, and I amongst the rest. The first thing that arrested my attention was the skirling of the pibroch, playing

" WILL YE NO COME BACK AGAIN ? "

and other old familiar Scottish airs, and the babbling of voices, mingling together with rather discordant music ringing in my ears. The sails were hoisted, and steam got up, and the anchor was weighed, and the bell was rung. Then the vessel steamed out of New York Harbour, bound for Glasgow. The stout vessel sailed o'er the mighty deep, and the passengers felt delighted, especially when an iceberg was sighted. I remember I saw two large ones while going to America. Now, on the return voyage one has been sighted, and a very big one, about ten feet high, which in the distance has a very ghostly appearance, standing there so white, which seemed most fearful to the passengers' sight. And some of the passengers were afraid that it might come towards the vessel, but it remained immovable, which the passengers and captain were very thankful for. Well, on sped the vessel for a week without anything dangerous happening until the sea began all of a sudden to swell, and the waves rose up like mountains high ; then the vessel began to roll from side to side in the trough of the sea, and the women began to scream and the children also.

The big waves swept o'er her deck, so much so that the hatches had to be nailed down, and we all expected to be drowned in that mighty ocean of waters. Some parts, the steward told me, were five miles deep. When he told me so I said to him, " Is that a fact ? " and he said it was really true. And I said to him how wonderful it was and how beautiful and dark blue the sea was, and how I had often heard of

THE DARK BLUE SEA,

but now I was sailing o'er it at last. The vessel all at once gave a lurch and slackened her speed, and the cause thereof was owing to the piston of one of the engines breaking in the centre, which rendered it unworkable, and it couldn't be repaired until the vessel arrived in Glasgow. By that break in the engine we were delayed three days longer at sea, and, strange to say, as I remarked to some of the passengers, " Isn't it wonderful to think that the sea calmed down all at once as soon as the piston broke ? " And some said it was and others said it wasn't, and I said in my opinion it was God that calmed the sea—that it was a Providential interference, for, if the sea hadn't calmed down, the vessel would have been useless amongst the big waves owing to the engine giving way, and would have sunk with us all to the bottom of the briny deep, and not one of us would have been saved. Well, my friends, after that I was looked upon as a prophet and a God-fearing man, and very much respected by the passengers and the chief steward. So on the next evening there was to be a concert held amongst the passengers, and they all felt happy that they were spared from a watery grave, and many of them thanked God for saving them from being drowned. So the next day the sea was as calm as a mirror, and the vessel skimmed o'er the smooth waters like a bird on the wing, and the passengers felt so delighted that some of them began to sing. When evening set in, and the passengers had got their tea, arrangements were made to hold the concert in the cabin saloon, as formerly, and, of course, I was invited, as before, to give my services. This is generally expected on board of all emigrant vessels. Any one known to be a singer or a reciter will join in the entertainment for the evening, because emigrants either going or returning from a foreign country are all like one family. There seems to be a brotherly and a sisterly feeling amongst them, more so at sea than on land. No doubt the reason is that they are more afraid of losing their lives at sea than on land.

A CONCERT AT SEA.

When it drew nigh to eight o'clock all those who intended to be present at the concert began to assemble in the cabin saloon, and by eight o'clock the saloon was well filled with a very select gathering of passengers. Of course, amongst them was the chief steward and myself as formerly. Of course he was elected as chairman, and as formerly he announced that all collections of money on board at concerts went for the benefit of the Lifeboat Fund. Now there was amongst the passengers an actor, who had been to New York in expectation of getting engagements there, and had failed, and was well known to the chief steward, and had consented

to give a recital along with a lady from the play of " The Lady of Lyons."
She was to read her part from the book, and he was to recite his part
from memory, he taking the part of Claude Mellnotte, and she " the Lady
of Lyons." So such being the case the audience thought they were going
to get a treat, so the chairman announced them as first on the programme
to give a recital, which was received with applause when announced.
But that was all the applause they received during their recital, for she
stammered all along in the reading of her part, and as for the actor he
wasn't much better. All the difference was he remembered his part, but
his voice was bad. Then when they had finished their recital I was
requested to give a recital, and I recited Othello's Apology, which was
received with great applause. Then I was encored, and for an encore I
sang " The Rattling Boy from Dublin," and received thunders of applause.
When I had finished several of the passengers shook hands with me
warmly, telling me I had done well. Then other songs followed from
ladies and gentlemen. And the chairman sang a song, and we all felt
quite jolly, and free from melancholy, while the vessel sped on steadily
as a rock. By this time it was near ten o'clock, and as it was near time
to finish up with the concert, I was requested by the chairman to give
another recital, which would conclude the evening's entertainment. So
I consented, and recited " The Battle of Tel-el-Kebir," and received the
general applause of the audience. This finished the evening's entertain-
ment. Then there was shaking of hands amongst the passengers, and
high compliments were paid to those that joined in the concert, myself
included. So we all retired to rest, highly pleased with the evening's
entertainment, and I slept fairly well that night. In the morning I was
awakened from my sleep by someone knocking at the door of my berth,
gently, and I asked who was there. A voice replied, " A friend." I arose
at once to see who had knocked, and there was one of the gentlemen who
had heard me recite at the concert, and he asked me if I was open to
receive from him a few shillings as

A TOKEN OF REWARD,

and his appreciation of my abilities as a reciter, telling me he considered
it a great shame for passengers to allow me to give them so much for
nothing. So I thanked him for his kindness, and he said—" Don't
mention it," and bade me good morning, saying he was going to have
breakfast, and that he would see me again. So in a short time the bell
rang for breakfast, and I was served, as well as others, with a small loaf
of bread and butter and a large tin of hot coffee, which in general is the
morning fare—quite enough, in my opinion, for any ordinary man. Well,
my friends, I have nothing more of any importance to relate concerning
my return from New York, any more than that we arrived safe and well
at Glasgow, after being fourteen days at sea on the home-coming voyage.
The next morning I took an early train bound for Dundee, and arrived
there shortly after one o'clock noon. When I arrived at home my family
were very glad to see me ; and also some of my old friends ; and as I had
written a diary regarding my trip to New York I sold it to a newspaper
reporter, who gave me 7s. 6d. for it.

FAREWELL TO DUNDEE.

Well, my dear friends, the next event in my life that I am going to relate is regarding me and my Mistress M'Gonagall leaving Dundee in the year 1894, resolving to return no more owing to the harsh treatment I had received in the city, as is well known for a truth without me recording it. Well, I went to the Fair City of Perth, one of the finest upon the earth, intending to remain there altogether. So I secured a small garret in the South Street, and me and my mistress lived there for eight months, and the inhabitants were very kind to us in many respects. But I remember receiving a letter from an Inverness gentleman requesting me to come through on the 16th October and give him and his friends an entertainment, and that all arrangements had been made with the directors of the Inverness Railway Company, and that I had only to show the letter. I went down to the Railway Station and showed the officials the letter from Inverness inviting me through, and when they read it they said it was all right. They had received a telegram regarding it, and they told me to come down in the morning a little before ten o'clock, so as I could leave Perth with the ten o'clock train, and they would give me a certificate that would make me all right for the return journey to Perth. So I thanked them, telling them I would be down in the morning, God willing, in good time. When I went home I told my wife that I had made all right for my railway trip to Inverness, and she was glad to hear that it was all right. When I had got my supper I went to bed, but I didn't sleep well, for I was thinking too much about venturing so far away entirely amongst strangers, but as I had been assured of

A HEARTY HIGHLAND WELCOME.

I considered I was safe in making the venture. So I screwed up my courage and all danger regarding my trip to Inverness vanished from my mind. In the morning I arose and donned my clothes, and partook of a hearty meal along with my good lady, and then made myself ready for going to Inverness. When ready I bade my mistress good-bye, and away I went to the railway station and saw the officials. When the train for Inverness was nearly ready to start they showed me into one of the carriages, and bade me good-bye.

The train steamed off with its long white curling cloud of steam which was most beautiful to be seen. The train passed rocky mountains and woodland scenery, and lochs and rivers, and clear crystal fountains gushing from the mountains, and the bleak, heathery hills made the scenery very romantic to the appearance I remember. But it was only a bird's eye view I had, the train passed on so quickly, but in the summer season I thought it would be delightful to be roaming at ease, and to be viewing the mountain scenery and the beautiful villas by the way near to the riverside, surrounded by trees and shrubberies. As for the angler, he could have excellent sport fishing in the lochs and the river in that Highland region near to Dalwhinnie and other beautiful places I noticed by the way. And while thinking so in my mind I was astonished to think that the train had arrived, before I knew, and there I was met at the station by the gentleman who had written to me. He asked me if I was the Poet M'Gonagall, and I said I was, and he grasped me by the hand kindly, and told me to follow him. I did so without fear, and he took me to a hotel. And as we entered it we were met by the landlord, to whom I was introduced. And the proprietor told me there and then not to be ashamed to ask for anything I liked that was in the house, and I would get it, because the gentleman that had fetched me through from Perth had told him so, and with that my friend left me to my own meditations. Then I told the hotel proprietor I would have for dinner some coffee, bread, and a beefsteak, so in a very short space of time my dinner was ready and served out to me by a servant girl, and I did ample justice to it because I felt hungry. By this time it was about five o'clock in the afternoon, so I went out to have a walk and view the beautiful scenery along the riverside, and after I did so it was within an hour for me to entertain the gentleman who had brought me from Perth, so I had some tea made ready, and ate heartily, and when finished my friend came in and asked me if I had been enjoying myself, and I told him I had. Then he said the gentlemen I was to entertain would soon drop in. So they began to drop in by twos and threes until the room was well filled. The large table in the room was well spread with costly viands. When we had all partaken of the good spread on the table a chairman was elected, a gentleman of the name of Mr Gossip, and a very nice gentleman he was. He began by saying—" Gentlemen! I feel proud to-night to be elected at this meeting of friends and acquaintances to hear the great poet, Mr M'Gonagall, displaying his poetic abilities from his own works and from other poets also, and I request, gentlemen, that we will give him a patient hearing, and I am sure if ye do ye will get a poetic treat, for his name is a household word at the present day. Therefore, gentlemen, with these few remarks I will call upon our distinguished guest, Mr M'Gonagall, to favour the company with a recital of his famous poem, ' Bannockburn.' "

I arose and said—" Gentlemen, I feel proud to-night to be amongst such a select company of gentlemen, and as far as my abilities will permit me I'll endeavour to please ye, and by your kind permission I will now begin to recite my Bannockburn poem."

Before I was halfway through, the cheering from the company was really deafening to my ears, so much so that I had to halt until the cheering subsided, and when I finished the company shook hands with me all round. After I sat down one of the gentlemen said he would sing a song on my behalf while I was resting, but he said he would need to get a glass of wine first. So when he got the glass of wine and drank to my health he began to sing that song of Burns', " Gae bring tae me a pint of wine." I can assure ye, my readers, he sang the song very well, and with so much vehemence that when he had finished

HE WAS FAIRLY EXHAUSTED,

and all for my sake. And when done his head fell upon his shoulder, and he seemed to be in the arms of Morpheus. Then other gentlemen sang songs, and the night passed by pleasantly, and all went well. Then the chairman said—" Gentlemen, as the night is far advanced I will now call upon our guest of the evening, Mr M'Gonagall, to give us a song— ' The Rattling Boy from Dublin,' of which he is the author."

Then I said—" Mr chairman and gentlemen, I am quite willing to do so, owing to the kind treatment I have met with, and the hearty Highland welcome ye have bestowed upon me, which I will not forget in a hurry. So I will begin to sing my song." Before I was halfway through, the gentleman who had fallen asleep in the chair awoke, and leapt on to the floor, and began to dance, until the chairman had to stop him from dancing, and when order was restored I went on with my song without any further interruption. And when I finished my song I recited " The Battle of Tel-el-Kebir," also a scene from Macbeth, which seemed to please the company very well. That was owing, I think, to Macbeth living in Inverness at one time.

Well, my dear friends, that concluded the evening's entertainment. Then the gentleman who had sent me the letter to come through to Inverness to give his friends an entertainment arose and said—" Mr chairman and friends,—It now falls to my lot to present to the great poet, M'Gonagall, this purse of silver, of which it is the desire of my friends and myself never to make known the contents. So saying, he handed me the purse and its contents, which I thanked him for and the company, telling them that I would never forget their kindness, and that in all my travels I had never met with such good treatment. Then the gentlemen all round shook hands with me, declaring they were well pleased with the entertainment I had given them. Wishing me good night and a sound sleep, they left me to my own meditations ; but my friend, before leaving me, conducted me to my bed in the hotel, and wishing me good-night, he said he would see me in the morning, and see me off in the train for Perth. So I went to bed, quite delighted with the treatment I had received from the gentlemen I had entertained in Inverness, and in the morning I was up with the lark, and had a good breakfast, and put a good luncheon piece in my pocket to eat by the way returning to Perth. My friend called on me in the morning, and accompanied me to the Railway Station, and saw me off by the ten o'clock train for Perth, and I arrived safe in Perth about half-past four o'clock on the afternoon of the 17th day of October, 1894.

Two days after my arrival from Inverness I composed a poem in praise of the Heather Blend Club banquet at Inverness, which is as follows :—

'Twas on the 16th of October, in the year 1894,
I was invited to Inverness, not far from the sea shore,
To partake of a banquet prepared by the Heather Blend Club,
Gentlemen who honoured me without any hubbub.

The banquet was held in the Gellion Hotel,
And the landlord, Mr Macpherson, treated me right well ;
Also the servant maids were very kind to me,
Especially the girl that polished my boots, most beautiful to see.

26

The banquet consisted of roast beef, potatoes, and red wine ;
Also hare soup and sherry and grapes most fine,
And baked pudding and apples lovely to be seen ;
Also rich sweet milk and delicious cream.

Mr Gossip, a noble Highlander, acted as chairman,
And when the banquet was finished the fun began ;
And I was requested to give a poetic entertainment,
Which I gave, and which pleased them to their hearts' content.

And for my entertainment they did me well reward
By titling me there the Heather Blend Club bard ;
Likewise I received an illuminated address,
Also a purse of silver, I honestly confess.

Oh, magnificent city of Inverness,
And your beautiful river, I must confess,
With its lovely scenery on each side,
Would be good for one's health there to reside.

There the blackbird and mavis together doth sing,
Making the woodlands with their echoes to ring
During the months of July, May, and June,
When the trees and the shrubberies are in full bloom.

And to see the River Ness rolling smoothly along,
Together with the blackbird's musical song,
While the sun shines bright in the month of May,
Will help to drive dull care away.

And Macbeth's Castle is grand to be seen,
Situated on Castle Hill, which is beautiful and green.
'Twas there Macbeth lived in days of old,
And a very great tyrant he was be it told.

I wish the members of the Heather Blend Club every success,
Hoping God will prosper them and bless ;
Long may Dame Fortune smile upon them,
For all of them I've met are kind gentlemen.

And in praise of them I must say
I never received better treatment in my day,
Than I received from my admirers in Bonnie Inverness.
This, upon my soul and conscience, I do confess.

My dear readers, I must now give you a brief account of my trip to
the mighty city of London. If I can remember, it might be either 19 or
20 years ago, and in the merry month of June, when trees and flowers
were in full bloom, and owing to my poverty I couldn't have gone to
London, only that I received a letter—a forged one—supposed to be

Written by Dion Boucicault, the Irish dramatist, inviting me down to Stratton's Restaurant at twelve o'clock noon to have lunch with him, as he intended to engage me for a provincial tour to give entertainments in the provincial towns throughout Britain, and he would give me a big salary. Well, my dear friends, of course I felt delighted when I read the letter, so I went to Stratton's Restaurant just as the town clock struck twelve. I was received very kindly, and shown upstairs to a little room. I think it was the smoking room, and I knocked at the door, and it was answered by one of the gentlemen. Of course I knew him, and he introduced me to the gentleman who was impersonating the character of Dion Boucicault, and he asked me how I was, and I told him I was very well, hoping to find him the same. Then he told me he had heard so much about my histrionic abilities that he would engage me and give me a salary of £20 weekly, food included, and the other gentlemen present said it was little enough for a man of my abilities ; but all the while I knew he was an impostor. Then he requested me to recite my famous poem, " Bruce at Bannockburn," and of course I did so, and when finished he declared if I would recite that before a Scottish audience in London it would pull down the house. Then he told one of the gentlemen to fetch in some refreshment for Mr M'Gonagall, for he was more than delighted with my Bannockburn recital. Then a gentleman waiter came in with a little refreshment on a tea tray, simply

<blockquote>
A penny sandwich and a tumbler of beer,
Thinking it would my spirits cheer.
</blockquote>

And I remember I looked at it with a scornful eye before I took it, nd I laid it down on a little round table beside me and screwed my courage to the sticking place, and stared the impostor Boucicault in the face, and he felt rather uneasy, like he guessed I knew he wasn't the original Boucicault, so he arose from his seat and made a quick retreat, and before leaving he bade me good-bye, telling me he would see me again. Then I kept silent, and I stared the rest of my pretended friends out of countenance until they couldn't endure the penetrating glance of my poetic eye, so they arose and left me alone in my glory. Then I partook of the grand penny luncheon I had received for my recital of " Bannockburn," and with indignation my heart did burn.

I went direct to the Theatre Royal, and inquired for Mr Hodge, the manager, and I saw him and I showed him the letter I had received from Dion Boucicault, as I didn't believe it was from him, and when he looked at it he said it wasn't his handwriting, and how I had met with a great disappointment no doubt, and asked me if I would allow him to make an extract from the letter and he would send it to Boucicault, so I said I would ; so he made an extract, telling me he mentioned my poor circumstances in it, and he had no doubt but Mr Boucicault would do something for me by way of solatium for my wounded feelings and for using his name in vain. He told me to come down to the theatre inside of three days, and he would have a letter from Boucicault by that time, he expected, so I thanked him for his kindness, and came away with my spirits light and gay.

28

Well, I waited patiently till the three days were expired, then called at the Theatre Royal and saw Mr Hodge, the manager, and he received me very kindly, telling me he had received a letter from Mr Boucicault with a £5 cheque in it on the Bank of Scotland, so he handed me five sovereigns in gold along with Boucicault's letter. I thanked him and came away, and in the letter Boucicault felt for me very much, saying practical jokers were practical fools, which in my opinion is really true. So, my dear readers, it was through me getting the £5 from Boucicault that I resolved to take a

TRIP TO LONDON.

A steerage return passage at that time was £1, so I purchased a ticket and made up my mind to go. I remember it was in the month of June, when trees and flowers were in full bloom, and on a Wednesday afternoon I embarked on board the steamer " London," and there were a few of my friends waiting patiently at the dockyard to see me off to London and wish me success in my perilous enterprise, and to give me a hearty cheer my spirits for to cheer, and a merry shake of hands all round, which made the dockyard loudly resound. Then when the handshakings were o'er the steam whistle began to roar. Then the engine started, and the steamer left the shore, while she sailed smoothly o'er the waters of the Tay, and the passengers' hearts felt light and gay. There weren't many passengers, I remember, but seemingly they all felt merry as the steamer drew near to Broughty Ferry, because the scenery in that direction is very fascinating to be seen, the seascape so lovely and green. When the steamer had passed by Broughty Ferry a few miles I remember the passengers began to get weary, and we were all sitting on the deck, and some of them proposed that they should have a song, so a lady sang a song, but I don't remember the name of it ; it's so long ago, but it's of no great consequence. When they had all sung I was requested to give a recital, and I gave them the " Battle of Tel-el-Kebir," which was well received, and I got an encore, and I gave them the " Rattling Boy from Dublin Town," and for which I received a small donation, and that finished the entertainment for the night. Then the steerage passengers bade me good-night and retired to their berths for the night, and me along with the rest. Well, the steamer sailed smoothly along during the night, and nothing happened that would the most timid heart affright, and the passengers slept well, including myself, owing to the smooth sailing of the good ship.

All went smoothly as a marriage bell until the good steamer landed us safe at the wharf, London, in the River Thames. Then there was shaking of hands and bidding each other good-bye, and each one took their own way, some on holiday, others on the look-out for work ; such was the case with me. Well, as soon as I got ashore I held on by the Fish Market, and as I drew near very discordant sounds broke upon my ear. The babbling of the fishmongers was disagreeable to hear ; and I had my properties with me in a black bag, and as I was passing along where there were about thirty men lounging near to the market-place they cried after me, " Hi! hi! Scottie, I'll carry your bag," but I paid no heed to them, because I would never have seen it if I had allowed any-one of them to have carried the bag. However, I made my way to Fetter Lane, Fleet Street, and secured my lodgings for a week in the White Horse Inn, Fetter Lane, at 4d. per night, so for the time being I was all right.

I PAID THE LANDLORD IN ADVANCE

for my lodging, and had some supper, and then I gave him my bag to lock up; then my mind felt quite at ease. Then I went out to have a walk, and resolved to call at the Lyceum Theatre and see—now Sir—Henry Irving. He wasn't Sir Henry then, my friends. Well, I made straight for the theatre and saw the janitor at the stage entrance, and I asked him if I could see Mr Irving, and he said snappishly I could not, and that Mr Irving wouldn't speak to the likes of me. Well, of course, I felt indignant, and I told him I considered myself to be as great a man as he is, and came away without delay; but he will speak to me now, my friends, and has done so in Edinburgh. Well, after I had come home to my lodgings from the theatre I made my supper quickly, and relished it with a good appetite. I requested the landlord to show me to bed, and he did so cheerfully, and wished me good-night and sweet repose. Each lodger had an enclosed apartment to himself of wood and a door, which he can lock if he likes to do so. However, I went to bed and slept soundly during the night, and arose in the morning, when the sun was shining bright. Then I donned my clothes, and made my breakfast, and took it with great gusto; then, when finished, I went out and wended my way towards London Bridge, and, oh! such a busy throng of cabs and 'buses rapidly whirling along. After viewing it, I returned to my lodging quite delighted with the sight I had seen, and then I prepared my dinner a few hours afterwards, and ate heartily. Then I went to some of the Music Halls looking for engagements, but, unfortunately, I didn't succeed. Owing to the disappointments I met with, I resolved to return home to Dundee as soon as possible. Well, when Sabbath came round, I went to the Tabernacle to hear Mr Spurgeon preach, and I most solemnly declare he is the greatest preacher I've ever heard, with the exception of Gilfillan.

However, as I resolved to return home to Dundee, I waited for the day Saturday to come. That was the day the steamer " London " would leave London for Dundee, and when Saturday came I left my lodgings in Fetter Lane, longing, of course, for to get hame, and embarked on board, with my heart light, and longing to see the Silvery Tay. So the stout steamer from the Thames sailed away, and arrived on Wednesday in the Silvery Tay, and the passengers' hearts were full of glee when they were landed safely in Dundee once again. I was glad to see it, especially my family. In conclusion, I will insert my poem,

" JOTTINGS OF LONDON."

As I stood upon London Bridge,
And viewed the mighty throng
Of thousands of people in cabs and 'buses
Rapidly whirling along,
And driving to and fro,
Up one street and down another
As quick as they could go.

Then I was struck with the discordant sounds
Of human voices there,
Which seemed to me like wild geese
Cackling in the air.

And as for the River Thames—
It is a most wonderful sight ;
To see the steamers and barges
Sailing up and down upon it
From early morn till night.

And as for the Tower of London—
It is most gloomy to behold,
And within it lies the Crown of England
Begemmed with precious stones and gold.

Kingly Henry the Sixth was murdered there
By the Duke of Gloster,
And when he killed him with his sword
He called him an impostor.

St. Paul's Cathedral is the finest building
That ever I did see ;
There's nothing can surpass it
In the town of Dundee,
For it is most magnificent to behold
With its beautiful dome and lofty spire glittering like gold.

And as for Nelson's Monument
That stands in Trafalgar Square—
It is a most stately statue
I most solemnly declare,
And towering very high,
Which arrests strangers' attention
When they are passing by.
And there's two beautiful water fountains
Spouting up very high,
Where the weary travellers can have a drink
When they feel dry

31

Then at the foot of Nelson's Monument
There's three figures of bronze lions in grand array,
Which ought to drive dull care away
As the stranger gazes thereon,
Unless he is very woebegone.

Then as for Mr Spurgeon,
He is a divine surgeon,
Which no one can gainsay.
I went to hear him preach on the Sabbath day,
Which made my heart feel light and gay
For to hear him preach and pray.

And the Tabernacle was crowded from ceiling to floor,
And many people were standing outside the door.
He is an eloquent preacher, I solemnly declare,
And I was struck with admiration as I on him did stare ;
For he is the only individual I heard
Speaking proper English during my stay there.

Then as for Petticoat Lane, I venture to say
It's a most wonderful place to see on the Sabbath day ;
For wearing apparel of every kind
Can be bought to suit the young and the old
For the ready money—silver, copper, or gold.

My Dear Readers,—I must now tell ye my reason for leaving the Fair City of Perth. It was because I found it to be too small for me making a living in. I must allow, the inhabitants were very kind to me during my stay mongst them. And while living there I received a letter, and when I opened it I was struck with amazement when I found a silver elephant enclosed, and I looked at it in amazement, and said— " I'll now have a look at this big letter enclosed. I was astonished to see that King Theebaw, of Burmah and the Andaman Islands, had conferred upon me the honorary title of Sir Wm. Topaz M'Gonagall, Knight of The White Elephant, Burmah, and for the benefit of my readers and the public, I consider I am justified in recording it in my autobiography, which runs as follows :—

Court of King Theebaw,
Andaman Islands,
Dec. 2, 1894.

Dear and Most Highly Honoured Sir,—Having the great honour to belong to the same holy fraternity of poets as yourself, I have been requested by our fellow-country-men at present serving our Queen and country in Her Majesty's great Indian Empire to send you the following address, and at the same time to inform you that you were lately appointed a Grand Knight of the Holy Order of the White Elephant, Burmah, by his Royal Highness upon representation being made to him by your fellow-countrymen out here.

King Theebaw, who is just now holding his Court in the Andaman Islands, expressed himself as being only too pleased to confer the highest honour possible upon merit, wheresoever found, if that merit were judged worthy by his Grand Topaz General. As the latter gentleman has long been impressed by the injustice with which you have been treated by Lord Rosebery in his position as chief adviser of Her Majesty, and since your great modesty upon several occasions has been noticed by His Royal Highness the King of Burmah, it gives him great pleasure to assure Theebaw, the King, that none more worthy of this high honour has ever lived in the East, whereat His Royal Highness called his Court together, and with much eclat and esteem caused it to be proclaimed throughout his present palace and kingdom that you were to be known henceforth as Topaz M'Gonagall, G.K.H.O.W.E.B.

Should you ever visit the Andaman Islands it will be his great pleasure to be presented to you, and to do all honour to you, according to the very ancient custom with which members of our mutual illustrious Order have always been treated by his ancestors.

That you will consent to accept the high honour now offered to you is the wish nearest the hearts of your countrymen in the East ; that you may be long spared to enrich British literature by your grand and thrilling works is their most sincere prayer.

His Majesty also expressed it as his opinion, and the opinion of his grandfathers as far back as the flood, that such talented works as those of their holy fraternity of poets were, had always been, and for ever would be, above all earthly praise, their value being inestimable. He further stated that he failed to conceive how Rosebery could have been so blind as not to have offered to such a man as yourself the paltry and mean stipend attached to the position of Poet Laureate of Great Britain and Ireland. It is indescribable to him that any man of ordinary rummel gumption could possibly offer remuneration to such a gift of the Gods as yours.

Should you see fit to do the ancient Kingdom of Burmah the honour of accepting the Ribbon of its highers Order, and will kindly pay its capital a visit at your earliest convenience, it is the King's order that you be received with all the ceremony due to the greatest ornament now living of the Holy Order of the White Elephant. You are to be immediately installed in the holy chair of the Knights of the above Order upon arrival, from which it is the custom of the holy fraternity to address the whole Eastern world.

King Theebaw will not injure your sensitive feelings by offering you any filthy lucre as payment for what you may compose in his honour after receiving the insignia of the Holy Order. He also states it will be his duty to see that your name is duly reverenced throughout the Kingdom.

I have the honour to be, most noble and illustrious sir, your most humble brother in the fraternity of poets.

(Per) C. MACDONALD, K.O.W.E.B.,
Poet Laureate of Burmah.

By order of His Royal Highness the King.

Topaz General.
Topaz Minister.
Secretary of State.
Holder of Seals.
Registrar-General.
Staff-Bearer.
Secretary of Letters Patent.
Keeper of the White Elephant.

My dear readers, this letter regarding my knighthood is a correct copy from the original as near as I can write it, with the exception of the Indian language therein, which means the names of the gentlemen that signed the Royal patent letter regarding my knighthood. That is all that is wanting, which I cannot write or imitate. Nor can I imitate the four red seals that are affixed to the Royal document. The insignia of the knighthood is a silver elephant attached to a green silk ribbon.

This, my dear readers, is the full particulars regarding my Indian knighthood, and, my dear friends and well-wishers, I must conclude this autobiography of mine by truthfully recording herein that since I came to beautiful Edinburgh, and that is more than six years now past, I have received the very best of treatment, and during my stay in Edinburgh I have given many entertainments from my own poetic works, also from Shakespeare.

I may say I have been highly appreciated by select audiences, and for their appreciation of my abilities I return them my sincere thanks for being so kind as to give me their support since I came to Edinburgh.—Mr dear friends, I am, yours faithfully,

SIR WM. TOPAZ M'GONAGALL,
Poet and Knight of the White Elephant,
Burmah.

McGONAGALL

THE DESTROYING ANGEL
OR THE POET'S DREAM

I dreamt a dream the other night
That an Angel appeared to me, clothed in white.
Oh! it was a beautiful sight,
Such as filled my heart with delight.

And in her hand she held a flaming brand,
Which she waved above her head most grand ;
And on me she glared with love-beaming eyes,
Then she commanded me from my bed to arise.

And in a sweet voice she said, " You must follow me,
And in a short time you shall see
The destruction of all the public-houses in the city,
Which is, my friend, the God of Heaven's decree."

Then from my bed in fear I arose,
And quickly donned on my clothes ;
And when that was done she said, " Follow me
Direct to the High Street, fearlessly."

So with the beautiful Angel away I did go,
And when we arrived at the High Street, Oh! what a show
I suppose there were about five thousand men there,
All vowing vengeance against the publicans, I do declare.

Then the Angel cried with a solemn voice aloud
To that vast and Godly assembled crowd,
" Gentlemen belonging the fair City of Dundee,
Remember I have been sent here by God to warn ye.

" That by God's decree ye must take up arms and follow me
And wreck all the public-houses in this fair City,
Because God cannot countenance such dens of iniquity.
Therefore, friends of God, come, follow me.

" Because God has said there's no use preaching against
strong drink,
Therefore, by taking up arms against it, God does think,
That is the only and the effectual cure
To banish it from the land, He is quite sure.

" Besides, it has been denounced in Dundee for fifty years
By the friends of Temperance, while oft they have shed tears.
Therefore, God thinks there's no use denouncing it any
longer,
Because the more that's said against it seemingly it grows
stronger."

And while the Angel was thus addressing the people,
The Devil seemed to be standing on the Townhouse Steeple,
Foaming at the mouth with rage, and seemingly much
annoyed,
And kicking the Steeple because the public-houses were
going to be destroyed.

Then the Angel cried, " Satan, avaunt! begone! "
Then he vanished in the flame, to the amazement of every-
one ;
And waving aloft the flaming brand,
That she carried in her right hand

She cried, " Now, friends of the Temperance cause, follow
me :
For remember it's God's high decree

36

To destroy all the public-houses in this fair City ;
Therefore, friends of God, let's commence this war immedi-
ately."

Then from the High Street we all did retire,
As the Angel, sent by God, did desire ;
And along the Perth Road we all did go,
While the Angel set fire to the public-houses along that row.

And when the Perth Road public-houses were fired, she
cried, " Follow me,
And next I'll fire the Hawkhill public-houses instantly."
Then away we went with the Angel, without dread or woe,
And she fired the Hawkhill public-houses as onward we
did go.

Then she cried, " Let's on to the Scouringburn, in God's
name."
And away to the Scouringburn we went, with our hearts
aflame,
As the destroying Angel did command.
And when there she fired the public-houses, which looked
very grand.

And when the public-houses there were blazing like a kiln,
She cried, " Now, my friends, we'll march to the Bonnet Hill,
And we'll fire the dens of iniquity without dismay,
Therefore let's march on, my friends, without delay."

And when we arrived at the Bonnet Hill,
The Angel fired the public-houses, as she did well.
Then she cried, " We'll leave them now to their fate,
And march on to the Murraygate."

Then we marched on to the Murraygate,
And the Angel fired the public-houses there, a most deserving
fate.
Then to the High Street we marched and fired them there,
Which was a most beautiful blaze, I do declare.

And on the High Street, old men and women were gathered
there,
And as the flames ascended upwards, in amazement they did
stare
When they saw the public-houses in a blaze,
But they clapped their hands with joy and to God gave
praise.

Then the Angel cried, " Thank God, Christ's Kingdom's near
at hand,
And there will soon be peace and plenty throughout the land,
And the ravages of the demon Drink no more will be seen."
But, alas, I started up in bed, and behold it was a dream!

LINES IN DEFENCE OF THE STAGE

Good people of high and low degree,
I pray ye all be advised by me,
And don't believe what the clergy doth say,
That by going to the theatre you will be led astray.

No, in the theatre we see vice punished and virtue rewarded,
The villain either hanged or shot, and his career retarded ;
Therefore the theatre is useful in every way,
And has no inducement to lead the people astray.

Because therein we see the end of the bad man,
Which must appal the audience—deny it who can—
Which will help to retard them from going astray,
While witnessing in a theatre a moral play.

The theatre ought to be encouraged in every respect,
Because example is better than precept,
And is bound to have a greater effect
On the minds of theatre-goers in every respect.

Sometimes in theatres, guilty creatures there have been
Struck to the soul by the cunning of the scene ;
By witnessing a play wherein murder is enacted,
They were proven to be murderers, they felt so distracted,

And left the theatre, they felt so much fear,
Such has been the case, so says Shakespeare.
And such is my opinion, I will venture to say,
That murderers will quake with fear on seeing murder in a
    play.

Hamlet discovered his father's murderer by a play
That he composed for the purpose, without dismay,
And the king, his uncle, couldn't endure to see that play,
And he withdrew from the scene without delay.

And by that play the murder was found out,
And clearly proven, without any doubt ;
Therefore, stage representation has a greater effect
On the minds of the people than religious precept.

We see in Shakespeare's tragedy of Othello, which is sub-
    lime,
Cassio losing his lieutenancy through drinking wine ;

And, in delirium and grief, he exclaims—
" Oh, that men should put an enemy in their mouths to steal
    away their brains! "

A young man in London went to the theatre one night
To see the play of George Barnwell, and he got a great fright;
He saw George Barnwell murder his uncle in the play,
And he had resolved to murder his uncle, but was stricken
    with dismay.

But when he saw George Barnwell was to be hung
The dread of murdering his uncle tenaciously to him clung,
That he couldn't murder and rob his uncle dear,
Because the play he saw enacted filled his heart with fear.

And, in conclusion, I will say without dismay,
Visit the theatre without delay,
Because the theatre is a school of morality,
And hasn't the least tendency to lead to prodigality.

CALAMITY IN LONDON

FAMILY OF TEN BURNED TO DEATH

'Twas in the year of 1897, and on the night of Christmas day,
That ten persons' lives were taken away,
By a destructive fire in London, at No. 9 Dixie Street,
Alas! so great was the fire, the victims couldn't retreat.

In Dixie Street, No. 9, it was occupied by two families,
Who were all quite happy, and sitting at their ease ;
One of these was a labourer, David Barber and his wife,
And a dear little child, he loved as his life.

Barber's mother and three sisters were living on the ground
floor,
And in the upper two rooms lived a family who were very
poor,
And all had retired to rest, on the night of Christmas day,
Never dreaming that by fire their lives would be taken away.

Barber got up on Sunday morning to prepare breakfast for
his family,
And a most appalling sight he then did see ;
For he found the room was full of smoke,
So dense, indeed, that it nearly did him choke.

Then fearlessly to the room door he did creep,
And tried to arouse the inmates, who were asleep ;
And succeeded in getting his own family out into the street,
And to him the thought thereof was surely very sweet.

And by this time the heroic Barber's strength was failing,
And his efforts to warn the family upstairs were unavailing ;
And, before the alarm was given, the house was in flames,
Which prevented anything being done, after all his pains.

Oh! it was a horrible and heart-rending sight
To see the house in a blaze of lurid light,
And the roof fallen in, and the windows burnt out,
Alas! 'tis pitiful to relate, without any doubt.

Oh, Heaven! 'tis a dreadful calamity to narrate,
Because the victims have met with a cruel fate ;
Little did they think they were going to lose their lives by
fire,
On that night when to their beds they did retire.

It was sometime before the gutted house could be entered in,
Then to search for the bodies the officers in charge did begin ;
And a horrifying spectacle met their gaze,
Which made them stand aghast in a fit of amaze.

Sometime before the Firemen arrived,
Ten persons of their lives had been deprived,
By the choking smoke, and merciless flame,
Which will long in the memory of their relatives remain.

Oh, Heaven! it was a frightful and pitiful sight to see
Seven bodies charred of the Jarvis' family ;
And Mrs Jarvis was found with her child, and both
    carbonised,
And as the searchers gazed thereon they were surprised.

And these were lying beside the fragments of the bed,
And in a chair the tenth victim was sitting dead ;
Oh, Horrible! Oh, Horrible! what a sight to behold,
The charred and burnt bodies of young and old.

Good people of high and low degree,
Oh! think of this sad catastrophe,
And pray to God to protect ye from fire,
Every night before to your beds ye retire.

THE BLACK WATCH MEMORIAL

Ye Sons of Mars, it gives me great content
To think there has been erected a handsome monument
In memory of the Black Watch, which is magnificent to see,
Where they first were embodied at Aberfeldy.

And as a Highland regiment they are worthy of what has
    been done for them,
Because a more courageous regiment we cannot find of men
Who have bravely fought and bled in defence of their
    country,
Especially in the Russian War and Soudan War they made
    their enemies flee.

The monument I hope will stand secure for many a long day,
And may the people of Aberfeldy always feel gay ;
As they gaze upon the beautiful Black Watch monument,
I hope they will think of the brave soldiers and feel content.

'Twas in the year of 1887, and on Saturday the 12th of
    November,
Which the people of Aberfeldy and elsewhere will remember,
Who came all the way from Edinburgh, Glasgow, Perth and
    Dundee,
Besides the Pitlochry Volunteers headed the procession right
    manfully.

And the Perthshire Rifles joined the procession with their
    pipe band,
Then followed a detachment of the 42nd Highlanders so
    grand,

43

Under the command of Lieutenant M'Leod,
Whose duty it was to represent the regiment of which he
    felt proud.

The pipe band of the Glasgow Highlanders also were there,
And Taymouth Brass Band, which discoursed sweet music
    I do declare ;
Also military officers and the magistrates of Aberfeldy,
While in the rear came the members of Committee.

There were also Freemasons, Foresters, all in a row,
And wearing their distinctive regalias, which made a great
    show ;
And the processionists were formed into three sides of a
    square
Around the monument, while the music of the bands did
    rend the air.

The noble Marquis of Breadalbane arrived on the ground at
    1.30,
Escorted by a guard of honour and his pipe band ;
Then the bands struck up, and the pipes were set a bumming,
And all with one accord played up the " Campbell's are
    Coming."

Then his Lordship ascended a platform on the north side of
    the monument,
And the bands played cheerfully till their breath was almost
    spent ;
Then his Lordship received three ringing cheers from the
    people there,
Then he requested the Rev. John M'Lean to open the
    proceedings with prayer.

44

And after the prayer, Major Menzies stepped forward
And said, " Ladies and gentlemen, for the Black Watch I
    have great regard ;
And the duty I have to perform gives me great content,
And that is to ask the noble Marquis to unveil this
    monument."

Then he handed the noble Marquis a Lochaber axe to unveil
    the Monument,
And the Marquis said, " Sir, to your request I most willingly
    consent."
Then he unveiled the monument in memory of the gallant
    Forty-twa,
While the bands played up the " Highland Laddie " as loud
    as they could blaw.

And when the bands ceased playing the noble Marquis said,
" This monument I declare is very elegantly made,
And its bold style is quite in keeping with the country I find,
And the Committee were fortunate in obtaining so able a
    designer as Mr. Rhind."

Then, turning to the Chief Magistrate of Aberfeldy,
He said, " Sir, I have been requested by the Committee
To give you the deed conveying the monument to your care,
With the feu-charter of the ground, therefore, sir, I'd have
    you beware."

Then the Chief Magistrate Forbes to Lord Breadalbane said,
" My noble Lord, I accept the charge, and you needn't be
    afraid.
Really it gives me much pleasure in accepting as I now do
    from thee
This Memorial, along with the deeds, on behalf of Aberfeldy."

Then Major Menzies proposed three cheers for the burgh of
Aberfeldy,
And three cheers were given right heartily.
Then the Taymouth Band played " God Save the Queen,"
Then the processionists marched to the New Public School,
happy and serene.

Then there was a banquet held in the school,
At which three hundred sat down and ate till they were full ;
And Lord Breadalbane presided, and had on his right,
Magistrates, Colonels, and Provosts, a most beautiful sight.

And the toasts of " The Queen," " Prince and Princess of
Wales," were given,
Wishing them prosperity while they are living ;
Then the noble Chairman proposed " The Army, Navy and
Volunteers,"
Which was loudly responded to with three loud cheers.

Then Colonel Smith, of the Highland Volunteers, from
Bonnie Dundee,
Replied for the Volunteers right manfully.
Then the noble Chairman said, " The toast I have now to
propose
Is long life and prosperity to the Royal Highlanders in spite
of their foes."

Then the toast was drunk with Highland honours and hearts
so true,
While Pipe-Major M'Dougall played " The 42nd March at
Waterloo."
So ended the proceedings in honour of the Black Watch, the
bravest of men,
And the company with one accord sung the National Anthem.

LOST ON THE PRAIRIE

In one of the States of America, some years ago,
There suddenly came on a violent storm of snow,
Which was nearly the death of a party of workmen,
Who had finished their day's work—nine or ten of them.

The distance was nearly twenty miles to their camp,
And with the thick falling snow their clothes felt damp,
As they set out for their camp, which was in a large grove,
And to reach it, manfully against the storm they strove.

The wind blew very hard, and the snow was falling fast,
Still, they plodded on, but felt a little downcast,
And the snow fell so fast they could scarcely see,
And they began to think they were lost on the wild prairie.

And they suddenly noticed marks of footsteps in the snow,
Which they found were their own tracks, as onward they
       did go,
Then they knew they were lost on the great prairie,
And what could they do in such a fearful extremity ?

Then their hearts began to sink with woe,
In dread of having to pass the night in the snow,
And they cried, " Oh, God! help us to find our way,
Or else we are lost on the lonely prairie."

And while they stood shivering with the cold,
One of the party a particular horse did behold,
Which was known by the name of Old Jack,
So to take off his bridle they were not slack.

When the horse was let free he threw up his head and tail,
Which seemed to say, " Follow me, and ye will not fail.
So come on, boys, and follow me,
And I'll guide ye home safely."
And they cried, " Old Jack can show us the way,
So let's follow his tracks without dismay " ;
And with the falling snow they were chilled to the bone,
But the horse seemed to say, " I'll show ye home."
And at last they gave a shout of delight
When they saw their camp fire burning bright,
Which was to them a cheerful sight,
And they caressed Old Jack for guiding them home that
    night.
And they felt thankful to God for their safety,
And they danced around Old Jack with their hearts full of glee,
And Old Jack became a favourite from that day,
Because he saved them from being lost on the wild prairie

THE IRISH CONVICT'S RETURN

Ye mountains and glens of Old Ireland,
    I've returned home to ye again ;
During my absence from ye
    My heart always felt great pain.

Oh, how I long'd to see you dear Nora,
    And the old folks at home ;
And the beautiful Lakes o' Killarney,
    Where we oft together did roam.

Ye beautiful Lakes of Killarney,
    Ye are welcome to me again ;
I will now reform my character,
    And from all bad company refrain.

Oh, how I have long'd to see my old father
    And my mother dearer than all ;
And my favour to dog Charlie
    That wont to come at my call.

Ye green hills and lakes of Old Ireland,
    Ye are dearer than life unto me ;
Many sleepless nights I have had
    Since my banishment from thee.

But to-night I will see the old folks
    And my dear Nora too . . .
And she and I will get married,
    And I'm sure we will never rue.

And we may have plenty of children,
    And for them I will work like a man.
And I hope Nora and I will live happy,
    And do the best we can.

For my own part, I will never grumble,
    But try and be content . . .
And walk in the paths of virtue,
    And remember my banishment.

And at night at the fireside with Nora,
    I will tell her of my limbs being bound,
And all my great hardships endured,
    And how I was lash'd like a hound.

And when my story is ended,
    Nora will sympathise with her tears,
Which will help to drown my sorrow,
    And help me through coming years.

49

LITTLE JAMIE

Ither laddies may ha'e finer claes, and may be better fed,
But nane o' them a' has sic a bonnie curly heid,
O sic a blythe blink in their e'e,
As my ain curly fair-hair'd laddie, Little Jamie.

When I gang oot tae tak' a walk wi' him, alang the Magdalen
    Green,
It mak's my heart feel lichtsome tae see him sae sharp and
    keen,
And he pu's the wee gowans, and gie's them to me,
My ain curly fair-hair'd laddie, Little Jamie.

When he rises in the mornin' an' gets oot o' bed,
He says, mither, mind ye'll need tae toast my faither's bread.
For he aye gie's me a bawbee ;
He's the best little laddie that ever I did see,
My ain curly fair-hair'd laddie, Little Jamie.

When I gang oot tae tak' a walk alang the streets o' Dundee,
And views a' the little laddies that I chance to see,
Nane o' them a' seems sae lovely to me,
As my ain curly fair-hair'd laddie, Little Jamie.

The laddie is handsome and fair to be seen,
He has a bonnie cheerie mou', and taw blue e'en,
And he prattles like an auld grandfaither richt merrily ;
He's the funniest little laddie that ever I did see,
My ain curly fair-hair'd laddie, Little Jamie.

Whene'er that he kens I am coming hame frae my wark,
He runs oot tae meet me as cheerful as the lark,
And he says, faither, I'm wanting just a'e bawbee,
My ain curly fair-hair'd laddie, Little Jamie.

AN ADDRESS TO THE REV. GEORGE GILFILLAN

All hail to the Rev. George Gilfillan of Dundee,
He is the greatest preacher I did ever hear or see.
He is a man of genius bright,
And in him his congregation does delight,
Because they find him to be honest and plain,
Affable in temper, and seldom known to complain.
He preaches in a plain straightforward way,
The people flock to hear him night and day,
And hundreds from the doors are often turn'd away,
Because he is the greatest preacher of the present day.
He has written the life of Sir Walter Scott,
And while he lives he will never be forgot,
Nor when he is dead,
Because by his admirers it will be often read ;
And fill their minds with wonder and delight,
And wile away the tedious hours on a cold winter's night.
He has also written about the Bards of the Bible,
Which occupied nearly three years in which he was not idle,
Because when he sits down to write he does it with might
    and main,
And to get an interview with him it would be almost vain,
And in that he is always right,
For the Bible tells us whatever your hands findeth to do,
Do it with all your might.
Rev. George Gilfillan of Dundee, I must conclude my muse,
And to write in praise of thee my pen does not refuse,
Nor does it give me pain to tell the world fearlessly, that
    when
You are dead they shall not look upon your like again.

AN ADDRESS TO SHAKESPEARE

Immortal! William Shakespeare, there's none can you excel,
You have drawn out your characters remarkably well,
Which is delightful for to see enacted upon the stage—
For instance, the love-sick Romeo, or Othello, in a rage ;
His writings are a treasure, which the world cannot repay,
He was the greatest poet of the past or of the present day—
Also the greatest dramatist, and is worthy of the name,
I'm afraid the world shall never look upon his like again.
His tragedy of Hamlet is moral and sublime,
And for purity of language, nothing can be more fine—
For instance, to hear the fair Ophelia making her moan,
At her father's grave, sad and alone. . . .
In his beautiful play, " As You Like It," one passage is very
    fine,
Just for instance in the forest of Arden, the language is
    sublime,
Where Orlando speaks of his Rosalind, most lovely and
    divine,
And no other poet I am sure has written anything more fine ;
His language is spoken in the Church and by the Advocate
    at the bar,
Here and there and everywhere throughout the world afar ;
His writings abound with gospel truths, moral and sublime,
And I'm sure in my opinion they are surpassing fine ;
In his beautiful tragedy of Othello, one passage is very fine,
Just for instance where Cassio looses his lieutenancy
. . . By drinking too much wine ;
And in grief he exclaims, " Oh! that men should put an
Enemy in their mouths to steal away their brains."
In his great tragedy of Richard the III., one passage is very
    fine

Where the Duchess of York invokes the aid of the Divine
For to protect her innocent babes from the murderer's
    uplifted hand,
And smite him powerless, and save her babes, I'm sure 'tis
    really grand.
Immortal! Bard of Avon, your writings are divine,
And will live in the memories of your admirers until the end
    of time ;
Your plays are read in family circles with wonder and
    delight,
While seated around the fireside on a cold winter's night.

THE FAIR MAID OF PERTH'S HOUSE

All ye good people, afar and near,
To my request pray lend an ear ;
I advise you all without delay to go
And see the Fair Maid's House—it is a rare show.

Some of the chairs there are very grand,
They have been cut and carved by a skilful hand ;
And kings, perchance, if the truth were told,
Have sat on them in days of old.

King James the First of Scotland was murdered there,
And his cries for mercy rent the air.
But the Highland robbers only laughed at him,
And murdered him in the dungeon and thought it no sin.

Then there's an ancient shrine upstairs,
Where the Monks and Saints said their prayers,
To the Holy Virgin, be it told ;
And the house, it is said, is six hundred years old.

The old cruisie lamps are there to be seen,
Which let the monks see to write from their sheen,
And if the walls could speak, they could tell a fearful tale,
Which would make the people's cheeks turn pale.

Then there's an old claymore dug up from Culloden Moor,
Which in its time shed innocent blood, I am sure,
If not at Culloden Moor, some other place,
Which no doubt the truth of it history might trace.

The interior of the house is magnificent to be seen,
And the wood panelling, I'm sure, would please the Queen;
And the old fire-place, with its big fire,
Is all that visitors could desire.

Then there's a ring in a big stone near by the door,
Where gentlemen tethered their horses in days of yore;
And on the staircase door there's a tirling pin
For making a rattling noise when anyone wanted in.

The mistress of the house is very kind,
A more affable woman would be hard to find;
And to visitors she is very good,
And well versed in history, be it understood.

THE QUEEN'S DIAMOND JUBILEE

CELEBRATIONS

'Twas in the year of 1897, and on the 22nd of June,
Her Majesty's Diamond Jubilee in London caused a great
    boom;
Because high and low came from afar to see,
The grand celebrations at Her Majesty's Diamond Jubilee.

People were there from almost every foreign land,
Which made the scene really imposing and grand ;
Especially the Queen's carriage, drawn by eight cream-
    coloured bays,
And when the spectators saw it joyous shouts they did
    raise.

Oh! it was a most gorgeous sight to be seen,
Numerous foreign magnates were there for to see the Queen ;
And to the vast multitude there of women and men,
Her Majesty for two hours showed herself to them.

The head of the procession looked very grand—
A party of the Horse Guards with their gold-belaced band ;
Which also headed the procession of the Colonial States,
While slowly they rode on until opposite the Palace gates.

Then the sound of the National Anthem was heard quite
    clear,
And the sound the hearts of the mighty crowd it did cheer ;
As they heard the loyal hymning on the morning air,
The scene was most beautiful and surpassing fair.

On the house tops thousands of people were to be seen,
All in eager expectation of seeing the Queen ;
And all of them seemed to be happy and gay,
Which enhanced the scene during the day.

And when Field Marshal Roberts in the procession passed by,
The cheers from thousands of people arose very high ;
And to see him on his war horse was inspiring to see,
Because he rode his charger most splendidly.

The Natal mounted troops were loudly cheered, they looked
     so grand,
And also the London Irish Emerald Isle Band ;
Oh it was a most magnificent sight to see.
The Malta Militia and Artillery,
And the Trinidad Artillery, and also bodies of infantry,
And, as the crowd gazed thereon, it filled their hearts with
     glee.

Her Majesty looked well considering her years,
And from the vast crowd burst forth joyous cheers ;
And Her Majesty bowed to the shouts of acclamation,
And smiled upon the crowd with a loving look of admiration.

His Excellency Chan Yin Hun in his carriage was a great
     attraction,
And his Oriental garb seemed to give the people great
     satisfaction ;
While the two little Battenberg's carriage, as it drove along,
Received from the people cheering loud and long.

And when the Dragoon Guards and the Hussars filed past
     at the walk,
Then loudly in their praise the people did talk ;
And the cavalry took forty minutes to trot past,
While the spectators in silent wonder stood aghast.

Her Majesty the Empress Frederick a great sensation made,
She was one of the chief attractions in the whole cavalcade ;
And in her carriage was the Princess Louise, the Marchioness
     of Lorne,
In a beautiful white dress, which did per person adorn.

The scene in Piccadilly caused a great sensation,
The grand decorations there were the theme of admiration ;
And the people in St. James Street were taken by
surprise,
Because the lovely decorations dazzled their eyes

The 42nd Highlanders looked very fine,
When they appeared and took up a position on the line ;
And the magnificent decorations in the Strand,
As far east as the Griffin was attractive and grand.

And the grandstand from Buckingham Palace to Temple
Bar,
Was crowded with eager eyes from afar,
Looking on the floral decorations and flags unfurled,
Which has been the grandest spectacle ever seen in the
world.

The corner building of St. James Street side was lovely to
view,
Ornamented with pink and white bunting and a screen of
blue ;
And to the eye, the inscription thereon most beautiful
seems :
" Thou art alone the Queen of earthly Queens."

The welcome given to Commander-in-Chief Lord Wolseley
was very flattering,
The people cheered him until the streets did ring ;
And the foreign princes were watched with rivetted
admiration,
And caused among the sight-seers great consternation.

And private householders seemed to vie with each
other,
In the lavishness of their decorations, and considered it no
bother ;
And never before in the memory of man,
Has there been a national celebration so grand.

And in conclusion, I most earnestly do pray,
May God protect Her Majesty for many a day ;
My blessing on her noble form and on her lofty head,
And may she wear a crown of glory hereafter when dead

AN ODE TO THE QUEEN

All hail to the Empress of India, Great Britain's Queen!
Long may she live in health, happy and serene ;
   Loved by her subjects at home and abroad ;
Blest may she be when lying down
   To sleep, and rising up, by the Eternal God ;
Happy may her visions be in sleep . . .
   And happy her thoughts in the day time ;
Let all loyal subjects drink to her health
   In a flowing bumper of Rhenish Wine.
And when the final hour shall come to summon her away,
May her soul be wafted to the realms of bliss,
   I most sincerely do pray, to sing with saints above,
Where all is joy, peace and love—
    In Heaven, for evermore to reign,
    God Save the Queen.　Amen.

THE DEATH OF THE QUEEN

Alas! our noble and generous Queen Victoria is dead,
And I hope her soul to Heaven has fled,
To sing and rejoice with saints above,
Where all is joy, peace, and love.

'Twas on January 22, 1901, in the evening she died at 6.30
    o'clock,
Which to the civilised world has been a great shock ;
She was surrounded by her children and grandchildren dear,
And for the motherly, pious Queen they shed many a tear.

She has been a model and faithful Queen,
Very few like her have been ;
She has acted virtuously during her long reign,
And I'm afraid the world will never see her like again.

And during her reign she was beloved by the high and the
    low,
And through her decease the people's hearts are full of woe,
Because she was kind to her subjects at home and abroad,
And now she's receiving her reward from the Eternal God.

And during her reign in this world of trouble and strife
Several attempts were made to take her life ;
Maclean he tried to shoot her, but he did fail,
But he was arrested and sent to an asylum, which made him
    bewail.

Victoria was a noble Queen, the people must confess,
She was most charitable to them while in distress ;
And in her disposition she wasn't proud nor vain,
And tears for her loss will fall as plentiful as rain.

The people around Balmoral will shed many tears
Owing to her visits amongst them for many years ;
She was very kind to the old, infirm women there,
By giving them provisions and occasionally a prayer.

And while at Balmoral she found work for men unemployed,
Which made the hearts of the poor men feel overjoyed ;
And for Her Majesty they would have laid down their lives,
Because sometimes she saved them from starving, and their
    wives.

Many happy days she spent at Balmoral,
Viewing the blooming heather and the bonnie Highland
    floral,
Along with Prince Albert, her husband dear,
But alas! when he died she shed many a tear.

She was very charitable, as everybody knows,
But the loss of her husband caused her many woes,
Because he cheered her at Balmoral as they the heather trod,
But I hope she has met him now at the Throne of God.

They ascended the Hill of Morven when she was in her
    fortieth year,
And Her Majesty was delighted as she viewed the Highland
    deer ;
Also dark Lochnagar, which is most beautiful to see,
Not far from Balmoral and the dark River Dee.

I hope they are walking in Heaven together as they did in life,
In the beautiful celestial regions, free from all strife,
Where God's family together continually meet,
Where the streets are paved with gold, and everything
    complete.

Alas! for the loss of Queen Victoria the people will mourn,
But she unto them can never return ;
Therefore to mourn for her is all in vain,
Knowing that she can never return again.

Therefore, good people, one and all,
Let us be prepared for death when God does on us call,
Like the good and noble Queen Victoria of renown,
The greatest and most virtuous Queen that ever wore a
    crown.

A HUMBLE HEROINE

'Twas at the Seige of Matagarda, during the Peninsular War,
That a Mrs Reston for courage outshone any man there by
    far ;
She was the wife of a Scottish soldier in Matagarda Fort,
And to attend to her husband she there did resort.

'Twas in the Spring of the year 1810,
That General Sir Thomas Graham occupied Matagarda with
    150 men ;
These consisted of a detachment from the Scots Brigade,
And on that occasion they weren't in the least afraid.

And Captain Maclaine of the 94th did the whole of them
    command,
And the courage the men displayed was really grand ;
Because they held Matagarda for fifty-four days,
Against o'erwhelming numbers of the French—therefore
    they are worthy of praise.

The British were fighting on behalf of Spain,
But if they fought on their behalf they didn't fight in vain ;
For they beat them manfully by land and sea,
And from the shores of Spain they were forced to flee.

Because Captain Maclaine set about repairing the old fort,
So as to make it comfortable for his men to resort ;
And there he kept his men at work day by day,
Filling sand-bags and stuffing them in the walls without delay.

There was one woman in the fort during those trying days,
A Mrs Reston, who is worthy of great praise ;
She acted like a ministering angel to the soldiers while there,
By helping them to fill sand-bags, it was her constant care.

Mrs Reston behaved as fearlessly as any soldier in the
    garrison,
And amongst the soldiers golden opinions she won,
For her presence was everywhere amongst the men,
And the service invaluable she rendered to them.

Methinks I see that brave heroine carrying her child,
Whilst the bullets were falling around her, enough to drive
    her wild ;
And bending over it to protect it from danger,
Because to war's alarms it was a stranger.

And while the shells shrieked around, and their fragments
    did scatter,
She was serving the men at the guns with wine and water ;
And while the shot whistled around, her courage wasn't
    slack,
Because to the soldiers she carried sand-bags on her back.

A little drummer boy was told to fetch water from the well,
But he was afraid because the bullets from the enemy
    around it fell ;
And the Doctor cried to the boy, Why are you standing
    there ?
But Mrs Reston said, Doctor, the bairn is feared, I do
    declare.

And she said, Give me the pail, laddie, I'll fetch the water,
Not fearing that the shot would her brains scatter ;
And without a moment's hesitation she took the pail,
Whilst the shot whirred thick around her, yet her courage
    didn't fail.

And to see that heroic woman the scene was most grand,
Because as she drew the water a shot cut the rope in her
    hand ;
But she caught the pail with her hand dexterously,
Oh! the scene was imposing and most beautiful to see.

The British fought bravely, as they are always willing to do,
Although their numbers were but few ;
So they kept up the cannonading with their artillery,
And stood manfully at their guns against the enemy.

And five times the flagstaff was shot away,
And as often was it replaced without dismay ;
And the flag was fastened to an angle of the wall,
And the British resolved to defend it whatever did befall.

So the French were beaten and were glad to run,
And the British for defeating them golden opinions have won ;
All through brave Captain Maclaine and his heroes bold,
Likewise Mrs Reston, whose name should be written in
    letters of gold.

NORA, THE MAID OF KILLARNEY

Down by the beautiful Lakes of Killarney,
Oft times I have met my own dear Barney,
In the sweet summer time of the year,
In the silvery moonlight so clear,
I've rambled with my sweetheart Barney,
Along the green banks of the Lakes of Killarney.

The Lakes of Killarney are most lovely to be seen
In the summer season when nature's face is green,
Especially in the beautiful silvery moonlight,
When its waters do shine like silver bright;
Such was the time when me and my Barney
Went to walk by the purty Lakes of Killarney.

My Barney was beautiful, gallant, and gay,
But, alas, he has left me and gone far away,
To that foreign country called Amerikay;
But when he returns we will get married without delay,
And again we will roam by the Lakes of Killarney,
Me and my sweetheart, charming Barney.

And until he returns I will feel rather sad,
For while walking with Barney I always felt glad;
May God send him home again safe to me,
And he will fill my sad heart with glee,
While we walk by the Lakes of Killarney.

I dreamt one night I was walking with Barney,
Down by the beautiful Lakes of Killarney,
And he said, " Nora, dear Nora, don't fret for me,
For I will soon come home to thee ;
And I will build a nice cabin near the Lakes of Killarney,
And Nora will live happy with her own dear Barney."

But, alas, I awoke from my beautiful dream,
For, och, it was a most lovely scene ;
But I hope it will happen some unexpected day,
When Barney comes home from Amerikay ;
Then Barney will relate his adventures to me,
As we walk by the silvery Lakes of Killarney.

We will ramble among its green trees and green bushes,
And hear the sweet songs of the blackbirds and thrushes,
And gaze on its lovely banks so green,
And its waters glittering like crystal in the moonlight's
    sheen ;
Och! how I long to be walking with Barney,
Along the green banks of the Lakes of Killarney.

Of all the spots in Ireland, Killarney for me,
For 'twas there I first met my dear Barney :
He was singing, I remember, right merrily ;
And his singing filled my heart with glee,
And he said, " Nora, dear Nora, will you walk with me,
For you are the prettiest girl I ever did see."

" Now, Barney," I said, " you are just mocking me,
When you say no other girl like me you can see " ;
Then he said, " Nora, you are the only girl I do love,
And this I do swear by the saints above,
I will marry you, dear Nora, without delay,
When I come home from Amerikay."

But when Barney landed in Amerikay,
He courted another girl without dismay,
And he married her in the month of May,
And when I heard it I fainted away ;
So maidens beware of such men as Barney,
Or else they will deceive ye with their flattering blarney.

LITTLE POPEET : THE LOST CHILD

Near by the silent waters of the Mediterranean,
And at the door of an old hut stood a coloured man,
Whose dress was oriental in style and poor with wear,
While adown his furrowed cheeks ran many a tear.

And the poor coloured man seemed very discontent,
And his frief overcame him at this moment ;
And he wrung his hands in agony wild,
And he cried, " Oh! help me, great God, to find my child.

" And Ada, my dear wife, but now she is dead,
Which fills my poor heart with sorrow and dread ;
She was a very loving wife, but of her I'm bereft,
And I and my lost child are only left.

And, alas! I know not where to find my boy,
Who is dear to me and my only joy ;
But with the help of God I will find him,
And this day in search of him I will begin."

So Medoo leaves Turkey and goes to France,
Expecting to find his boy there perhaps by chance ;
And while there in Paris he was told
His boy by an Arab had been sold

To a company of French players that performed in the street,
Which was sad news to hear about his boy Popeet ;
And while searching for him and making great moan,
He was told he was ill and in Madame Mercy's Home.

Then away went Medoo with his heart full of joy,
To gaze upon the face of his long-lost boy ;
Who had been treated by the players mercilessly,
But was taken to the home of Madame Celeste.

She was a member of the players and the leader's wife,
And she loved the boy Popeet as dear as her life,
Because she had no children of her own ;
And for the poor ill-treated boy often she did moan.

And when Popeet's father visited the Home,
He was shown into a room where Popeet lay alone,
Pale and emaciated, in his little bed ;
And when his father saw he he thought he was dead.

And when Popeet saw his father he lept out of bed,
And only that his father caught him he'd been killed dead ;
And his father cried, " Popeet, my own darling boy,
Thank God I've found you, and my heart's full of joy."

Then Madame Mercy's tears fell thick and fast,
When she saw that Popeet had found his father at last ;
Then poor Popeet was taken home without delay,
And lived happy with his father for many a day.

THE LITTLE MATCH GIRL

It was biting cold, and the falling snow,
Which filled a poor little match girl's heart with woe,
Who was bareheaded and barefooted, as she went along the
    street,
Crying, " Who'll buy my matches ? for I want pennies to
    buy some meat! "

When she left home she had slippers on ;
But, alas! poor child, now they were gone.
For she lost both of them while hurrying across the street,
Out of the way of two carriages which were near by her feet.

So the little girl went on, while the snow fell thick and fast ;
And the child's heart felt cold and downcast,
For nobody had bought any matches that day,
Which filled her little mind with grief and dismay.

Alas! she was hungry and shivering with cold ;
So in a corner between two houses she made bold
To take shelter from the violent storm.
Poor little waif! wishing to herself she'd never been born.

And she grew colder and colder, and feared to go home
For fear of her father beating her ; and she felt woe-begone
Because she could carry home no pennies to buy bread,
And to go home without pennies she was in dread.

The large flakes of snow covered her ringlets of fair hair ;
While the passers-by for her had no care,
As they hurried along to their homes at a quick pace,
While the cold wind blew in the match girl's face.

As night wore on her hands were numb with cold,
And no longer her strength could her uphold,
When an idea into her little head came :
She'd strike a match and warm her hands at the flame.

And she lighted the match, and it burned brightly,
And it helped to fill her heart with glee ;
And she thought she was sitting at a stove very grand ;
But, alas! she was found dead, with a match in her hand!

Her body was found half-covered with snow,
And as the people gazed thereon their hearts were full of woe;
And many present let fall a burning tear
Because she was found dead on the last night of the year,

In that mighty city of London, wherein is plenty of gold—
But, alas! their charity towards street waifs is rather cold.
But I hope the match girl's in Heaven, beside her Saviour
    dear,
A bright reward for all the hardships she suffered here.

A TALE OF ELSINORE

A little child stood thinking, sorrowfully and ill at ease,
In a forest beneath the branches of the tall pine trees—
And his big brown eyes with tears seemed dim,
While one soft arm rested on a huge dog close by him.

And only four summers had passed o'er his baby head,
And, poor little child, his twin brother was dead,
Who had died but a few days before,
And now he must play alone, for he'd see him no more.

And for many generations 'tis said for a truth
That the eldest born of the Cronberg family died early in
    youth,
Owing to a curse that pursued them for many a day,
Because the Cronberg chief had carried a lovely maiden
    away,

That belonged, 'tis said, to the bold Viking chief,
And her aged mother could find no relief ;
And she cursed the Cronberg family in accents wild,
For the loss of her darling, beautiful child.

So at last the little child crept back to its home,
And entered the silent nursery alone,
Where he knew since morning his twin brother had lain,
But, alas! they would never walk hand in hand again.

And, pausing breathless, he gazed into the darkened room,
And there he saw in the dark gloom
The aged Gudrun keeping her lonely watch o'er the dead,
Sad and forlorn at the head of the bed.

Then little Olaf sprang joyfully into the room,
And bounding upon the bed, not fearing the corpse in the
    gloom ;
And crept close beside the white form,
That was wont to walk by his side night and morn.

And with his dimpled hands his brother he did stroke,
And with grief his little heart almost broke ;
And he whispered in baby talk his brother's name,
But, alas! to him no answer came.

But his good old nurse let little Olaf be,
The more it was very sad to see ;
But she could not check the child, nor on him frown,
And as she watched him, the tears came trickling down.

Then Olaf cried, " Oh, nursey, when will he speak again ? "
And old Gudrun said, " My lamb, 'tis all in vain,
He is singing sweet songs with the angels now,"
And kissed him fondly on cheek and brow.

And the same evening, Olaf wandered out on the green,
Which to him and his brother oft a playground had been ;
And lying down on the mossy bank, their old play place,
He fell asleep with a heavenly smile upon his face.

And as he slept it seemed to him an angel drew near,
And bending o'er him seemed to drop a tear,
And swept his closed eyes with her downy wing,
Then in whispers softly she did sing—

" Love God and be good to all, and one day
You'll meet your brother in Heaven in grand array,
On that bright and golden happy shore,
Where you and your brother shall part no more."

Then the angel kissed him and vanished away,
And Olaf started to his feet in great dismay ;
Then he turned his eyes to Heaven, for his heart felt sore,
And from that day the house of Cronberg was cursed no
    more.

THE BONNIE SIDLAW HILLS

Bonnie Clara, will you go to the bonnie Sidlaw hills
And pu' the blooming heather, and drink from their rills ?
There the cranberries among the heather grow,
Believe me, dear Clara, as black as the crow.

Chorus—

Then, bonnie Clara, will you go
And wander with me to and fro ?
And with joy our hearts will o'erflow
When we go to the bonnie Sidlaws O.

And the rabbits and hares sport in mirthful glee
In the beautiful woods of Glen Ogilvy,
And innocent trout do sport and play
In the little rivulet of Glen Ogilvy all the day.

Chorus—

And in the bonnie woods of Sidlaw the blackbird doth sing,
Making the woodlands with his notes to ring,
Which ought to make a dull heart feel gay,
And help to cheer us on our way.

Chorus—

And there the innocent sheep are to be seen
Browsing on the purple heather and pastures green ;
And the shepherd can be heard shouting to his dog
As he chases the sheep from out of the bog.

Chorus—

And from the tops of the Sidlaws can be seen
The beautiful Howe of Strathmore with its trees and
    shrubberies green ;
Likewise Lochee and its spinning mills
Can be seen on a clear day from the Sidlaw hills.

Chorus—

Therefore, bonnie Clara, let's away
To Sidlaw hills without delay,
And pu' the cranberries and bonnie blooming heather
While we wander to and fro on the Sidlaws together.

Chorus—

There the lovers can enjoy themselves free from care
By viewing the hilly scenery and inhaling the fresh air,
And return home at night with their hearts full of glee
After viewing the beauties of the Sidlaw hills and Glen
    Ogilvy.

Chorus—

BONNIE CALLANDER

Chorus—

Bonnie Helen, will you go to Callander with me
And gaze upon its beauties and romantic scenery ?
Dear Helen, it will help to drive all sorrow away ;
Therefore come, sweet Helen, and let's have a holiday.

Callander is a pretty little town most lovely to see,
Situated in the midst of mountains towering frowningly;
And Ben Ledi is the chief amongst them and famous in
    history,
Looking stern and rugged in all its majesty.

Chorus—

And as for Bracklinn Falls, they are impressive to sight,
Especially the Keltie, which will the visitor's heart delight,
With its bonnie banks bordered with beautiful trees,
And the effect would be sure the spectator to please.

Chorus—

The hawthorn hedges and the beautiful wild flowers
Will help to enliven the scene and while away the hours ;
And as the spectator gazes upon Keltie waterfall,
The rumbling and tumbling of the water does his heart appal.

Chorus—

As it makes one fearful plunge into a yawning abyss below,
Fifty or sixty feet beneath, where it splashes to and fro,
And seethes and boils in a great deep pool,
And the sweet, fragrant air around it is very cool.

Chorus—

'Tis said two lovers met there with a tragic fate.
Alas! poor souls, and no one near to extricate.
The rail of the bridge upon which they were leaning gave
way,
And they were drowned in the boiling gulf. Oh, horror and
dismay!

Chorus—

The Pass of Leny is most wild and amazing to see,
With its beetling crags and towering mountains and romantic
scenery ;

And the brawling Leny, with its little waterfalls,
Will repay the visitor for the time occupied any time he calls.

Chorus—

Then lovers of the picturesque make haste and go away
To the pretty little village of Callander without delay,
And breathe the fresh air in the harvest time,
And revel amongst romantic scenery in the beautiful
    sunshine.

BONNIE KILMANY

Bonnie Kilmany, in the County of Fife,
Is a healthy spot to reside in to lengthen one's life.
The scenery there in the summer time is truly grand,
Especially the beautiful hills and the woodland.

Chorus—

    Then, bonnie Annie, will you go with me
    And leave the crowded city of Dundee,
    And breathe the pure, fragrant air
    In the Howe of Kilmany, so lovely and fair ?

And the little village in the Howe is lovely to see,
In the midst of green trees and shrubbery ;
And the little rivulet, as it wimples along,
Can be heard singing aloud an aquatic song.

Chorus—

And the old church there is built on a knoll,
And on the Sabbath mornings the church bell does toll,
Inviting the people to join in prayer,
While the echoes of the bell is heard in mid-air.

Chorus—

Then there's a little schoolroom, surrounded by trees,
A favourite haunt for butterflies and busy bees,
And an old red-tiled smithy near by,
And the clink of the hammers can be heard sounding high.

Chorus—

And there's a wood sawmill by the roadway,
And the noise can be heard by night and day,
As the circular saw wheels round and round,
Making the village with its echoes resound.

Chorus—

And in the harvest time on a fine summer morn
The Howe looks most beautiful when the corn is shorn ;
And to hear the beautiful lark singing on high
Will make you exclaim, " Dull care, good-bye."

Chorus—

BONNIE MONTROSE

Beautiful town of Montrose, I will now commence my lay,
And I will write in praise of thee without dismay ;
And, in spite of all your foes,
I will venture to call thee Bonnie Montrose.

Your Chain Bridge is most magnificent to be seen,
Spanning the River Esk, a beautiful tidal stream,
Which abounds with beautiful trout and salmon,
And can be had for the catching without any gammon.

Then as for the Mid Links, it is most charming to be seen,
And I'm sure it's a very nice bowling green ;
There the people can enjoy themselves and inhale pure air
Emanating from the sea and beautiful flowers there.

And as for the High Street, it's most beautiful to see,
There's no street can surpass it in the town of Dundee,
Because it is so long and wide
That the people can pass on either side
Without jostling one another
Or going to any bother.

Beautiful town of Montrose near by the seaside,
With your fine ships and streets so wide ;
'Tis health for the people that in you reside,
Because they inhale the pure, fragrant air
Emanating from the sea waves and shrubberies there ;
And the inhabitants of Montrose ought to feel gay
Because you are one of the bonniest towns in Scotland at the
    present day.

BEAUTIFUL COMRIE

AND ITS SURROUNDINGS

Ye lovers of the picturesque, away, away!
To beautiful Comrie and have a holiday ;
And bask in the sunshine and inhale the fragrant air
Emanating from the woodlands and shrubberies there.

The charming village of Comrie is most lovely to be seen,
Especially in the summer season when the trees are green ;
And near by is Loch Earn and its waters sparkling clear,
And as the tourist gazes thereon his spirits it will cheer.

Then St. Fillans is a beautiful spot, I must confess,
It is really a picture of rural loveliness;
Because out of the quiet lake the river ripples merrily,
And all round are hills beautiful in shape and nothing
uncomely.

The rocky knoll to the south is a most seductive place,
And in the hotel there visitors will find every solace ;
And the flower-decked cottages are charming to see,
Also handsome villas suitable for visitors of high and low
degree.

Then there's St. Fillan's Hill, a prehistoric fort,
And visitors while there to it should resort ;
And to the tourist the best approach is from the west,
Because in climbing the hill his strength it will test.

And descending the hill as best one may,
The scene makes the tourist's heart feel gay ;
And by the west side is reached a wooded dell,
And about two hundred yards from that there's St. Fillan's
 Well.

Oh, charming Comrie! I must conclude my lay,
And to write in praise of thee I virtually do say
That your lovely mountains and silver birches will drive dull
 care away :
Therefore lovers of the picturesque, away, away!

To beautiful Comrie and have a holiday,
And I'm sure you will return with spirits light and gay,
After viewing the Sylvan beauties and hoary beeches there,
Also pines, ferns, and beautiful oaks, I do declare.

BEAUTIFUL NORTH BERWICK

AND ITS SURROUNDINGS

North Berwick is a watering-place with golfing links green,
With a fine bathing beach most lovely to be seen ;
And there's a large number of handsome villas also,
And often it's called the Scarborough of Scotland, as
 Portobello.

The greatest attraction is Tantallon Castle, worthy of
 regard,
About three miles distant to the eastward ;
Which in time of war received many a shock,
And it's deemed impregnable and built on a perpendicular
 rock.

The castle was built in times unknown to history,
But 'tis said it belonged to the Douglas family ;
And the inside is a labyrinth of broken staircases,
Also ruined chambers and many dismal places.

Then there's the Berwick Law Hill, 612 feet high,
Which no doubt is very attractive to the eye,
And skirted with a wood and a public walk,
Where visitors can enjoy themselves and have a social talk.

The wood is really lovely and enchanting to be seen,
In the spring or summer season when the trees are green ;
And as ye listen to the innocent birds singing merrily there,
'Twill help to elevate your spirits and drive away dull care.

Then near by Tantallon is the fishing village of Canty Bay,
Where boats can be hired to the Bass Rock, about two miles
        away ;
And the surrounding scenery is magnificent to see,
And as the tourists view the scene it fills their hearts with
        glee.

Then away! then away! pleasure-seekers in bands,
And view Gullane with its beautiful sands,
Which stretch along the sandy shores of Fife,
Where the tourist can enjoy himself and be free from strife·

BEAUTIFUL CRIEFF

Ye lovers of the picturesque, if ye wish to drown your grief,
Take my advice, and visit the ancient town of Crieff ;
The climate is bracing, and the walks lovely to see
Besides, ye can ramble over the district, and view the
    beautiful scenery.

The town is admirably situated from the cold winter winds,
And the visitors, during their stay there, great comfort finds,
Because there is boating and fishing, and admission free,
Therefore they can enjoy themselves right merrily.

There is also golf courses, tennis greens, and good roads,
Which will make the travelling easier to tourists with great
    loads,
And which will make the bicyclists' hearts feel gay,
Because they have everything there to make an enjoyable
    holiday.

The principal river there is the Earn, rolling on its way,
And which flows from Loch Earn, and joins the silvery Tay
Above Newburgh, after a course of more than thirty miles ;
And as the tourist views the scene with joy he smiles.

The princely domain of Drummond Castle is most beautiful
    to be seen,
Especially when the woody landscape is blown full green,
And from the entrance gate to the castle an avenue extends
    all the way,
And to view the branches of the trees interlacing makes the
    heart feel gay.

Drummond Castle's flowery gardens are really very grand ;
They cannot be surpassed in Great Britain,
And in the summer-time the bee and the butterfly are there
    on the wing,
And with the carolling of birds the gardens doth ring.

And from Knock Hill on the north and west,
The view from its summit is considered the best ;
Because the Grampians and the Ochils can be seen,
While the beautiful rich fertile valley lies between.

And there are many seats where the weary traveller can rest,
And there is also a fountain of water, the very best,
While visitors can drink of while resting there,
And gaze on the magnificent scenery and inhale the pure air.

Then there's Lady Mary's Walk near the Bridge of
    Turret,
Which I hope visitors will go and see and not forget,
Because near by grows a magnificent oak most lovely
    to see,
Which is known by the name of Eppie Callum's Tree.

And at each end of this walk the visitors can ascend Laggan
    Hill,
And as they view the woods and fields with joy their hearts
    will thrill ;
And they will find seats plenteous on this elevated bower,
On which they may rest and wile away the hour.

The Hydropathic is situated on an eminence most grand,
And is one of the largest buildings in fair Scotland ;
And capable of accommodating five hundred visitors, who
    often call there,
To recuperate their health and breathe the fragrant air.

Then there's Abercairny, which is most beautiful to view,
And Her Majesty the Queen visited the grounds in 1842 ;
And the park and the trees has the aspect of a southern
    scene,
And the lovely appearance of it gladdened the heart of our
    Queen.

Then there's the village of Foulis, which tourists ought to
    see,
Because the scenery there is charming and pretty ;
And there's a sycamore tree there that was planted 300 years
    ago,
And I'm sure the sight thereof will please both high and low.

Therefore, in conclusion, to all lovers of the beautiful I will
    say,
If ye really wish to spend an enjoyable holiday,
I would recommend Crieff for lovely scenery and pure air ;
Besides, the climate gives health to many visitors during
    their stay there.

BEATIFUL BALMORAL

Ye lovers of the picturesque, away and see
Beautiful Balmoral, near by the River Dee ;
There ye will see the deer browsing on the heathery hills,
While adown their sides run clear sparkling rills.

Which the traveller can drink of when he feels dry,
And admire the dark River Dee near by,
Rolling smoothly and silently on its way,
Which is most lovely to see on a summer day.

There the trout do sport and play
During the live-long summer day ;
Also plenty of salmon are there to be seen,
Glittering like silver in the sun's sheen.

And the mountains are rugged and wild to be seen,
But the woodlands are beautiful when Nature's face is green;
There numerous rabbits do gambol all day
Amongst the green shrubbery all lively and gay.

There's one charming spot most magnificent to be seen,
'Tis Balmoral Castle, the Highland Home of our Queen ;
The surrounding scenery is enchanting to see,
While near by rolls past the lovely River Dee.

Therefore, ye lovers of the picturesque, away and see
Beautiful Balmoral Castle and its grand scenery,
And the sight will fill your hearts with glee,
As ye walk along the bonnie banks o' the River Dee.

THE BEAUTIFUL VILLAGE OF PENICUIK

The village of Penicuik, with its neighbouring spinning mills,
Is most lovely to see, and the Pentland Hills ;
And though of a barren appearance and some parts steep,
They are covered with fine pasture and sustain flocks of
    sheep.

There, tourists while there should take a good look,
By viewing the surrounding beauties of Penicuik ;
About three miles south-west is the romantic locality
Of Newhall, which is most fascinating and charming to see.

Then about half a mile above Newhall the River Esk is seen,
Which sparkles like crystal in the sun's sheen ;
And on the Esk there's a forking ridge forming a linn
Betwixt two birch trees, which makes a noisy din.

And on a rocky protuberance close by is Mary Stuart's bower,
Where Scotland's ill-starred Queen spent many an hour,
Which is composed of turf and a nice round seat
Commanding a full view of the linn—the sight is quite a
    treat.

Then there's Habbie's Howe, where the beauties of summer
    grow,
Which cannot be excelled in Scotland for pastoral show ;
'Tis one of the most beautiful landscapes in fair Scotland,
For the scenery there is most charming and grand.

Then ye tourists to the village of Penicuik haste away,
And there spend the lovely summer day
By climbing the heathy, barren Pentland Hills,
And drink the pure water from their crystal rills.

BEAUTIFUL NAIRN

All ye tourists who wish to be away
From the crowded city for a brief holiday ;
The town of Nairn is worth a visit, I do confess,
And it's only about fifteen miles from Inverness.

And in the summer season it's a very popular bathing-place,
And the visitors from London and Edinburgh finds solace,
As they walk along the yellow sand beach inhaling fresh air ;
Besides, there's every accommodation for ladies and gentle-
     men there.

Then there's a large number of bathing coaches there,
And the climate is salubrious, and very warm the air ;
And every convenience is within the bathers' reach,
Besides, there's very beautiful walks by the sea beach.

The visitors to Nairn can pass away the time agreeably,
By viewing Tarbetness, which slopes downwards to the sea ;
And Queen Street is one of the prettiest thoroughfares,
Because there's splendid shops in it, and stocked with
    different wares.

And there's ornamental grounds, and lovely shady nooks,
Which is a great advantage to visitors while reading their
    books ;
And there's a certain place known as the Ladies' Beach,
So private that no intruder can them reach.

And there's many neat cottages with gardens very nice,
And picturesque villas, which can be rented at a reasonable
    price ;
Besides, there's a golf course for those that such a game seeks,
Which would prove a great attraction to the knights of clubs
    and cleeks.

The surrounding scenery of Nairn is magnificent to be seen,
Especially its fertile fields and woodlands so green ;
Besides, not far from Nairn, there's Cawdor Castle, the
    ancient seat
Of the noble Thanes of Cawdor, with its bold turrets so neat.

And its massive proportions is very imposing to see,
Because the arched entrance is secured by a drawbridge and
    a fosse ;
And visitors will be allowed all over the grounds to roam,
Besides shown over the castle if the Earl is not at home.

The scenery surrounding the castle is charming in the
    summer-time,
And the apples in the orchard there is very fine,
Also the flower-beds are most beautiful to see,
Especially in the month of June, when the birds sing merrily.

Then there's the ancient stronghold of the Hays of Lochloy,
And visitors when they see it will it heartily enjoy ;
And a little further on there's the blasted heath of Macbeth,
And a hillock where the witches are wont to dance till out
    of breath.

And as the visitors to Nairn walk along the yellow sand,
They can see, right across the Moray Firth, the Black Island
    so grand,
With its productive fields and romantic scenery,
And as the tourist gazes thereon his heart fills with ecstasy.

And Darnaway Castle is well worthy of praise,
And to oblige all visitors there are open days,
When they can see the castle where one thousand warriors
    in all
Oft have assembled in the Earl of Randolph's Hall.

And in conclusion I will say for good bathing Nairn is the
    best,
And besides its pleasant scenery is of historical interest ;
And the climate gives health to many visitors while there,
Therefore I would recommend Nairn for balmy pure air.

BEAUTIFUL TORQUAY

All ye lovers of the picturesque, away
To beautiful Torquay and spend a holiday ;
'Tis health for invalids for to go there
To view the beautiful scenery and inhale the fragrant air,
Especially in the winter and spring-time of the year,
When the weather is not too hot, but is balmy and clear.

Torquay lies in a very deep and well-sheltered spot,
And at first sight by strangers it won't be forgot ;
'Tis said to be the mildest place in all England,
And surrounded by lofty hills most beautiful and grand.

'Twas here that William of Orange first touched English
    ground,
And as he viewed the beautiful spot his heart with joy did
    rebound ;
And an obelisk marks the spot where he did stand,
And which for long will be remembered throughout England.

Torquay, with its pier and its diadem of white,
Is a most beautiful andi very dazzling sight,
With its white villas glttering on the sides of its green hills,
And as the tourist gazes thereon with joy his heart fills.

The heights around Torquay are most beautiful to be seen,
Especially when the trees and shrubberies are green,
And to see the pretty houses under the cliff is a treat,
And the little town enclosed where two deep valleys meet.

There is also a fine bathing establishment near the pier,
Where the tourist can bathe without any fear ;
And as the tourists there together doth stroll,
I advise them to visit a deep chasm called Daddy's Hole.

Then there's Bablicome, only two miles from Torquay,
Which will make the stranger's heart feel gay,
As he stands on the cliff four hundred feet above the sea,
Looking down, 'tis sure to fill his heart with ecstasy.

The lodging-houses at Bablicome are magnificent to be seen,
And the accommodation there would suit either king or
    queen,
And there's some exquisite cottages embowered in the
    woodland,
And sloping down to the sea shore, is really very grand.

You do not wonder at Napoleon's exclamation
As he stood on the deck of the " Bellerophon," in a fit of
    admiration,
When the vessel was lying to windbound,
He exclaimed—" Oh, what a beautiful country! " his joy
    was profound.

And as the tourist there in search of beautiful spots doth
    rove,
Let them not forget to enquire for Anstey's Cove,
And there they will see a beautiful beach of milky white,
And the sight will fill their hearts with delight.

Oh! beautiful Torquay, with your lovely scenery,
And your magnificent cottages sloping down to the sea,
You are the most charming spot in all England,
With your picturesque bay and villas most grand.

And, in conclusion, to tourists I will say,
Off! off to Torquay and make no delay,
For the scenery is magnificent, and salubrious the air,
And 'tis good for the health to reside there.

THE ANCIENT TOWN OF LEITH

Ancient town of Leith, most wonderful to be seen,
With your many handsome buildings, and lovely links so
    green,
And the first buildings I may mention are the Courthouse
    and Town Hall,
Also Trinity House, and the Sailors' Home of Call.

Then as for Leith Fort, it was erected in 1779, which is
    really grand,
And which is now the artillery headquarters in Bonnie
    Scotland ;
And as for the Docks, they are magnificent to see,
They comprise five docks, two piers, 1,141 yards long
    respectively.

And there's steamboat communication with London and the
    North of Scotland,
And the fares are really cheap and the accommodation most
    grand ;
Then there's many public works in Leith, such as flour mills,
And chemical works, where medicines are made for curing
    many ills.

Besides, there are sugar refineries and distilleries,
Also engineer works, saw-mills, rope-works, and breweries,
Where many of the inhabitants are daily employed,
And the wages they receive make their hearts feel over-
    joyed.

In past times Leith shared the fortunes of Edinboro',
Because it withstood nine months' siege, which caused them
    great sorrow ;
They fought against the Protestants in 1559 and in '60,
But they beat them back manfully and made them flee.

Then there's Bailie Gibson's fish shop, most elegant to be
    seen,
And the fish he sells there are beautiful and clean ;
And for himself, he is a very good man,
And to deny it there's few people can.

The suburban villas of Leith are elegant and grand,
With accommodation that might suit the greatest lady in
the land ;
And the air is pure and good for the people's health,—
And health, I'm sure, is better by far than wealth.

The Links of Leith are beautiful for golfers to play,
After they have finished the toils of the day ;
It is good for their health to play at golf there,
On that very beautiful green, and breathe the pure air.

The old town of Leith is situated at the junction of the River
of Leith,
Which springs from the land of heather and heath ;
And no part in the Empire is growing so rapidly,
Which the inhabitants of Leith are right glad to see.

And Leith in every way is in itself independent,
And has been too busy to attend to its own adornment ;
But I venture to say and also mention
That the authorities to the town will pay more attention.

Ancient town of Leith, I must now conclude my muse,
And to write in praise of thee my pen does not refuse,
Because the inhabitants to me have been very kind,
And I'm sure more generous people would be hard to find.

They are very affable in temper and void of pride,
And I hope God will always for them provide ;
May He shower His blessings upon them by land and sea,
Because they have always been very kind to me.

THE CITY OF PERTH

Beautiful Ancient City of Perth,
One of the fairest on the earth,
With your stately mansions and scenery most fine,
Which seems very beautiful in the summer time ;
And the beautiful silvery Tay,
Rolling smoothly on its way,
And glittering like silver in the sunshine—
And the Railway Bridge across it is really sublime.
The scenery is very beautiful when in full bloom,
It far excels the river Doon—
For the North Inch and South Inch is most beautiful to
    behold,
Where the buttercups do shine in the sunshine like gold.

And there's the Palace of Scone, most beautiful to be seen,
Near by the river Tay and the North Inch so green,
Whereon is erected the statue of Prince Albert, late husband
    of the Queen,
And also the statue of Sir Walter Scott is most beautiful to
    be seen,
Erected on the South Inch, which would please the Queen,
And recall to her memory his novels she has read—
And cause her to feel a pang for him that is dead.

Beautiful City of Perth, along the river Tay, I must conclude
    my lay,
And to write in praise of thee my heart does not gainsay,
To tell the world fearlessly, without the least dismay—
With your stately mansions and the beautiful river Tay,
You're one of the fairest Cities of the present day.

BONNIE DUNDEE IN 1878

Oh, Bonnie Dundee ! I will sing in thy praise
A few but true simple lays,
Regarding some of your beauties of the present day—
And virtually speaking, there's none can them gainsay ;
There's no other town I know of with you can compare
For spinning mills and lasses fair,
And for stately buildings there's none can excel
The beautiful Albert Institute or the Queen's Hotel,
For it is most handsome to be seen,
Where accommodation can be had for Duke, Lord or Queen,
And the four pillars of the front are made of Aberdeen
    granite, very fine,
And most beautiful does shine, just like a looking glass,
And for beauty and grandeur there's none can them surpass.
And your fine shops in Reform Street,
Very few can with them compete
For superfine goods, there's none can excel,
From Inverness to Clerkenwell.
And your Tramways, I must confess,
That they have proved a complete success,
Which I am right glad to see . . .
And a very great improvement to Bonnie Dundee.
And there's the Royal Arch, most handsome to be seen,
Erected to the memory of our Most Gracious Queen—
Most magnificent to see,
And a very great honour to the people of Dundee.
Then there's the Baxter Park, most beautiful to see,
And a great boon it is to the people of Dundee,
For there they can enjoy themselves when they are free from
    care,

By inhaling the perfumed air,
Emanating from the sweet flowers and green trees and
    shrubs there.
Oh, Bonnie Dundee! I must conclude my muse,
And to write in praise of thee, my pen does not refuse,
Your beauties that I have alluded to are most worthy to see,
And in conclusion, I will call thee Bonnie Dundee!

LOCH NESS

Beautiful Loch Ness,
The truth to express,
Your landscapes are lovely and gay,
Along each side of your waters, to Fort Augustus all the
    way,
Your scenery is romantic . . .
With rocks and hills gigantic . . .
Enough to make one frantic,
As they view thy beautiful heathery hills,
And their clear crystal rills,
And the beautiful woodlands so green,
On a fine summer day . . .
From Inverness all the way . . .
Where the deer and the roe together doth play ;
And the beautiful Falls of Foyers with its crystal spray,
As clear as the day,
Enchanting and gay,
To the traveller as he gazes thereon,
That he feels amazed with delight,
To see the water falling from such a height,
That his head feels giddy with the scene,
As he views the Falls of Foyers and the woodlands so green,

That he exclaims in an ecstasy of delight—
Oh, beautiful Loch Ness!
I must sincerely confess,
That you are the most beautiful to behold,
With your lovely landscapes and water so cold.
And as he turns from the scene, he says with a sigh—
Oh, beautiful Loch Ness! I must bid you good-bye.

A DESCRIPTIVE POEM ON THE
SILVERY TAY

Beautiful silvery Tay,
With your landscapes, so lovely and gay,
Along each side of your waters, to Perth all the way ;
No other river in the world has got scenery more fine,
Only I am told the beautiful Rhine,
Near to Wormit Bay, it seems very fine,
Where the Railway Bridge is towering above its waters
    sublime,
And the beautiful ship Mars,
With her Juvenile Tars,
Both lively and gay,
Does carelessly lie
By night and by day,
In the beautiful Bay
Of the silvery Tay.
Beautiful, beautiful! silvery Tay,
Thy scenery is enchanting on a fine summer day,
Near by Balmerino it is beautiful to behold,
When the trees are in full bloom and the cornfields seems
    like gold—

And nature's face seems gay,
And the lambkins they do play,
And the humming bee is on the wing,
It is enough to make one sing,
While they carelessly do stray,
Along the beautiful banks of the silvery Tay,
Beautiful silvery Tay, rolling smoothly on your way,
Near by Newport, as clear as the day,
Thy scenery around is charming I'll be bound . . .
And would make the heart of any one feel light and gay on a
    fine summer day,
To view the beautiful scenery along the banks of the silvery
    Tay.

THE DEN O' FOWLIS

Beautiful Den o' Fowlis, most charming to be seen
In the summer season, when your trees are green ;
Especially in the bright and clear month of June,
When your flowers and shrubberies are in full bloom.

There visitors can enjoy themselves during the holidays,
And be shaded by the trees from the sun's rays,
And admire the beautiful primroses that grow there ;
And inhale their sweet perfume that fills the air.

There the little children sport and play,
Blythe and gay during the live-long summer day,
In its beautiful green and cool shady bowers,
Chasing the bee and butterfly, and pulling the flowers.

There the Minnows loup and play ;
In the little rivulet all the day ;
Right in the hollow of that fairy-like Den,
Together in little shoals of nine or ten.

And the Mavis and Blackbird merrily sing,
Making the Den with their notes to ring ;
From high noon till sunset at night,
Filling the visitor's heart with delight.

Tis most lovely to see the trees arched overhead,
And the little rivulet rolling o'er its pebbly bed,
Ane near by is an old Meal Mill ;
Likewise an old Church and Churchyard where the dead lie
    still.

The Den is always cool in the summer time,
Because it is so closely shaded from the sunshine,
By the spreading branches of the trees,
While the murmuring of the rivulet is heard on the night
    breeze.

It is a very magnificent spot the Den o' Fowlis,
And where oft the wintry wind it howls,
Among its bare and leafless withered trees,
And with fear would almost make one's heart to freeze.

To be walking through it on a dark wintry night,
Because the bare trees seem like spectres to your sight,
And everything around seems dark and drear,
And fills the timid mind with an undefinable fear.

But in the summer season it is most lovely to see ;
With its fair flowers and romantic scenery,
Where the people can enjoy themselves all the day,
In the months of July, June, or May.

There the people can drink pure water when they are dry ;
From the wells of spring water in the Den near by,
Which God has provided for his creatures in that lonely spot,
And such a blessing to the people shouldn't be forgot.

THE INAUGURATION OF THE
HILL O' BALGAY

Beautiful Hill o' Balgay,
With your green trees and flowers fair,
'Tis health for the old and young
For to be walking there,
To breathe the fragrant air
Emanating from the green bushes
And beautiful flowers there,
Then they can through the burying-ground roam,
And read the epitaphs on the tombstones
Before they go home.
There the lovers can wander safe arm in arm,
For policemen are there to protect them from harm
And to watch there all day,
So that no accident can befall them
In the Hill o' Balgay.
Then there's Harry Scott's mansion,
Most beautiful to be seen,
Also the Law Hill, likewise the Magdalen Green,

And the silvery Tay,
Rolling on its way.
And the coast of Fife,
And the beautiful town of St. Andrews,
Where Cardinal Beaton lost his life ;
And to be seen on a clear summer day,
From the top of the beautiful Hill o' Balgay.
On the opening day of the Hill o' Balgay,
It was a most beautiful sight to see
Numerous bands, with flags and banners, assembled in
    Dundee,
All in grand procession, with spirits light, that day,
March'd out the Blackness Road to the Hill o' Balgay.
The Earl o' Dalhousie was there on the opening day,
Also Harry Scott, the young laird o' Balgay,
And he made a great speech to the people there,
And they applauded him with cries that rent the air.
The Earl o' Dalhousie made a fine speech in his turn,
And said there was only one thing that caus'd him to
    mourn,—
There was no protection from the rain in the Hill o' Balgay,
And he would give another five hundred pounds away
For to erect a shed for the people upon a rainy day,
To keep them dry and comfortable on the Hill o' Balgay.
Then the people applauded him with three loud cheers,
For their hearts were all opened, and flowed with joyous
    tears,
So they all dispers'd quietly with spirits light that day,
And that ended the inauguration of the Hill o' Balgay.

THE BONNIE LASS O' DUNDEE

O' a' the toons that I've been in,
   I dearly love Dundee,
It's there the bonnie lassie lives,
   The lass I love to see.
Her face is fair, broon is her hair,
   And dark blue is her e'e,
And aboon a' the lasses e'er I saw,
   There's nane like her to me—
The bonnie broon-hair'd lassie o' Bonnie Dundee.

I see her in my night dreams,
   Wi' her bonnie blue e'e,
And her face it is the fairest,
   That ever I did see ;
And aboon a' the lassies e'er I saw,
   There's nane like her to me,
For she makes my heart feel lichtsome,
   And I'm aye richt glad to see—
The bonnie broon-hair'd lassie o' Bonnie Dundee.

Her eyes, they beam with innocence,
   Most lovely for to see,
And her heart it is as free from guile,
   As a child on its mother's knee ;
And aboon a' the lasses e'er I saw,
   There's nane like her to me,
For she aye seems so happy,
   And has a blythe blink in her e'e—
The bonnie broon-hair'd lassie o' Bonnie Dundee.

The lassie is tidy in her claes,
  Baith neat and clean to see ;
And her body's sma and slender,
  And a neat foot has she ;
And aboon a' the lassies e'er I saw,
  There's nane like her to me—
The bonnie broon-hair'd lassie o' Bonnie Dundee.

She sings like the nightingale,
  Richt merrily, or a wee lintie,
Wi' its heart fou' o' glee,
  And she's as frisky as a bee ;
And aboon a' the lassies e'er I saw,
  There's nane like her to me—
The bonnie broon-hair'd lassie o' Bonnie Dundee.

The lassie is as handsome
  As the lily on the lea,
And her mou' it is as red
  As a cherry on the tree ;
And she's a' the world to me,
  The bonnie broon-hair'd lassie
Wi' the bonnie blue e'e,
  She's the joy o' my heart
And the flower o' Dundee.

THE BONNIE LASS OF RUILY

'Twas in the village of Ruily there lived a bonnie lass
With red, pouting lips which few lasses could surpass,
And her eyes were as azure the blue sky,
Which caused Donald McNeill to heave many a love sigh.

Beyond the township of Ruily she never had been,
This pretty maid with tiny feet and aged eighteen ;
And when Donald would ask her to be his wife,
" No," she would say, " I'm not going to stay here all my
    life."

" I'm sick of this life," she said to Donald one day,
" By making the parridge and carrying peats from the bog
    far away."
" Then marry me, Belle, and peats you shall never carry
    again,
And we might take a trip to Glasgow and there remain."

Then she answered him crossly, " I wish you wouldn't
    bother me,
For I'm tired of this kind of talk, as you may see."
So at last there came a steamer to Ruily one day,
So big that it almost seemed to fill the bay.

Then Belle and Effie Mackinnon came to the door with a
    start,
While Belle's red, pouting lips were wide apart ;
But when she saw the Redcoats coming ashore
She thought she had never seen such splendid men before.

One day after the steamer "Resistless" had arrived,
Belle's spirits seemed suddenly to be revived ;
And as Belle was lifting peats a few feet from the door
She was startled by a voice she never heard before.

The speaker wore a bright red coat and a small cap,
And she thought to herself he is a handsome chap ;
Then the speaker said, " 'Tis a fine day," and began to
    flatter,
Until at last he asked Belle for a drink of watter.

Then she glanced up at him shyly, while uneasy she did feel,
At the thought of having to hoist the peat-creel ;
And she could see curly, fair hair beneath his cap,
Still, she thought to herself, he is a good-looking chap.

And his eyes were blue and sparkling as the water in the
    bay,
And he spoke in a voice that was pleasant and gay ;
Then he took hold of the peat-creel as he spoke,
But Belle only laughed and considered it a joke.

Then Belle shook her head and lifted the peats on her
    back,
But he followed her home whilst to her he did crack ;
And by and by she brought him a drink of watter,
While with loving words he began Belle to flatter.

And after he had drank the watter and handed back the jug,
He said, " You are the sweetest flower that's to be found in
    Ruily " ;
And he touched her bare arm as he spoke,
Which proved to be sailor Harry's winning stroke.

104

But it would have been well for Belle had it ended there,
But it did not, for the sailor followed her, I do declare ;
And he was often at old Mackinnon's fireside,
And there for hours on an evening he would abide.

And Belle would wait on him with love-lit eyes,
While Harry's heart would heave with many love sighs.
At last, one night Belle said, " I hear you're going away."
Then Harry Lochton said, " 'Tis true, Belle, and I must
    obey.

But, my heather Belle, if you'll leave Ruily with me
I'll marry you, with your father's consent, immediately."
Then she put her arms around his neck and said, " Harry,
    I will."
Then Harry said, " You'll be a sailor's wife for good or ill."

In five days after Belle got married to her young sailor lad,
And there was a grand wedding, and old Mackinnon felt
    glad ;
And old Mackinnon slapped his son-in-law on the back
And said, " I hope good health and money you will never
    lack."

At last the day came that Harry had to go away,
And Harry said, " God bless you, Belle, by night and day ;
But you will come to Portsmouth and I will meet you there,
Remember, at the railway platform, and may God of you
    take care."

And when she arrived in Portsmouth she was amazed at the
    sight,
But when she saw Harry her heart beat with delight ;
And when the train stopped, Harry to her quickly ran,
And took her tin-box from the luggage van.

Then he took her to her new home without delay,
And the endless stairs and doors filled her heart with dismay;
But for that day the hours flew quickly past,
Because she knew she was with her Harry at last.

But there came a day when Harry was ordered away,
And he said, " My darling, I'll come back some unexpected
    day."
Then he kissed her at parting and " Farewell " he cries,
While the tears fell fast from her bonnie blue eyes.

Then when Harry went away she grew very ill,
And she cried, " If Harry stays long away this illness will
    me kill."
At last Harry came home and found her ill in bed,
And he cried, " My heather Belle, you're as pale as the
    dead."

Then she cried, " Harry, sit so as I may see your face,
Beside me here, Harry, that's just the place."
Then on his shoulder she gently dropped her head ;
Then Harry cried, " Merciful heaven, my heather Belle is
    dead! "

MARY, THE MAID OF THE TAY

Ye banks and braes o' bonnie Tay,
Whaur me and my Mary oft did stray ;
But noo she is dead and gane far away,
Sae I maun mourn for lovely Mary, the Maid o' the Tay.

The first time I met her 'twas in the month of May,
And the sun was shining bricht on the Silvery Tay ;
I asked her name and she modestly did say,
" Some fouks ca's me lovely Mary, the Maid o' the Tay."

Oh, charming Mary o' the Tay,
Queen o' my soul by nicht and day ;
But noo thou'rt gane and left me here
To weep for you, sweet Mary dear.

Oh, bonnie Mary o' the Tay,
Joy o' my heart and Queen o' May ;
With thee I aye felt happy and gay
While rambling with thee on the banks o' the Tay.

Ye banks and braes o' bonnie Tay,
With my Mary ye seemed ever gay ;
But noo ye seem baith dark and drear,
For my puir heart ye canna cheer.

My Mary was handsome and fair to be seen,
She had bonnie fair hair and twa blue een ;
And she was aye happy while we carelessly did stray
Alang the banks o' the Silvery Tay.

Oh, Mary dear, I mourn thy loss,
To me the world seems nought but dross ;
Sae I maun mourn baith nicht and day
For my lovely Mary, the Maid o' the Tay.

THE HEATHERBLEND CLUB BANQUET

'Twas on the 16th of October, in 1894,
I was invited to Inverness, not far from the seashore,
To partake of a Banquet prepared by the Heatherblend
  Club,
Gentlemen who honoured me without any hubbub.

The Banquet was held in the Gellion Hotel,
And the landlord, Mr Macpherson, treated me right
  well ;
Also the servant maids were very kind to me,
Especially the girl who polished my boots most beautiful to
  see.

The Banquet consisted of roast beef, potatoes, and red
  wine,
Also hare soup and sherry, and grapes most fine,
And baked pudding and apples, lovely to be seen,
Also rick sweet milk and delicious cream.

Mr Gossip, a noble Highlander, acted as chairman,
And when the Banquet was finished the fun began ;
And I was requested to give a poetic entertainment,
Which I gave, and which pleased them to their hearts'
  content.

And for the entertainment they did me well reward
By entitling me the Heatherblend Club Bard ;
Likewise I received an Illuminated Address,
Also a purse of silver, I honestly confess.

Mr A. J. Stewart was very kind to me,
And tried all he could to make me happy ;
And several songs were sung by gentlemen there—
It was the most social gathering I've been in, I do declare.

Oh, magnificent town of Inverness!
With its lovely scenery on each side,
And your beautiful river, I must confess,
'Twould be good for one's health there to reside.

There the blackbird and the mavis doth sing,
Making the woodland with their echoes to ring ;
During the months of July, May and June,
When the trees and shrubberies are in full bloom.

And to see the River Ness rolling smoothly along,
Together with the blackbird's musical song ;
As the sun shines bright in the month of May,
'Twill help to drive dull care away.

And Macbeth's Castle is grand to be seen,
Situated on Castle Hill, which is beautiful and green,
'Twas there Macbeth lived in days of old,
And a great tyrant he was, be it told.

I wish the Heatherblend members every success,
Hoping God will prosper them and bless ;
Long May Dame Fortune smile upon them,
For all of them I've met are kind gentlemen.

And, in conclusion, I must say
I never received better treatment in my day
Than I received from my admirers in bonnie Inverness ;
This on my soul and conscience I do confess.

A SUMMARY HISTORY OF SIR WILLIAM
WALLACE

Sir William Wallace of Ellerslie,
I'm told he went to the High School in Dundee,
For to learn to read and write,
And after that he learned to fight.
While at the High School in Dundee,
The Provost's son with him did disagree,
Because Wallace he did wear a dirk,
He despised him like an ignorant stirk,
Which with indignation he keenly felt,
And told him it would become him better in his belt.

Then Wallace's blood began to boil,
Just like the serpent in its coil,
Before it leaps upon its prey ;
And unto him he thus did say :
" Proud, saucy cur, come cease your prate,
For no longer I shall wait,
For to hear you insult me,
At the High School in Dundee ;
For such insolence makes my heart to smart,
And I'll plunge my dagger in your heart."

Then his heart's blood did quickly flow,
And poor Wallace did not know where to go ;
And he stood by him until dead.
Then far from him he quickly fled,
Lamenting greatly the deed he had done,
The murdering of the Provost's son.

The scene shifts to where he was fishing one day,
Where three English soldiers met him by the way,
And they asked him to give them some fish,

And from them they would make a delicious dish.
Then Wallace gave them share of his fish,
For to satisfy their wish ;
But they seemed dissatisfied with the share they got,
So they were resolved to have all the lot.

Then Wallace he thought it was time to look out,
When they were resolved to have all his trout ;
So he swung his fishing-rod with great force round his head,
And struck one of them a blow that killed him dead ;
So he instantly seized the fallen man's sword,
And the other two fled without uttering a word.

Sir William Wallace of Ellerslie,
You were a warrior of great renown,
And might have worn Scotland's crown ;
Had it not been for Monteith, the base traitor knave,
That brought you to a premature grave ;
Yes! you were sold for English gold,
And brought like a sheep from the fold,
To die upon a shameful scaffold high,
Amidst the derisive shouts of your enemies standing by.

But you met your doom like a warrior bold,
Bidding defiance to them that had you sold,
And bared your neck for the headsman's stroke ;
And cried, "Marion, dear, my heart is broke ;
My lovely dear, I come to thee,
Oh! I am longing thee to see!"
But the headsman was as stolid as the rock,
And the axe fell heavily on the block,
And the scaffold did shake with the terrible shock,
As the body of noble Wallace fell,
Who had fought for Scotland so well.

111

LINES IN PRAISE OF TOMMY ATKINS

Success to Tommy Atkins, he's a very brave man,
And to deny it there's few people can ;
And to face his foreign foes he's never afraid,
Therefore he's not a beggar, as Rudyard Kipling has said.

No, he's paid by our Government, and is worthy of his hire;
And from our shores in time of war he makes our foes retire,
He doesn't need to beg ; no, nothing so low ;
No, he considers it more honourable to face a foreign foe.

No, he's not a beggar, he's a more useful man,
And, as Shakespeare has said, his life's but a span ;
And at the cannon's mouth he seeks for reputation,
He doesn't go from door to door seeking a donation.

Oh, think of Tommy Atkins when from home far away,
Lying on the battlefield, earth's cold clay ;
And a stone or his knapsack pillowing his head,
And his comrades lying near by him wounded and dead.

And while lying there, poor fellow, he thinks of his wife at
    home,
And his heart bleeds at the thought, and he does moan ;
And down his cheek flows many a silent tear,
When he thinks of his friends and children dear.

Kind Christians, think of him when far, far away,
Fighting for his Queen and Country without dismay ;
May God protect him wherever he goes,
And give him strength to conquer his foes.

To call a soldier a beggar is a very degrading name,
And in my opinion it's a very great shame ;
And the man that calls him a beggar is not the soldier's
    friend,
And no sensible soldier should on him depend.

A soldier is a man that ought to be respected,
And by his country shouldn't be neglected ;
For he fights our foreign foes, and in danger of his life,
Leaving behind him his relatives and his dear wife.

Then hurrah for Tommy Atkins, he's the people's friend,
Because when foreign foes assail us he does us defend ;
He is not a beggar, as Rudyard Kipling has said,
No, he doesn't need to beg, he lives by his trade.

And in conclusion I will say,
Don't forget his wife and children when he's far away ;
But try and help them all you can,
For remember Tommy Atkins is a very useful man.

THE RELIEF OF MAFEKING

Success to Colonel Baden-Powell and his praises loudly
    sing,
For being so brave in relieving Mafeking,
With his gallant little band of eight hundred men,
They made the Boers fly from Mafeking like sheep escaping
    from a pen.

'Twas in the year of 1900 and on the 18th of May,
That Colonel Baden-Powell beat the Boers without dismay,
And made them fly from Mafeking without delay,
Which will be handed down to posterity for many a day.

Colonel Baden-Powell is a very brave man,
And to deny it, I venture to say, few men can ;
He is a noble hero be it said,
For at the siege of Mafeking he never was afraid.

And during the siege Colonel Baden was cheerful and gay,
While the starving population were living on brawn each
    day ;
And alas! the sufferings of the women and children were
    great,
Yet they all submitted patiently to their fate.

For seven months besieged they fought the Boers without
    dismay,
Until at last the Boers were glad to run away ;
Because Baden-Powell's gallant band put them to flight
By cannon shot and volleys of musketry to the left and
    right.

Then long live Baden-Powell and his brave little band,
For during the siege of Mafeking they made a bold stand
Against yelling thousands of Boers who were thirsting for
    their blood,
But as firm as a rock against them they fearlessly stood.

114

Oh! think of them living on brawn extracted from horse
    hides,
While the inhuman Boers their sufferings deride,
Knowing that the women's hearts with grief were torn
As they looked on their children's faces that looked sad and
    forlorn.

For 217 days the Boers tried to obtain Mafeking's surrender,
But their strategy was futile owing to its noble defender,
Colonel Baden-Powell, that hero of renown,
Who, by his masterly generalship, saved the town.

Methinks I see him and his gallant band,
Looking terror to the foe : Oh! The sight was really grand,
As he cried, " Give it them, lads ; let's do or die ;
And from Mafeking we'll soon make them fly,
And we'll make them rue their rash undertaking
The day they laid siege to the town of Mafeking."

Long life and prosperity to Colonel Baden-Powell,
For there's very few generals can him excel ;
And he is now the Hero of Mafeking, be it told,
And his name should be engraved on medals of gold.

I wish him and his gallant little band every success,
For relieving the people of Mafeking while in distress ;
They made the Boers rue their rash undertaking
The day they laid siege to the town of Mafeking.

For during the defence of Mafeking
From grief he kept the people's hearts from breaking,
Because he sang to them and did recite
Passages from Shakespeare which did their hearts delight.

115

THE BATTLE OF GLENCOE

Twas in the month of October, and in the year of 1899,
Which the Boers will remember for a very long time,
Because by the British Army they received a crushing blow ;
And were driven from Smith's Hill at the Battle of Glencoe.

The Boers' plan of the battle was devised with great skill,
And about 7000 men of them were camped on Smith's Hill ;
And at half-past five the battle began,
And the Boers behaved bravely to a man.

At twenty minutes to six two of the British batteries opened
    fire,
And early in the fight some of the Boers began to retire ;
And in half an hour the Boers' artillery had ceased to fire,
And from the crest of the hill they began to retire.

And General Symons with his staff was watching every detail,
The brave hero whose courage in the battle didn't fail ;
Because he ordered the King's Royal Rifles and the Dublin
    Fusiliers,
To advance in skirmishing order, which they did with three
    cheers.

Then they boldly advanced in very grand style,
And encouraged by their leaders all the while ;
And their marching in skirmishing order was beautiful to see,
As they advanced boldly to attack the enemy.

For over an hour the advance continued without dismay,
Until they had to take a breath by the way ;
They felt so fatigued climbing up Smith's Hill,
But, nevertheless, the brave heroes did it with a will.

They they prepared to attack the enemy,
And with wild battle-cries they attacked them vigorously ;
And with one determined rush they ascended the hill,
And drove the Boers from their position sore against their
    will.

But, alas, General Symons received a mortal wound,
Which caused his soldiers' sorrow to be profound ;
But still they fought on manfully without any dread ;
But, alas, brave General Symons now is dead.

Oh! It was a most inspiring and a magnificent sight,
To see the Hussars spurring their steeds with all their might ;
And charging the Boers with their lances of steel,
Which hurled them from their saddles and made them reel.

The battle raged for six hours and more,
While British cannon Smith's Hill up tore ;
Still the Boers fought manfully, without dismay,
But in a short time they had to give way.

For the Gordon Highlanders soon put an end to the fight,
Oh! it was a most gorgeous and thrilling sight,
To see them with their bagpipes playing, and one ringing
    cheer,
And from Smith's Hill they soon did the Boers clear.

And at the charge of the bayonet they made them fly,
While their leaders cried, " Forward, my lads, do or die,"
And the Boers' blood copiously they did spill,
And the Boers were forced to fly from Smith's Hill.

And in conclusion I hope and pray
The British will be successful when from home far away ;
And long may the Gordons be able to conquer the foe,
At home or abroad, wherever they go.

THE CAPTURE OF HAVANA

'Twas in the year 1762 that France and Spain
Resolved, allied together, to crush Britain ;
But the British Army sailed from England in May,
And arrived off Havana without any delay.

And the British Army resolved to operate on land,
And the appearance of the British troops were really grand ;
And by the Earl of Albemarle the British troops were
    commanded,
All eager for to fight as soon as they were landed.

Arduous and trying was the work the British had to do,
Yet with a hearty goodwill they to it flew ;
While the tropical sun on them blazed down,
But the poor soldiers wrought hard and didn't frown.

The bombardment was opened on the 30th of June,
And from the British battleships a fierce cannonade did
    boom ;
And continued from six in the morning till two o'clock in
    the afternoon,
And with grief the French and Spaniards sullenly did
    gloom.

And by the 26th of July the guns of Fort Moro were
    destroyed,
And the French and Spaniards were greatly annoyed ;
Because the British troops entered the Fort without dismay,
And drove them from it at the bayonet charge without
    delay.

But for the safety of the city the Governor organised a night
    attack,
Thinking to repulse the British and drive them back;
And with fifteen hundred militia he did the British attack,
But the British trench guards soon drove them back.

Then the Spandiards were charged and driven down the
    hill,
At the point of the bayonet sore against their will ;
And they rushed to their boats, the only refuge they could
    find,
Leaving a trail of dead and wounded behind.

Then Lieutenant Forbes, at the head of his men,
Swept round the ramparts driving all before them ;
And with levelled bayonets they drove them to and fro,
Then the British flag was hoisted over the bastions of
    Moro.

Then the Governor of the castle fell fighting sword in hand,
While rallying his men around the flagstaff the scene was
    grand ;
And the Spaniards fought hard to save their ships of war,
But the British destroyed their ships and scattered them
    afar.

And every man in the Moro Fort was bayonet or shot,
Which in Spanish history will never be forgot ;
And on the 10th of August Lord Albemarle sent a flag of
    truce,
And summoned the Governor to surrender, but he seemed to
    refuse.

Then from the batteries the British opened a terrific fire,
And the Spaniards from their guns were forced to retire,
Because no longer could they the city defend ;
Then the firing ceased and hostilities were at an end.

Then the city of Havana surrendered unconditionally,
And terms were settled, and the harbour, forts, and city,
With a district of one hundred miles to the westward,
And loads of gold and silver were the British troops' reward.

And all other valuable property was brought to London,
The spoils that the British Army had won ;
And it was conveyed in grand procession to the Tower of
    London,
And the Londoners applauded the British for the honours
    they had won.

THE BATTLE OF WATERLOO

'Twas in the year 1815, and on the 18th day of June,
That British cannon, against the French army, loudly did
    boom,
Upon the ever memorable bloody field of Waterloo ;
Which Napoleon remembered while in St. Helena, and
    bitterly did rue.

The morning of the 18th was gloomy and cheerless to behold,
But the British soon recovered from the severe cold
That they had endured the previous rainy night ;
And each man prepared to burnish his arms for the coming
    fight.

Then the morning passed in mutual arrangements for battle,
And the French guns, at half-past eleven, loudly did rattle ;
And immediately the order for attack was given,
Then the bullets flew like lightning till the Heaven's seemed
    riven.

The place from which Bonaparte viewed the bloody field
Was the farmhouse of La Belle Alliance, which some pro-
    tection did yield ;
And there he remained for the most part of the day,
Pacing to and fro with his hands behind him in doubtful
    dismay.

The Duke of Wellington stood upon a bridge behind La Haye,
And viewed the British army in all their grand array,
And where danger threatened most the noble Duke was
    found
In the midst of shot and shell on every side around.

Hougemont was the key of the Duke of Wellington's position,
A spot that was naturally very strong, and a great acqusition
To the Duke and his staff during the day,
Which the Coldstream Guards held to the last, without
dismay.

The French 2nd Corps were principally directed during the
day
To carry Hougemont farmhouse without delay ;
So the farmhouse in quick succession they did attack,
But the British guns on the heights above soon drove them
back.

But still the heavy shot and shells ploughed through the
walls ;
Yet the brave Guards resolved to hold the place no matter
what befalls ;
And they fought manfully to the last, with courage un-
shaken,
Until the tower of Hougemont was in a blaze but still it
remained untaken.

By these desperate attacks Napoleon lost ten thousand men,
And left them weltering in their gore like sheep in a pen ;
And the British lost one thousand men—which wasn't very
great,
Because the great Napoleon met with a crushing defeat.

The advance of Napoleon on the right was really very fine,
Which was followed by a general onset upon the British line,
In which three hundred pieces of artillery opened their
cannonade ;
But the British artillery played upon them, and great
courage displayed.

For ten long hours it was a continued succession of attacks ;
Whilst the British cavalry charged them in all their draw-
   backs ;
And the courage of the British Army was great in square at
   Waterloo,
Because hour after hour they were mowed down in numbers
   not a few.

At times the temper of the troops had very nearly failed,
Especially amongst the Irish regiments who angry railed ;
And they cried : " When will we get at them ? Show us the
   way
That we may avenge the death of our comrades without
   delay ? "

" But be steady and cool, my brave lads," was their officers'
   command,
While each man was ready to charge with gun in hand ;
Oh, Heaven! it was pitiful to see their comrades lying
   around,
Dead and weltering in their gore, and cumbering the
   ground.

It was a most dreadful sight to behold,
Heaps upon heaps of dead men lying stiff and cold ;
While the cries of the dying was lamentable to hear ;
And for the loss of their comrades many a soldier shed
   a tear.

Men and horses fell on every side around,
Whilst heavy cannon shot tore up the ground ;
And musket balls in thousands flew,
And innocent blood bedewed the field of Waterloo.

Methinks I see the solid British square,
Whilst the shout of the French did rend the air,
As they rush against the square of steel.
Which forced them back and made them reel.

And when a gap was made in that square,
The cry of " Close up! Close up! " did rend the air,
" And charge them with your bayonets, and make them fly !
And Scotland for ever! be the cry."

The French and British closed in solid square,
While the smoke of the heavy cannonade darkened the air ;
Then the noble Picton deployed his division into line,
And drove back the enemy in a very short time.

Then Lord Anglesey seized on the moment, and charging
    with the Greys,
Whilst the Inniskillings burst through everything, which
    they did always ;
Then the French infantry fell in hundreds by the swords of
    the Dragoons ;
Whilst the thundering of the cannonade loudly booms.

And the Eagles of the 45th and 105th were all captured that
    day,
And upwards of 2000 prisoners, all in grand array ;
But, alas! at the head of his division, the noble Picton fell,
While the Highlanders played a lament for him they loved
    so well.

Then the French cavalry receded from the square they
    couldn't penetrate,
Still Napoleon thought to weary the British into defeat ;
But when he saw his columns driven back in dismay,
He cried, " How beautifully these English fight, but they
    must give way."

And well did British bravery deserve the proud encomium,
Which their enduring courage drew from the brave Napoleon;
And when the close column of infantry came on the British
    square,
Then the British gave one loud cheer which did rend the air.

Then the French army pressed forward at Napoleon's
    command,
Determined, no doubt, to make a bold stand ;
Then Wellington cried, " Up Guards and break their ranks
    through,
And chase the French invaders from off the field of Watei -
    loo! "

Then, in a moment, they were all on their feet,
And they met the French, sword in hand, and made them
    retreat ;
Then Wellington in person directed the attack,
And at every point and turning the French were beaten
    back.

And the road was choked and encumbered with the dead ;
And, unable to stand the charge, the French instantly fled,
And Napoleon's army of yesterday was now a total wreck,
Which the British manfully for ten long hours held in check.

Then, panic-struck, the French were forced to yield,
And Napoleon turned his charger's head, and fled from the
    field,
With his heart full of woe, no doubt—
Exclaiming, " Oh, Heaven! my noble army has met with a
    total rout! "

THE ALBION BATTLESHIP CALAMITY

'Twas in the year of 1898, and on the 21st of June,
The launching of the Battleship Albion caused a great
    gloom,
Amongst the relatives of many persons who were drowned
    in the River Thames,
Which their relatives will remember while life remains.

The vessel was christened by the Duchess of York,
And the spectators' hearts felt as light as cork
As the Duchess cut the cord that was holding the fine ship,
Then the spectators loudly cheered as the vessel slid down
    the slip.

The launching of the vessel was very well carried out,
While the guests on the stands cheered without any
    doubt,
Under the impression that everything would go well ;
But, alas ! instantaneously a bridge and staging fell.

Oh ! little did the Duchess of York think that day
That so many lives would be taken away
At the launching of the good ship Albion,
But when she heard of the catastrophe she felt woebegone.

But accidents will happen without any doubt,
And often the cause thereof is hard to find out ;
And according to report, I've heard people say,
'Twas the great crowd on the bridge caused it to give
    way.

Just as the vessel entered the water the bridge and staging
gave way,
Immersing some three hundred people which caused great
dismay
Amongst thousands of spectators that were standing there,
And in the faces of the bystanders were depicted despair.

Then the police boats instantly made for the fatal spot,
And with the aid of dockyard hands several people were
got,
While some scrambled out themselves, the best way they
could—
And the most of them were the inhabitants of the neighbour-
hood.

Part of them were the wives and daughters of the dockyard
hands,
And as they gazed upon them they in amazement
stands ;
And several bodies were hauled up quite dead,
Which filled the onlookers' hearts with pity and dread.

One of the first rescued was a little baby,
Which was conveyed away to a mortuary ;
And several were taken to the fitter's shed, and attended to
there
By the firemen and several nurses with the greatest care.

Meanwhile heartrending scenes were taking place,
Whilst the tears ran down many a Mother and Father's
face,
That had lost their children in the River Thames,
Which they will remember while life remains.

Oh, Heaven! it was horrible to see the bodies laid out
in rows,
And as Fathers and Mothers passed along, adown their
cheeks the tears flows,
While their poor, sickly hearts were throbbing with fear.

A great crowd had gathered to search for the missing
dead,
And many strong men broke down because their heart with
pity bled,
As they looked upon the distorted faces of their relatives
dear,
While adown their cheeks flowed many a silent tear.

The tenderest sympathy, no doubt, was shown to them,
By the kind hearted Police and Firemen ;
The scene in fact was most sickening to behold,
And enough to make one's blood run cold,
To see tear-stained men and women there
Searching for their relatives, and in their eyes a pitiful
stare.

There's one brave man in particular I must mention,
And I'm sure he's worthy of the people's attention :
His name is Thomas Cooke, of No. 6 Percy Road, Canning
Town,
Who's name ought to be to posterity handed down,
Because he leapt into the River Thames, and heroically did
behave,
And rescued five persons from a watery grave.

128

Mr Wilson, a young Electrician, got a terrible fright,
When he saw his mother and sister dead—he was shocked at
    the sight,
Because his sister had not many days returned from her
    honeymoon,
And in his countenance, alas ! there was a sad gloom.

Her Majesty has sent a message of sympathy to the bereaved
    ones in distress,
And the Duke and Duchess of York have sent 25 guineas I
    must confess,
And £1000 from the Directors of the Thames Ironworks and
    Shipbuilding Company,
Which I hope will help to fill the bereaved one's hearts with
    glee.

And in conclusion I will venture to say,
That accidents will happen by night and by day ;
And I will say without any fear,
Because to me it appears quite clear,
That the stronger we our houses do build,
The less chance we have of being killed.

AN ALL NIGHT SEA FIGHT

Ye sons of Mars, come list to me,
And I will relate to ye
A great and heroic naval fight,
Which will fill your hearts with delight.

The fight was between the French Frigate " Pique " and the
  British Frigate " Blanche,"
But the British crew were bold and staunch ;
And the battle was fought in West Indian waters in the year
  of 1795,
And for to gain the victory the French did nobly strive.

And on the morning of the 4th of January while cruising off
  Gadulope,
The look-out man from the foretop loudly spoke,
And cried, " Sail ahoy! " " Where away ? "
" On the lee bow, close in shore, sir," was answered without
  delay.

Then Captain Faulkner cried, " Clear the decks! "
And the French vessel with his eyeglass he inspects ;
And he told his men to hoist the British flag,
And " prepare my heroes to pull down that French rag."

Then the "Blanche" made sail and bore away
In the direction of the "Pique" without delay ;
And Captain Faulkner cried, " Now, my lads, bear down on
  him,
And make ready quickly and begin."

It was about midnight when the Frenchman hove in sight,
And could be seen distinctly in the starlight ;
And for an hour and a half they fired away
Broadsides into each other without dismay.

And with the rapid flashes the Heavens were aflame,
As each volley from the roaring cannons came ;
And the incessant roll of musketry was awful to hear,
As it broke over the silent sea and smote upon the ear.

The French vessel had nearly 400 men,
Her decks were literally crowded from stem to stern ;
And the musketeers kept up a fierce fire on the " Blanche,"
But still the "Blanche" on them did advance.

And the "Blanche's" crew without dismay
Fired a broadside into the "Pique" without delay,
Which raked her fore and aft, and knocked her to smash,
And the mizenmast fell overboard with a terrible crash.

Then the Frenchmen rushed forward to board the
    " Blanche,"
But in doing so they had a very poor chance,
For the British Tars in courage didn't lack,
Because thrice in succession on their own deck they were
    driven back.

Then "Bravo, my lads!" Captain Faulkner loudly cries,
"Lash her bowsprit to our capstan, she's our prize" ;
And he seized some ropes to lash round his foe,
But a musket ball pierced his heart and laid him low.

Then a yell of rage burst from the noble crew,
And near to his fallen body they drew ;
And tears for his loss fell fast on the deck,
Their grief was so great their tears they couldn't check.

The crew was very sorry for their captain's downfall,
But the sight didn't their brave hearts appal ;
Because they fastened the ropes to the "Pique" at the
    capstan,
And the " Pique " was dragged after the " Blanche," the
    sight was grand.

Yet the crew of the "Pique" maintained the fight,
Oh! most courageously they fought in the dead of night ;
And for two hours they kept up firing without dismay,
But it was a sacrifice of human life, they had to give way.

And about five o'clock in the morning the French cried for
    quarter,
Because on board there had been a great slaughter ;
Their Captain Cousail was mortally wounded in the fight
Along with many officers and men ; oh! it was a heart-
    rending sight
To see the wounded and dead weltering in their gore
After thecannonading had ceased and the fighting was o'er.

THE WRECK OF THE STEAMER "STELLA"

'Twas in the month of March and in the year of 1899,
Which will be remembered for a very long time ;
The wreck of the steamer "Stella" that was wrecked on the
    Casquet Rocks,
By losing her bearings in a fog, and received some terrible
    shocks.

The "Stella" was bound for the Channel Islands on a holiday
    trip,
And a number of passengers were resolved not to let the
    chance slip ;
And the hearts of the passengers felt light and gay,
As the "Stella" steamed out of the London Docks without
    delay.

The vessel left London at a quarter-past eleven,
With a full passenger list and a favourable wind from
　heaven ;
And all went well until late in the afternoon,
When all at once a mist arose, alas! too soon.

And as the Channel Islands were approached a fog set in,
Then the passengers began to be afraid and made a chatter-
　ing din ;
And about half-past three o'clock the fog settled down,
Which caused Captain Reeks and the passengers with fear
　to frown.

And brave Captain Reeks felt rather nervous and discontent,
Because to him it soon became quite evident ;
And from his long experience he plainly did see
That the fog was increasing in great density.

Still the "Stella" sailed on at a very rapid rate,
And, of, heaven! rushed headlong on to her fate,
And passed o'er the jagged rocks without delay,
And her side was ripped open : Oh! horror and dismay!

Then all the passengers felt the terrible shock,
As the "Stella" stuck fast upon the first ledge of rock ;
And they rushed to the deck in wild alarm,
While some of them cried : " Oh! God protect us from
　harm."

Then men clasped wives and daughters, and friends shook
　hands,
And unmoved Captain Reeks upon the bridge stands ;
And he shouted, " Get out the boats without delay! "
Then the sailors and officers began to work without dismay.

Again Captain Reeks cried in a manly clear voice,
" Let the women and children be our first choice! "
Then the boats were loaded in a speedy way,
And with brave seamen to navigate them that felt no
dismay.

Then the "Stella" began rapidly for to settle down,
And Captain Reeks gave his last order without a frown,
Shouting, "Men, for yourselves, you'll better look out! "
Which they did, needing no second bidding, without fear or
doubt.

Then the male passengers rushed to the boats in wild
despair,
While the cries of the women and children rent the air ;
Oh, heaven ! such a scene ! 'twas enough to make one weep,
To see mothers trying to save their children that were fast
asleep.

Brave Captain Reeks stood on the bridge till the ship went
down,
With his eyes uplifted towards heaven, and on his face no
frown ;
And some of the passengers jumped from the ship into the
sea,
And tried hard to save their lives right manfully.

But the sufferings of the survivors are pitiful to hear,
And I think all Christian people for them will drop a tear,
Because the rower of the boats were exhausted with damp
and cold ;
And the heroine of the wreck was Miss Greta Williams, be it
told.

She remained in an open boat with her fellow-passengers and
  crew,
And sang "O rest in the Lord, and He will come to our
  rescue" ;
And for fourteen hours they were rowing on the mighty
  deep,
And when each man was done with his turn he fell asleep.

And about six o'clock in the morning a man shrieked out,
"There's a sailing boat coming towards us without any
  doubt " ;
And before the sailing boat could get near, a steamer hove
  in sight,
Which proved to be the steamer " Lynx," to their delight.

And they were conveyed to Guernsey without delay,
Poor souls, with their hearts in a state of joy and dismay ;
But alas! more than eighty persons have been lost in the
  briny deep,
But I hope their souls are now in heaven in safe keep.

THE WRECK OF THE STEAMER

"STORM QUEEN"

Ye landsmen, all pray list to me,
While I relate a terrible tale of the sea,
Concerning the screw steamer "Storm Queen"
Which was wrecked, alas! a most heart-rending scene.

From Sebastopol, with a cargo of grain, she was on her way,
And soon after entering the Bay of Biscay,
On the 21st of December, they experienced a fearful storm
Such as they never experienced since they were born.

The merciless sea was running mountains high,
And to save themselves from a watery grave manfully they
    did try ;
But the vessel became unmanageable, but still they worked
    away,
And managed to launch two small boats without dismay.

They wrought most manfully and behaved very well,
But a big wave smashed a small boat before they left the
    vessel ;
Still the Captain, Mr Jaques, and five of the crew
Clung to the "Storm Queen" until she sank beneath the
    waters blue.

While the sea lashed itself into white foam and loudly did
    roar,
And with a gurgling sound the big waves covered the vessel
    o'er ;
So perished Captain Jaques and five of the crew
Who stuck to the vessel, as brave sailors would do.

But before the vessel sank a raft was made,
And a few men got on to it who were not afraid ;
And oh! it was enough to make one's blood to freeze
To see them jumping off the steamer into the yawning
    seas.

So they were tossed about on the big billows the whole
    night,
And beneath the big waves they were engulphed before
    daylight ;
But 22 that reached the boats were saved in all
By the aid of God, on whom they did call.

And on the next morning before daylight
The Norwegian barque "Gulvare" hove in sight ;
Then they shouted and pulled towards her with all their
    might,
While the seas were running high, oh ! what a fearful sight.

The poor souls were prevented from getting along side
Of the barque "Gulvare" by the heavy seas and tide ;
And as the boats drew near the barque the storm increases
Until the boats struck against her and were dashed to pieces.

It was almost beyond human efforts with the storm to cope,
But most fortunately they were hauled on board by a rope,
While the big waves did lash the barque all over,
But by a merciful providence they were landed safely at
    Dover.

The survivors when rescued were in a destitute state,
But nevertheless they seemed resigned to their fate,
And they thanked God that did them save
Most timely from a cold and watery grave.

And during their stay in Dover they received kind treatment,
For which they, poor creatures, felt very content ;
And when they recovered from their ills they met at sea,
The authorities sent them home to their own country.

But as for Captain Jaques, few men like him had been,
Because he couldn't be persuaded to desert the "Storm
    Queen,"
As he declared he wouldn't leave her whatever did betide ;
So the brave hero sank with her beneath the waters wide.

THE WRECK OF THE
"ABERCROMBIE ROBINSON"

'Twas in the year of 1842 and on the 27th of May
That six Companies of the 91st Regiment with spirits light
    and gay,
And forming the Second Battalion, left Naas without delay,
Commanded by Captain Bertie Gordon, to proceed to the
    Cape straightaway.

And on the second of June they sailed for the Cape of Good
    Hope
On board the "Abercrombie Robinson," a vessel with which
    few vessels could cope ;
And in August the 25th they reached Table Bay,
Where a battalion of the 91st was warned for service without
    delay.

To relieve the 91st, which was to be stationed at Cape
    Town,
An order which the 91st obeyed without a single frown ;
And all the officers not on duty obtained leave to go
    ashore,
Leaving only six aboard, in grief to deplore.

138

There were 460 men of the 91st seemingly all content,
Besides a draft of the Cape Mounted Rifles and a draft of
the 27th Regiment ;
But, alas an hour after midnight on the same night
A strong gale was blowing, which filled the passengers'
hearts with fright.

The ship pitched heavily and could be felt touching the
ground,
Then Captain Gordon warned the Sergeant-Major and officers
all round,
That they might expect a storm, to him it seemed plain;
And, as he predicted, it blew a terrific hurricane.

And the passengers' hearts were filled with dismay,
And a little after three o'clock in the morning the cable
broke away,
Then the ship drifted helplessly before the merciless storm,
While the women and children looked sad, pale and
forlorn.

Then the thunder roared and the lightning flashed in bright
array,
And was one of the greatest storms ever raged over Table
Bay,
And the ill-fated vessel drove in towards the shore,
While the Storm Fiend did laugh and loudly did roar.

And the ship rolled and heaved with the raging tide,
While the seas poured down the hatchways and broke over
her side,
And the ship wrought for herself a bed in the sand ;
Still Captain Bertie hoped all might get safely to land.

'Twas about seven o'clock when daylight did appear,
And when the storm ceases the passengers gave a cheer,
Who had been kept below during the awful night,
Then in small groups they came on deck, a most pitiful
    sight.

Alas! sad and dejected, sickly looking, pale and forlorn,
Owing to the close confinement during the storm ;
And for a time attempts were made to send a rope
    ashore,
But these proved futile owing to the raging billows which
    loudly did roar.

Then one of the ship's cutters was carefully lowered over
    the side,
And her crew towards the shore merrily did glide,
And succeeded in reaching the shore with a leading line,
And two boats were conveyed to the sinking ship just in
    time.

And to save the women and children from being drowned,
Captain Gordon gave orders to the 91st all round
For the women and children to disembark immediately,
Who to God were crying for help most frantically.

And the 91st made a most determined stand,
While lowering the women and children it was awful and
    grand,
As they lowered them gently into the boats over the ship's
    side,
Regardless of their own lives whatever would betide.

140

Then the sick were to disembark after the women and
  children,
And next the 27th Regiment and Cape Mounted Riflemen;
And from half-past eight till ten o'clock the disembarkation
  went on,
While the women and children looked ghastly pale and woe
  begone.

The disembarkation of the 91st came at last,
And as there were only two boats available they stood
  aghast,
Because the boats only carried each time thirty;
Still, the work went on for four hours most manfully.

And at half-past three the last boat left the ship's side,
And o'er the raging billows the small boats did glide,
Containing the officers and crew who remained to the last,
To see the women and children saved and all danger past.

And after a night of great danger and through a raging sea
Seven hundred souls were carried from a sinking ship provi-
  dentially;
And among them were trembling children and nervous
  women also,
And sick men who were dying with their hearts full of woe.

But thank God they were all saved and brought to land,
All through Colonel Bertie Gordon, who wisely did com-
  mand
The 91st to see to the women and children's safety,
An order which they obeyed right manfully;
And all honour is due to the 91st for their gallantry,
Likewise Captain Bertie Gordon, who behaved so heroically.

THE LOSS OF THE "VICTORIA"

Alas ! Now o'er Britannia there hangs a gloom,
Because over 400 British Tars have met with a watery tomb;
Who served aboard the " Victoria," the biggest ship in the
    navy,
And one of the finest battleships that ever sailed the sea.

And commanded by Sir George Tyron, a noble hero bold,
And his name on his tombstone should be written in letters
    of gold ;
For he was skifull in naval tactics, few men could with him
    cope,
And he was considered to be the nation's hope.

'Twas on Thursday, She twenty-second of June,
And off the coast of tyria, and in the afternoon,
And in the year of our Lord eighteen ninety-three,
That the ill-fated "Victoria" sank to the bottom of the sea.

The "Victoria" sank in fifteen minutes after she was rammed,
In eighty fathoms of water, which was smoothly calmed ;
The monster war vessel capsized bottom uppermost,
And, alas, lies buried in the sea totally lost.

The "Victoria" was the flagship of the Mediterranean Fleet,
And was struck by the "Camperdown" when too close they
    did meet,
While practising the naval and useful art of war,
How to wheel and discharge their shot at the enemy
    afar.

Oh, Heaven ! Methinks I see some men lying in their
    beds,
And some skylarking, no doubt, and not a soul dreads
The coming avalanche that was to seal their doom,
Until down came the mighty fabric of the engine room.

Then death leaped on them from all quarters in a moment,
And there were explosions of magazines and boilers rent ;
And the fire and steam and water beat out all life,
But I hope the drowned ones are in the better world free
    from strife.

Sir George Tyron was on the bridge at the moment of the
    accident
With folded arms, seemingly quite content ;
And seeing the vessel couldn't be saved he remained till the
    last,
And went down with the "Victoria" when all succour was
    past.

Methinks I see him on the bridge like a hero brave,
And the ship slowly sinking into the briny wave ;
And when the men cried, " Save yourselves without
    delay,"
He told them to save themselves, he felt no dismay.

'Twas only those that leaped from the vessel at the first
    alarm,
Luckily so, that were saved from any harm
By leaping into the boats o'er the vessel's side,
Thanking God they had escaped as o'er the smooth water
    they did glide.

At Whitehall, London, mothers and fathers did call,
And the pitiful scene did the spectators' hearts appal ;
But the most painful case was the mother of J. P. Scarlet,
Who cried, " Oh, Heaven, the loss of my son I'll never
    forget."

Oh, Heaven! Befriend the bereaved ones, hard is their fate,
Which I am sorry at heart to relate ;
But I hope God in His goodness will provide for them,
Especially the widows, for the loss of their men.

Alas! Britannia now will mourn the loss of her naval com-
    mander,
Who was as brave as the great Alexander ;
And to his honour be it fearlessly told,
Few men would excel this hero bold.

Alas ! 'Tis sad to be buried in eighty fathoms of Syrian sea,
Which will hide the secret of the "Victoria" to all eternity;
Which causes Britannia's sorrow to be profound
For the brave British Tars that have been drowned.

THE BURNING OF THE SHIP "KENT"

Good people of high and low degree,
I pray ye all to list to me,
And I'll relate a harrowing tale of the sea
Concerning the burning of the ship "Kent" in the Bay of
    Biscay,
Which is the most appalling tale of the present century.

She carried a crew, including officers, of 148 men,
And twenty lady passengers along with them ;
Besides 344 men of the 31st Regiment,
And twenty officers with them, all seemingly content.

Also the soldiers' wives, which numbered forty-three,
And sixty-six children, a most beautiful sight to see ;
And in the year of 1825, and on the 19th of February,
The ship "Kent" sailed from the Downs right speedily,
While the passengers' hearts felt light with glee.

And the beautiful ship proceeded on her way to Bengal,
While the passengers were cheerful one and all ;
And the sun shone out in brilliant array,
And on the evening of the 28th they entered the Bay of
    Biscay.

But a gale from the south-west sprang up that night,
Which filled the passengers' hearts with fright ;
And it continued to increase in violence as the night wore on,
Whilst the lady passengers looked very woe-begone.

Part of the cargo in the hold consisted of shot and shell,
And the vessel rolled heavily as the big billows rose and fell ;
Then two sailors descended the forehold carrying a light,
To see if all below was safe and right.

And they discovered a spirit cask and the contents oozing
    rapidly,
And the man with the light stooped to examine it immedi-
    ately ;
And in doing so he dropped the lamp while in a state of
    amaze,
And, oh horror! in a minute the forehold was in a blaze.

It was two o'clock in the morning when the accident took
place,
And, alas! horror and fear was depicted in each face ;
And the sailors tried hard to extinguish the flame,
But, oh Heaven! all their exertions proved in vain.

The inflammable matter rendered their efforts of no avail,
And the brave sailors with over-exertion looked very pale ;
And for hours in the darkness they tried to check the fire,
But the flames still mounted higher and higher.

But Captain Cobb resolved on a last desperate experiment,
Because he saw the ship was doomed, and he felt discontent ;
Then he raised the alarm that the ship was on fire,
Then the passengers quickly from their beds did retire.

And women and children rushed to the deck in wild despair,
And, paralysed with terror, many women tore their hair ;
And some prayed to God for help, and wildly did screech,
But, alas ! poor souls, help was not within their reach.

Still the gale blew hard, and the waves ran mountains high,
While men, women, and children bitterly did cry
To God to save them from the merciless fire ;
But the flames rose higher and higher.

And when the passengers had lost all hope, and in great
dismay,
The look-out man shouted, " Ho! a sail coming this way " ;
Then every heart felt light and gay,
And signals of distress were hoisted without delay.

Then the vessel came to their rescue, commanded by Captain
 Cook,
And he gazed upon the burning ship with a pitiful look ;
She proved to be the brig " Cambria," bound for Vera Cruz,
Then the captain cried, " Men, save all ye can, there's no
 time to lose."

Then the sailors of the "Cambria" wrought with might and
 main,
While the sea spray fell on them like heavy rain ;
First the women and children were transferred from the
 "Kent"
By boats, ropes, and tackle without a single accident.

But, alas ! the fire had reached the powder magazine,
Then followed an explosion, oh! what a fearful scene ;
But the explosion was witnessed by Captain Babby of the
 ship "Carline,"
Who most fortunately arrived in the nick of time.

And fourteen additional human beings were saved from the
 " Kent,"
And they thanked Captain Babby and God, who to them
 succour sent,
And had saved them from being burnt, and drowned in the
 briny deep ;
And they felt so overjoyed that some of them did weep ;
And in the first port in England they landed without delay,
And when their feet touched English soil their hearts felt
 gay.

THE WRECK OF THE "INDIAN CHIEF"

'Twas on the 8th of January 1881,
That a terrific gale along the English Channel ran,
And spread death and disaster in its train,
Whereby the "Indian Chief" vessel was tossed on the raging
   main.

She was driven ashore on the Goodwin Sands,
And the good captain fearlessly issued his commands,
" Come, my men, try and save the vessel, work with all your
   might,"
Although the poor sailors on board were in a fearful plight.

They were expecting every minute her hull would give way,
And they, poor souls, felt stricken with dismay,
And the captain and some of the crew clung to the main
   masts,
Where they were exposed to the wind's cold blasts.

A fierce gale was blowing and the sea ran mountains high,
And the sailors on board heaved many a bitter sigh ;
And in the teeth of the storm the lifeboat was rowed bravely
Towards the ship in distress, which was awful to see.

The ship was lifted high on the crest of a wave,
While the sailors tried hard their lives to save,
And implored God to save them from a watery grave,
And through fear some of them began to rave.

The waves were miles long in length,
And the sailors had lost nearly all their strength,
By striving hard their lives to save,
From being drowned in the briny wave.

A ration of rum and a biscuit was served out to each man,
And the weary night passed, and then appeared the morning
dawn ;
And when the lifeboat hove in sight a sailor did shout,
" Thank God, there's she at last without any doubt."

But, with weakness and the biting cold,
Several of the sailors let go their hold ;
And, alas, fell into the yawning sea,
Poor souls! and were launched into eternity.

Oh, it was a most fearful plight,
For the poor sailors to be in the rigging all night ;
While the storm fiend did laugh and roar,
And the big waves lashed the ship all o'er.

And as the lifeboat drew near,
The poor sailors raised a faint cheer ;
And all the lifeboat men saw was a solitary mast,
And some sailors clinging to it, while the ship was sinking
fast.

Charles Tait, the coxswain of the lifeboat, was a skilful
boatman,
And the bravery he and his crew displayed was really grand ;
For his men were hardy and a very heroic set,
And for bravery their equals it would be hard to get.

But, thank God, out of twenty-nine eleven were saved,
Owing to the way the lifeboat men behaved ;
And when they landed with the eleven wreckers at Rams-
gate,
The people's joy was very great.

CAPTAIN TEACH *alias* BLACK BEARD

Edward Teach was a native of Bristol, and sailed from that
    port
On board a privateer, in search of sport,
As one of the crew, during the French War in that station,
And for personal courage he soon gained his Captain's
    approbation.

'Twas in the spring of 1717, Captain Harnigold and Teach
    sailed from Providence
For the continent of America, and no further hence ;
And in their way captured a vessel laden with flour,
Which they put on board their own vessels in the space of
    an hour.

They also seized two other vessels and took some gallons of
    wine,
Besides plunder to a considerable value, and most of it most
    costly design ;
And after that they made a prize of a large French Guinea-
    man,
Then to act an independent part Teach now began.

But the news spread throughout America, far and near,
And filled many of the inhabitants' hearts with fear ;
But Lieutenant Maynard with his sloops of war directly
    steered,
And left James River on the 17th November in quest of
    Black Beard,
And on the evening of the 21st came in sight of the pirate ;
And when Black Beard spied his sloops he felt elate.

When he saw the sloops sent to apprehend him,
He didn't lose his courage, but fiendishly did grin;
And told his men to cease from drinking and their tittle-
tattle,
Although he had only twenty men on board, and prepare for
battle.

In case anything should happen to him during the engage-
ment,
One of his men asked him, who felt rather discontent,
Whether his wife knew where he had buried his pelf,
When he impiously replied that nobody knew but the devil
and himself.

In the Morning Maynard weighed and sent his boat to sound,
Which, coming near the pirate, unfortunately ran aground;
But Maynard lightened his vessel of the ballast and water,
Whilst from the pirates' ship small shot loudly did clatter.

But the pirates' small shot or slugs didn't Maynard appal,
He told his men to take their cutlasses and be ready upon
his call;
And to conceal themselves every man below,
While he would remain at the helm and face the foe.

Then Black Beard cried, " They're all knocked on the head,"
When he saw no hands upon deck he thought they were
dead;
Then Black Beard boarded Maynard's sloop without dismay,
But Maynard's men rushed upon deck, then began the
deadly fray.

Then Black Beard and Maynard engaged sword in hand,
And the pirate fought manfully and made a bold stand ;
And Maynard with twelve men, and Black Beard with
fourteen,
Made the most desperate and bloody conflict that ever was
seen.

At last with shots and wounds the pirate fell down dead,
Then from his body Maynard severed the pirate's head,
And suspended it upon his bowsprit-end,
And thanked God Who so mercifully did him defend.

Black Beard derived his name from his long black beard,
Which terrified America more than any comet that had ever
appeared ;
But, thanks be to God, in this age we need not be afeared,
Of any such pirates as the inhuman Black Beard.

THE DISASTROUS FIRE AT SCARBOROUGH

'Twas in the year of 1898, and on the 8th of June,
A mother and six children met with a cruel doom
In one of the most fearful fires for some years past—
And as the spectators gazed upon them they stood aghast.

The fire broke out in a hairdresser's, in the town of Scarborough,
And as the fire spread it filled the people's hearts with sorrow ;
But the police and the fire brigade were soon on the ground,
Then the hose and reel were quickly sent round.

Oh ! it was horrible to see the flames leaping up all around,
While amongst the spectators the silence was profound,
As they saw a man climb out to the parapet high,
Resolved to save his life, or in the attempt to die!

And he gave one half frantic leap, with his heart full of woe,
And came down upon the roof of a public-house 20 feet below ;
But, alas! he slipped and fell through the skylight,
And received cuts and bruises : oh, what a horrible sight!

He was the tenant of the premises, Mr Brookes,
And for his wife and family he enquires, with anxious looks,
But no one could tell him, it did appear,
And when told so adown his cheeks flowed many a tear.

He had been sleeping by himself on the second floor,
When suddenly alarmed, he thought he'd make sure,
And try to escape from the burning pile with his life,
And try and save his family and his wife.

The fire brigade played on the first floor with great speed,
But the flames had very inflammable fuel upon which to
feed,
So that the fire spread with awful rapidity,
And in twenty minutes the building was doomed to the
fourth storey.

The firemen wrought with might and main,
But still the fire did on them gain,
That it was two hours before they could reach the second
floor,
The heat being so intense they could scarcely it endure.

And inside all the time a woman and six children were there,
And when the firemen saw them, in amazement they did
stare ;
The sight that met their eyes made them for to start—
Oh, Heaven! the sight was sufficient to rend the strongest
heart.

For there was Mrs Brookes stretched dead on the floor,
Who had fallen in trying her escape for to procure.
She was lying with one arm over her ten months old child,
And her cries for help, no doubt, were frantic and wild ;
And part of her arm was burned off as it lay above
The child she was trying to shield, which shows a mother's
love.

For the baby's flesh was partly uninjured by the flames,
Which shows that the loving mother had endured great
pains ;
It, however, met its death by suffocation,
And as the spectators gazed thereon, it filled their hearts
with consternation.

The firemen acted heroically, without any dread,
And when they entered the back premises they found the
    six children dead ;
But Mr Brookes, 'tis said, is still alive,
And I hope for many years he will survive.

Oh, Heaven! it is cruel to perish by fire,
Therefore let us be watchful before to our beds we retire,
And see that everything is in safe order before we fall asleep,
And pray that God o'er us in the night watch will keep.

THE BURIAL OF MR. GLADSTONE

THE GREAT POLITICAL HERO

Alas! the people now do sigh and moan
For the loss of Wm. Ewart Gladstone,
Who was a very great politician and a moral man,
And to gainsay it there's few people can.

'Twas in the year of 1898, and on the 19th of May,
When his soul took its flight for ever and aye,
And his body lies interred in Westminster Abbey ;
But I hope his soul has gone to that Heavenly shore,
Where all trials and troubles cease for evermore.

He was a man of great intellect and genius bright,
And ever faithful to his Queen by day and by night,
And always foremost in a political fight ;
And for his services to mankind, God will him requite.

155

The funeral procession was affecting to see,
Thousands of people were assembled there, of every degree ;
And it was almost eleven o'clock when the procession left
    Westminster Hall,
And the friends of the deceased were present—physicians
    and all.

A large force of police was also present there,
And in the faces of the spectators there was a pitiful air,
Yet they were orderly in every way,
And newspaper boys were selling publications without delay.

Present in the procession was Lord Playfair,
And Bailie Walcot was also there,
Also Mr Macpherson of Edinboro—
And all seemingly to be in profound sorrow.

The supporters of the coffin were the Earl Rosebery,
And the Right Honourable Earl of Kimberley,
And the Right Honourable Sir W. Vernon he was there,
And His Royal Highness the Duke of York, I do declare.

George Armitstead, Esq., was there also,
And Lord Rendal, with his heart full of woe ;
And the Right Honourable Duke of Rutland,
And the Right Honourable Arthur J. Balfour, on the right
    hand ;
Likewise the noble Marquis of Salisbury,
And His Royal Highness the Prince of Wales, of high degree.

And immediately behind the coffin was Lord Pembroke,
The representative of Her Majesty, and the Duke of Norfolk,
Carrying aloft a beautiful short wand,
The insignia of his high, courtly office, which looked very
    grand.

And when the procession arrived at the grave, Mrs Glad-
    stone was there,
And in her countenance was depicted a very grave air ;
And the dear, good lady seemed to sigh and moan
For her departed, loving husband, Wm. Ewart Gladstone.

And on the opposite side of her stood Lord Pembroke,
And Lord Salisbury, who wore a skull cap and cloak ;
Also the Prince of Wales and the Duke of Rutland,
And Mr Balfour and Lord Spencer, all looking very bland.

And the clergy were gathered about the head of the grave,
And the attention of the spectators the Dean did crave ;
Then he said, " Man that is born of woman hath a short
    time to live,
But, Oh, Heavenly Father! do thou our sins forgive."

Then Mrs Gladstone and her two sons knelt down by the grave,
Then the Dean did the Lord's blessing crave,
While Mrs Gladstone and her sons knelt,
While the spectators for them great pity felt.

The scene was very touching and profound,
To see all the mourners bending their heads to the ground,
And, after a minute's most silent prayer,
The leave-taking at the grave was affecting, I do declare.

Then Mrs Gladstone called on little Dorothy Drew,
And immediately the little girl to her grandmamma flew,
And they both left the grave with their heads bowed down,
While tears from their relatives fell to the ground.

Immortal Wm. Ewart Gladstone! I must conclude my muse,
And to write in praise of thee my pen does not refuse—
To tell the world, fearlessly, without the least dismay,
You were the greatest politician in your day.

THE DEATH OF THE REV. DR. WILSON

'Twas in the year of 1888 and on the 17th of January
That the late Rev. Dr. Wilson's soul fled away ;
The generous-hearted Dr. had been ailing for some time,
But death, with his dart, did pierce the heart of the learned
    divine.

He was a man of open countenance and of great ability,
And late minister of Free St. Paul's Church, Dundee,
And during the twenty-nine years he remained as minister
    in Dundee
He struggled hard for the well-being of the community.

He was the author of several works concerning great
    men,
In particular the Memoirs of Dr. Candlish and Christ turning
    His face towards Jerusalem ;
Which is well worthy of perusal, I'm sure,
Because the style is concise and the thoughts clear and
    pure.

And as for his age, he was in his eightieth year,
And has left a family of one son and five daughters dear,
And for his loss they will shed many a tear,
Because in their hearts they loved him most dear.

He was a man of a very kindly turn,
And many of his old members for him will mourn,
Because as a preacher he was possessed of courage bold,
Just like one of Covenanting heroes of old.

158

But I hope he is landed safe on Canaan's bright shore,
To sing with bright angels for evermore
Around that golden throne where God's family doth meet
To sing songs night and day, most sacred and sweet.

The coffin containing the remains was brought on Tuesday
evening from Edinboro,
And as the relatives witnessed its departure their hearts
were full of sorrow,
And the remains were laid inside Free St. Paul's Church,
Dundee,
And interred on Wednesday in the Western Cemetery.

The funeral service began at half-past one o'clock in the
afternoon,
And with people the church was filled very soon,
And the coffin was placed in the centre of the platform,
And the lid was covered with wreaths which did the coffin
adorn.

There were beautiful wreaths from the grandchildren of the
deceased,
Whom I hope is now from all troubles released
Also there were wreaths from Mrs and Miss Young, Windsor
Street, Dundee,
Which certainly were most beautiful to see.

Besides the tributes of Miss Morrison and Miss H. Morrison
were a beautiful sight,
Also the tributes of Miss Strong and Mr I. Martin White,
Also Mrs and the Misses Henderson's, West Park, Dundee,
Besides the Misses White Springrove were magnificent
to see.

The members and office-bearers of the church filled the pews on the right,
Which was a very impressive and solemn sight ;
And psalms and hymns were sung by the congregation,
And the Rev. W. I. Cox concluded the service with great veneration.

Then the coffin was carried from the church and placed in the hearse,
While the congregation allowed the friends to disperse,
Then followed the congregation without delay,
Some to join the procession, while others went home straightaway.

The procession consisted of the hearse and 47 carriages no less,
Which were drawn up in the Nethergate, I do confess,
And as the cortege passed slowly along the Nethergate,
Large crowds watched the procession and ungrudgingly did wait.

And when the hearse reached the cemetery the Rev. R. Waterson offered up a prayer,
Then the coffin was lowered into the grave by the pall-bearers there ;
'Twas then the friends began to cry for their sorrow was profound,
Then along with the people assembled there they left the burying-ground.

THE DEATH OF CAPTAIN WARD

'Twas about the beginning of the past century
Billy Bowls was pressed into the British Navy,
And conveyed on board the " Waterwitch " without delay,
Scarce getting time to bid farewell to the villagers of Fairway.

And once on board the " Waterwitch " he resolved to do his
    duty,
And if he returned safe home he'd marry Nelly Blyth, his
    beauty ;
And he'd fight for old England like a jolly British tar,
And the thought of Nelly Blyth would solace him during
    the war.

Poor fellow, he little thought what he had to go through,
But in all his trials at sea he never did rue ;
No, the brave tar became reconciled to his fate,
And felt proud of his commander, Captain Ward the Great.

And on board the " Waterwitch " was Tom Riggles, his old
    comrade,
And with such a comrade he seldom felt afraid ;
Because the stories they told each other made the time pass
    quickly away,
And made their hearts feel light and gay.

'Twas on a Sunday morning and clear to the view,
Captain Ward the attention of his men he drew ;
" Look! " he cried, " There's two French men-of-war on
    our right,
Therefore prepare, my lads, immediately to begin the fight."

K   161

Then the " Waterwitch " was steered to the ship that was
most near,
While every man resolved to sell their lives most dear ;
But the French commander disinclined to engage in the
fight,
And he ordered his men to put on a press of canvas and
take to flight.

Then Captain Ward gave the order to fire,
Then Billy Bowls cried, " Now we'll get fighting to our
hearts' desire " ;
And for an hour a running fight was maintained,
And the two ships of the enemy near upon the "Waterwitch"
gained.

Captain Ward walked the deck with a firm tread,
When a shot from the enemy pierced the ship, yet he felt no
dread ;
But with a splinter Bill Bowls was wounded on the left arm,
And he cried, " Death to the frog-eaters, they have done me
little harm."

Then Captain Ward cried, " Fear not, my men, we will win
the day,
Now, men, pour in a broadside without delay " ;
Then they sailed around the " St. Denis " and the " Gloire,"
And in their cabin windows they poured a deadly fire.

The effect on the two ships was tremendous to behold,
But the Frenchmen stuck to their guns with courage
bold ;
And the crash and din of artillery was deafening to the ear,
And the cries of the wounded men were pitiful to hear.

Then Captain Ward to his men did say,
" We must board the Frenchman without delay " ;
Then he seized his cutlass as he spoke,
And jumped on board the " St. Denis " in the midst of the
    smoke.

Then Bill Bowls and Tom Riggles hastily followed him,
Then, hand to hand, the battle did begin ;
And the men sprang upon their foe and beat them back,
And hauled down their colours and hoisted the Union
    Jack.

But the men on board the " St. Denis " fought desperately
    hard,
And just as the " St. Denis " was captured a ball struck
    Captain Ward
Right on the forehead, and he fell without a groan,
And for the death of Captain Ward the men did moan.

Then the first lieutenant who was standing near by,
Loudly to the men did cry,
" Come, men, and carry your noble commander below ;
But there's one consolation, we have beaten the foe."

And thus fell Captain Ward in the prime of life,
But I hope he is now in the better world free from strife;
But, alas! 'tis sad to think he was buried in the mighty
    deep,
Where too many of our brave seamen silently sleep.

McGONAGALL'S ODE TO THE KING

Oh! God, I thank Thee for restoring King Edward the
   Seventh's health again,
And let all his subjects throughout the Empire say Amen ;
May God guard him by night and day,
At home and abroad, when he's far away.

May angels guard his bed at night when he lies down,
And may his subjects revere him, and on him do not frown ;
May he be honoured by them at home and abroad,
And may he always be protected by the Eternal God.

My blessing on his noble form, and on his lofty head,
May all good angels guard him while living and when dead ;
And when the final hour shall come to summons him away,
May his soul be wafted to the realms of bliss I do pray.

Long may he reign, happy and serene,
Also his Queen most beautiful to be seen ;
And may God guard his family by night and day,
That they may tread in the paths of virtue and not go astray.

May God prosper King Edward the Seventh wherever he
   goes,
May he always reign victorious over his foes ;
Long may he be spared to wear the British Crown,
And may God be as a hedge around him at night when he
   lies down ;
May God inspire him with wisdom, and long may he reign
As Emperor of India and King Edward the VII.—Amen.

A SOLDIER'S REPRIEVE

'Twas in the United States of America some years ago
An aged father sat at his fireside with his heart full of woe,
And talking to his neighbour, Mr Allan, about his boy
  Bennie
That was to be shot because found asleep doing sentinel duty.

" Inside of twenty-four hours, the telegram said,
And, oh! Mr Allan, he's dead, I am afraid.
Where is my brave Bennie now to me is a mystery."
" We will hope with his heavenly Father," said Mr Allan,
  soothingly.

" Yes, let us hope God is very merciful," said Mr Allan.
" Yes, yes," said Bennie's father, " my Bennie was a good
  man.
He said, ' Father, I'll go and fight for my country.'
' Go, then, Bennie,' I said, ' and God be with ye.' "

Little Blossom, Bennie's sister, sat listening with a blanched
  cheek,
Poor soul, but she didn't speak,
Until a gentle tap was heard at the kitchen door,
Then she arose quickly and tripped across the floor.

And opening the door, she received a letter from a neigh-
  bour's hand,
And as she looked upon it in amazement she did stand.
Then she cried aloud, " It is from my brother Bennie.
Yes, it is, dear father, as you can see."

And as his father gazed upon it he thought Bennie was dead,
Then he handed the letter to Mr Allan and by him it was read,
And the minister read as follows : " Dear father, when this
   you see
I shall be dead and in eternity.

" And, dear father, at first it seemed awful to me
The thought of being launched into eternity.
But, dear father, I'm resolved to die like a man,
And keep up my courage and do the best I can.

" You know I promised Jemmie Carr's mother to look after
   her boy,
Who was his mother's pet and only joy.
But one night while on march Jemmie turned sick,
And if I hadn't lent him my arm he'd have dropped very
   quick.

" And that night it was Jemmie's turn to be sentry,
And take poor Jemmie's place I did agree,
But I couldn't keep awake, father, I'm sorry to relate,
And I didn't know it, well, until it was too late.

"Good-bye, dear father, God seems near me,
But I'm not afraid now to be launched into eternity.
No, dear father, I'm going to a world free from strife,
And see my Saviour there in a better, better life."

That night, softly, little Blossom, Bennie's sister, stole out
And glided down the footpath without any doubt.
She was on her way to Washington, with her heart full of
   woe,
To try and save her brother's life, blow high, blow low.

And when Blossom appeared before President Lincoln,
Poor child, she was looking very woebegone.
Then the President said, " My child, what do you want with
me ? "
"Please, Bennie's life, sir," she answered timidly.

" Jemmie was sick, sir, and my brother took his place."
" What is this you say, child ? Come here and let me see
your face."
Then she handed him Bennie's letter, and he read it care-
fully,
And taking up his pen he wrote a few lines hastily.

Then he said to Blossom, " To-morrow, Bennie will go with
you."
And two days after this interview
Bennie and Blossom took their way to their green mountain
home,
And poor little Blossom was footsore, but she didn't moan.

And a crowd gathered at the mill depot to welcome them
back,
And to grasp the hand of his boy, Farmer Owen wasn't
slack,
And tears flowed down his cheeks as he said fervently,
" The Lord be praised for setting my dear boy free."

RICHARD PIGOTT, THE FORGER

Richard Pigott, the forger, was a very bad man,
And to gainsay it there's nobody can,
Because for fifty years he pursued a career of deceit,
And as a forger few men with him could compete.

For by forged letters he tried to accuse Parnell
For the Phoenix Park murders, but mark what befel.
When his conscience smote him he confessed to the fraud,
And the thought thereof no doubt drove him mad.

Then he fled from London without delay,
Knowing he wouldn't be safe there night nor day,
And embarked on board a ship bound for Spain,
Thinking he would escape detection there, but 'twas all in
    vain.

Because while staying at a hotel in Spain
He appeared to the landlord to be a little insane.
And he noticed he was always seemingly in dread,
Like a person that had committed a murder and afterwards
    fled.

And when arrested in the hotel he seemed very cool,
Just like an innocent schoolboy going to school.
And he said to the detectives, " Wait until my portmanteau
    I've got."
And while going for his portmanteau, himself he shot.

So perished Richard Pigott, a forger bold,
Who tried to swear Parnell's life away for the sake of gold,
But the vengeance of God overtook him,
And Parnell's life has been saved, which I consider no sin.

Because he was a man that was very fond of gold,
Not altogether of the miser's craving, I've been told,
But a craving desire after good meat and drink,
And to obtain good things by foul means he never did shrink.

He could eat and drink more than two ordinary men,
And to keep up his high living by foul means we must him
    condemn,
Because his heart's desire in life was to fare well,
And to keep up his good living he tried to betray Parnell.

Yes, the villain tried hard to swear his life away,
But God protected him by night and by day,
And during his long trial in London, without dismay,
The noble patriot never flinched nor tried to run away.

Richard Pigott was a man that was blinded by his own
    conceit.
And would have robbed his dearest friend all for good meat,
To satisfy his gluttony and his own sensual indulgence,
Which the inhuman monster considered no great offence.

But now in that undiscovered country he's getting his
    reward,
And I'm sure few people have for him little regard,
Because he was a villain of the deepest dye,
And but few people for him will heave a sigh.

When I think of such a monster my blood runs cold,
He was like Monteith, that betrayed Wallace for English
    gold ;
But I hope Parnell will prosper for many a day
In despite of his enemies that tried to swear his life away.

Oh! think of his sufferings and how manfully he did stand.
During his long trial in London, to me it seems grand.
To see him standing at the bar, innocent and upright,
Quite cool and defiant, a most beautiful sight.

And to the noble patriot, honour be it said,
He never was the least afraid
To speak on behalf of Home Rule for Ireland,
But like a true patriot nobly he did take his stand.

And may he go on conquering and conquer to the end,
And hoping that God will the right defend,
And protect him always by night and by day,
At home and abroad when far away.

And now since he's set free, Ireland's sons should rejoice
And applaud him to the skies, all with one voice,
For he's their patriot, true and bold,
And an honest, true-hearted gentleman be it told.

THE TROUBLES OF MATTHEW MAHONEY

In a little town in Devonshire, in the mellow September
    moonlight,
A gentleman passing along a street saw a pitiful sight,
A man bending over the form of a woman on the pavement.
He was uttering plaintive words and seemingly discontent.

" What's the matter with the woman ? " asked the gentle-
    man,
As the poor, fallen woman he did narrowly scan.
" There's something the matter, as yer honour can see,
But it's not right to prate about my wife, blame me."

" Is that really your wife ? " said the gentleman.
" Yes, sor, but she looks very pale and wan."
" But surely she is much younger than you ? "
" Only fourteen years, sor, that is thrue.

" It's myself that looks a deal oulder nor I really am,
Throuble have whitened my hair, my good gintleman,
Which was once as black as the wings of a crow,
And it's throuble as is dyed it as white as the snow.

Come, my dear sowl, Bridget, it's past nine o'clock,
And to see yez lying there it gives my heart a shock."
And he smoothed away the raven hair from her forehead,
And her hands hung heavily as if she had been dead.

The gentleman saw what was the matter and he sighed
    again,
And he said, " It's a great trial and must give you pain,
But I see you are willing to help her all you can."
But the encouraging words was not lost upon the Irishman.

" Thrial! " he echoed, " Don't mintion it, yer honour,
But the blessing of God rest upon her.
Poor crathur, she's good barrin' this one fault,
And by any one I don't like to hear her miscault."

" What was the reason of her taking to drink ? "
" Bless yer honour, that's jest what I oftentimes think,
Some things is done without any rason at all,
And, sure, this one to me is a great downfall.

' Ah, Bridget, my darlin', I never dreamt ye'd come to
   this,"
And stooping down, her cheek he did kiss.
While a glittering tear flashed in the moonlight to the ground,
For the poor husband's grief was really profound.

" Have you any children ? " asked the gentleman.
" No, yer honour, bless the Lord, contented I am,
I wouldn't have the lambs know any harm o' their mother,
Besides, sor, to me they would be a great bother."

" What is your trade, my good man ? "
" Gardening, sor, and mighty fond of it I am.
Kind sor, I am out of a job and I am dying with sorrow."
" Well, you can call at my house by ten o'clock to-morrow.

" And I'll see what I can do for you.
Now, hasten home with your wife, and I bid you adieu.
But stay, my good man, I did not ask your name."
" My name is Matthew Mahoney, after Father Matthew of
   great fame."

Then Mahoney stooped and lifted Bridget tenderly,
And carried her home in his arms cheerfully,
And put her to bed while he felt quite content,
Still hoping Bridget would see the folly of drinking and
   repent.

And at ten o'clock next morning Matthew was at Blandford
   Hall,
And politely for Mr Gillespie he did call,
But he was told Mrs Gillespie he would see,
And was invited into the parlour cheerfully.

And when Mrs Gillespie entered the room
She said, " Matthew Mahoney, I suppose you want to know your doom.
Well, Matthew, tell your wife to call here to-morrow."
" I'll ax her, my lady, for my heart's full of sorrow."

So Matthew got his wife to make her appearance at Blandford Hall,
And, trembling, upon Mrs Gillespie poor Bridget did call,
And had a pleasant interview with Mrs Gillespie,
And was told she was wanted for a new lodge-keeper immediately.

" But, Bridget, my dear woman, you musn't drink any more,
For you have got a good husband you ought to adore,
And Mr Gillespie will help you, I'm sure,
Because he is very kind to deserving poor."

And Bridget's repentance was hearty and sincere,
And by the grace of God she never drank whisky, rum, or beer,
And good thoughts come into her mind of Heaven above,
And Matthew Mahoney dearly does her love.

DAVID WINTER AND SON LTD., PRINTERS, DUNDEE

LAST
POETIC GEMS

SELECTED FROM THE WORKS

OF

WILLIAM McGONAGALL

Poet and Tragedian

Died in Edinburgh, 29th September 1902

Edited by
James L. Smith

DUNDEE:
DAVID WINTER & SON LTD.
15 SHORE TERRACE

LONDON:
GERALD DUCKWORTH & CO. LTD
3 HENRIETTA ST., W.C.2

1968

" A Summary History of Poet McGonagall" and " Requisition to the Queen " are reproduced by kind permission of the Corporation of Dundee and are copyright

CONTENTS

Page

CONTENTS

Page

A SUMMARY HISTORY OF POET McGONAGALL

Poet McGonagall was born In the Month of March 1825. His parents were Irish and his Father left Ireland, shortly after His marriage and came to Scotland. And got settled down In Ayrshire In a place call'd Maybole as a Cotton Weaver, and lived there for About ten years untill the Cotton Weaving began to fail there, and Then he was Induced to leave it owing to the very small demand There was for Cotton weaving In that part of Scotland. Then he and his family left Maybole, and came to Edinburgh Where he got settled down again to work Cotton fabrics which there was a greater demand for, than in Maybole. and by this time they family consisted of two Sons, And three daughters. William, The Poet, was the youngest, and was born in Edinburgh. And the rest of the family was born in Maybole And Dundee. his Father lived in Edinburgh for more than eight years, untill the Cotton Weaving began to fail, then his Father and they family left Edinburgh, And travelled to the Orkney Isles, And to a house for they family to live in the Island of Southronaldsay And his father bought the Living as a Pedlar, and supported the family by selling hardware, among they peasantry In the Orkney Isles, and returning home every night to his family, when circumstances would permit him. Charles the eldest son was herding Cows to a Farmer in the Island of South-ronaldsay, and his eldest Sister Nancy, was in the service of a Farmer in the same locality, and William, the Poet, and Thomas, the second eldest brother, was sent to School to be teached by Mr. James Forbes, the parish Schoolmaster, Who was a very Strict Dominie indeed, of which our readers shall hear of as a proof of his strictness, a rather curious incident. William, the Poet, chanced to be one day in his garden behind the school, and Chanc'd to espy a live, Tortoise, that the Dominie kept in the garden. and never having seen such a curious kind of a reptile before, his Curiousity was therefore excited no doubt to see it, and he stooped down and lifted the Tortoise with both hands, thereon admiring the varied beautiful Colours of its shell. when behold it dunged upon both hands of William the poet, which was rather aggravating to William, no doubt, and he dash'd the Tortoise on the ground which almost killed it. And the Dominie Chanc'd to see him, at the time through the back window of the Schoolroom, and he rattled on the window with his Cane to William, which startled him, and as soon as William came in to the School, he layd hold of him and began to beat him unmercifully about the body and face, untill his face was blackened in many places, with his hard Taws. and persisted in it untill some of the elder Scholars cried out to him to Stop! beating William. and when William went home to his dinner, and told his kind father all about it as it had happened his father flew into a rage and said he would be revenged upon him for beating William so unmerciful, and accordingly he went to a Magistrate, with William, and related the Case to him as it had happened. and when the Magistrate examined Williams face, and seen the marks, the Dominie had left thereon he ask'd Williams father if he was willing to put him from ever being a Schoolmaster in the parish again, but Williams Father would not consent to hear of that owing to the Kindness he had shown towards his Son, Thomas, and he simply ask'd the Magistrate, to give him a line, to certify, to Mr. Forbes, that he could put him from ever being a Schoolmaster in that parish again if he would just say the word. so Williams Father went with him to the Dominie, and showed him the line he had got from the Magistrate, to

6

certify that he could put him from being a Schoolmaster again in the parish if he would say the word. and when the Dominie read he was very much surprised and began to make an Apology to Williams Father for what he had done, and promised he would never do the like again. so William and his Father were well satisfied for getting such a sweet revenge, upon that Dominie, and ever after that William was a great favourite of the Dominies and just acted as he pleased and was always very unwilling to go to School. Williams Father had to beat him very often before he would go to School, so that he never got a very great share of education.

William has been like the Immortal Shakspeare he had learn'd more from nature than ever he learn'd at School. William has been from his Boyhood a great admirer of every thing that is Considered to be beautiful sush as beautiful Rivers and mountain Scenery and beautiful land-scapes, and great men such as Shakspeare and great preachers, such as the Rev. George Gilfillan, and Great Poets such as Burns, or Tannahill, and Campbell &c. but again I must return to Williams Father he stay'd in the Island of Southronaldsay for about three years, and then left it with the Family, and came to Dundee, and settled down in it. and those of the family that were able to work were sent to the Mills and some of his Sons wrought at the handloom in the Factory along with himself, that was Thomas, and Charles, and William wrought in the Mill for a few years. and then his Father took him from the Mill, and learnd him the handloom himself and he has followed that occupation up to the present when he Can get it to do. he has always had a great liking for Theatrical representation and has made several appearances upon the Stage, In the Theatre Royal Dundee, In the Character of Macbeth, under the Management of Mr. Caple. he has also play'd the Characters of Hamlet and Othello, Macbeth, and Richard III, In the Music Hall under the Management of Forrest Knowles, to delighted and crowded audiences. and it is only recently ago that he discovered himself to be a poet. the desire for writing Poetry came upon him In the Month of June 1877 that he could not resist the desire for writing poetry the first piece he wrote was An address to the Rev. George Gilfillan, to the Weekly News, only giving the Initials of his name, W. M. G. Dundee which was received with eclat, then he turned his muse to the Tay Bridge, and sung it successfully and was pronounced by the press the Poet Laurete of The Tay Bridge then he unfolded himself to they public, and honestly gave out to them his own name. then he wrote an Address to Robert Burns. Also upon Shakspeare, which he sent printed Copies of to her Majesty, and received her Royal Patronage for so doing. he has also Composed the following effusions, the Bonnie broon haird Lassie o' Bonnie Dundee, and A Companion to it Little Jeemie, also the Convicts return home again to Scotland and the Silvery Tay, and a host of others to numerous to mention, which will be publish'd shortly.

© *The Corporation of Dundee*

8

A REQUISITION TO THE QUEEN

Smiths Buildings No. 19
Patons Lane,
Dundee.
Sept the 6th. 1877.

1. Most August! Empress of India, and of great Britain the
   Queen,
   I most humbly beg your pardon, hoping you will not
   think it mean
   That a poor poet that lives in Dundee,
   Would be so presumptous to write unto Thee

2. Most lovely Empress of India, and Englands generous
   Queen,
   I send you an Address, I have written on Scotlands Bard,
   Hoping that you will accept it, and not be with me to
   hard,
   Nor fly into a rage, but be as Kind and Condescending
   As to give me your Patronage

3. Beautiful Empress, of India, and Englands Gracious
   Queen,
   I send you a Shakespearian Address written by me.
   And I think if your Majesty reads it, right pleased you
   will be.
   And my heart it will leap with joy, if it is patronized by
   Thee.

4. Most Mighty Empress, of India, and Englands beloved
   Queen,
   Most Handsome to be Seen.
   I wish you every Success.
   And that heaven may you bless.

9

For your Kindness to the poor while they are in distress.
I hope the Lord will protect you while living
    And hereafter when your Majesty is . . . dead.
I hope Thee Lord above will place an eternal Crown!
        upon your Head.
    I am your Gracious Majesty ever faithful to Thee,
William McGonagall, The Poor Poet,
    That lives in Dundee.

A NOTE ON THE TEXT

'A Summary History of Poet McGonagall' and 'A Requisition to the Queen' are printed exactly as they appear in McGonagall's handwriting in the Dundee Public Library, by whose courtesy they are here reproduced. The remaining poems are printed from the earliest broadsheets and newspapers, and are transcribed without correction to preserve as far as possible the poet's original grammar, spelling and punctuation.

—*Ed.*

McGONAGALL

THE DEMON DRINK

Oh, thou demon Drink, thou fell destroyer;
Thou curse of society, and its greatest annoyer.
What hast thou done to society, let me think ?
I answer thou hast caused the most of ills, thou demon
    Drink.

Thou causeth the mother to neglect her child,
Also the father to act as he were wild,
So that he neglects his loving wife and family dear,
By spending his earnings foolishly on whisky, rum, and beer.

And after spending his earnings foolishly he beats his wife—
The man that promised to protect her during life—
And so the man would if there was no drink in society,
For seldom a man beats his wife in a state of sobriety.

And if he does, perhaps he finds his wife fou',
Then that causes, no doubt, a great hullaballoo ;
When he finds his wife drunk he begins to frown,
And in a fury of passion he knocks her down.

And in the knock down she fractures her head,
And perhaps the poor wife is killed dead,
Whereas, if there was no strong drink to be got,
To be killed wouldn't have been the poor wife's lot.

Then the unfortunate husband is arrested and cast into jail,
And sadly his fate he does bewail ;
And he curses the hour that ever he was born,
And paces his cell up and down very forlorn.

And when the day of his trial draws near,
No doubt for the murdering of his wife he drops a tear,
And he exclaims, "Oh, thou demon Drink, through thee I
    must die,"
And on the scaffold he warns the people from drink to fly,

Because whenever a father or a mother takes to drink,
Step by step on in crime they do sink,
Until their children loses all affection for them,
And in justice we cannot their children condemn.

The man that gets drunk is little else than a fool,
And is in the habit, no doubt, of advocating for Home Rule ;
But the best Home Rule for him, as far as I can understand,
Is the abolition of strong drink from the land.

And the men that get drunk in general wants Home Rule ;
But such men, I rather think, should keep their heads cool,
And try and learn more sense, I most earnestly do pray,
And help to get strong drink abolished without delay.

If drink was abolished how many peaceful homes would
    there be,
Just, for instance, in the beautiful town of Dundee ;
Then this world would be a heaven, whereas it's a hell,
And the people would have more peace in it to dwell.

Alas ! strong drink makes men and women fanatics,
And helps to fill our prisons and lunatics ;
And if there was no strong drink such cases wouldn't be,
Which would be a very glad sight for all Christians to see.

I admit, a man may be a very good man,
But in my opinion he cannot be a true Christian
As long as he partakes of strong drink,
The more that he may differently think.

But, no matter what he thinks, I say nay,
For by taking it he helps to lead his brother astray,
Whereas, if he didn't drink, he would help to reform society,
And we would soon do away with all inebriety.

Then, for the sake of society and the Church of God,
Let each one try to abolish it at home and abroad;
Then poverty and crime would decrease and be at a stand,
And Christ's Kingdom would soon be established throughout
the land.

Therefore, brothers and sisters, pause and think,
And try to abolish the foul fiend, Drink.
Let such doctrine be taught in church and school,
That the abolition of strong drink is the only Home Rule.

GRIF, OF THE BLOODY HAND

In an immense wood in the south of Kent,
There lived a band of robbers which caused the people
discontent;
And the place they infested was called the Weald,
Where they robbed wayside travellers and left them dead on
the field.

13

Their leader was called Grif, of the Bloody Hand,
And so well skilled in sword practice there's few could him
    withstand;
And sometimes they robbed villages when nothing else
    could be gained,
In the year of 1336, when King Edward the III. reigned.

The dress the robbers wore was deep coloured black,
And in courage and evil deeds they didn't lack;
And Grif, of the Bloody Hand, called them his devils,
Because they were ever ready to perform all kinds of ills.

'Twas towards the close of a very stormy day,
A stranger walked through the wood in search of Grif,
    without dismay;
And as the daylight faded he quickened his pace and ran,
Never suspecting that in his rear he was followed by a man.

And as the man to the stranger drew near,
He demanded in a gruff voice, what seek you here;
And when the stranger saw him he trembled with fear,
Because upon his head he wore a steel helmet, and in his
    hand he bore a spear.

What seek you here repeated the dark habited man,
Come, sir, speak out, and answer me if you can;
Are you then one of the devils demanded the stranger
    faintly,
That I am said the man, now what matters that to thee.

Then repeated the stranger, sir, you have put me to a stand,
But if I guess aright, you are Grif, of the Bloody Hand;
That I am replied Grif, and to confess it I'm not afraid,
Oh! well then I require your service and you'll be well paid.

14

But first I must know thy name, I, that's the point,
Then you shall have the help of my band conjoint;
Before any of my men on your mission goes,
Well then replied the stranger call me Martin Dubois.

Well sir, come tell me what you want as quick as you can,
Well then replied Dubois do you know one Halbert Evesham
That dwells in the little village of Brenchley,
Who has a foster child called Violet Evesham of rare beauty.

And you seek my aid to carry her off,
Ha! ha! a love affair, nay do not think I scoff;
For you shall enjoy her sir before this time to morrow,
If that will satisfy you, or help to drown your sorrow.

And now sir what is your terms with me,
Before I carry off Violet Evesham from the village of
    Brenchley;
Well Grif, one thousand marks shall be the pay,
'Tis agreed then cried Grif, and you shall enjoy her without
    delay.

Then the bargains struck, uttered Grif, how many men will
    you require,
Come sir, speak, you can have all my band if you desire;
Oh, thanks sir, replied Dubois, I consider four men will do,
That's to say sir if the four men's courage be true.

And to-morrow sir send the men to Brenchley without delay,
And remember one thousand merks will be the pay;
And the plan I propose is to carry her to the wood,
And I will be there to receive her, the plan is good.

And on the next morning Grif, of the Bloody Hand,
Told off four of his best men and gave them strict command;
To carry off Violet Evesham from the village of Brenchley,
And to go about it fearlessly and make no delay.

And when ye have captured her carry her to the wood,
Now remember men I wish my injunctions to be understood;
All right, captain, we'll do as we've be told,
And carry her off all right for the sake of the gold.

So on the next morning before the villagers were out of bed,
The four robbers marched into the village of Brenchley
    without any dread;
And boldly entered Violet Evesham's house and carried her,
    away,
While loudly the beautiful girl shrieked in dismay.

But when her old father missed her through the village he
    ran,
And roused the villagers to a man;
And a great number of them gathered, and Wat Tyler at
    their head,
And all armed to the teeth, and towards the wood they
    quickly sped.

And once within the wood Wat Tyler cried, where is Violet
    Evesham,
Then Grif, of the Bloody Hand cried, what ails the man;
My dear sir I assure you that Violet Evesham is not here.
Therefore good people I advise ye to retire from here.

No! I'll not back cried Wat Tyler, until I rescue Violet
    Evesham,
Therefore liar, and devil, defend thyself if you can;
Ay replied Grif, that I will thou braggart loon,
And with my sword you silly boy prepare for thy doom.

Then they rained their blows on each other as thick as hail,
Until at last Grif's strength began to fail;
Then Wat leaped upon him and threw him to the ground,
Then his men fled into the wood that were standing around.

Then the villagers shouted hurrah for Wat Tyler and
    victory,
And to search for Violet Evesham they willingly did agree;
And they searched the wood and found her at the foot of a
    tree,
And when she was taken home the villagers danced with
    glee.

And 'tis said Wat Tyler married Violet Evesham,
And there was great rejoicing among the villagers at the
    marriage so grand;
And Wat Tyler captured Dubois, and bound him to a tree,
And left him there struggling hard to gain his liberty.

A SUMMARY HISTORY OF LORD CLIVE

About a hundred and fifty years ago,
History relates it happened so,
A big ship sailed from the shores of Britain
Bound for India across the raging main.

And many of the passengers did cry and moan
As they took the last look of their old home,
Which they were fast leaving far behind,
And which some of them would long bear in mind.

Among the passengers was a youth about seventeen years
    old,
Who had been a wild boy at home and very bold,
And by his conduct had filled his parents' hearts with woe,
Because to school he often refused to go.

And now that he was going so far away from home,
The thought thereof made him sigh and groan,
For he felt very sad and dejected were his looks,
And he often wished he had spent more time at his books.

And when he arrived in India he searched for work there,
And got to be clerk in a merchant's office, but for it he didn't
    care;
The only pleasure he found was in reading books,
And while doing so, sad and forlorn were his looks.

One day while feeling unhappy he fired a pistol at his own
    head,
Expecting that he would kill himself dead;
But the pistol wouldn't go off although he tried every plan,
And he felt sorry, and resolved to become a better man.

So Clive left his desk and became a soldier brave,
And soon rose to be a captain and manfully did behave;
For he beat the French in every battle,
After all their foolish talk and prattle.

Then he thought he would take a voyage home to his friends,
And for his bad behaviour towards them he would make
    some amends;
For he hadn't seen them for many years,
And when he thought of them he shed briny tears.

And when he arrived in London
The people after him in crowds did run;
And they flocked to see him every minute,
Because they thought him the most famous man in it.

And all the greatest people in the land
Were proud to shake him by the hand;
And they gave him a beautiful sword because he had fought
    so well
And of his bravery the people to each other did tell.

And when his own friends saw him they to him ran,
And they hardly knew him, he looked so noble a man;
And his parents felt o'erjoyed when they saw him home
    again,
And when he left his parents again for India it caused them
    great pain.

But it was a good thing Clive returned to India again,
Because a wicked prince in his territory wouldn't allow the
    British to remain,
And he resolved to drive them off his land,
And marched upon them boldly with thousands of his band

But the bad prince trembled when he heard that Clive had
    come,
Because the British at the charge of the bayonet made his
    army run;
And the bad prince was killed by one of his own band,
And the British fortunately got all his land.

And nearly all India now belongs to this country,
Which has been captured by land and by sea,
By some of the greatest men that ever did live,
But the greatest of them all was Robert Clive.

THE BATTLE OF THE NILE

'Twas on the 18th of August in the year of 1798,
That Nelson saw with inexpressible delight
The City of Alexandria crowded with the ships of France,
So he ordered all sail to be set, and immediately advance.

And upon the deck, in deep anxiety he stood,
And from anxiety of mind he took but little food;
But now he ordered dinner to be prepared without delay,
Saying, I shall gain a peerage to-morrow, or Westminster
    Abbey.

The French had found it impossible to enter the port of
    Alexandria,
Therefore they were compelled to withdraw;
Yet their hearts were burning with anxiety the war to begin,
But they couldn't find a pilot who would convey them
    safely in.

20

Therefore Admiral Brueys was forced to anchor in Aboukir
    Bay,
And in a compact line of battle, the leading vessel lay
Close to a shoal, along a line of very deep water,
There they lay, all eager to begin the murderous slaughter.

The French force consisted of thirteen ships of the line,
As fine as ever sailed on the salt sea brine;
Besides four Frigates carrying 1,196 guns in all,
Also 11,230 men as good as ever fired a cannon ball.

The number of the English ships were thirteen in all,
And carrying 1012 guns, including great and small;
And the number of the men were 8,068,
All jolly British tars and eager for to fight.

As soon as Nelson perceived the position of the enemy,
His active mind soon formed a plan immediately;
As the plan he thought best, as far as he could see,
Was to anchor his ships on the quarter of each of the enemy.

And when he had explained his mode of attack to his officers
    and men,
He said, form as convenient, and anchor at the stern;
Then first gain the victory, and make the best use of it you
    can,
Therefore I hope every one here to-day, will do their duty to
    a man.

When Captain Berry perceived the boldness of the plan,
He said, my Lord, I'm sure the men will do their duty to a
    man;
And, my Lord, what will the world say, if we gain the
    victory ?
Then Nelson replied, there's no if in the case, and that you'll
    see.

21

Then the British tars went to work without delay,
All hurrying to and fro, making ready for the fray;
And there wasn't a man among them, but was confident
   that day,
That they would make the French to fly from Aboukir Bay.

Nelson's Fleet did not enter Aboukir Bay at once,
And by adopting that plan, that was his only chance;
But one after another, they bore down on the enemy;
Then Nelson cried, now open fire my heroes, immediately!

Then the shores of Egypt trembled with the din of the war,
While sheets of flame rent the thick clouds afar;
And the contending fleets hung incumbent o'er the bay,
Whilst our British tars stuck to their guns without the least
   dismay.

And loudly roared the earthly thunder along the river Nile,
And the British ship Orion went into action in splendid
   style;
Also Nelson's Ship Vanguard bore down on the foe,
With six flags flying from her rigging high and low.

Then she opened a tremendous fire on the Spartiate,
And Nelson cried, fear not my lads we'll soon make them
   retreat!
But so terrific was the fire of the enemy on them,
That six of the Vanguards guns were cleared of men.

Yet there stood Nelson, the noble Hero of the Nile,
In the midst of death and destruction on deck all the while;
And around him on every side, the cannon balls did rattle,
But right well the noble hero knew the issue of the battle.

But suddenly he received a wound on the head,
And fell into the arms of Captain Berry, but fortunately not
    dead;
And the flow of blood from his head was very great,
But still the hero of the Nile was resigned to his fate.

Then to the Cockpit the great Admiral was carried down,
And in the midst of the dying, he never once did frown;
Nor he did'nt shake with fear, nor yet did he mourne,
But patiently sat down to wait his own turn.

And when the Surgeon saw him, he instantly ran,
But Nelson said, Surgeon, attend to that man;
Attend to the sailor you were at, for he requires your aid,
Then I will take my turn, don't be the least afraid.

And when his turn came, it was found that his wound was
    but slight,
And when known, it filled the sailors hearts with delight;
And they all hoped he would soon be able to command in the
    fight,
When suddenly a cry arose of fire! which startled Nelson
    with affright.

And unassisted he rushed upon the deck, and to his amaze,
He discovered that the Orient was all in a blaze;
Then he ordered the men to lower the boats, and relieve the
    enemy,
Saying, now men, see and obey my orders immediately.

Then the noble tars manned their boats, and steered to the
    Orient,
While the poor creatures thanked God for the succour He
    had sent;
And the burning fragments fell around them like rain,
Still our British tars rescued about seventy of them from the
    burning flame,

And of the thirteen sail of the French the British captured
    nine,
Besides four of their ships were burnt, which made the scene
    sublime,
Which made the hero of the Nile cry out thank God we've
    won the day,
And defeated the French most manfully in Aboukir Bay.

Then the victory was complete and the French Fleet
    annihilated,
And when the news arrived in England the peoples' hearts
    felt elated,
Then Nelson sent orders immediately through the fleet,
That thanksgiving should be returned to God for the victory
    complete.

BEAUTIFUL ABERFOYLE

The mountains and glens of Aberfoyle are beautiful to sight,
Likewise the rivers and lakes are sparkling and bright;
And its woods were frequented by the Lady of the Lake,
And on its Lakes many a sail in her boat she did take.

The scenery there will fill the tourist with joy,
Because 'tis there once lived the bold Rob Roy,
Who spent many happy days with his Helen there,
By chasing the deer in the woods so fair.

The little vale of Aberfoyle and its beautiful river
Is a sight, once seen, forget it you'll never;
And romantic ranges of rock on either side
Form a magnificent background far and wide.

And the numerous lochs there abound with trout
Which can be had for the taking out,
Especially from the Lochs Chon and Ard,
There the angler can make a catch which will his toil reward.

And between the two lochs the Glasgow Water Works are
    near,
Which convey water of Loch Katrine in copious streams
    clear
To the inhabitants of the Great Metropolis of the West,
And for such pure water they should think themselves blest.

The oak and birch woods there are beautiful to view,
Also the Ochil hills which are blue in hue,
Likewise the Lake of Menteith can be seen far eastward,
Also Stirling Castle, which long ago the English besieged
    very hard.

Then away to Aberfoyle, Rob Roy's country,
And gaze on the magnificent scenery.
A region of rivers and mountains towering majestically
Which is lovely and fascinating to see.

But no words can describe the beautiful scenery.
Aberfoyle must be visited in order to see,
So that the mind may apprehend its beauties around,
Which will charm the hearts of the visitors I'll be bound.

As for the clachan of Aberfoyle, little remains but a hotel,
Which for accommodation will suit the traveller very well.
And the bedding there is clean and good,
And good cooks there to cook the food.

Then away to the mountains and lakes of bonnie Aberfoyle,
Ye hard-working sons and daughters of daily toil;
And traverse its heathery mountains and view its lakes so
    clear,
When the face of Nature's green in the spring of the year.

THE CONVICT'S RETURN

Ye mountains and glens of fair Scotland I'm with ye once
    again,
During my absence from ye my heart was like to break in
    twain;
Oh! how I longed to see you and the old folks at home,
And with my lovely Jeannie once more in the green woods
    to roam.

Now since I've returned safe home again
I will try and be content
With my lovely Jeannie at home,
And forget my banishment.

26

My Jeannie and me will get married,
And I will be to her a good man,
And we'll live happy together,
And do the best we can.

I hope my Jeannie and me
Will always happy be,
And never feel discontent;
And at night at the fireside
I'll relate to her the trials of my banishment.

But now I will never leave my Jeannie again
Until the day I die;
And before the vital spark has fled
I will bid ye all good-bye.

THE BATTLE OF ALEXANDRIA, OR
THE RECONQUEST OF EGYPT

It was on the 21st of March in the year of 1801,
The British were at their posts every man;
And their position was naturally very strong,
And the whole line from sea to lake was about a mile long.

And on the ruins of a Roman Palace, rested the right,
And every man amongst them was eager for the fight,
And the reserve was under the command of Major General
    Moore,
A hero brave, whose courage was both firm and sure.

And in the valley between the right were the cavalry,
Which was really a most beautiful sight to see;
And the 28th were posted in a redoubt open in the rear,
Determined to hold it to the last without the least fear.

And the Guards and the Inniskillings were eager for the fray,
Also the Gordon Highlanders and Cameron Highlanders in
    grand array;
Likewise the dismounted Cavalry and the noble Dragoons,
Who never fear'd the cannons shot when it loudly booms.

And between the two armies stretched a sandy plain,
Which the French tried to chase the British off, but it was
    all in vain,
And a more imposing battle-field seldom has been chosen,
But alack the valour of the French soon got frozen.

Major General Moore was the general officer of the night,
And had galloped off to the left and to the right,
The instant he heard the enemy briskly firing;
He guessed by their firing they had no thought of retiring.

Then a wild broken huzza was heard from the plain below,
And followed by a rattle of musketry from the foe;
Then the French advanced in column with their drums
    loudly beating,
While their officers cried forward men and no retreating.

Then the colonel of the 58th reserved his fire,
Until the enemy drew near, which was his desire;
Then he ordered his men to attack them from behind the
    palace wall,
Then he opened fire at thirty yards, which did the enemy
    appal.

And thus assailed in front, flank, and rear,
The French soon began to shake with fear;
Then the 58th charged them with the bayonet, with courage
unshaken,
And all the enemy that entered the palace ruins were killed
or taken.

Then the French Invincibles, stimulated by liquor and the
promise of gold,
Stole silently along the valley with tact and courage bold,
Proceeded by a 6 pounder gun, between the right of the
guards,
But brave Lieutenant-Colonel Stewart quickly their
progress retards.

Then Colonel Stewart cried to the right wing,
Forward! my lads, and make the valley ring,
And charge them with your bayonets and capture their gun,
And before very long they will be glad to run.

Then loudly grew the din of battle, like to rend the skies,
As Major Stirling's left wing faced, and charged them
likewise;
Then the Invincibles maddened by this double attack,
Dashed forward on the palace ruins, but they soon were
driven back.

And by the 58th, and Black Watch they were brought to
bay, here,
But still they were resolved to sell their lives most dear,
And it was only after 650 of them had fallen in the fray,
That the rest threw down their arms and quickly ran away.

Then unexpected, another great body of the enemy was seen,
With their banners waving in the breeze, most beautiful and
green;
And advancing on the left of the redoubt,
But General Moore instantly ordered the Black Watch out.

And he cried, brave Highlanders you are always in the
hottest of the fight,
Now make ready for the bayonet charge with all your might;
And remember our country and your forefathers
As soon as the enemy and ye foregathers.

Then the Black Watch responded with a loud shout,
And charged them with their bayonots without fear or
doubt;
And the French tried hard to stand the charge, but it was all
in vain,
And in confussion they all fled across the sandy plain.

Oh! it was a glorious victory, the British gained that day,
But the joy of it, alas! was unfortunately taken away,
Because Sir Ralph Abercrombie, in the hottest of the fight,
was shot,
And for his undaunted bravery, his name will never be
forgot.

SAVED BY MUSIC

At one time, in America, many years ago,
Large gray wolves wont to wander to and fro;
And from the farm yards they carried pigs and calves away,
Which they devoured ravenously, without dismay.

But, as the story goes, there was a negro fiddler called old
    Dick,
Who was invited by a wedding party to give them music,
In the winter time, when the snow lay thick upon the ground,
And the rivers far and near were frozen all around.

So away went Dick to the wedding as fast as he could go,
Walking cautiously along o'er the crisp and crackling snow,
And the path was a narrow one, the greater part of the way
Through a dark forest, which filled his heart with dismay.

And when hurrying onward, not to be late at the festival,
He heard the howl of a wolf, which did his heart appal,
And the howl was answered, and as the howl came near
Poor Old Dick, fiddle in hand, began to shake with fear.

And as the wolves gathered in packs from far and near,
Old Dick in the crackling bushes did them hear,
And they ran along to keep pace with him,
Then poor Dick began to see the danger he was in.

And every few minutes a wolf would rush past him with a
    snap,
With a snapping sound like the ring of a steel trap,
And the pack of wolves gathered with terrible rapidity,
So that Dick didn't know whether to stand or flee.

And his only chance, he thought, was to keep them at bay
By preserving the greatest steadiness without dismay,
Until he was out of the forest and on open ground,
Where he thought a place of safety might be found.

He remembered an old hut stood in the clearing,
And towards it he was slowly nearing,
And the hope of reaching it urged him on,
But he felt a trifle dispirited and woe-begone.

And the poor fellow's heart with fear gave a bound,
When he saw the wolves' green eyes glaring all around,
And they rushed at him boldly, one after another,
Snapping as they passed, which to him was great bother.

And Dick sounded his fiddle and tried to turn them back,
And the sound caused the wolves to leap back in a crack,
When Dick took to his heels at full run,
But now poor Dick's danger was only begun :

For the wolves pursued him without delay,
But Dick arrived at the hut in great dismay,
And had just time to get on the roof and play,
And at the strains of the music the wolves felt gay.

And for several hours he sat there in pain,
Knowing if he stopped playing the wolves would be at him
    again,
But the rage of the wolves abated to the subduing strains,
And at last he was rewarded for all his pains :

For the wedding-party began to weary for some music,
And they all came out to look for Old Dick,
And on the top of the hut they found him fiddling away,
And they released him from his dangerous position without
    delay.

BEAUTIFUL NEWPORT ON THE BRAES
O' THE SILVERY TAY

Bonnie Mary, the Maid o' the Tay,
Come! let's go, and have a holiday
In Newport, on the braes o' the silvery Tay,
'Twill help to drive dull care away.

The scenery there is most enchanting to be seen,
Especially the fine mansions with their shrubbery green;
And the trees and ivy are beautiful to view
Growing in front of each stately home in the avenue.

There the little birds and beautiful butterflies
Are soaring heavenwards almost to the skies,
And the busy bees are to be seen on the wing,
As from flower to flower they hummingly sing,

As they gather honey all the day,
From the flowery gardens of Newport on the braes o' the
     Tay.
And as we view the gardens our hearts will feel gay
After being pent up in the workshop all the day.

Then there's a beautiful spot near an old mill,
Suitable for an artist to paint of great skill,
And the trees are arched o'erhead, lovely to be seen,
Which screens ye from the sunshine's glittering sheen.

Therefore, holiday makers, I'd have ye resort
To Newport on the braes o' the Tay for sport,
And inhale the pure air with its sweet perfume,
Emanating from the flowery gardens of Newport and the
     yellow broom.

And when bright Sol sinks in the West
You'll return home at night quite refreshed,
And dream in your beds of your rambles during the day
Along the bonnie braes o' the silvery Tay.

THE BATTLE OF CORUNNA

'Twas in the year of 1808, and in the autumn of the year,
Napoleon resolved to crush Spain and Portugal without fear;
So with a mighty army three hundred thousand strong
Through the passes of the Pyrenees into Spain he passed
along.

But Sir John Moore concentrated his troops in the north,
And into the west corner of Spain he boldly marched forth;
To cut off Napoleon's communications with France
He considered it to be advisable and his only chance.

And when Napoleon heard of Moore's coming, his march he
did begin,
Declaring that he was the only General that could oppose
him;
And in the month of December, when the hills were clad
with snow,
Napoleon's army marched over the Guadiana Hills with
their hearts full of woe.

And with fifty thousand cavalry, infantry, and artillery,
Napoleon marched on, facing obstacles most dismal to see:
And performed one of the most rapid marches recorded in
history,
Leaving the command of his army to Generals Soult and
Ney.

And on the 5th of January Soult made his attack,
But in a very short time the French were driven back;
With the Guards and the 50th Regiment and the 42d
    conjoint,
They were driven from the village of Elnina at the bayonet's
    point.

Oh! it was a most gorgeous and inspiring sight
To see Sir John Moore in the thickest of the fight,
And crying aloud to the 42d with all his might,
"Forward, my lads, and charge them with your bayonets
    left and right."

Then the 42d charged them with might and main,
And the French were repulsed again and again;
And although they poured into the British ranks a withering
    fire,
The British at the charge of the bayonet soon made them
    retire.

Oh! that battlefield was a fearful sight to behold,
'Twas enough to make one's blood run cold
To hear the crack, crack of the musketry and the cannon's
    roar,
Whilst the dead and the dying lay weltering in their gore.

But O Heaven! it was a heartrending sight,
When Sir John Moore was shot dead in the thickest of the
    fight;
And as the soldiers bore him from the field they looked
    woebegone,
And the hero's last words were "Let me see how the battle
    goes on."

Then he breathed his last with a gurgling sound,
And for the loss of the great hero the soldiers' sorrow was
    profound,
Because he was always kind and served them well,
And as they thought of him tears down their cheeks trickling
    fell.

Oh! it was a weird and pathetic sight
As they buried him in the Citadel of Corunna at the dead of
    night,
While his staff and the men shed many tears
For the noble hero who had commanded them for many
    years.

Success to the British Army wherever they go,
For seldom they have failed to conquer the foe;
Long may the Highlanders be able to make the foe reel,
By giving them an inch or two of cold steel.

A TALE OF CHRISTMAS EVE

'Twas Christmastide in Germany,
And in the year of 1850,
And in the city of Berlin, which is most beautiful to the eye;
A poor boy was heard calling out to the passers-by.

"Who'll buy my pretty figures," loudly he did cry,
Plaster of Paris figures, but no one inclined to buy;
His clothes were thin and he was nearly frozen with cold,
And wholly starving with hunger, a pitiful sight to behold.

And the twilight was giving place to the shadows of
    approaching night,
And those who possessed a home were seeking its warmth
    and light;
And the market square was dark and he began to moan,
When he thought of his hungry brother and sisters at home.

Alas! the poor boy was afraid to go home,
Oh, Heaven! hard was his lot, for money he'd none;
And the tears coursed down his cheeks while loudly he did
    cry,
"Buy my plaster of Paris figures, oh! please come buy."

It was now quite dark while he stood there,
And the passers-by did at the poor boy stare,
As he stood shivering with cold in the market square;
And with the falling snow he was almost frozen to the bone.
And what would it avail him standing there alone,
Therefore he must make up his mind to return home.

Then he tried to hoist the board and figures on to his head,
And for fear of letting the board fall he was in great dread;
Then he struggled manfully forward without delay,
But alas! he fell on the pavement, oh! horror and dismay.

And his beautiful figures were broken and scattered around
    him,
And at the sight thereof his eyes grew dim;
And when he regained his feet he stood speechless like one
    bowed down,
Then the poor boy did fret and frown.

Then the almost despairing boy cried aloud,
And related his distress to the increasing crowd;
Oh! What a pitiful sight on a Christmas eve,
But the dense crowd didn't the poor boy relieve,

Until a poor wood-cutter chanced to come along,
And he asked of the crowd what was wrong;
And twenty ready tongues tells him the sad tale,
And when he heard it the poor boy's fate he did bewail.

And he cried, "Here! Something must be done and quickly too,
Do you hear! Every blessed soul of you;
Come, each one give a few pence to the poor boy,
And it will help to fill his heart with joy."

Then the wood-cutter gave a golden coin away,
So the crowd subscribed largely without delay;
Which made the poor boy's heart feel gay,
Then the wood-cutter thanked the crowd and went away.

So the poor boy did a large subscription receive,
And his brother, mother, and sisters had a happy Christmas eve;
And he thanked the crowd and God that to him the money sent,
And bade the crowd good-night, then went home content.

THE BATTLE OF GUJRAT

'Twas in the year of 1849, and on the 20th of February,
Lord Gough met and attacked Shere Sing right manfully.
The Sikh Army numbered 40,000 in strength,
And showing a front about two miles length.

It was a glorious morning, the sun was shining in a cloudless
    sky;
And the larks were singing merrily in the heavens high;
And 'twas about nine o'clock in the morning the battle was
    begun,
But at the end of three hours the Sikhs were forced to run.

Lord Gough's force was a mixture of European and native
    infantry,
And well supported with artillery and cavalry;
But the British Army in numbers weren't so strong,
Yet, fearlessly and steadily, they marched along.

Shere Sing, the King, had taken up a position near the town,
And as he gazed upon the British Army he did frown;
But Lord Gough ordered the troops to commence the battle,
With sixty big guns that loudly did rattle.

The Sikhs were posted on courses of deep water,
But the British in a short time soon did them scatter.
Whilst the British cannonading loudly bums,
And in the distance were heard the enemy's drums.

Then the Sikhs began to fight with their artillery,
But their firing didn't work very effectively;
Then the British lines advanced on them right steadily,
Which was a most inspiring sight to see.

Then the order was given to move forward to attack,
And again—and again—through fear the enemy drew back.
Then Penny's brigade, with a ringing cheer, advanced
    briskly,
And charged with their bayonets very heroically.

Then the Sikhs caught the bayonets with their left hand,
And rushed in with their swords, the scene was heroic and
    grand.
Whilst they slashed and cut with great dexterity,
But the British charge was irresistible, they had to flee.

And with 150 men they cleared the village of every living
    thing,
And with British cheers the village did ring;
And the villagers in amazement and terror fled,
Because the streets and their houses were strewn with their
    dead.

The chief attack was made on the enemy's right
By Colin Campbell's brigade—a most magnificent sight.
Though they were exposed to a very galling fire,
But at last the Sikhs were forced to retire.

And in their flight everything was left behind,
And the poor Sikhs were of all comfort bereft,
Because their swords, cannon, drums, and waggons were left
    behind,
Therefore little pleasure could they find.

Then Shere Sing fled in great dismay,
But Lord Gough pursued him without delay,
And captured him a few miles away;
And now the Sikhs are our best soldiers of the present day,
Because India is annexed to the British Dominions, and they
    must obey.

BILL BOWLS THE SAILOR

Bill Bowels was an amiable gentle youth,
And concerning him I'll relate the truth;
His Mother wanted to make him a Tailor,
But Bill's Father said he was cut out for a Sailor.

Dancing bareheaded under heavy rain was his delight,
And wading in ponds and rivers by day and night;
And he was as full of mischief as an Egg is full of meat,
And tumbling and swimming in deep pools to him was a
    treat.

His Father was a Mill Wright, and lived near a small lake,
And many a swim in that lake, Bill used to take;
And many a good lesson his good dad gave to him,
To keep always in shoal water till he could swim.

One day he got hold of a very big plank,
And with it he resolved to play some funny prank,
So he launched the plank into the lake,
Crying now I'll have some rare fun and no mistake.

And on the plank he went with a piece broken paling for an
    oar,
But suddenly a squall came down on the lake which made
    him roar,
And threw him on his beam ends into the water,
And the clothes he had on him were drenched every tatter.

'Twas lucky for Bill his Father heard his cries,
And to save poor Bill he instantly flies,
And he leaped into the lake and dragged Bill ashore,
While Bill for help did lustily roar.

41

Then after that he joined a ship bound for China,
With a pair of light breeches and his heart full of glee,
But his heart soon became less buoyant
When he discovered his Captain was a great tyrant.

One evening as Bill stood talking to the steersman,
And the weather at the time was very calm;
Tom Riggles said, Bill we're going to have dirty weather,
But with the help of God, we'll weather it together.

That night the Captain stood holding to on the shrouds,
While scudding across the sky were thick angry clouds
And the ship was running unsteady before the wind,
And the Captain was drunk must be borne in mind.

Then a cry is heard which might have chilled the stoutest
    heart,
Which caused every man on board with fear to start;
Oh! heavens, rocks ahead, shouted the mate, above the gale,
While every face on board turned ghastly pale.

Then, port! port! hard-a-port! shouted the men
All over the ship, from bow to stern,
And the order was repeated by the mate
Who sprang to the wheel, fearlessly resigned to his fate.

At last a heavy wave struck the ship with a terrible dash,
Which made every plank quiver and give way with a crash,
While wave on the back of wave struck her with fearful
    shocks,
Until at last she was lifted up and cast on the rugged rocks.

42

Oh! heaven, it must have been an awful sight,
To witness in the dusky moon-light;
Men clinging to the rigging with all their might,
And others trying to put the ship all right.

Then the wind it blew a terrific blast,
Which tore the rigging away and the missen-mast;
And the big waves lashed her furiously,
And the Captain was swept with the wreck into the sea.

Then every man struggled manfully to gain the shore,
While the storm fiend did loudly laugh and roar,
But alas! they all perished but Tom Riggles and Bill Bowls,
And they were cast on a rocky islet where on the tempest
    howls

And they lived on shell fish while they were there,
Until one day they began to despair,
But thank God they espied a vessel near at hand,
And they were taken on board and landed safe in fair
    England.

THE BATTLE OF THE ALMA. FOUGHT IN 1854

'Twas on the heights of Alma the battle began,
But the Russians turned and fled every man;
Because Sir Colin Campbell's Highland Brigade put them to
    flight,
At the charge of the bayonet, which soon ended the fight.

Sir Colin Campbell he did loudly cry,
Let the Highlanders go forward, they will win or die,
We'll hae nane but Hieland bonnets here,
So forward, my lads, and give one ringing cheer.

Then boldly and quickly they crossed the river,
But not one amongst them with fear did shiver,
And ascended the height, forming quietly on the crest,
While each man seemed anxious to do his best.

The battle was fought by twenty against one,
But the gallant British troops resolved to die to a man,
While the shot was mowing them down and making ugly
    gaps,
And shells shrieking and whistling and making fearful
    cracks.

On the heights of Alma it was a critical time,
And to see the Highland Brigade it was really sublime,
To hear the officers shouting to their men,
On lads, I'll show you the way to fight them.

Close up! Close up! Stand firm, my boys,
Now be steady, men, steady and think of our joys;
If we only conquer the Russians this day,
Our fame will be handed down to posterity for ever and aye.

Still forward! Forward! my lads was the cry,
And from the redoubt make them fly;
And at length the Russians had to give way,
And fled from the redoubt in wild dismay.

Still the fate of the battle hung in the balance,
But Sir Colin knew he had still a chance,
But one weak officer in fear loudly shouted,
Let the Guards fall back, or they'll be totally routed.

Then Sir Colin Campbell did make reply,
'Tis better, Sir, that every man of the Guards should die,
And to be found dead on this bloody field,
Than to have it said they fled and were forced to yield.

Then the Coldstreams on the Highlanders' right
Now advanced to engage the enemy in the fight,
But then they halted, unable to go forward,
Because the Russians did their progress retard.

But now came the turning point of the battle,
While the Russian guns loudly did rattle;
Then Sir Colin turned to the plumed Highland array,
And in stirring tones to them did say—

Be steady, keep silence, my lads, don't be afraid,
And make me proud of my Highland Brigade;
Then followed the command, sharp and clear,
While the war notes of the 42d bagpipes smote the ear.

The soldiers, though young, were cool and steady,
And to face the enemy they were ever ready,
And still as the bare-kneed line unwavering came on
It caused the Russians to shake and look woebegone.

And now as the din of the fight grew greater,
Fear filled the hearts of the Russian giants in stature,
Because the kilted heroes they fought so well
That they thought they had come from the regions of hell.

Oh! it was a most beautiful and magnificent display
To see the Highland Brigade in their tartan array,
And their tall bending plumes in a long line,
The scene was inspiring and really sublime.

Then, terror-stricken by this terrible advancing line,
The Russians broke down and began to whine,
And they turned round and fled with a moaning cry,
Because they were undone and had to fly.

Then the crisis was past and the victory won,
Which caused Sir Colin Campbell to cry, Well done,
And, raising his hand, gave the signal to cheer,
Which was responded to by hurrahs, loud and clear.

BEAUTIFUL ROTHESAY

Beautiful Rothesay, your scenery is most grand,
You cannot be surpassed in fair Scotland.
Tis healthy for holiday makers, to go there,
For the benefit of their health, by inhaling the pure air

And to hear the innocent birds, on a fine Summer day,
Carolling their sweet songs, so lively and gay,
Therefore, holiday makers, be advised by me,
And visit beautiful Rothesay, by the side of the Sea.

Then Sweet Jessie, let us go,
To Scotlands garden of Eden O!
And spend the lovely Summer day,
In the beautiful village of Rothesay.

There you can see the ships, passing to and fro,
Which will drive away dull care, and woe,
And, the heavens breath smells wooingly there,
Therefore, lets away dear Jessie, to inhale the balmy air.

The mansions, there, are most beautiful to be seen,
Likewise the trees, and shrubberies, green.
Therefore, we will feel happy and gay,
Walking hand in hand, together the live long day.

Along the beautiful walks with our hearts fu' cheerie,
My dear love! until we grow weary.
Then, return home at night, with our spirits light and gay,
After viewing the beautiful scenery of Rothesay.

THE BATTLE OF INKERMANN

'Twas in the year of 1854, and on the 5th of November,
Which Britain will no doubt long remember,
When the Russians plotted to drive the British army into
    the sea,
But at the bayonet charge the British soon made them flee

With fourteen hundred British, fifteen thousand Russians
    were driven back,
At half-past seven o'clock in the morning they made the
    attack,
But the Grenadiers and Scottish Fusilier Guards, seven
    hundred strong,
Moved rapidly and fearlessly all along.

47

And their rifles were levelled ready for a volley,
But the damp had silenced their fire which made the men
 feel melancholy,
But the Russians were hurled down the ravine in a
 disordered mass
At the charge of the bayonet—an inspiring sight!—nothing
 could it surpass.

General Cathcart thought he could strike a blow at an
 unbroken Russian line;
Oh! the scene was really very sublime,
Because hand to hand they fought with a free will,
And with one magnificent charge they hurled the Russians
 down the hill.

But while General Cathcart without any dread
Was collecting his scattered forces, he fell dead,
Pierced to the heart with a Russian ball,
And his men lamented sorely his downfall.

While the Duke of Cambridge with the colours of two
 Regiments of Guards
Presses forward, and no obstacle his courage retards,
And with him about one hundred men,
And to keep up their courage he was singing a hymn to them.

Then hand to hand they fought the Russians heroically,
Which was a most inspiring sight to see;
Captain Burnaby with thirteen Guardsmen fighting
 manfully,
And they drove the Russians down the hillside right
 speedily.

The French and Zouaves aided the British in the fight,
And they shot down and killed the Russians left and right,
And the Chasseurs also joined in the fight,
And the Russians fell back in great afright.

Then the Russians tried again and again
To drive the British from the slopes of Inkermann, but all in
    vain,
For the French and British beat them back without dismay,
Until at last the Russians had to give way.

And the French and British fought side by side
Until the Russians no longer the bayonet charge could abide,
And the Russians were literally scorched by the musketry
    fire,
And in a short time the Russians were forced to retire.

Then the British and French pursued them into the depths
    of the ravine,
Oh! it was a grand sight—the scene was really sublime—
And at half-past one o'clock the Russians were defeated,
And from the field of Inkermann they sullenly retreated.

Then the Battle of Inkermann was won,
And from the field the Russians were forced to run,
But the loss of the British was terrible to behold;
The dead lay in heaps stiff and cold,
While thousands of Russians were dying with no one to aid
    them,
Alas! pitiful to relate, thousands of innocent men.

LITTLE PIERRE'S SONG

In a humble room in London sat a pretty little boy,
By the bedside of his sick mother her only joy,
Who was called Little Pierre, and who's father was dead;
There he sat poor boy, hungry and crying for bread.

There he sat humming a little song, which was his own,
But to the world it was entirely unknown,
And as he sang the song he felt heartsick,
But he resolved to get Madame Malibran to sing his song in
    public

Then he paused for a moment and clasped his hands,
And running to the looking-glass before it he stands,
Then he smoothed his yellow curls without delay,
And from a tin box takes a scroll of paper worn and grey.

Then he gave one fond eager glance at his mother,
Trying hard brave boy his grief to smother,
As he gazed on the bed where she lay,
But he resolved to see Madame Malibran without delay.

Then he kissed his mother while she slept,
And stealthly from the house he crept,
And direct to Madame Malibran's house he goes,
Resolved to see her no matter who did him oppose.

And when he reached the door he knocked like a brave
    gallant
And the door was answered by her lady servant,
Then he told the servant Madame Malibran he wished to see
And the servant said, oh yes, I'll tell her immediately.

Then away the servant goes feeling quite confident,
And told her a little boy wished to see her just one moment
Oh! well, said Madame Malibran, with a smile,
Fetch in the little boy he will divert me a while.

So Little Pierre was brought in with his hat under his arm
And in his hand a scroll of paper, thinking it no harm,
Then walked straight up to Madame Malibran without dread
And said, dear lady my mother is sick and in want of bread.

And I have called to see if you would sing my little song,
At some of your grand concerts, Ah! say before long,
Or perhaps you could sell it to a publisher for a small sum,
Then I could buy food for my mother and with it would run.

Then Madame Malibran rose from her seat most costly and
    grand
And took the scroll of paper from Pierre's hand
And hummed his little song, to a plaintive air,
Then said, your song is soul stirring I do declare.

Dear child did you compose the words she asked Pierre,
Oh yes my dear lady just as you see,
Well my dear boy I will sing your song to-night,
And you shall have a seat near me on the right.

Then Pierre, said, Oh! lady I cannot leave my mother,
But my dear boy, as for her you need not bother,
So dear child don't be the least cast down,
And in the meantime here is a crown.

And for your mother you can buy food and medicine,
So run away and be at the concert to-night in time
Then away he ran and bought many little necessary things
And while doing so his little song he hums and sings.

Then home to his poor sick mother he quickly ran,
And told her of his success with Madame Malibran,
Then his mother cried, Oh! Pierre, you are a very good boy,
And to hear of your success my heart is full of joy.

Dear mother, I am going to the concert hall to-night,
To hear Madame Malibran, which will my heart delight,
Oh! well said his mother, God speed you my little man,
I hope you will be delighted to hear Madame Malibran.

So to the concert hall he goes, and found a seat there,
And the lights and flashing of diamonds made him stare,
And caused a joyous smile to play upon his face,
For never had he been in so grand a place.

There the brave boy sat and Madame Malibran came at last
And with his eyes rivetted on her he stared aghast,
And to hear her sing, Oh! how he did long,
And he wondered if the lady would really sing his song.

At last the great singer commenced his little song,
And many a heart was moved and the plaudits loud and
     long
And as she sang it Pierre clapped his hands for joy.
That he felt as it were free from the world's annoy.

When the concert was over his heart felt as light as the air
And as for money now he didn't seem to care,
Since the great singer in Europe had sung his little song,
But he hoped that dame fortune would smile on him ere
   long

The next day he was frightened by a visit from Madame
   Malibran
And turning to his mother, she said your little boy Madame
Will make a fortune for himself and you before long,
Because I've been offered a large sum for his little song.

And Madame thank God you have such a gifted son,
But dear Madame heavens will must be done,
Then Pierre knelt and prayed that God would the lady bless
For helping them in the time of their distress.

And the memory of Pierre's prayer made the singer do more
   good
By visiting the poor and giving them clothing and food
And Pierre lightened her last moments ere her soul fled away
And he came to be one of the most talented composers of the
   day.

THE CAPTURE OF LUCKNOW

'Twas near the Begum Kothie the battle began,
Where innocent blood as plentiful as water ran ;
The Begum Kothie was a place of honour given to the 93rd,
Which heroically to a man they soon did begird.

And the 4th Punjaub Rifles were their companions in glory,
And are worthy of their names enrolled in story,
Because they performed prodigious wonders in the fight,
By killing and scattering the Sepoys left and right.

The 93rd Highlanders bivouacked in a garden surrounded
  by mud walls,
Determined to capture the Begum Kothie no matter what
  befalls—,
A place strongly fortified and of enormous strength,
And protected by strong earthworks of very great length.

And added to these obstacles was the most formidable of
  all—
A broad deep ditch that ran along the wall,
Which the storming party not even guessed at before;
But this barrier the British soon did climb o'er.

But early the next morning two batteries of Artillery were
  pounding away,
And the fight went on for the whole day;
And the defenders of the building kept up rattling musketry
  fire,
And when night fell the British had to retire.

Next day the contest was renewed with better success,
And the 93rd in all their beauty forward did press,
And moved on toward the position without firing a shot,
And under cover of some ruined buildings they instantly got.

And here for a few minutes they kept themselves under
    cover,
While each man felt more anxious than another
To attack the merciless rebels while it was day,
Because their blood was up and eager for the fray.

Still the enemy kept up a blazing fire at them pell-mell,
But they fired too high and not a man of them fell;
And the bullets whistled around them again and again,
Still on went the unwavering Highlanders with might and
    main.

But when they reached the ditch they were taken by
    surprise,
By the unexpected obstacle right before their eyes;
But Captain Middleton leapt into the ditch and showed
    them the way,
And immediately the whole of the men were after him
    without delay.

Leith Hay himself was among the first across,
And gained a footing on the other side without any personal
    loss;
And he assisted in helping the rest out of the ditch,
While the din of war was at the highest pitch.

'Twas then the struggle commenced in terrible earnest :
While every man was resolved to do his best;
And the enemy barricaded every entrance so as a single man
    could only pass,
Determined to make a strong resistance, and the British to
    harass.

But barrier after barrier soon was passed;
And the brave men no doubt felt a little harassed,
But they fought desperately and overturned their foes at
    every point,
And put the rebels to flight by shot and bayonet conjoint.

The Sheiks and the Horse Guards behaved right well—
Because beneath their swords, by the score, the Sepoys fell;
And their beautiful war steeds did loudly neigh and roar,
While beneath their hoofs they trampled them all o'er.

And as for John McLeod—the pipe-major of the 93rd,
He kept sounding his bagpipes and couldn't be stirred—
Because he remembered his duty in the turmoil,
And in the battlefield he was never known to recoil.

And as for Major General McBain—he was the hero in the
    fight;
He fought heroically—like a lion—with all his might;
And again and again he was met by desperate odds,
But he scattered them around him and made them kiss the
    sods.

And he killed eleven of the enemy with sword in hand,
Which secured for him the proudest of all honours in the
    land,
Namely, that coveted honour called the Victoria Cross,
Of which many a deserving hero has known the loss.

And as for brave Hodson—he was a warrior born,
And military uniform did his body adorn;
And his voice could be heard in the battle afar,
Crying—"Come on my boys there is nothing like war!"

But, in a moment, a volley was discharged at him,
And he fell mortally wounded, while the Sepoys did grin;
Then the Highlanders closed with their foes and made them
    retreat,
And left them not till every rebel lay dead at their feet.

Then Sir Colin Campbell to his men did say,—
"Men, I feel proud that we have captured Lucknow this
    day;
Therefore strike up the bagpipes and give one hearty cheer,
And enjoy yourselves, my heroes, while ye are here."

THE BURNS STATUE
(A fragment)

This Statue, I must confess, is magnificent to see,
And I hope will long be appreciated by the people of Dundee;
It has been beautifully made by Sir John Steell,
And I hope the pangs of hunger he will never feel.

This Statue is most elegant in its design,
And I hope will defy all weathers for a very long time;
And I hope strangers from afar with admiration will stare
On this beautiful statue of thee, Immortal Bard of Ayr.

Fellow-citizens, this Statue seems most beautiful to the eye,
Which would cause Kings and Queens for such a one to sigh,
And make them feel envious while passing by
In fear of not getting such a beautiful Statue after they die.

THE HERO OF KALAPORE : AN INCIDENT
OF THE INDIAN MUTINY

The 27th Regiment has mutinied at Kalapore:
That was the substance of a telegram, which caused a great
    uproar
At Sattara, on the evening of the 8th of July,
And when the British officers heard it, they heaved a bitter
    sigh.

'Twas in the year of 1857,
Which will long be remembered : Oh! Heaven!
That the Sepoys revolted, and killed their British officers
    and their wives;
Besides, they killed their innocent children, not sparing one
    of their lives.

There was one man there who was void of fear,
He was the brave Lieutenant William Alexander Kerr;
And to face the rebels boldly it was his intent,
And he assured his brother officers his men were true to the
    Government.

And now that the danger was so near at hand,
He was ready to put his men to the test, and them
    command;
And march to the rescue of his countrymen at Kalapore,
And try to quell the mutiny and barbarous uproar.

And in half an hour he was ready to start,
With fifty brave horsemen, fearless and smart;
And undaunted Kerr and his horsemen rode on without
    dismay,
And in the middle of the rainy season, which was no child's
    play.

And after a toilsome march they reached Kalapore,
To find their countrymen pressed very hard and sore;
The mutineers had attacked and defeated the Kalapore
    Light Infantry,
Therefore their fellow countrymen were in dire extremity.

Then the Sepoys established themselves in a small square
    fort;
It was a place of strength, and there they did resort;
And Kerr had no guns to batter down the gate,
But nevertheless he felt undaunted, and resigned to his
    fate.

And darkness was coming on and no time was to be lost,
And he must attack the rebels whatever be the cost;
Therefore he ordered his troopers to prepare to storm the
    fort,
And at the word of command towards it they did resort.

And seventeen troopers advanced to the attack,
And one of his men, Gumpunt Row Deo Kerr, whose
    courage wasn't slack;
So great was his courage he couldn't be kept back,
So he resolved with Lieutenant Kerr to make the attack.

Then with crowbars they dashed at the doors vigorously,
Whilst bullets rained around them, but harmlessly;
So they battered on the doors until one gave way,
Then Lieutenant Kerr and his henchmen entered without
    dismay.

Then Kerr's men rushed in sword in hand,
Oh! what a fearful onslaught, the mutineers couldn't it
    withstand,
And Kerr's men with straw set the place on fire,
And at last the rebels were forced to retire.

And took refuge in another house, and barricaded it fast,
And prepared to defend themselves to the last;
Then Lieutenant Kerr and Row Deo Kerr plied the
    crowbars again,
And heavy blows on the woodwork they did rain.

Then the door gave way and they crawled in,
And they two great heroes side by side did begin
To charge the mutineers with sword in hand, which made
    them grin,
Whilst the clashing of swords and bayonets made a fearful
    din.

Then hand to hand, and foot to foot, a fierce combat
    began,
Whilst the blood of the rebels copiously ran,
And a ball cut the chain of Kerr's helmet in two,
And another struck his sword, but the man he slew.

Then a Sepoy clubbed his musket and hit Kerr on the
    head,
But fortunately the blow didn't kill him dead;
He only staggered, and was about to be bayoneted by a
    mutineer,
But Gumpunt Kerr laid his assailant dead without fear.

Kerr's little party were now reduced to seven,
Yet fearless and undaunted, and with the help of Heaven,
He gathered his small band possessed of courage bold,
Determined to make a last effort to capture the stronghold.

Then he cried, "My men, we will burn them out,
And suffocate them with smoke, without any doubt!"
So bundles of straw and hay were found without delay,
And they set fire to them against the doors without dismay.

Then Kerr patiently waited till the doors were consumed,
And with a gallant charge, the last attack was resumed,
And he dashed sword in hand into the midst of the
    mutineers,
And he and his seven troopers played great havoc with their
    sabres.

So by the skillful war tactics of brave Lieutenant Kerr,
He defeated the Sepoy mutineers and rescued his country-
    men dear;
And but for Lieutenant Kerr the British would have met
    with a great loss,
And for his great service he received the Victoria Cross.

JACK HONEST, OR THE WIDOW AND HER SON

Jack Honest was only eight years of age when his father
    died,
And by the death of his father, Mrs Honest was sorely
    tried;
And Jack was his father's only joy and pride,
And for honesty Jack couldn't be equalled in the
    country-side.

So a short time before Jack's father died,
'Twas loud and bitterly for Jack he cried,
And bade him sit down by his bedside,
And then told him to be honest whatever did betide.

John, he said, looking him earnestly in the face,
Never let your actions your name disgrace,
Remember, my dear boy, and do what's right,
And God will bless you by day and night.

Then Mr Honest bade his son farewell, and breathed his
    last,
While the hot tears from Jack's eyes fell thick and fast;
And the poor child did loudly sob and moan,
When he knew his father had left him and his mother
    alone.

So, as time wore on, Jack grew to be a fine boy,
And was to his mother a help and a joy;
And, one evening, she said, Jack, you are my only prop,
I must tell you, dear, I'm thinking about opening a shop.

Oh! that's a capital thought, mother, cried Jack,
And to take care of the shop I won't be slack;
Then his mother said, Jackey, we will try this plan,
And look to God for his blessing, and do all we can.

So the widow opened the shop and succeeded very well,
But in a few months fresh troubles her befell—
Alas! poor Mrs Honest was of fever taken ill,
But Jack attended his mother with a kindly will.

But, for fear of catching the fever, her customers kept
  away,
And once more there wasn't enough money the rent to
  pay;
And in her difficulties Mrs Honest could form no plan to
  get out,
But God would help her, she had no doubt.

So, one afternoon, Mrs Honest sent Jack away
To a person that owed her some money, and told him not
  to stay,
But when he got there the person had fled,
And to return home without the money he was in
  dread.

So he saw a gentleman in a carriage driving along at a
  rapid rate,
And Jack ran forward to his mansion and opened the
  lodge-gate,
Then the gentleman opened his purse and gave him, as he
  thought, a shilling
For opening the lodge-gate so cleverly and so willing.

Then Jack stooped to lift up the coin, when, lo and
  behold!
He found to his surprise it was a piece of gold!
And Jack cried oh! joyful, this will make up my mother's
  loss,
Then he ran home speedily, knowing his mother wouldn't
  be cross.

63

And when he got home he told his mother of his ill
  success,
And his adventure with the gentleman, then she felt deep
  distress;
And when Jack showed her the sovereign, the gentleman
  gave him,
She cried, We mustn't keep that money, it would be a sin.

Dear mother, I thought so, there must be some mistake,
But in the morning, to Squire Brooksby, the sovereign
  I'll take;
So, when morning came, he went to Squire Brooksby's
  Hall,
And at the front door for the Squire he loudly did call.

Then the hall door was opened by a footman, dressed in
  rich livery,
And Jack told him he wished Mr Brooksby to see;
Then to deliver Jack's message the footman withdrew,
And when the footman returned he said, Master will see you.

Then Jack was conducted into a rich furnished room,
And to Mr Brooksby he told his errand very soon,
While his honest heart, with fear, didn't quake,
Saying, Mr Brooksby, you gave me a sovereign yesterday
  in a mistake.

Why, surely I have seen you before, said Mr Brooksby;
Yes, Sir, replied Jack Honest, bowing very politely;
Then what is your name, my honest lad ? asked Mr
  Brooksby;
John Honest, sir, replied Jack, right fearlessly.

Then, my brave lad, you are Honest by name, and honest
    by nature,
Which, really, you appear to be in every feature,
But, I am afraid, such boys as you are very few,
But, I dare say, your mother has taught you.

Then Jack laid the sovereign down on the table before
    Mr Brooksby;
But Mr Brooksby said, No! my lad, I freely give it to thee;
Then Jack said, Oh, sir, I'm obliged to you I'm sure,
Because, sir, this money will help my mother, for she is
    poor.

Mrs Brooksby came to see Mrs Honest in a few days,
And for Jack's honesty she was loud in praise;
And she took Jack into her service, and paid him liberally,
And she gave Mrs Honest a house, for life, rent free.

Now, I must leave Jack Honest and his mother in fresh-
    found glory,
Hoping my readers will feel interested in this story,
And try always to imitate the hero—Jack Honest—
And I'm sure they will find it the safest and the best!

THE DOWNFALL OF DELHI

'Twas in the year of 1857 and on the 14th of September
That the Sepoy rebels at Delhi were forced to surrender;
The attack was first to be made by Brigadier Nicholson,
And he was ordered to attack the Cashmere Bastion.

The British were entirely in command
Of Major-General Reid, assisted by Brigadier-Generals
    Wilson and Burnand;
After a long march, fighting through a hostile country,
And the brave heroes took up a position before the city.

Delhi gates were encircled with a fringe of fire,
But the British resolved to die rather than retire;
And the brave fellows rushed towards the gate
Carrying the powder bags that were to seal the Sepoys'
    fate.

Here their progress was checked, for the drawbridge was
    destroyed,
But the British felt very little annoyed,
Because a few planks were across the chasm thrown,
Then a match was applied to the powder bags, and into
    atoms the gate was blown.

Then the rebel artillerymen with terror fled,
For the streets were strewn by the Sepoy dead;
Then the British charged them without fear,
Shouting "On boys, on, for our Queen and Country dear."

Then Lieutenant Home gave orders to advance,
And charge them with your bayonets, it is our only
    chance;
And with a ringing British cheer they charged them
    fearlessly,
And they drove the enemy before them through the
    streets of the city.

Then the young bugler blew a blast loud and clear,
Which was answered by a British ringing cheer;
But General Nicholson was killed, which was a great loss,
And afterwards the bugler was decorated with the Victoria
Cross.

General Jones formed a junction with Colonel Campbell's
Regiment,
And to enter by the Cashmere Gate they were bent;
And they advanced through the streets without delay,
And swept all before them through the gate without
dismay.

The streets were filled with mutineers who fought
savagely,
Determined to fight to the last and die heroically,
While the alarm drums did beat, and the cannons did roar,
And the dead and the dying lay weltering in their gore.

And the rebels fought for King Timour like tigers in a cage,
He was a very old man, more than ninety years of age;
And their shouts and yells were fearful to hear,
While the shrill sound of the bugle smote on the ear.

The British dash at Delhi will never be forgot,
For the chief instigators of the mutiny were shot;
And their bodies in the Mayor's Court were hung,
And as the people gazed thereon, their hearts with anguish
were wrung.

And that evening General Wilson drank the health of the
    Queen,
Also his officers hailed her Empress of India, which
    enhanced the scene;
While the assembled thousands shouted "God save the
    Queen!"
Oh! it was a most beautiful scene.

Delhi was a glorious prize, for the city was full of jewels
    and gold,
Besides a hundred pieces of cannon, be it told;
But dearly was the victory gained,
But in the book of fame the British are famed;
Oh, it was a glorious and heroic victory,
And will be handed down to posterity.

THE RIVER OF LEITH

As I stood upon the Dean Bridge and viewed the beautiful
    scenery,
I felt fascinated and my heart was full of glee,
And I exclaimed in an ecstasy of delight,
In all my travels I never saw such a sight.

The scenery is so enchanting to look upon
That all tourists will say, "Dull care, be gone."
'Tis certainly a most lovely spot,
And once seen it can never be forgot.

Then away! away! to the River of Leith,
That springs from the land of heather and heath,
And view the gorgeous scenery on a fine summer day.
I'm sure it will drive dull care away.

The water-fall near the Bridge is most beautiful to be
    seen,
As it falls and shines like crystal in the sunsheen;
And the sound can be heard all day long,
While the innocent trouts sing an aquatic song.

The glen is a cool spot in the summer time.
There the people can be shaded from the sunshine
Under the spreading branches of the big trees,
And there's seats there to rest on if they please.

Then near St. Bernard's Well there's a shady bower,
Where the lovers, if they like, can spend an hour;
And while they rest there at their ease
They can make love to each other if they please.

The water of St. Bernard's Well is very nice,
But to get a drink of it one penny is the price.
I think in justice the price is rather high,
To give a penny for a drink when one feels dry.

The braes of the River Leith is most charming to be seen,
With its beautiful trees and shrubberies green,
And as the tourist gazes on the river in the valley below,
His heart with joy feels all aglow.

There the little trouts do sport and play
During the live-long summer day,
While the bee and butterfly is on the wing,
And with the singing of birds the glen doth ring.

The walk underneath the Dean Bridge is lovely to see.
And as ye view the scenery it will fill your heart with glee.
It is good for the people's health to be walking there
As they gaze on the beauties of Nature and inhale pure
air.

The Dean Bridge is a very magnificent sight,
Because from the basement it is a great height.
And it seems most attractive to the eye,
And arrests the attention of strangers as they pass by.

The braes of Belgrave Crescent is lovely to see,
With its beautiful walks and green shrubbery.
'Tis health for the people that lives near by there
To walk along the bonny walks and breathe the sweet air.

Therefore all lovers of the picturesque, be advised by me
And the beautiful scenery of the River Leith go and see,
And I am sure you will get a very great treat,
Because the River of Leith scenery cannot be beat.

THE ASHANTEE WAR.   THE FALL OF COOMASSIE

'Twas in the year of 1874, and on New Year's Day,
The British Army landed at Elmina without dismay,
And numbering in all, 1400 bayonets strong,
And all along the Cape Coast they fearlessly marched
along,
Under the command of Sir Garnet Wolseley, a hero bold,
And an honour to his King and country, be it told.

And between them and Coomassie, lay a wilderness of
  jungle,
But they marched on boldly without making a stumble,
And under a tropical sun, upwards of an hundred miles,
While their bayonets shone bright as they marched on in
  files.

Coomassie had to be reached and King Coffee's power
  destroyed,
And, before that was done the British were greatly
  annoyed,
Lieutenant Lord Gifford, with his men gained the Crest of
  the Adenisi Hills,
And when they gained the top, with joy their hearts fills.

Sir John McLeod was appointed General of the Black
  Brigade,
And a great slaughter of the enemy they made,
And took possession of an Ashantee village,
And fought like lions in a fearful rage.

While the British troops most firmly stood,
And advanced against a savage horde concealed in a wood,
Yet the men never flinched, but entered the wood fearlessly,
And all at once the silence was broken by a roar of musketry.

And now the fight began in real earnest,
And the Black Watch men resolved to do their best,
While the enemy were ambushed in the midst of the wood,
Yet the Highlanders their ground firmly stood.

71

And the roar of the musketry spread through the jungle,
Still the men crept on without making a stumble,
And many of the Black Watch fell wounded and dead,
And Major Macpherson was wounded, but he rallied his
 men without dread.

The battle raged for five hours, but the Highlanders were
 gaining ground,
Until the bagpipes struck up their wild clarion sound,
Then the dusky warriors fled in amazement profound,
Because their comrades were falling on every side around.

Sir Archibald Alison led on the Highland Brigade,
And great havoc amongst the enemy they made,
And village after village they captured and destroyed,
Until King Coffee lost heart and felt greatly annoyed.

Sir John McLeod took the command of his own regiment,
And with a swinging pace into the jaws of death they
 went,
Fearlessly firing by companies in rotation,
And dashed into a double Zone of Fire without hesitation.

And in that manner the Black Watch pressed onward,
And the enemy were powerless their progress to retard,
Because their glittering bayonets were brought into play,
And panic stricken the savage warriors fled in great dismay.

Then Sir Garnet Wolseley with his men entered Coomassie
 at night,
Supported by half the rifles and Highlanders—a most
 beautiful sight,
And King Coffee and his army had fled,
And thousands of his men on the field were left dead.

72

And King Coffee, he was crushed at last,
And the poor King felt very downcast,
And his sorrow was really profound,
When he heard that Coomassie was burned to the ground.

Then the British embarked for England without delay,
And with joy their hearts felt gay,
And by the end of March they reached England,
And the reception they received was very grand.

THE BEAUTIFUL CITY OF PERTH

Beautiful and ancient city of Perth,
One of the grandest upon the earth,
With your stately mansions and streets so clean,
And situated betwixt two Inches green,
Which are most magnificent to be seen.

The North Inch is beautiful to behold,
Where the daisies and butter-cups their petals unfold,
In the warm summer time of the year,
While the clear silvery Tay rolls by quite near,
And such a scene will your spirits cheer.

The South Inch is lovely, be it said,
And a splendid spot for military parade,
While along the highway there are some big trees,
Where the soldiers can rest or stand at ease,
Whichever way their commanders please.

The surrounding woodland scenery is very grand,
It cannot be surpassed in fair Scotland,
Especially the elegant Palace of Scone, in history renowned,
Where some of Scotland's kings were crowned.

And the Fair Maid of Perth's house is worthy to be seen,
Which is well worth visiting by Duke, Lord, or Queen;
The Fair Maid of Perth caused the battle on the North Inch
'Twixt the Clans Chattan and Kay, and neither of them did
    flinch,
Until they were cut up inch by inch.

The scenery is lovely in the month of June,
When trees and flowers are in full bloom,
Especially near by the Palace of Scone,
Where the blackbird is heard whistling all day
While near by rolls on the clear silvery Tay.

Of all the cities in Scotland, beautiful Perth for me,
For it is the most elegant city that ever I did see,
With its beautiful woodland scenery along the river Tay,
Which would make the tourist's heart feel gay,
While fishing for trout on a fine summer day.

There, the angler, if he likes to resort
For a few day's fishing, can have excellent sport,
And while he is fishing during the day,
He will feel delighted with the scenery along the river Tay.
And the fish he catches will drive dull care away,
And his toil will be rewarded for the fatigues of the day.

Beautiful city of Perth, magnificent to be seen,
With your grand statues and Inches green,
And your lovely maidens fair and gay,
Which, in conclusion, I will venture to say,
You cannot be surpassed at the present day.

74

GENERAL ROBERTS IN AFGHANISTAN

'Twas in the year of 1878, and the winter had set in,
Lord Roberts and the British Army their march did begin,
On their way to Afghanistan to a place called Cabul;
And the weather was bitter cold and the rivers swollen and
    full.

And the enemy were posted high up amongst the hills,
And when they saw the British, with fear their blood thrills;
The savages were camped on the hillsides in war array,
And occupying a strong position which before the British
    lay.

And viewed from the front their position was impregnable,
But Lord Roberts was a general of great skill;
Therefore to surprise the enemy he thought it was right,
To march upon the enemy in the dead of night.

Then the men were mustered without delay,
And each man of them was eager for the fray;
And in the silent darkness they felt no dismay,
And to attack the enemy they marched boldly away.

And on they marched bravely without fear or doubt,
And about daybreak the challenge of an Afghan sentinel
    rang out,
And echoed from rock to rock on the frosty biting air;
But the challenge didn't the British scare.

Then the Highlanders attacked them left and right,
And oh! it was a gorgeous and an inspiring sight;
For a fierce hand to hand struggle raged for a time,
While the pibrochs skirled aloud, oh! the scene was
    sublime.

Then the Ghoorkas did the Afghans fiercely attack,
And at every point and turning they were driven back;
And a fierce hand to hand struggle raged for a time,
While in the morning sunshine the British bayonets did
  shine.

And around the ridge or knoll the battle raged for three
  hours,
And British bullets fell amongst them in showers;
For Captain Kelso brought us his mountain battery,
And sent his shells right into the camp of the enemy,
Then the left of the Afghans was turned, and began to flee.

Meanwhile, on the enemy's strong position Lord Roberts
  launched an attack,
And from their position they could hardly be driven back
Because the Afghans were hid amongst the woods and hills,
Still with undaunted courage, the British blood thrills.

And the Afghans pressed the British hotly, but they didn't
  give way,
For the 8th Ghoorkas and the 72nd kept them at bay;
And the mountain guns shells upon them did fire,
Then the 8th Punjaub, bounding up the heights, made
  them retire.

Then Major White seized a rifle from one of his men and
  did retire,
And levelled the piece fearlessly and did fire;
And with a steady and well-timed shot
He shot the Afghan leader dead on the spot.

Then the British with a wild cheer dashed at them,
And on each side around they did them hem;
And at the bayonet charge they drove them down the hill,
And in hundreds they did them kill.

Then in a confused mass they fled down the opposite side
  of the hill
In hundreds, driven by sheer force sore against their will;
And helter-skelter they did run,
For all their positions were carried and the victory won.

Then on the 8th of August again Lord Roberts' march
  began
For to fight the rebel Ayoob Khan;
And with an army about seven thousand strong
On his way to Candahar he fearlessly marched along.

And the battle that followed at Candahar was a complete
  victory,
And Lord Roberts' march to Candahar stands unrivalled
  in history;
And let's thank God that sent Lord Roberts to conquer
  Ayoob Khan,
For from that time there's been no more war in
  Afghanistan.

Success to Lord Roberts; he's a very brave man,
For he conquered the Afghans in Afghanistan,
With an army about seven thousand strong,
He spread death and desolation all along.

FAREWELL ADDRESS AT THE ARGYLE HALL,
TUESDAY, JUNE 22, 1880

Fellow Citizens of Dundee.
I now must bid farewell to ye.
For I am going to London far away.
But when I will return again I cannot say.

Farewell! Farewell! to the bonnie banks o' the Silvery Tay.
Also the beautiful Hill o' Balgay.
And the ill fated Bridge o' the Silvery Tay.
Which I will remember when I am far away.

Farewell! to my friends and patrons all.
That rallied around me in the Music Hall.
And those that has rallied around me to night,
I shall not forget when out of sight.

And if I ever return to Dundee again,
I hope it will be with the laurels of fame.
Plac'd on my brow by dame fortune that fickle Jade.
And to Court her favour I am not afraid.

Farewell! to every one in the Argyle Hall.
That has Come to hear McGonagall.
Recite, and sing, his Songs to night.
Which I hope will long be remember'd when I'm out of
    sight.

Adieu to all my enemies that want to mock me when
    passing by.
But I excuse them for their ignorance and leave them to
    the most high.
And, once again, my friends, and enemies. I bid ye all
    good bye.
And when I am gone ye will for me heave a sigh :—

78

I return my thanks to my Chairman and my Committee,
For the Kindness they have always shown to me.
I hope the Lord! will protect them when I am far away.
And prosper them in all their undertakings by night and
    by day.

THE LAST BERKSHIRE ELEVEN: THE HEROES OF MAIWAND

'Twas at the disastrous battle of Maiwand, in Afghanistan,
Where the Berkshires were massacred to the last man;
On the morning of July the 27th, in the year eighteen
    eighty,
Which I'm sorry to relate was a pitiful sight to see.

Ayoub Khan's army amounted to twelve thousand in all,
And honestly speaking it wasn't very small,
And by such a great force the Berkshires were killed to the
    last man,
By a murderous rebel horde under the command of Ayoub
    Khan.

The British force amounted to about 2000 strong in all,
But although their numbers were but few it didn't them
    appal;
They were commanded by General Burrows, a man of
    courage bold,
But, alas! the British army was defeated be it told.

The 66th Berkshire Regiment stood as firm as a wall,
Determined to conquer or die whatever would befall,
But in the face of overwhelming odds, and covered to the
last,
The broken and disordered Sepoys were flying fast

Before the victorious Afghan soldiers, whose cheers on the
air arose,
But the gallant band poured in deadly volleys on their foes ;
And, outnumbered and surrounded, they fell in sections like
ripe grain ;
Still the heroes held their ground, charging with might and
main.

The British force, alas! were shut up like sheep in a pen,
Owing to the bad position General Burrows had chosen for
his men ;
But Colonel Galbraith with the Berkshires held the enemy
at bay,
And had the Sepoys been rallied the Afghans would not
have won the day.

But on the Berkshires fell the brunt of the battle,
For by the Afghan artillery they fell like slaughtered
cattle ;
Yet the wild horsemen were met with ringing volleys of
musketry,
Which emptied many a saddle ; still the Afghans fought
right manfully.

And on came the white cloud like a whirlwind ;
But the gallant Berkshires, alas! no help could find,
While their blood flowed like water on every side around,
And they fell in scores, but the men rallied and held their
ground

The brave Berkshires under Colonel Galbraith stood firm in
the centre there,
Whilst the shouts of the wild Ghazis rent the air;
But still the Berkshires held them at bay,
At the charge of the bayonet, without dismay.

Then the Ghazis, with increased numbers, made another
desperate charge
On that red line of British bayonets, which wasn't very
large;
And the wild horsemen were met again with ringing volleys
of musketry,
Which was most inspiring and frightful to see.

Then Ayoub concentrated his whole attack on the Berkshire
Regiment,
Which made them no doubt feel rather discontent,
And Jacob's Rifles and the Grenadiers were a confused and
struggling mass,
Oh heaven! such a confused scene, nothing could it surpass.

But the Berkshires stood firm, replying to the fire of the
musketry,
While they were surrounded on all sides by masses of
cavalry;
Still that gallant band resolved to fight for their Queen and
country,
Their motto being death before dishonour, rather than flee.

At last the gallant British soldiers made a grand stand,
While most of the officers were killed fighting hand to hand,
And at length the Sepoys fled from the enclosure, panic-
stricken and irate,
Alas! leaving behind their European comrades to their fate.

The Berkshires were now reduced to little more than one
    hundred men,
Who were huddled together like sheep in a pen;
But they broke loose from the enclosure, and back to back,
Poured volley after volley in the midst of the enemy, who
    wern't slack.

And one by one they fell, still the men fought without
    dismay,
And the regimental pet dog stuck to the heroes throughout
    the day;
And their cartridge pouches were empty, and of shot they
    were bereft,
And eleven men, most of them wounded, were all that were
    left.

And they broke from the enclosure, and followed by the
    little dog,
And with excitement it was barking savagely, and leaping
    like a frog;
And from the field the last eleven refused to retire,
And with fixed bayonets they charged on the enemy in that
    sea of fire.

Oh, heaven! it was a fearful scene the horrors of that
    day,
When I think of so many innocent lives that were taken
    away;
Alas! the British force were massacred in cold blood,
And their blood ran like a little rivulet in full flood.

And the Ghazis were afraid to encounter that gallant little
    band
At the charge of the bayonet : Oh! the scene was most
    grand;
And the noble and heroic eleven fought on without dismay,
Until the last man in the arms of death stiff and stark lay.

THE SUNDERLAND CALAMITY

'Twas in the town of Sunderland, and in the year of 1883,
That about 200 children were launch'd into eternity
While witnessing an entertainment in Victoria Hall,
While they, poor little innocents, to God for help did call.

The entertainment consisted of conjuring, and the ghost
    illusion play,
Also talking waxworks, and living marionettes, and given
    by Mr. Fay;
And on this occasion, presents were to be given away,
But in their anxiety of getting presents they wouldn't
    brook delay,
And that is the reason why so many lives have been taken
    away;
But I hope their precious souls are in heaven to-day.

As soon as the children began to suspect
That they would lose their presents by neglect,
They rush'd from the gallery, and ran down the stairs
    pell-mell,
And trampled one another to death, according as they fell.

As soon as the catastrophe became known throughout the
   boro'
The people's hearts were brim-full of sorrow,
And parents rush'd to the Hall terror-stricken and wild,
And each one was anxious to find their own child.

Oh! it must have been a most horrible sight
To see the dear little children struggling with all their
   might
To get out at the door at the foot of the stair,
While one brave little boy did repeat the Lord's Prayer.

The innocent children were buried seven or eight layers
   deep,
The sight was heart-rending and enough to make one weep;
It was a most affecting spectacle and frightful to behold
The corpse of a little boy not above four years old,

Who had on a top-coat much too big for him,
And his little innocent face was white and grim,
And appearing to be simply in a calm sleep—
The sight was enough to make one's flesh to creep.

The scene in the Hall was heart-sickening to behold,
And enough to make one's blood run cold.
To see the children's faces, blackened, that were trampled
   to death,
And their parents lamenting o'er them with bated breath.

Oh! it was most lamentable for to hear
The cries of the mothers for their children dear;
And many mothers swooned in grief away
At the sight of their dead children in grim array.

84

There was a parent took home a boy by mistake,
And after arriving there his heart was like to break
When it was found to be the body of a neighbour's child;
The parent stood aghast and was like to go wild.

A man and his wife rush'd madly in the Hall,
And loudly in grief on their children they did call,
And the man searched for his children among the dead
Seemingly without the least fear or dread.

And with his finger pointing he cried. "That's one! two!
Oh! heaven above, what shall I do;"
And still he kept walking on and murmuring very low,
Until he came to the last child in the row;

Then he cried, "Good God! all my family gone
And now I am left to mourn alone;"
And staggering back he cried, "Give me water, give me
    water!"
While his heart was like to break and his teeth seem'd to
    chatter.

Oh, heaven! it must have been most pitiful to see
Fathers with their dead children upon their knee
While the blood ran copiously from their mouths and ears
And their parents shedding o'er them hot burning tears.

I hope the Lord will comfort their parents by night and by
    day,
For He gives us life and He takes it away,
Therefore I hope their parents will put their trust in Him,
Because to weep for the dead it is a sin.

Her Majesty's grief for the bereaved parents has been
   profound,
And I'm glad to see that she has sent them £50;
And I hope from all parts of the world will flow relief
To aid and comfort the bereaved parents in their grief.

THE INAUGURATION OF THE UNIVERSITY COLLEGE, DUNDEE

Good people of Dundee, your voices raise,
And to Miss Baxter give great praise;
Rejoice and sing and dance with glee,
Because she has founded a College in Bonnie Dundee.

Therefore loudly in her praise sing,
And make Dundee with your voices ring,
And give honour to whom honour is due,
Because ladies like her are very few.

'Twas on the 5th day of October, in the year of 1883,
That the University College was opened in Dundee,
And the opening proceedings were conducted in the College
   Hall,
In the presence of ladies and gentlemen both great and small.

Worthy Provost Moncur presided over the meeting,
And received very great greeting;
And Professor Stuart made an eloquent speech there,
And also Lord Dalhousie, I do declare.

Also, the Right Hon W. E. Baxter was there on behalf of
    his aunt,
And acknowledged her beautiful portrait without any rant,
And said that she requested him to hand it over to the
    College,
As an incentive tc others to teach the ignorant masses
    knowledge,

Success to Miss Baxter, and praise to the late Doctor Baxter,
    John Boyd,
For I think the Dundonians ought to feel overjoyed
For their munificent gifts to the town of Dundee,
Which will cause their names to be handed down to
    posterity.

The College is most handsome and magnificent to be seen,
And Dundee can now almost cope with Edinburgh or
    Aberdeen,
For the ladies of Dundee can now learn useful knowledge
By going to their own beautiful College.

I hope the ladies and gentlemen of Dundee will try and
    learn knowledge
At home in Dundee in their nice little College,
Because knowledge is sweeter than honey or jam,
Therefore let them try and gain knowledge as quick as they
    can.

It certainly is a great boon and an honour to Dundee
To have a College in our midst, which is most charming to
    see,
All through Miss Baxter and the late Dr Baxter, John Boyd,
Which I hope by the people of Dundee will long be enjoyed.

Now since Miss Baxter has lived to see it erected,
I hope by the students she will long be respected
For establishing a College in Bonnie Dundee,
Where learning can be got of a very high degree.

"My son, get knowledge," so said the sage,
For it will benefit you in your old age,
And help you through this busy world to pass,
For remember a man without knowledge is just like an ass.

I wish the Professors and teachers every success,
Hoping the Lord will all their labours bless;
And I hope the students will always be obedient to their
    teachers,
And that many of them may learn to be orators and
    preachers.

I hope Miss Baxter will prosper for many a long day
For the money that she has given away,
May God shower his blessings on her wise head,
And may all good angels guard her while living and
    hereafter when dead.

THE GREAT FRANCHISE DEMONSTRATION, DUNDEE, 20th SEPTEMBER 1884

'Twas in the year of 1884, and on Saturday the 20th of
    September,
Which the inhabitants of Dundee will long remember
The great Liberal Franchise Demonstration,
Which filled their minds with admiration.

88

Oh! it was a most magnificent display,
To see about 20 or 30 thousand men all in grand array;
And each man with a medal on his breast;
And every man in the procession dressed in his best.

The banners of the processionists were really grand to see—
The like hasn't been seen for a long time in Dundee;
While sweet music from the bands did rend the skies,
And every processionist was resolved to vote for the
   Franchise.

And as the procession passed along each street,
The spectators did loudly the processionists greet;
As they viewed their beautiful banners waving in the wind,
They declared such a scene would be ever fresh in their
   mind.

The mustering of the processionists was very grand,
As along the Esplanade each man took his stand,
And as soon as they were marshalled in grand array,
To the Magdalen Green, in haste, they wended their way.

And when they arrived on the Magdalen Green,
I'm sure it was a very beautiful imposing scene—
While the cheers of that vast multitude ascended to the
   skies,
For the "Grand Old Man," Gladstone, the Hero of the
   Franchise,

Who has struggled very hard for the people's rights,
Many long years, and many weary nights;
And I think the "Grand Old Man" will gain the Franchise,
And if he does, the people will laud him to the skies.

And his name should be written in letters of gold :
For he is a wise statesman—true and bold—
Who has advocated the people's rights for many long years;
And when he is dead they will thank him with their tears.

For he is the man for the working man,
And without fear of contradiction, deny it who can;
Because he wishes the working man to have a good coat,
And, both in town and country, to have power to vote.

The reason why the Lords wont pass the Franchise Bill :
They fear that it will do themselves some ill;
That is the reason why they wish to throw it out,
Yes, believe me, fellow citizens, that's the cause without
    doubt.

The emblems and mottoes in the procession, were really
    grand,
The like hasn't been seen in broad Scotland;
Especially the picture of Gladstone—the nation's hope,
Who is a much cleverer man than Sir John Cope.

There were masons and ploughmen all in a row,
Also tailors, tenters, and blacksmiths, which made a grand
    show;
Likewise carters and bakers which was most beautiful to be
    seen,
To see them marching from the Esplanade to the Magdalen
    Green.

I'm sure it was a most beautiful sight to see,
The like has never been seen before in Dundee;
Such a body of men, and Gladstone at the helm,
Such a sight, I'm sure, 'twould the Lords o'erwhelm.

Oh! it was grand to see that vast crowd,
And to hear the speeches, most eloquent and loud,
That were made by the speakers, regarding the Franchise;
While the spectators applauded them to the skies.

And for the "Grand Old Man" they gave three cheers,
Hoping he would live for many long years;
And when the speeches were ended, the people's hearts were
    gay,
And they all dispersed quietly to their homes without delay.

THE WRECK OF THE BARQUE "LYNTON" WHILE BOUND FOR ASPINWALL, HAVING ON BOARD 1000 TONS OF COAL

A sad tale of the sea, I will unfold,
About Mrs Lingard, that Heroine bold;
Who struggled hard in the midst of the hurricane wild,
To save herself from being drowned, and her darling child.

'Twas on the 8th of September, the Barque "Lynton"
    sailed for Aspinwall,
And the crew on board, numbered thirteen in all;
And the weather at the time, was really very fine,
On the morning that the ill-fated vessel left the Tyne.

And on the 19th of November, they hove in sight of
    Aspinwall,
But little did they think there was going to be a squall;
When all on a sudden, the sea came rolling in,
And a sound was heard in the heavens, of a rather peculiar
    din.

Then the vivid lightning played around them, and the
thunder did roar,
And the rain came pouring down, and lashed the barque all
o'er;
Then the Captain's Wife and Children were ordered below,
And every one on board began to run to and fro.

Then the hurricane in all its fury, burst upon them,
And the sea in its madness, washed the deck from stem to
stem;
And the rain poured in torrents, and the waves seemed
mountains high,
Then all on board the barque, to God for help, did loudly
cry.

And still the wind blew furiously, and the darkness was
intense,
Which filled the hearts of the crew with great suspense,
Then the ill-fated vessel struck, and began to settle down,
Then the poor creatures cried, God save us, or else we'll
drown!

Then Mrs Lingard snatched to her breast, her darling child,
While loudly roared the thunder, and the hurricane wild;
And she cried, oh! God of heaven, save me and my darling
child,
Or else we'll perish in the hurricane wild.

'Twas then the vessel turned right over, and they were
immersed in the sea,
Still the poor souls struggled hard to save their lives, most
heroically;
And everyone succeeded in catching hold of the keel
garboard streak,
While with cold and fright, their hearts were like to break.

Not a word or a shriek came from Mrs Lingard, the Captain's
  wife,
While she pressed her child to her bosom, as dear she loved
  her life;
Still the water dashed over them again and again,
And about one o'clock, the boy, Hall, began to complain.

Then Mrs Lingard put his cold hands into her bosom,
To warm them because with cold he was almost frozen,
And at the same time clasping her child Hilda to her breast,
While the poor boy Hall closely to her prest.

And there the poor creatures lay huddled together with
  fear,
And the weary night seemed to them more like a year,
And they saw the natives kindling fires on the shore,
To frighten wild animals away, that had begun to roar.

Still the big waves broke over them, which caused them to
  exclaim,
Oh! God, do thou save us for we are suffering pain;
But, alas, the prayers they uttered were all in vain,
Because the boy Hall and Jonson were swept from the
  wreck and never rose again.

Then bit by bit the vessel broke up, and Norberg was swept
  away,
Which filled the rest of the survivors hearts with great
  dismay;
But at length the longed for morning dawned at last,
Still with hair streaming in the wind, Mrs Lingard to the
  wreck held fast.

Then Captain Lingard still held on with Lucy in his arms,
Endeavouring to pacify the child from the storms alarms;
And at last the poor child's spirits began to sink,
And she cried in pitiful accents, papa! papa! give me a
  drink.

And in blank amazement the Captain looked all round
  about,
And he cried Lucy dear I cannot find you a drink I doubt,
Unless my child God sends it to you,
Then he sank crying Lucy, my dear child, and wife, adieu!
  adieu!

'Twas then a big wave swept Lucy and the Carpenter away,
Which filled Mrs Lingard's heart with great dismay,
And she cried Mr Jonson my dear husband and child are
  gone,
But still she held to the wreck while the big waves rolled on.

For about 38 hours they suffered on the wreck,
At length they saw a little boat which seemed like a speck,
Making towards them on the top of a wave,
Buffetting with the billows fearlessly and brave.

And when the boat to them drew near,
Poor souls they gave a feeble cheer,
While the hurricane blew loud and wild,
Yet the crew succeeded in saving Mrs Lingard and her
  child.

Also, the Steward and two sailors named Christophers and
    Eversen,
Able-bodied and expert brave seamen.
And they were all taken to a French Doctor's and attended
    to,
And they caught the yellow fever, but the Lord brought
    them through.

And on the 6th of December they embarked on board the
    ship Moselle,
All in high spirits, and in health very well,
And arrived at Southampton on the 29th of December,
A day which the survivors will long remember.

THE GREAT YELLOW RIVER INUNDATION
IN CHINA

'Twas in the year of 1887, and on the 28th of September,
Which many people of Honan, in China, will long
    remember;
Especially those that survived the mighty deluge,
That fled to the mountains, and tops of trees, for refuge.

The river burst its embankments suddenly at dead of night,
And the rushing torrent swept all before it left and right;
All over the province of Honan, which for its fertility,
Is commonly called by historians, the garden of China.

The river was at its fullest when the embankment gave way,
And when the people heard it, oh! horror and dismay;
'Twas then fathers and mothers leaped from their beds
    without delay,
And some saved themselves from being drowned, but
    thousands were swept away.

Oh! it was a horrible and most pitiful scene,
To hear fathers and mothers and their children loudly
    scream;
As the merciless water encircled their bodies around,
While the water spirits laughed to see them drowned.

Oh! heaven, it must have been an appalling sight,
To witness in the dead stillness of the night
Frantic fathers and mothers, struggling hard against the
    roaring flood,
To save themselves and little ones, their own flesh and
    blood.

The watchmen tried to patch the breach, but it was all in
    vain,
Because the banks were sodden with the long prolonged
    rain;
And driven along by a high wind, which brought the last
    strain,
Which caused the water with resistless fury to spread o'er
    the plain.

And the torrent poured into the valley of the La Chia river,
Sweeping thousands of the people before it ere a helping
    hand could them deliver;
Oh! it was horrible to hear the crashing of houses fallen on
    every side,
As the flood of rushing waters spread far and wide.

The Chinese offer sacrifices to the water spirits twice a year,
And whether the water spirits or God felt angry I will not
    aver;
But perhaps God has considered such sacrifices a sin,
And has drowned so many thousands of them for not
    worshipping Him.

How wonderful are the works of God,
At times among His people abroad;
Therefore, let us be careful of what we do or say,
For fear God doth suddenly take our lives away.

The province of Honan is about half the size of Scotland,
Dotted over with about 3000 villages, most grand;
And inhabited by millions of people of every degree,
And these villages, and people were transformed into a
    raging sea.

The deluge swept on over the fertile and well-cultivated
    land,
And the rushing of the mighty torrent no power could
    withstand;
And the appalling torrent was about twenty feet deep,
And with resistless fury everything before it it did sweep.

Methinks I see the waste of surging waters, and hear its
    deafening roar,
And on its surface I see corpses of men and women by the
    score;
And the merciless torrent in the darkness of the night,
Sportively tossing them about, oh! what a horrible sight.

Besides there were buffaloes and oxen, timber, straw, and
    grain,
Also three thousand villages were buried beneath the waters
    of the plain;
And multitudes beneath their own roofs have found a
    watery grave,
While struggling hard, no doubt, poor souls their lives to
    save.

Therefore good people at home or abroad,
Be advised by me and trust more in God,
Than the people of Honan, the benighted Chinese,
For fear God punished you likewise for your iniquities.

THE DEATH OF FRED. MARSDEN, THE AMERICAN PLAYWRIGHT

A pathetic tragedy I will relate,
Concerning poor Fred. Marsden's fate,
Who suffocated himself by the fumes of gas,
On the 18th of May, and in the year of 1888, alas!

Fred. Marsden was a playwright, the theatrical world
    knows,
And was highly esteemed by the people, and had very few
    foes;
And in New York, in his bedroom, he took his life away,
And was found by his servant William in his bedroom where
    he lay.

The manner in which he took his life : first he locked the
    door,
Then closed down the window, and a sheet to shreds he tore,
And then stopped the keyholes and chinks through which
    air might come,
Then turned on the single gas-burner, and soon the deed
    was done.

About seven o'clock in the evening he bade his wife
    good-night,
And she left him, smoking, in his room, thinking all was
    right,
But when morning came his daughter said she smelled gas,
Then William, his servant, called loudly on him, but no
    answer, alas!

Then suspicion flashed across William's brain, and he broke
    open the door,
Then soon the family were in a state of uproar,
For the room was full of gas, and Mr Marsden quite dead,
And a more kind-hearted father never ate of the world's
    bread.

And by his kindness he spoiled his only child,
His pretty daughter Blanche, which made him wild;
For some time he thought her an angel, she was so very
    civil,
But she dishonoured herself, and proved herself a devil.

Her father idolised her, and on her spared no expense,
And the kind-hearted father gave her too much indulgence,
Because evening parties and receptions were got up for her
    sake,
Besides, he bought her a steam yacht to sail on Schroon
    Lake.

His means he lavished upon his home and his wife,
And he loved his wife and daughter as dear as his life;
But Miss Blanche turned to folly, and wrecked their home
    through strife,
And through Miss Marsden's folly her father took his life.

She wanted to ride, and her father bought her a horse,
And by giving her such indulgences, in morals she grew
    worse;
And by her immoral actions she broke her father's heart;
And, in my opinion, she has acted a very ungrateful part.

At last she fled from her father's house, which made him
    mourn,
Then the crazy father went after her and begged her to
    return,
But she tore her father's beard, and about the face beat
    him,
Then fled to her companions in evil, and thought it no sin.

Then her father sent her one hundred dollars, and found her
    again,
And he requested her to come home, but it was all in vain;
For his cruel daughter swore at him without any dread,
And, alas! next morning, he was found dead in his bed.

And soon theatrical circles were shocked to learn,
Of the sudden death of genial Fred. Marsden,
Whose house had been famous for its hospitality,
To artists, litterateurs, and critics of high and low degree.

And now dear Mrs Marsden is left alone to mourn
The loss of her loving husband, whom to her will ne'er
    return;
But I hope God will be kind to her in her bereavement,
And open her daughter's eyes, and make her repent

For being the cause of her father's death, the generous Fred,
Who oft poor artists and mendicants has fed;
But, alas! his bounties they will never receive more,
Therefore poor artists and mendicants will his loss
    deplore.

Therefore, all ye kind parents of high and low degree,
I pray ye all, be advised by me,
And never pamper your children in any way,
Nor idolise them, for they are apt to go astray,

And treat ye, like pretty Blanche Marsden,
Who by her folly has been the death of one of the finest
    men;
So all kind parents, be warned by me,
And remember always this sad Tragedy!

AN EXCURSION STEAMER SUNK IN THE TAY

'Twas in the year of 1888, and on July the 14th day,
That an alarming accident occurred in the River Tay.
Which resulted in the sinking of the Tay Ferries' Steamer
    "Dundee,"
Which was a most painful and sickening sight to see.

The Steamer was engaged by the Independent Order of
    Rechabites,
And all were resolved to see some rural sights;
And the place they selected was the village of Newburgh;
While each heart was happy and free from sorrow.

And the weather was sunny, and really very fine,
And 900 souls had agreed to while away the time;
And they left the Craig Pier at half-past two o'clock,
Never thinking they would meet with an accidental
shock.

And after passing underneath the Bridge of Tay,
Then they took the Channel on the south side without
dismay;
And Captain Methven stood on the Steamer's bridge, I do
declare,
And for the passengers he seemed to have very great care.

And all went well on board for some time,
And the silvery Tay shone beautiful in the sunshine;
And the passengers' hearts felt light and gay,
While they gazed on the bonnie banks of the silvery Tay.

To do justice to the passengers, they were a goodly band,
For their behaviour, 'tis said, was truly grand;
But to the eastward of Newburgh, the Steamer was too close
inshore,
And on passing a boatman, he warningly to them did roar,—

Warning them not to come inshore so near,
But his warning voice the helmsman didn't hear;
Neither the Captain or passengers his warning dreads,
Until the Steamer struck a number of boulders, known as
The Heads.

And close to the point where the Pow falls into the Tay,
Which the people that escaped drowning will remember for
    many a day,
Because many of the passengers were thrown off their
    balance;
But, most fortunately, they were all saved merely by
    chance.

And owing to the suddenness of the shock, many women
    fainted away,
Which filled the rest of the passengers' hearts with dismay;
But they soon regained their composure when close to the
    land,
Especially when they saw that succour was near at hand.

The engines were kept going at full speed,
And God helped His people in time of need;
And in a short time Newburgh was reached,
While many women wept bitterly, and loudly screeched.

Because by this time the forehold was nearly filled with
    water,
Which caused the passengers' teeth with fear to chatter;
Because the Steamer was settling down forward,
While to land the passengers safe Captain Methven struggled
    hard.

But before one-half of them had got ashore,
The women and children were in a state of uproar,
Because the forepart of the Steamer was submerged in the
    Tay,
Which filled the passengers' hearts with dismay.

But, thanks be to God! all the passengers were sent to
  Dundee
By the Steamers Renown, Forfarshire, Protector, and the
  Lass o' Gowrie,
Which certainly was a most beautiful sight to see,
When they landed 900 passengers safe on the pier at
  Dundee.

Then, good people, away to the mountains, glens, and lakes,
And drink of milk and pure water, and eat oaten cakes;
And sit down on the margin of a little burn in the sunshine,
And enjoy yourselves heartily during the holiday time.

THE FUNERAL OF THE LATE EX-PROVOST
ROUGH, DUNDEE

'Twas in the year of 1888, and on the 19th of November,
Which the friends of the late Ex-Provost Rough will long
  remember,
Because 'twas on the 19th of November his soul took its
  flight
To the happy land above, the land of pure delight.

Take him for all in all, he was a very good man,
And during his Provostship he couldn't be equalled in
  Great Britain,
Which I proclaim to the world without any dread,
Because while Provost he reduced the public-houses to
  three hundred.

104

Whereas at the time there were 620 public-houses in the
    town,
But being a friend of the temperance cause he did frown,
Because he saw the evils of intemperance every day
While sitting on the bench, so he resolved to sweep public-
    houses away.

And in doing so the good man, in my opinion, was right,
Because the evils of intemperance is an abomination in
    God's sight;
And all those that get drunk are enemies to Him,
Likewise enemies to Christ's kingdom, which is a great sin.

The late Ex-Provost Rough was President of the Dundee
    Temperance Society,
An office which he filled with great ability;
Besides Vice-President of the Scottish Temperance League
    for many years,
And no doubt the friends of temperance for his loss will
    shed tears.

Because many a hungry soul he relieved while in distress,
And for doing so I hope the Lord will him bless,
For his kindness towards the poor people in Dundee,
Besides for his love towards the temperance cause, and his
    integrity.

And when the good man's health began to decline
The doctor ordered him to take each day two glasses of
    wine,
But he soon saw the evil of it, and from it he shrunk,
The noble old patriarch, for fear of getting drunk.

And although the doctor advised him to continue taking the
    wine,
Still the hero of the temperance cause did decline,
And told the doctor he wouldn't of wine take any
    more,
So in a short time his spirit fled to heaven, where all
    troubles are o'er.

I'm sure very little good emanates from strong drink,
And many people, alas! it leads to hell's brink!
Some to the scaffold, and some to a pauper's grave,
Whereas if they would abstain from drink, Christ would
    them save.

'Twas on Friday afternoon, in November the 23rd day,
That the funeral cortege to the Western Cemetery wended
    its way,
Accompanied by the Magistrates, and amongst those
    present were—
Bailie Macdonald and Bailie Black, also Lord Provost
    Hunter I do declare.

There were also Bailie Foggie, Bailie Craig, and Bailie
    Stephenson,
And Ex-Provost Moncur, and Ex-Provost Ballingall
    representing the Royal Orphan Institution;
Besides there were present the Rev. J. Jenkins and the Rev.
    J. Masson,
With grief depicted in their faces and seemingly
    woe-begone.

There were also Mr Henry Adams, representing the Glover
    trade,
Also Mr J. Carter, who never was afraid
To denounce strong drink, and to warn the people from it
    to flee,
While agent of the Temperance Society in Dundee.

And when the funeral cortege arrived at the Western
    burying-ground,
Then the clergyman performed the funeral service with a
    solemn sound;
While from the eyes of the spectators fell many a tear
For the late Ex-Provost Rough they loved so dear.

And when the coffin was lowered into its house of clay,
Then the friends of the deceased homewards wended their
    way,
Conversing on the good qualities of the good man,
Declaring that the late Ex-Provost Rough couldn't be
    equalled in Great Britain.

THE CRUCIFIXION OF CHRIST
COMPOSED, BY SPECIAL REQUEST, 18TH JUNE 1890

Then Pilate, the Roman Governor, took Jesus and scourged
    Him,
And the soldiers platted a crown of thorns, and thought it
    no sin
To put it on His head, while meekly Jesus stands;
They put on Him a purple robe, and smote Him with their
    hands.

Then Pilate went forth again, and said unto them,
Behold, I bring Him forth to you, but I cannot Him
condemn,
And I would have you to remember I find no fault in Him,
And to treat Him too harshly 'twould be a sin.

But the rabble cried, Hail, King of the Jews, and crucify
Him;
But Pilate saith unto them, I find in Him no sin;
Then Jesus came forth, looking dejected and wan,
And Pilate saith unto them, Behold the Man.

Then the Jews cried out, By our laws He ought to die,
Because He made Himself the Son of God the Most High;
And when Pilate heard that saying the Jews had made,
He saw they were dissatisfied, and he was the more afraid.

And to release Jesus Pilate did really intend,
But the Jews cried angrily, Pilate, thou art not Caesar's
friend,
Remember, if thou let this vile impostor go,
It only goes to prove thou art Caesar's foe.

When Pilate heard that he felt very irate,
Then he brought Jesus forth, and sat down in the
judgment-seat,
In a place that is called the Pavement,
While the Blessed Saviour stood calm and content.

The presence of His enemies did not Him appal,
When Pilate asked of Him, before them all,
Whence art Thou, dost say from on High ?
But Jesus, the Lamb of God, made no reply.

Then saith Pilate unto Him, Speakest Thou not unto me,
Remember, I have the power to crucify Thee;
But Jesus answered, Thou hast no power at all against me,
Except from above it were given to thee.

Then Pilate to the Jews loudly cried,
Take Him away to be crucified;
Then the soldiers took Jesus and led Him away,
And He, bearing His Cross, without dismay.

And they led Him to a place called Golgotha,
But the Saviour met His fate without any awe,
And there crucified Him with two others, one on either side,
And Jesus in the midst, whilst the Jews did Him deride.

Then Pilate tried to pacify the Jews, they felt so morose,
And he wrote a title, and put it on the Cross;
And the title he wrote did the Jews amuse,
The writing was, Jesus of Nazareth the King of the Jews.

This title read many of the Jews without any pity;
And the place where Jesus was crucified was nigh to the
    city;
And the title was written in Hebrew, and Greek, and Latin,
And wh le reading the title the Jews did laugh and grin.

While on the Cross the sun refused to shine,
And there was total darkness for a long time;
The reason was God wanted to hide His wounds from view,
And He kept the blessed sun from breaking through.

And to quench His thirst they gave Him vinegar and
    hyssop,
While the blood from His wounded brow copiously did
    drop,
Then He drank of it willingly, and bowed His head,
And in a few minutes the dear Saviour was dead.

Then Joseph of Arimathea sadly did grieve,
And he asked if Pilate would give him leave
To take the body of Jesus away,
And Pilate told him to remove it without delay.

Then Joseph took the body of Jesus away,
And wound it in linen, which was the Jewish custom of
    that day,
And embalmed his body with spices sweet,
Then laid it in a new sepulchre, as Joseph thought meet.

But death could not hold Him in the grave,
Because He died poor sinners' souls to save;
And God His Father took Him to Heaven on high;
And those that believe in Jesus shall never die.

Oh! think of the precious Blood our Saviour did loss,
That flowed from His wounds while on the Cross,
Especially the wound in His side, made with a spear,
And if you are a believer, you will drop a silent tear.

And if you are not a believer, try and believe,
And don't let the devil any longer you deceive,
Because the precious Blood that Jesus shed will free you
    from all sin,
Therefore, believe in the Saviour, and Heaven you shall
    enter in!

DEATH AND BURIAL OF LORD TENNYSON

Alas! England now mourns for her poet that's gone—
The late and the good Lord Tennyson.
I hope his soul has fled to heaven above,
Where there is everlasting joy and love.

He was a man that didn't care for company,
Because company interfered with his study,
And confused the bright ideas in his brain,
And for that reason from company he liked to abstain.

He has written some fine pieces of poetry in his time,
Especially the May Queen, which is really sublime;
Also the gallant charge of the Light Brigade—
A most heroic poem, and beautifully made.

He believed in the Bible, also in Shakspeare,
Which he advised young men to read without any fear;
And by following the advice of both works therein,
They would seldom or never commit any sin.

Lord Tennyson's works are full of the scenery of his
    boyhood,
And during his life all his actions were good;
And Lincolnshire was closely associated with his history,
And he has done what Wordsworth did for the Lake
    Country.

His remains now rest in Westminster Abbey,
And his funeral was very impressive to see;
It was a very touching sight, I must confess,
Every class, from the Queen, paying a tribute to the poet's
    greatness.

The pall-bearers on the right of the coffin were Mr W. E. H. Lecky,
And Professor Butler, Master of Trinity, and the Earl of Rosebery;
And on the left were Mr J. A. Froude and the Marquis of Salisbury,
Also Lord Selborne, which was an imposing sight to see.

There were also on the left Professor Jowett,
Besides Mr Henry Whyte and Sir James Paget,
And the Marquis of Dufferin and the Duke of Argyll,
And Lord Salisbury, who seemed melancholy all the while.

The chief mourners were all of the Tennyson family,
Including the Hon. Mr and Mrs Hallam Tennyson, and Masters Lionel and Aubrey,
And Mr Arthur Tennyson, and Mr and Mrs Horatio Tennyson;
Also Sir Andrew Clark, who was looking woe begone.

The bottom of the grave was thickly strewn with white roses,
And for such a grave kings will sigh where the poet now reposes;
And many of the wreaths were much observed and commented upon,
And conspicuous amongst them was one from Mrs Gladstone.

The Gordon boys were there looking solemn and serene,
Also Sir Henry Ponsonby to represent the Queen;
Likewise Henry Irving, the great tragedian,
With a solemn aspect, and driving his brougham.

And, in conclusion, I most earnestly pray,
That the people will erect a monument for him without
    delay,
To commemorate the good work he has done,
And his name in gold letters written thereon!

A NEW YEAR'S RESOLUTION TO LEAVE DUNDEE

Welcome! thrice welcome! to the year 1893,
For it is the year that I intend to leave Dundee,
Owing to the treatment I receive,
Which does my heart sadly grieve.
Every morning when I go out
The ignorant rabble they do shout
'There goes Mad McGonagall'
In derisive shouts, as loud as they can bawl,
And lifts stones and snowballs, throws them at me;
And such actions are shameful to be heard in the City of
    Dundee.
And I'm ashamed, kind Christians, to confess,
That from the Magistrates I can get no redress.
Therefore I have made up my mind, in the year of
    1893,
To leave the Ancient City of Dundee,
Because the citizens and me cannot agree.
The reason why ?—because they disrespect me,
Which makes me feel rather discontent.
Therefore, to leave them I am bent;
And I will make my arrangements without delay,
And leave Dundee some early day.

LINES IN REPLY TO THE BEAUTIFUL POET,
WHO WELCOMED NEWS OF McGONAGALL'S
DEPARTURE FROM DUNDEE

Dear Johnny, I return my thanks to you;
But more than thanks is your due
For publishing the scurrilous poetry about me
Leaving the Ancient City of Dundee.

The rhymster says, we'll weary for your schauchlin' form;
But if I'm not mistaken I've seen bonnier than his in a field
    of corn;
And, as I venture to say and really suppose,
His form seen in a cornfield would frighten the crows.

But, dear Johnny, as you said, he's just a lampoon,
And as ugly and as ignorant as a wild baboon;
And, as far as I can judge or think,
He is a vendor of strong drink.

He says my nose would make a peasemeal warrior weep;
But I've seen a much bonnier sweep,
And a more manly and wiser man
Than he is by far, deny it who can!

And, in conclusion, I'd have him to beware,
And never again to interfere with a poet's hair,
Because Christ the Saviour wore long hair,
And many more good men, I do declare.

Therefore I laugh at such bosh that appears in print.
So I hope from me you will take the hint,
And never publish such bosh of poetry again,
Or else you'll get the famous *Weekly News* a bad name.

LINES IN MEMORIAM REGARDING THE ENTERTAINMENT I GAVE ON THE 31st MARCH, 1893, IN REFORM STREET HALL, DUNDEE

'Twas on the 31st of March, and in the year of 1893,
I gave an entertainment in the city of Dundee,
To a select party of gentlemen, big and small,
Who appreciated my recital in Reform Street Hall.

The meeting was convened by J. P. Smith's manager,
  High Street,
And many of J. P. Smith's employes were there me to
  greet,
And several other gentlemen within the city,
Who were all delighted with the entertainment they got
  from me.

Mr Green was the chairman for the night,
And in that capacity he acted right;
He made a splendid address on my behalf,
Without introducing any slang or chaff.

I wish him success during life;
May he always feel happy and free from strife,
For the kindness he has ever shown to me
During our long acquaintance in Dundee.

I return my thanks to Mr J. P. Smith's men,
Who were at my entertainment more than nine or ten;
And the rest of the gentlemen that were there,
Also deserves my thanks, I do declare.

Because they showered upon me their approbation,
And got up for me a handsome donation,
Which was presented to me by Mr Green,
In a purse most beautiful to be seen.

Which was a generous action in deed,
And came to me in time of need.
And the gentlemen that so generously treated me
I'll remember during my stay in Dundee.

LINES IN PRAISE OF MR J. GRAHAM HENDERSON, HAWICK

Success to Mr J. Graham Henderson, who is a good man,
And to gainsay it there's few people can,
I say so from my own experience,
And experience is a great defence.

He is a good man, I venture to say,
Which I declare to the world without dismay,
Because he's given me a suit of Tweeds, magnificent to
    see,
So good that it cannot be surpassed in Dundee.

The suit is the best of Tweed cloth in every way,
And will last me for many a long day;
It's really good, and in no way bad,
And will help to make my heart feel glad.

He's going to send some goods to the World's Fair,
And I hope of patronage he will get the biggest share;
Because his Tweed cloth is the best I ever did see,
In the year of our Lord eighteen hundred and ninety-three.

At the International Exhibition, and the Isle of Man
    Exhibition,
He got a gold medal from each, in recognition
Of his Scotch Tweeds, so good and grand,
Which cannot be surpassed in fair Scotland.

Therefore, good people, his goods are really grand,
And manufactured at Weensforth Mill, Hawick, Scotland;
Where there's always plenty of Tweeds on hand,
For the ready cash at the people's command.

Mr Tocher measured me for the suit,
And it is very elegant, which no one will dispute,
And I hope Mr Henry in Reform Street
Will gain customers by it, the suit is so complete.

THE TERRIFIC CYCLONE OF 1893

'Twas in the year of 1893, and on the 17th and 18th of
    November,
Which the people of Dundee and elsewhere will long
    remember,
The terrific cyclone that blew down trees,
And wrecked many vessels on the high seas.

All along the coast the Storm Fiend did loudly roar,
Whereby many ships were wrecked along the shore,
And many seamen lost their lives,
Which caused their children to mourn and their wives.

117

Alas! they will never see their husbands again,
And to weep for them 'tis all in vain,
Because sorrow never could revive the dead,
Therefore they must weep, knowing all hope is fled.

The people's hearts in Dundee were full of dread
For fear of chimney-cans falling on their heads,
And the roofs of several houses were hurled to the ground,
And the tenants were affrighted, and their sorrow was
    profound,

And scores of wooden sheds were levelled to the ground,
And chimney stalks fell with a crashing rebound :
The gale swept everything before it in its way;
No less than 250 trees and 37 tombstones were blown down
    at Balgay.

Oh! it was a pitiful and a terrible sight
To see the fallen trees lying left and right,
Scattered about in the beautiful Hill of Balgay,
Also the tombstones that were swept away.

At Broughty Ferry the gale made a noise like thunder,
Which made the inhabitants shake with fear and wonder
If their dwellings would be blown to the ground,
While the slates and chimney-cans were falling all around.

Early on the 18th a disaster occurred on the Tay :
The wreck of the steamer "Union,"—Oh! horror and
    dismay!
Whereby four lives have been taken away,
Which will make their friends mourn for many a day.

The steamer left Newburgh for Dundee with a cargo of
    sand,
And the crew expected they would safely land,
But by the time the steamer was opposite Dundee,
Alas! stronger blew the gale, and heavier grew the sea.

And in order to prevent stranding the anchor was let go,
And with the cold the hearts of the crew were full of woe,
While the merciless Storm Fiend loudly did roar,
As the vessel was driven towards the Fife shore.

Then the crew took shelter in the stokehole,
From the cold wind they could no longer thole,
But the high seas broke over her, one finding its way
Right into the stokehole, which filled the crew's hearts with
    dismay.

Then one of the crew, observing that the steamer had
    broached to,
Immediately went on deck to see what he could do,
And he tried hard to keep her head to the sea,
But the big waves dashed over her furiously.

Then Strachan shouted that the "Union" was sinking fast,
Which caused his companions to stand aghast,
And Strachan tried to lower the small boat,
But alas! the vessel sunk, and the boat wouldn't float,

And before he could recover himself he was struggling in the
    sea,
And battling with the big waves right manfully,
But his companions sank with the "Union" in the Tay,
Which filled Strachan's heart with sorrow and dismay,

And after a great struggle he reached the beach,
Fortunately so, which he never expected to reach,
For often he was drawn back by the back-wash,
As the big waves against his body did dash.

But, when nearly exhausted, and near to the land,
A piece of wreckage was near him, which he grasped with
his hand,
Which providentially came within his reach,
And bruised, and battered, he was thrown on the
beach.

He was so exhausted, he was unable to stand upright,
He felt so weakly, he was in such a plight,
Because the big waves had done him bodily harm,
Yet on hands and knees he crept to a house at Northfield
farm.

He arrived there at ten minutes past four o'clock,
And when he awakened the inmates, their nerves got a
shock,
But under their kind treatment he recovered speedily,
And was able to recount the disaster correctly.

Oh! it was a fearful, and a destructive storm!
I never mind the like since I was born,
Only the Tay Bridge storm of 1879,
And both these storms will be remembered for a very 'ong
time.

A TRIBUTE TO DR MURISON

Success to the good and skilful Dr Murison,
For golden opinions he has won
From his patients one and all,
And from myself, McGonagall.

He is very skilful and void of pride;
He was so to me when at my bedside,
When I turned badly on the 25th of July,
And was ill with inflammation, and like to die.

He told me at once what was ailing me;
He said I had been writing too much poetry,
And from writing poetry I would have to refrain,
Because I was suffering from inflammation on the brain.

And he has been very good to me in my distress,
Good people of Dundee, I honestly confess,
And to all his patients as well as me
Within the Royal city of Dundee.

He is worthy of the public's support,
And to his shop they should resort
To get his advice one and all;
Believe me on him ye ought to call.

He is very affable in temper and a skilful man,
And to cure all his patients he tries all he can;
And I wish him success for many a long day,
For he has saved me from dying, I venture to say;
The kind treatment I received surpasses all
Is the honest confession of McGonagall.

THE KESSACK FERRY-BOAT FATALITY

'Twas on Friday the 2nd of March in the year of 1894,
That the Storm Fiend did loudly laugh and roar
Along the Black Isle and the Kessack Ferry shore,
Whereby six men were drowned, which their friends will
    deplore.

The accident is the most serious that has occurred for many
    years,
And their relatives no doubt will shed many tears,
Because the accident happened within 200 yards of the
    shore,
While Boreas he did loudly rail and roar.

The ferry-boat started from the north or Black Isle,
While the gusty gales were blowing all the while
From the south, and strong from the south-west,
And to get to land the crew tried their utmost best.

The crew, however, were very near the land,
When the gusts rose such as no man could withstand,
With such force that the ferry-boat flew away
From her course, down into the little bay,

Which opens into the Moray Firth and the river Ness,
And by this time the poor men were in great distress,
And they tried again and again to get back to the pier,
And to save themselves from being drowned they began to
    fear.

And at last the poor men began to despair,
And they decided to drop anchor where they were,
While the Storm Fiend did angry roar,
And the white-crested billows did lash the shore.

And the water poured in, but was baled out quickly,
And the men's clothes were wet, and they felt sickly,
Because they saw no help in the distance,
Until at last they blew the fog-horn for assistance.

And quickly in response to their cry of distress,
Four members of the coastguard, in coastguard dress,
Whose station overlooked the scene, put off in a small boat,
And with a desperate struggle they managed to keep her
    afloat.

Then the coastguards and boat drifted rapidly away,
Until they found themselves in the little bay,
Whilst the big waves washed o'er them, again and again,
And they began to think their struggling was all in vain.

But they struggled on manfully until they came upon a
    smaller boat,
Which they thought would be more easily kept afloat,
And to which the hawser was soon transferred,
Then for a second time to save the ferrymen all was
    prepared.

Then the coastguards drifted down alongside the ferry-boat,
And with great difficulty they kept themselves afloat,
Because the big waves were like mountains high,
Yet the coastguards resolved to save the ferrymen or die.

Then at last the ferrymen got into the coastguard boat,
And they all toiled manfully to keep her afloat,
Until she was struck as she rose on the crest of the wave,
Then each one tried hard his life to save.

And the poor men's hearts with grief were rent,
For they were thrown into the merciless sea in a moment,
And out of the eight men two have been saved,
All owing to their swimming abilities, and how they
    behaved.

Oh! it must have been a fearful sight,
To see them striving hard with all their might
To save themselves from a watery grave,
While the Storm Fiend did laugh and angry did rave.

LINES IN PRAISE OF THE LYRIC CLUB BANQUET,
WHICH WAS HELD
IN THE QUEEN'S HOTEL, PERTH.
ON THE EVENING OF THE 5TH OF SEPTEMBER 1894

'Twas in the year of 1894, and on the 5th of September,
Which for a long time I will remember,
And the gentlemen I entertained in the city of Perth,
Which is one of the grandest cities upon the earth.

At the Banquet there were gentlemen of high degree,
And the viands they partook of filled their hearts with glee;
There was Beef, Fish, and Potatoes galore,
And we all ate until we could eat no more

The gentlemen present were very kind to me,
And the entertainment I gave them filled their hearts with
glee;
Especially the Recital I gave them from "Macbeth",
They were so much fascinated they almost lost their breath.

The audience were orderly and all went well,
As cheerily and as smoothly as a marriage bell.
Mr James Speedie was the chairman, and behaved right
manfully,
And sang a beautiful song, which filled our hearts with glee.

But when I sang my "Rattling Boy from Dublin Town",
The audience were like to pull the house down
With the hearty applause they showered upon me,
Because I sang the song so merrily.

But, in conclusion, I must honestly say
I haven't been so well treated for many a day;
Because I got a Splendid Bed in the Queen's Hotel,
And the breakfast I got there I liked right well.

The treatment I received there would please the Queen,
Because the cooking is most excellent and the beds are
clean;
And, in conclusion, I return my thanks to one and all,
Especially the members of the Lyric Club, big and small,
Also the landlord of the Queen's Hotel, yours truly,

McGONAGALL.

LINES IN PRAISE OF PROFESSOR BLACKIE

Alas! the people's hearts are now full of sorrow
For the deceased Professor Blackie, of Edinboro';
Because he was a Christian man, affable and kind,
And his equal in charitable actions would be hard to find

'Twas in the year of 1895, March the 2nd, he died at
    10 o'clock.
Which to his dear wife, and his adopted son, was a great
    shock;
And before he died he bade farewell to his adopted son
    and wife.
Which, no doubt, they will remember during life.

Professor Blackie celebrated his golden wedding three
    years ago,
When he was made the recipient of respect from high and
    low.
He leaves a widow, but, fortunately, no family,
Which will cause Mrs. Blackie to feel less unhappy.

Professor Blackie will be greatly missed in Edinboro;
Especially those that met him daily will feel great sorrow,
When they think of his never-failing plaid and hazel rung,
For, although he was an old man, he considered he was
    young.

He had a very striking face, and silvery locks like a seer,
And in the hearts of the Scottish people he was loved
    most dear;
And many a heart will mourn for him, but all in vain,
Because he never can return to them again.

He was a very kind-hearted man, and in no way vain,
And I'm afraid we ne'er shall look upon his like again;
And to hear him tell Scotch stories, the time did quickly
    pass,
And for singing Scotch songs few could him surpass.

But I hope he is in heaven, singing with saints above,
Around God's throne, where all is peace and love;
There, where God's children daily doth meet
To sing praises to God, enchanting and sweet.

He had visited almost every part of Europe in his time,
And, like Lord Byron, he loved the Grecian clime;
Nor did he neglect his own dear country,
And few men knew it more thoroughly than he.

On foot he tramped o'er most of bonnie Scotland,
And in his seventies he climbed the highest hills most
    grand.
Few men in his day could be compared to him,
Because he wasn't hard on fallen creatures when they did
    sin.

Oh, dearly beloved Professor Blackie, I must conclude my
    muse,
And to write in praise of thee my pen does not refuse;
Because you were a very Christian man, be it told,
Worthy of a monument, and your name written thereon
    in letters of gold.

THE FUNERAL OF THE LATE PRINCE HENRY
OF BATTENBERG

Alas! Prince Henry of Battenberg is dead!
And, I hope, has gone to heaven, its streets to tread,
And to sing with God's saints above,
Where all is joy and peace and love.

'Twas in the year of 1896, and on the 5th of February,
Prince Henry was buried at Whippingham—a solemn
    sight to see.
As the funeral moved off, it was a very impressive sight—
First came the military, and police, and volunteers from
    the Isle of Wight.

Then came the carriage party of the Scots Guards;
While the people uncovered their heads as it passed
    onwards
And many of them did sob and sigh
When the gun carriage with the coffin was passing by.

Prince Henry's charger was led by Richter, his stud groom;
And depicted in the people's faces there was a sad gloom
When they saw the noble charger of the dead—
It seemed that all joy from them had fled.

The Queen's carriage was followed by the Princess of
    Wales, and other Princesses,
All clad in gorgeous mourning dresses;
And there was a number of military representatives, which
    enhanced the scene;
And as the procession moved along it was solemn in the
    extreme.

Her Majesty looked very sad and serene,
Leaning back in her carriage could plainly be seen;
And the carriage was drawn by a pair of greys in grand
    harness;
And Her Majesty seemed to be in deep distress.

By Her Majesty's side sat the Princess Beatrice
And the two younger Battenberg children, looking very
    nice;
And by the coffin walked the elder Prince, immediately
Between Prince Louis and Prince Joseph, holding their
    hands tenderly.

The "Dead March" was played by the Marine Band;
And the music was solemn and very grand,
And accompanied by the roll of muffled drums;
Whilst among the spectators were heard sighs and hums.

And when the procession arrived at the church of
    Whippingham,
Then the coffin was carried inside—of the good man—
And was then laid in its resting place,
While sorrow was depicted in every face.

Then there was the firing of guns, with their earthly
    thunder
Which made the people start and wonder;
And the tolling of the village bells,
While the solemn music on the air swells.

And the people said, "Prince Henry was a good man,
But now he's laid low in the church of Whippingham."
But when the Grim King his dart does throw,
None can escape death, high or low.

The funeral service was certainly very nice—
Which was by the request of Princess Beatrice—
Which was the rendering of Sullivan's anthem, "Brother,
    before us thou art gone"—
I hope unto thy heavenly home.

No Doubt the Princess Beatrice will mourn for him—
But to mourn for the dead it is a sin!
Therefore I hope God will comfort her alway,
And watch o'er her children night and day.

Prince Henry was a God-fearing man—
And to deny it few people can—
And very kind to his children dear,
And for the loss of him they will drop a tear.

His relatives covered the coffin lid with wreaths of flowers
While adown their cheeks flowed tears in showers.
Then the service concluded with "Christ will gather His
    own";
And each one left with a sad heart and went home.

THE BURNING OF THE PEOPLE'S VARIETY
THEATRE, ABERDEEN

'Twas in the year of 1896, and on the 30th of September,
Which many people in Aberdeen will long remember;
The burning of the People's Variety Theatre, in Bridge
    Place,
Because the fire spread like lightning at a rapid pace.

130

The fire broke out on the stage, about eight o'clock,
Which gave to the audience a very fearful shock;
Then a stampede ensued, and a rush was made pell-mell,
And in the crush, trying to get out, many people fell.

The stage flies took fire owing to the gas
Not having room enough by them to pass;
And with his jacket Mr. Macaulay tried to put out the
    flame,
But oh! horrible to relate, it was all in vain.

Detective Innes, who was passing at the time of the fire,
Rendered help in every way the audience could desire,
By helping many of them for to get out,
Which was a heroic action, without any doubt.

Oh! it was a pitiful and fearful sight,
To see both old and young struggling with all their might,
For to escape from that merciless fire,
While it roared and mounted higher and higher.

Oh! it was horrible to hear the cries of that surging crowd,
Yelling and crying for "Help! help!" aloud;
While one old woman did fret and frown
Because her clothes were torn off when knocked down.

A lady and gentleman of the Music Hall company, Monti
    & Spry,
Managed to make their escape by climbing up very high,
To an advertisement board, and smashing the glass of the
    fanlight,
And squeezed themselves through with a great fight.

A little boy's leg was fractured while jumping from the
     gallery,
And by doing so he saved his life miraculously;
And every one of the artistes were in a sorry plight,
Because all their properties was burnt on that night.

There were about 400 or 500 people present on that night,
And oh! to them it was a most appalling sight;
When the flames swept the roof at one stroke,
'Twas then that a fearful yell from the audience broke.

And in a short time the interior was one mass of flames,
And nothing but the bare walls now remains;
But thank God it did not occur on Monday night,
Or else it would have been a more pitiable sight.

Because there was an over-crowded audience on Monday
     night.
The theatre was packed in every corner left and right,
Which certainly was a most pleasant sight,
And seemingly each heart was filled with delight.

The courage of Mr. T. Turner was wonderful to behold,
A private in the 92nd Highlanders, he was a hero bold;
Because he cast off his tunic and cap without delay,
And rescued several of the people without dismay.

Yet many were burned and disfigured in the face,
While trying hard to escape from that burning place;
Because with fear and choking smoke
Many of their hearts were almost broke.

But accidents will happen both on sea and land,
And the works of the Almighty is hard to understand;
And thank God there's only a few has fallen victims to
the fire,
But I hope they are now in Heaven, amongst the Heavenly
choir.

THE STORMING OF DARGAI HEIGHTS

'Twas on the 20th of November, and in the year of 1897,
That the cheers of the Gordon Highlanders ascended to
heaven,
As they stormed the Dargai heights without delay,
And made the Indian rebels fly in great dismay.

"Men of the Gordon Highlanders," Colonel Mathias said,
"Now, my brave lads, who never were afraid,
Our General says ye must take Dargai heights to-day;
So, forward, and charge them with your bayonets without
dismay!"

Then with a ringing cheer, and at the word of command,
They bounded after their leaders, and made a bold stand;
And, dashing across the open ground with their officers at
their head,
They drove the enemy from their position without any
dread.

In that famous charge it was a most beautiful sight
To see the regimental pipers playing with all their might;
But, alas! one of them was shot through both ankles, and
fell to the ground,
But still he played away while bullets fell on every side
around.

Oh! it must have been a gorgeous sight that day,
To see two thousand Highlanders dressed up in grand
array,
And to hear the pibroch sounding loud and clear
While the Highlanders rushed upon the foe with a loud
cheer.

The Gordon Highlanders have gained a lasting fame
Which for ages to come will long remain :
The daring gallantry they displayed at the storming of
Dargai,
Which will be handed down to posterity.

Methinks I see that gallant and heroic band
When brave Colonel Mathias gave them the command,
As they rushed upon the rebel horde, which was their
desire,
Without the least fear through a sheet of fire.

Then the rebels fled like frightened sprites,
And the British were left masters of the Dargai heights;
But, alas! brave Captain Robinson was mortally wounded
and cut down,
And for his loss many tears from his comrades fell to the
ground.

Success to the Gordon Highlanders wherever they go.
May they always be enabled to conquer the foe;
And may God guard them always in the fight,
And give them always strength to put their enemies to
flight.

134

SAVING A TRAIN

A poor old woman lived on the line of the Ohio Railway,
Where the train passed near by night and day :
She was a widow, with only one daughter,
Who lived with her in a log-hut near a deep gorge of
    water.

Which was spanned o'er from ridge to ridge,
By a strong metal railway bridge;
And she supported herself by raising and selling poultry,
Likewise eggs and berries, in great variety.

She often had to walk to the nearest town,
Which was many miles, but she seldom did frown;
And there she sold her basket of produce right quickly,
Then returned home with her heart full of glee.

The train passed by her hut daily to the town.
And the conductor noticed her on the line passing down,
So he gave her a lift, poor soul, many a time,
When he chanced to see her travelling along the line.

The engineman and brakesman to her were very good,
And resolved to help her all they could;
And thought they were not wronging the railway
    company
By giving the old woman a lift when she felt weary.

And, by thinking so, they were quite right,
For soon an accident occurred in the dead of night,
Which filled the old woman's heart with fright,
When she heard the melted torrents of snow descending
    in the night.

Then the flood arose, and the railway bridge gave way
With a fearful crash and plash,—Oh, horror and dismay!
And fell into the seething and yawning gulf below,
Which filled the old woman's heart with woe.

Because in another half-hour the train would be due,
So the poor old woman didn't know what to do;
And the rain fell in a flood, and the wind was howling,
And the heavens above seemed angry and scowling.

And alas! there was no telegraph along the line,
And what could she do to warn the train in time,
Because a light wouldn't live a moment in the rain,
But to save the train she resolved to strain every vein.

Not a moment was to be lost, so to work she went,
And cut the cords of her bed in a moment;
Then shouldered the side-pieces and head-pieces in all,
Then shouted to her daughter to follow as loud as she
    could bawl.

Then they climbed the steep embankment, and there
    fearlessly stood,
And piled their furniture on the line near the roaring
    flood,
And fired the dry combustibles, which blazed up bright,
Throwing its red light along the line a weird-like sight.

Then the old woman tore her red gown from her back,
And tying it to the end of a stick she wasn't slack;
Then ran up the line, waving it in both hands,
While before, with a blazing chair-post, her daughter
    stands.

Then round a curve the red eye of the engine came at last,
Whilst the poor old woman and her daughter stood aghast;
But, thank God, the engine stopped near the roaring fire,
And the train was saved, as the old woman did desire.

And such an old woman is worth her weight in gold,
For saving the train be it told;
She was a heroine, true and bold,
Which should be written on her tombstone in letters of
    gold.

THE BATTLE OF ATBARA

Ye Sons of Great Britain, pray list to me,
And I'll tell ye of a great victory.
Where the British defeated the Dervishes, without delay,
At the Battle of Atbara, without dismay.

The attack took place, 'twas on the 8th of April, in the
    early morning dawn,
And the British behaved manfully to a man;
And Mahmud's front was raked fearfully, before the
    assault began,
By the disposition of the force under Colonel Long:
Because the cannonading of their guns was very strong.

The main attack was made by General Gatacre's British
    Brigade,
And a heroic display they really made;
And General Macdonald's and General Maxwell's Brigade
    looked very fine,
And the Cameron Highlanders were extended along the
    line.

And behind them came the Lincolnshire Regiment, on the right,
And the Seaforth Highlanders in the centre, 'twas a most gorgeous sight,
And the Warwickshire Regiment were on the left,
And many of the Dervishes' heads by them were cleft.

General Macdonald's Brigade was on the right centre in similar formation,
And the 9th Battalion also in line in front rotation;
Then the whole force arrived about four o'clock,
And each man's courage was as firm as the rock.

At first the march was over a ridge of gravel,
But it didn't impede the noble heroes' travel;
No, they were as steady as when marching in the valley below,
And each man was eager to attack the foe.

And as the sun shone out above the horizon,
The advancing army, with banners flying, came boldly marching on;
The spectacle was really imposing to see,
And a dead silence was observed throughout the whole army.

Then Colonel Murray addressed the Seaforth Highlanders, and said,
"Come now my lads, don't be afraid,
For the news of the victory must be in London to-night,
So ye must charge the enemy with your bayonets, left and right."

General Gatacre also delivered a stirring address,
Which gave courage to the troops, I must confess;
He told the troops to drive the Dervishes into the
river,
And go right through the zereba, and do not shiver.

Then the artillery on the right opened fire with grapnel
and percussion shell,
Whereby many of the Dervishes were wounded and fell,
And the cannonading raked the whole of the Dervishes'
camp, and did great execution,
Which to Mahmud and his followers has been a great
retribution.

Then the artillery ceased fire, and the bugles sounded the
advance,
And the Cameron Highlanders at the enemy were eager to
get a chance;
So the pipers struck up the March of the Cameron Men,
Which reminded them of the ancient Camerons marching
o'er mountain and glen.

The business of this regiment was to clear the front with
a rifle fire,
Which to their honour, be it said, was their greatest
desire;
Then there was a momentary pause until they reached the
zereba,
Then the Dervishes opened fire on them, but it did not
them awe.

And with their pipes loudly sounding, and one ringing
    cheer,
Then the Cameron Highlanders soon did the zereba clear,
And right through the Dervish camp they went without
    dismay,
And scattered the Dervishes across the desert, far, far
    away.

Then the victory was complete, and the British gave three
    cheers,
While adown their cheeks flowed burning tears
For the loss of their commanders and comrades who fell
    in the fray,
Which they will remember for many a day.

Captain Urquhart's last words were "never mind me my
    lads, fight on,"
While, no doubt, the Cameron Highlanders felt woe-
    begone
For the loss of their brave captain, who was foremost in
    the field,
Death or glory was his motto, rather than yield.

There have been 4,000 prisoners taken, including Mahmud
    himself,
Who is very fond of dancing girls, likewise drink and pelf;
Besides 3,000 of his followers have been found dead,
And the living are scattered o'er the desert with their
    hearts full of dread.

Long life and prosperity to the British army,
May they always be able to conquer their enemies by land
    and by sea,
May God enable them to put their enemies to flight,
And to annihilate barbarity, and to establish what is right.

BEAUTIFUL BALMERINO

Beautiful Balmerino on the bonnie banks of Tay,
It's a very bonnie spot in the months of June or May;
The scenery there is charming and fascinating to see,
Especially the surroundings of the old Abbey,

Which is situated in the midst of trees on a rugged hill,
Which visitors can view at their own free will;
And the trees and shrubberies are lovely to view,
Especially the trees on each side of the avenue

Which leads up to the Abbey amongst the trees;
And in the summer time it's frequented with bees,
And also crows with their unmusical cry,
Which is a great annoyance to the villagers that live
    near by.

And there in the summer season the mavis sings,
And with her charming notes the woodland rings;
And the sweet-scented zephyrs is borne upon the gale,
Which is most refreshing and invigorating to inhale.

Then there's the stately Castle of Balmerino
Situated in the midst of trees, a magnificent show,
And bordering on the banks o' the silvery Tay,
Where visitors can spend a happy holiday.

As they view the castle and scenery around
It will help to cheer their spirits I'll be bound;
And if they wish to view Wormit Bay
They can walk along the braes o' the silvery Tay.

THE BATTLE OF OMDURMAN

Ye Sons of Great Britain! come join with me
And sing in praise of the gallant British Armie,
That behaved right manfully in the Soudan,
At the great battle of Omdurman.

'Twas in the year of 1898, and on the 2nd of September,
Which the Khalifa and his surviving followers will long
    remember,
Because Sir Herbert Kitchener has annihilated them
    outright,
By the British troops and Soudanese in the Omdurman
    fight.

The Sirdar and his Army left the camp in grand array,
And marched on to Omdurman without delay,
Just as the brigades had reached the crest adjoining the
    Nile,
And became engaged with the enemy in military style.

The Dervishes had re-formed under cover of a rocky
    eminence,
Which to them, no doubt, was a strong defence,
And they were massed together in battle array
Around the black standard of the Khalifa, which made a
    grand display.

But General Maxwell's Soudanese brigade seized the
    eminence in a short time,
And General Macdonald's brigade then joined the firing
    line;
And in ten minutes, long before the attack could be driven
    home,
The flower of the Khalifa's army was almost overthrown.

Still manfully the dusky warriors strove to make headway,
But the Soudanese troops and British swept them back
    without dismay,
And their main body were mown down by their deadly
    fire—
But still the heroic Dervishes refused to retire.

And defiantly they planted their standards and died by
    them,
To their honour be it said, just like brave men;
But at last they retired, with their hearts full of woe,
Leaving the field white with corpses, like a meadow dotted
    with snow.

The chief heroes in the fight were the 21st Lancers;
They made a brilliant charge on the enemy with ringing
    cheers,
And through the dusky warriors bodies their lances they
    did thrust,
Whereby many of them were made to lick the dust.

Then at a quarter past eleven the Sirdar sounded the
    advance,
And the remnant of the Dervishes fled, which was their
    only chance,
While the cavalry cut off their retreat while they ran;
Then the Sirdar, with the black standard of the Khalifa,
    headed for Omdurman.

And when the Khalifa saw his noble army cut down,
With rage and grief he did fret and frown;
Then he spurred his noble steed, and swiftly it ran,
While inwardly to himself he cried, "Catch me if you
    can!"

And Mahdism now has received a crushing blow,
For the Khalifa and his followers have met with a complete
  overthrow;
And General Gordon has been avenged, the good Christian,
By the defeat of the Khalifa at the battle of Omdurman.

Now since the Khalifa has been defeated and his rule at
  an end,
Let us thank God that fortunately did send
The brave Sir Herbert Kitchener to conquer that bad man,
The inhuman Khalifa, and his followers at the battle of
  Omdurman.

Success to Sir Herbert Kitchener! he is a great
  commander,
And as skilful in military tactics as the great Alexander,
Because he devised a very wise plan,
And by it has captured the town of Omdurman.

I wish success to the British and Soudanese Army,
May God protect them by land and by sea,
May he enable them always to conquer the foe,
And to establish what's right wherever they go.

THE VILLAGE OF TAYPORT AND ITS
SURROUNDINGS

All ye pleasure-seekers, where'er ye be,
I pray ye all be advised by me,
Go and visit Tayport on the banks o' the Tay,
And there ye can spend a pleasant holiday.

The village and its surroundings are magnificent to be
    seen,
And the shops on the High Street are tidy and clean,
And the goods, I'm sure, would please the Queen,
They cannot be surpassed in Edinburgh or Aberdeen.

And the villagers' gardens are lovely to be seen,
There sweet flowers grow and gooseberries green.
And the fragrant air will make you feel gay
While viewing the scenery there on the banks of the Tay.

Scotscraig is an ancient and a most charming spot,
And once seen by visitors will never be forgot.
'Twas there that Archbishop Sharp lived long ago,
And the flower-garden there is a very grand show.

The flower beds there are very beautiful to see,
They surpass the Baxter Park flower beds in Dundee,
And are all enclosed in a round ring,
And there the bee and the butterfly are often on the wing.

Scotscraig farm-house is magnificent to see
With its beautiful rich fields of wheat and barley,
And the farm-house steading is certainly very fine,
And the scenery is charming in the summer time.

The Serpentine Walk is a secluded spot in Scotscraig
    wood,
And to be walking there 'twould do one's heart good.
There the lovers can enjoy themselves in its shady bowers
By telling tales of love to wile away the tedious hours.

There innocent rabbits do sport and play
During the livelong summer day
Amongst the ivy and shrubberies green,
And screened all day from the sun's sheen.

Then, lovers of the picturesque, off and away
To the village of Tayport on the banks o' the Tay,
And ramble through Scotscraig wood,
It will, I'm sure, do your bodies good.

And, as ye walk along the Serpentine Walk,
With each other ye can have a social talk,
And ye will hear the birds singing away,
Which will make your hearts feel light and gay.

And while walking underneath the branches of the trees,
Ye will hear the humming of the bees.
Therefore, pleasure-seekers, make no delay,
But visit Scotscraig wood on a fine summer day.

There visitors can be shaded from the sun in the summer
    time,
While walking along the secluded Serpentine,
By the spreading branches of the big trees,
Or from the undergrowth ivy, if they please.

Do not forget to visit the old Tower,
Where Archbishop Sharp spent many an hour,
Viewing the beautiful scenery for miles away
Along the bonnie banks o' the silvery Tay.

THE BLIND GIRL

Kind Christians, pray list to me,
And I'll relate a sad story,
Concerning a little blind girl, only nine years of age,
Who lived with her father in a lonely cottage.

Poor girl, she had never seen the blessed light of day,
Nor the beautiful fields of corn and hay,
Nor the sparrows, that lifted their heads at early morn
To bright Sol that does the hills adorn.

And near the cottage door there was an elm tree;
But that stunted elm tree she never did see,
Yet her little heart sometimes felt gay
As she listened to the thrushes that warbled the live-long
    day.

And she would talk to the wren when alone,
And to the wren she would her loneliness bemoan,
And say, "Dear little wren, come again to-morrow;
Now be sure and come, your singing will chase away my
    sorrow."

She was motherless, but she had a drunken father,
Who in his savage moods drank all he could gather,
And would often cruelly beat her until she would cry,
"Dear father, if you beat me I will surely die."

She spent the days in getting ready her father's food,
Which was truly for her drunken father's good;
But one night he came home, reeling drunk,
And the poor child's heart with fear sunk;

And he cried, "You were at the door when I came up the
   lane;
Take that, you good-for-nothing slut; you're to blame
For not having my supper ready; you will find
That's no excuse, Sarah, because you are blind."

And with a stick he struck her as he spoke
Across the shoulders, until the stick almost broke;
Crying aloud, "I'll teach you better, you little sneak;"
And with the beating, Sarah's heart was like to break.

Poor little Sarah had never seen the snow;
She knew it was beautiful white, some children told her so;
And in December, when the snow began to fall,
She would go to the door and make a snowball.

One day she'd been very cheerless and alone,
Poor child, and so cold, almost chilled to the bone;
For her father had spent his wages in drink,
And for want of fire she was almost at death's brink.

Her face was pinched with hunger but she never
   complained,
And her little feet with cold were chilblained,
And her father that day had not come home for dinner,
And the dull grey sky was all of a shimmer.

So poor Sarah was very sick when her father came home;
So bad, little dear, that she did sigh and moan,
And when her father saw her in bed
He was heart-stricken with fear and dread.

So within a few days poor Sarah did die,
And for the loss of Sarah the drunken father did cry,
So the loss of his child soon converted him
From drinking either whisky, rum, or gin.

WRECK OF THE STEAMER MOHEGAN

Good people of high and low degree,
I pray ye all to list to me,
And I'll relate a terrible tale of the sea
Concerning the unfortunate steamer, Mohegan,
That against the Manacles Rocks, ran.

'Twas on Friday, the 14th of October, in the year of
    ninety-eight,
Which alas! must have been a dreadful sight;
She sailed out of the river Thames on Thursday,
While the hearts of the passengers felt light and gay.

And on board there were 133 passengers and crew,
And each one happier than another seemingly to view;
When suddenly the ship received some terrible shocks,
Until at last she ran against the Manacles Rocks.

Dinner was just over when the shock took place,
Which caused fear to be depicted in every face;
Because the ship was ripped open, and the water rushed in,
It was most dreadful to hear, it much such a terrific din.

Then the cries of children and women did rend the air,
And in despair many of them tore their hair
As they clung to their babies in wild despair,
While come of them cried—'Oh, God, do Thou my babies
    spare!'

The disaster occurred between seven and eight o'clock at
night,
Which caused some of the passengers to faint with fright;
As she struck on the Manacles Rocks between Falmouth
and Lizard Head,
Which filled many of the passengers' hearts with dread.

Then the scene that followed was awful to behold,
As the captain hurried to the bridge like a hero bold;
And the seamen rushed manfully to their posts,
While many of the passengers with fear looked as pale as
ghosts.

And the poor women and children were chilled to the
heart,
And crying aloud for their husbands to come and take
their part;
While the officers and crew did their duty manfully,
By launching the boats immediately into the sea.

Then lifebelts were tied round the women and children
By the brave officers and gallant seamen;
While the storm fiend did laugh and angry did roar,
When he saw the boats filled with passengers going
towards the shore.

One of the boats, alas! unfortunately was swamped,
Which caused the officers and seamens' courage to be a
little damped;
But they were thankful the other boats got safely away,
And tried hard to save the passengers without dismay.

Then a shriek of despair arose as the ship is sinking
    beneath the wave,
While some of the passengers cried to God their lives to
    save;
But the angry waves buffetted the breath out of them,
Alas, poor sickly children, also women and men.

Oh, heaven, it was most heartrending to see
A little girl crying and imploring most piteously,
For some one to save her as she didn't want to die,
But, alas, no one seemed to hear her agonizing cry.

For God's sake, boys, get clear, if ye can,
Were the captain's last words spoken like a brave man;
Then he and the officers sank with the ship in the briny
    deep,
Oh what a pitiful sight, 'tis enough to make one weep.

Oh think of the passengers that have been tempest
    tossed,
Besides, 100 souls and more, that have been lost;
Also, think of the mariner while on the briny deep,
And pray to God to protect him at night before ye sleep.

THE HERO OF RORKE'S DRIFT

Twas at the camp of Rorke's Drift, and at tea-time,
And busily engaged in culinary operations was a private
    of the line;
But suddenly he paused, for he heard a clattering din,
When instantly two men on horseback drew rein beside
    him.

"News from the front!" said one, "Awful news!" said the
  other,
"Of which, we are afraid, will put us to great bother,
For the black Zulus are coming, and for our blood doth
  thirst,"
"And the force is cut up to pieces!" shouted the first.

"We're dead beat," said both, "but we've got to go on,"
And on they rode both, looking very woebegone;
Then Henry Hook put all thought of cooking out of his
  mind,
For he was surrounded with danger on every side he did
  find.

He was a private of the South Wales Borderers, Henry
  Hook,
Also a brave soldier, and an hospital cook;
A soldier of the Queen, who was always ready to obey,
And willing to serve God by night and day.

Then away to the Camp he ran, with his mind all in a
  shiver,
Shouting, "The force is cut up, sir, on the other side of
  the river!"
Which caused the officer in command with fear to quiver,
When Henry Hook the news to him did deliver.

Then Henry Hook saluted, and immediately retired,
And with courage undaunted his soul was fired,
And the cry rang out wildly, "The Zulus are coming!"
Then the alarm drums were instantly set a-drumming.

Then "Fall in! Fall in!" the commanders did cry,
And the men mustered out, ready to do and to die,
As British soldiers are always ready to do,
But, alas, on this occasion their numbers were but few.

They were only eighty in number, that brave British band,
And brave Lieutenant Broomhead did them command;
He gave orders to erect barricades without delay,
"It's the only plan I can see, men, to drive four thousand
savages away."

Then the mealie bags and biscuit boxes were brought out,
And the breastwork was made quickly without fear or
doubt,
And barely was it finished when some one cried in dismay,
"There's the Zulus coming just about twelve hundred
yards away."

Methinks I see the noble hero, Henry Hook,
Because like a destroying angel he did look,
As he stood at the hospital entrance defending the patients
there,
Bayoneting the Zulus, while their cries rent the air,
As they strove hard the hospital to enter in,
But he murdered them in scores, and thought it no sin.

In one of the hospital rooms was stationed Henry Hook,
And every inch a hero he did look,
Standing at his loophole he watched the Zulus come,
All shouting, and yelling, and at a quick run.

On they came, a countless host of savages with a rush,
But the gallant little band soon did their courage crush,
But the cool man Henry Hook at his post began to fire,
And in a short time those maddened brutes were forced to retire.

Still on came the savages into the barricade,
And still they were driven back, but undismayed.
Again they came into the barricade, yet they were driven back,
While darkness fell swift across the sun, dismal and black.

Then into the hospital the savages forced their way,
And in a moment they set fire to it without dismay,
Then Henry Hook flew to assist the patients in the ward,
And the fighting there was fearful and hard.

With yell and shriek the Zulus rushed to the attack,
But for the sixth time they were driven back
By the brave British band, and Henry Hook,
Who was a brave soldier, surgeon, and hospital cook.

And when Lord Chelmsford heard of the victory that day,
He sent for Henry Hook without delay,
And they took the private before the commander,
And with his braces down, and without his coat, in battle array grandeur.

Then Lord Chelmsford said, "Henry Hook, give me your hand,
For your conduct to day has been hereoic and grand,
And without your assistance to-day we'd been at a loss,
And for your heroic behaviour you shall receive the Victoria Cross."

BEAUTIFUL EDINBURGH

Beautiful city of Edinburgh, most wonderful to be seen,
With your ancient palace of Holyrood and Queen's Park
    Green,
And your big, magnificent, elegant New College,
Where people from all nations can be taught knowledge.

The New College of Edinburgh is certainly very grand
Which I consider to be an honour to fair Scotland,
Because it's the biggest in the world, without any doubt,
And is most beautiful in the inside as well as out.

And the Castle is wonderful to look upon,
Which has withstood many angry tempests in years
    bygone;
And the rock it's built upon is rugged and lovely to be
    seen
When the shrubberies surrounding it are blown full green.

Morningside is lovely and charming to be seen;
The gardens there are rich with flowers and shrubberies
    green
And sweet scented perfumes fill the air,
Emanating from the sweet flowers and beautiful plants
    there.

And as for Braidhill, it's a very romantic spot,
But a fine place to visit when the weather is hot;
There the air is nice and cool, which will help to drive
    away sorrow
When ye view from its summit the beautiful city of
    Edinburgh.

And as for the statues, they are very grand—
They cannot be surpassed in any foreign land;
And the scenery is attractive and fascinating to the eye,
And arrests the attention of tourists as they pass by.

Lord Melville's Monument is most elegant to be seen,
Which is situated in St. Andrew's Square, amongst
    shrubberies green,
Which seems most gorgeous to the eye,
Because it is towering so very high.

The Prince Albert Consort Statue looks very grand,
Especially the granite blocks whereon it doth stand,
Which is admired by all tourists as they pass by,
Because the big granite blocks seem magnificent to the eye.

Princes Street West End Garden is fascinating to be seen,
With its beautiful big trees and shrubberies green,
And its magnificent water fountain in the valley below
Helps to drive away from the tourist all care and woe.

The Castle Hotel is elegant and grand,
And students visit it from every foreign land,
And the students of Edinburgh often call there
To rest and have luncheon, at a very cheap fare.

Queen Street Garden seems charming to the eye,
And a great boon it is to the tenantry near by,
As they walk along the grand gravel walks near there,
Amongst the big trees and shrubberies, and inhale pure air.

Then, all ye tourists, be advised by me,
Beautiful Edinburgh ye ought to go and see.
It's the only city I know of where ye can wile away the time
By viewing its lovely scenery and statues fine.

Magnificent city of Edinburgh, I must conclude my muse,
But to write in praise of thee I cannot refuse.
I will tel' the world boldly without dismay
You have the biggest college in the world at the present
    day.

Of all the cities in the world, Edinburgh for me;
For no matter where I look, some lovely spot I see;
And for picturesque scenery unrivalled you do stand.
Therefore I pronounce you to be the Pride of Fair
    Scotland.

WOMEN'S SUFFRAGE

Fellow men! why should the lords try to despise
And prohibit women from having the benefit of the
    parliamentary Franchise ?
When they pay the same taxes as you and me,
I consider they ought to have the same liberty.

And I consider if they are not allowed the same liberty,
From taxation every one of them should be set free;
And if they are not, it is really very unfair,
And an act of injustice I most solemnly declare.

Women, farmers, have no protection as the law now
   stands;
And many of them have lost their property and lands,
And have been turned out of their beautiful farms
By the unjust laws of the land and the sheriffs' alarms.

And in my opinion, such treatment is very cruel;
And fair play, 'tis said, is a precious jewel;
But such treatment causes women to fret and to dote,
Because they are deprived of the parliamentary Franchise
   vote.

In my opinion, what a man pays for he certainly should
   get;
And if he does not, he will certainly fret;
And why wouldn't women do the very same ?
Therefore, to demand the parliamentary Franchise they
   are not to blame.

Therefore let them gather, and demand the parliamentary
   Franchise;
And I'm sure no reasonable man will their actions despise,
For trying to obtain the privileges most unjustly withheld
   from them;
Which Mr. Gladstone will certainly encourage and never
   condemn.

And as for the working women, many are driven to the
   point of starvation,
All through the tendency of the legislation;
Besides, upon members of parliament they have no claim
As a deputation, which is a very great shame.

Yes, the Home Secretary of the present day,
Against working women's deputations, has always said—
    nay;
Because they haven't got the parliamentary Franchise,
That is the reason why he does them despise.

And that, in my opinion, is really very unjust;
But the time is not far distant, I most earnestly trust,
When women will have a parliamentary vote,
And many of them, I hope, will wear a better petticoat.

And I hope that God will aid them in this enterprise,
And enable them to obtain the parliamentary Franchise;
And rally together, and make a bold stand,
And demand the parliamentary Franchise throughout
  Scotland.

And do not rest day nor night—
Because your demands are only right
In the eyes of reasonable men, and God's eyesight;
And Heaven, I'm sure, will defend the right.

Therefore go on brave women! and never fear,
Although your case may seem dark and drear,
And put your trust in God, for He is strong;
And ye will gain the parliamentary Franchise before very
    long.

LORD ROBERTS' TRIUMPHAL ENTRY INTO PRETORIA

'Twas in the year of 1900, and on the 5th of June,
Lord Roberts entered Pretoria in the afternoon;
His triumphal entry was magnificent to see,
The British Army marching behind him fearlessly.

With their beautiful banners unfurled to the breeze,
But the scene didn't the Boers please;
And they immediately made some show of fight,
But at the charge of the bayonet they were put to flight.

The troops, by the people, were received with loud cheers,
While many of them through joy shed joyous tears;
Because Lord Roberts from bondage had set them free,
Which made them dance and sing with glee.

Lord Roberts' march into Pretoria was inspiring to see,
It is reckoned one of the greatest achievements in our
    military history;
Because the Boers were watching him in front and behind,
But he scattered them like chaff before the wind.

Oh! it was a most beautiful and inspiring sight
To see the British bayonets glittering in the sunlight,
Whilst the bands played "See the conquering hero comes,"
While the people in ecstasy towards them run.

The British marched into Pretoria like the rushing tide,
And the Boers around Pretoria there no longer could abide,
Because the British at the charge of the bayonet made them
    run with fear,
And fly from Pretoria just like wild dear.

Then Lord Roberts cried, "Pull down the Transvaal Flag,
And hoist the Union Jack instead of the Transvaal rag;
And shout 'Britannia for ever,' and 'Long live our Queen,'
For she is the noblest Queen the world has ever seen."

Then the Union Jack was hoisted and unfurled to the breeze,
Which certainly did the Boers displease,
When they saw the Union Jack flying o'er their capital,
The sight thereof amazed them, and did them appall.

And when old Kruger saw Lord Roberts he shook with
    fright,
Then he immediately disguised himself and took to flight,
Leaving his poor wife in Pretoria behind,
But the British troops have treated her very kind.

Now let us all thank Lord Roberts for his great bravery,
Who has gained for the people of Pretoria their liberty,
By his skillful tactics and great generalship, be it told,
And the courage of his soldiers, who fought like lions bold.

Lord Roberts is a brave man, be it said,
Who never was the least afraid
To defend his Queen and country when called upon;
And by his valorous deeds great battles he has won.

Then success to Lord Roberts and the British Army,
May God protect them by land and by sea;
And enable them always to conquer the Boers,
And beat all foreign foes from our shores.

A TRIBUTE TO MR J. GRAHAM HENDERSON,
THE WORLD'S FAIR JUDGE

Thrice welcome home to Hawick, Mr J. Graham Henderson,
For by your Scotch tweeds a great honour you have won;
By exhibiting your beautiful tweeds at the World's Fair
You have been elected judge of Australian and American
    wools while there.

You had to pass a strict examination on the wool trade,
But you have been victorious, and not the least afraid,
And has been made judge of wools by Sir Henry Truman
 Good,
And was thanked by Sir Henry where he stood.

You have been asked by Sir Henry to lecture on wools
 there,
And you have consented to do so, which made your
 audience stare
When you let them see the difference betwixt good wool
 and bad;
You'll be sure to gain fresh honours, they will feel so glad.

To think they have found a clever man indeed,
That knows good wool and how to manufacture Scotch
 tweed,
I wish you success for many a long day,
Because your Scotch tweeds are the best, I venture to say.

May you always be prosperous wherever you go,
Always gaining fresh friends, but never a foe,
Because you are good and a very clever man,
And to gainsay it there's few people can.

THE WRECK OF THE COLUMBINE

Kind Christians, all pay attention to me,
And Miss Mouat's sufferings I'll relate to ye;
While on board the Columbine, on the merciless sea,
Tossing about in the darkness of night in the storm
 helplessly.

She left her home (Scatness), on Saturday morning, bound
    for Lerwick,
Thinking to get cured by a man she knew, as she was very
    sick;
But for eight days she was tossed about on the stormy main,
By a severe storm of wind, hail, and rain.

The waves washed o'er the little craft, and the wind
    loudly roared,
And the Skipper, by a big wave, was washed overboard;
Then the crew launched the small boat on the stormy
    main,
Thinking to rescue the Skipper, but it was all in vain.

Nevertheless, the crew struggled hard his life to save,
But alas! the Skipper sank, and found a watery grave;
And the white crested waves madly did roar,
Still the crew, thank God, landed safe on shore.

As soon as Miss Mouat found she was alone,
Her mind became absorbed about her friends at home;
As her terrible situation presented itself to her mind,
And her native place being quickly left far behind.

And as the big waves lashed the deck with fearful shocks,
Miss Mouat thought the vessel had struck upon a reef of
    rocks;
And she thought the crew had gone to get help from land,
While she held to a rope fastened to the cabin roof by her
    right hand.

And there the poor creature was in danger of being thrown
to the floor,
Whilst the heavy showers of spray were blown against the
cabin door,
And the loosened sail was reduced to tatters and flapping
with the wind,
And the noise thereof caused strange fears to arise in her
mind.

And after some hours of darkness had set in,
The table capsized with a lurch of the sea which made a
fearful din,
Which helped to put the poor creature in a terrible fright,
To hear the drawers of the table rolling about all the night.

And there the noble heroine sat looking very woe-begone,
With hands uplifted to God making her moan,
Praying to God above to send her relief,
While in frantic screams she gave vent to her pent up grief.

And loud and earnestly to God the noble heroine did cry,
And the poor invalid's bosom heaved many a sigh;
Oh! heaven, hard was the fate of this woman of sixty years
of age,
Tossing about on the briny deep, while the storm fiend did
rage.

Oh! think of the poor soul crouched in the cabin below,
With her heart full of fear, cold, hunger, and woe,
And the pitless storm of rain, hail, and snow,
Tossing about her tiny craft to and fro.

And when the morning came she felt very sick,
And she expected the voyage would be about three hours
    to Lerwick,
And her stock of provisions was but very small,
Only two half-penny biscuits and a quart bottle of milk in
    all

Still the heavy snow kept falling, and the sky was
    obscured,
And on Sabbath morning she made her first meal on
    board,
And this she confined to a little drop of milk and half a
    biscuit,
Which she wisely considered was most fit.

And to the rope fastened to the cabin roof she still held on
Until her hands began to blister, and she felt woe-begone,
But by standing on a chest she could look out of the
    hatchway,
And spend a little time in casting her eyes o'er the sea
    each day.

When Wednesday morning came the weather was very
    fine,
And the sun in the heavens brightly did shine,
And continued so all the live long day;
Then Miss Mouat guessed that land to the norward lay.

Then the poor creature sat down to her last meal on board,
And with heartfelt thanks she praised the Lord;
But when Thursday morning came no more food could be
    had,
Then she mounted a box about seven o'clock while her heart
    felt sad.

And she took her usual gaze o'er the sea with a wistful eye,
Hoping that some passing vessel she might descry,
And to the westward she espied a bright red light,
But as the little craft passed on it vanished from her sight.

But alas; no vessel could she see around anywhere,
And at last the poor soul began to despair,
And there the lonely woman sat looking out to the heavens
 above,
Praying to God for succour with her heart full of love.

At last the Columbine began to strike on submerged rocks,
And with the rise and fall of the sea she received some
 dreadful shocks,
And notwithstanding that the vessel was still rolling
 among the rocks,
Still the noble heroine contrived once more to raise herself
 upon the box.

Still the Columbine sped on, and ran upon a shingly
 beach,
And at last the Island of Lepsoe, Miss Mouat did reach,
And she was kindly treated by the inhabitants in everyway
 that's grand,
And conveyed to Aalesund and there taking steamer to fair
 England.

BALMORAL CASTLE

Beautiful Balmoral Castle,
  Most handsome to be seen,
Highland home of the Empress of India,
  Great Britain's Queen.

Your woods and waters and
  Mountains high are most
Beautiful to see,
  Near by Balmoral Castle
And the dark river Dee.

Then there's the hill of Cairngorm
  To be seen from afar,
And the beautiful heathery hills
  Of dark Lochnagar,
And the handsome little village—
  The Castleton o' Braemar—
Which is most beautiful to see,
  Near by Balmoral Castle
And the dark river Dee.

Then there's the handsome little church
  Of Crathie—most beautiful to be seen;
And the Queen goes there on Sunday
  To hear the Word of God
Most solemn and serene,
  Which is most beautiful to see,
Nor far from Balmoral Castle
  And the dark river Dee.

Then, when she finds herself
  At leisure, she goes for to see
Her old female acquaintances
  That lives on the river Dee,
And reads the Bible unto them,
  Which is most beautiful to see,
Near by Balmoral Castle
  And the dark river Dee.

Beautiful Balmoral Castle!
   In the summer season of the year
The Queen comes to reside in thee,
   Her spirits for to cheer,
And to see her hiland deer,
   And in the green woods to roam
And admire the hiland cataracts,
   With their misty foam,
Which is most beautiful to see,
   Near by Balmoral Castle
And the dark river Dee.

Beautiful Balmoral Castle,
   With your green swards and flowers fair,
Thee Queen of great Britain
   Is always welcome there;
For they young and they old
   Tries to do for her all they can,
And they faithful Highlanders there
   Will protect her to a man,
Which is most beautiful to see,
   Near by Balmoral Castle
And thee dark river Dee.

A NEW TEMPERANCE POEM, IN MEMORY OF MY DEPARTED PARENTS, WHO WERE SOBER LIVING & GOD FEARING PEOPLE

My parents were sober living, and often did pray,
For their family to abstain from intoxicating drink alway;
Because they knew it would lead them astray,
Which no God fearing man will dare to gainsay.

Some people do say that God made strong drink,
But he is not so cruel I think;
To lay a stumbling block in his children's way,
And then punish them for going astray.

No! God has more love for his children, than mere man.
To make strong drink their souls to damn;
His love is more boundless than mere man's by far,
And to say not it would be an unequal par.

A man that truly loves his family wont allow them to
    drink,
Because he knows seldom about God they will think,
Besides he knows it will destroy their intellect,
And cause them to hold their parents in disrespect.

Strong drink makes the people commit all sorts of evil,
And must have been made by the Devil
For to make them quarrel, murder, steal, and fight,
And prevent them from doing what is right.

The Devil delights in leading the people astray,
So that he may fill his kingdom with them without delay;
It is the greatest pleasure he can really find,
To be the enemy of all mankind.

The Devil delights in breeding family strife,
Especially betwixt man and wife;
And if the husband comes home drunk at night,
He laughs and crys, ha! ha! what a beautiful sight.

169

And if the husband asks his supper when he comes in,
The poor wife must instantly find it for him;
And if she cannot find it, he will curse and frown,
And very likely knock his loving wife down.

Then the children will scream aloud,
And the Devil no doubt will feel very proud,
If he can get the children to leave their own fireside,
And to tell their drunken father, they won't with him
   reside.

Strong drink will cause the gambler to rob and kill his
   brother,
Aye! also his father and his mother,
All for the sake of getting money to gamble,
Likewise to drink, cheat, and wrangle.

And when the burglar wants to do his work very handy,
He plies himself with a glass of Whisky, Rum, or Brandy,
To give himself courage to rob and kill,
And innocent people's blood to spill.

Whereas if he couldn't get Whisky, Rum, or Brandy,
He wouldn't do his work so handy;
Therefore, in that respect let strong drink be abolished in
   time,
And that will cause a great decrease in crime.

Therefore, for this sufficient reason remove it from
   society,
For seldom burglary is committed in a state of sobriety;
And I earnestly entreat ye all to join with heart and hand,
And to help to chase away the Demon drink from bonnie
   Scotland.

I beseech ye all to kneel down and pray,
And implore God to take it away;
Then this world would be a heaven, whereas it is a hell,
And the people would have more peace in it to dwell.

Ah! pity the sorrows of a poor poet, when unable to pay
   his rent;
And help him to pay it, and he will feel content.

· DAVID WINTER AND SON LTD., PRINTERS, DUNDEE